CLASSROOM MANAGEMENT

Perspectives on the Social Curriculum

RICHARD R. POWELL

University of Colorado, Denver

H. JAMES McLAUGHLIN

University of Georgia

TOM V. SAVAGE

California State University, Fullerton

STANLEY ZEHM

University of Nevada at Las Vegas

Merrill
Prentice Hall

Upper Saddle River, New Jersey
Columbus, Ohio

Library of Congress Cataloging-in-Publication Data

Classroom management: perspectives on the social curriculum/Richard R. Powell ... [et al.].
   p. cm.
Includes bibliographical references and index.
ISBN 0-13-460908-5
  1. Classroom management–Social aspects. I. Powell, Richard R.

LB3013.C5274 2001
371.102'4–dc21   99-086567

Vice President and Publisher: Jeffery W. Johnston
Editor: Debra A. Stollenwerk
Editorial Assistant: Penny S. Burleson
Production Editor: Mary Harlan
Design Coordinator: Diane C. Lorenzo
Photo Coordinator: Nancy Harre Ritz
Cover Design: Tanya Burgess
Cover Art: SuperStock
Text Design and Illustrations: Carlisle Publishers Services
Production Coordination: Amy Gehl, Carlisle Publishers Services
Production Manager: Pamela D. Bennett
Director of Marketing: Kevin Flanagan
Marketing Manager: Amy June
Marketing Services Manager: Krista Groshong

This book was set in Palatino by Carlisle Communications, Ltd. It was printed and bound by R. R. Donnelley & Sons Company. The cover was printed by Phoenix Color Corp.

Photo Credits: Anne Vega/Merrill, 2, 116, 260; Anthony Magnacca/Merrill, 22, 48, 68, 230; Laima Druskis/ PH College, 92; Scott Cunningham/Merrill, 144, 196; Robert Vega/Merrill, 174; Tom Watson/Merrill, 288.

Merrill
Prentice Hall

10 9 8 7 6 5 4 3 2
ISBN 0-13-460908-5

To the memory of
Stanley Zehm

P R E F A C E

This book is intended to help readers consider management strategies for contemporary school classrooms. The book engages readers in a number of activities that focus on cultural dimensions of classroom management. An assumption underlying many books on classroom management, especially those reflective of behavioristic perspectives, is that preservice teachers should first learn theoretical principles of management, then somehow connect these principles to their practice during field experiences in teacher education programs or during the first year of teaching. We have learned from research that this kind of theory-practice connection is problematic, and that preservice teachers who learn management theory in such a manner often express concerns over the impracticality of their teacher education experience.

Purely behaviorist approaches to classroom management tend to decontextualize classroom management by discussing it apart from the whole of classroom practice. These approaches also focus in theory on explicit behavior of learners irrespective of biographical or cultural influences. However, the position we take in this book is that decontextualized approaches to classroom management are misaligned with contemporary constructivist thinking on preservice and in-service teacher education and also with the globalization of local school classrooms. Consequently, this book engages readers in readings, activities, and action research projects that proactively link contemporary thinking in classroom management to actual classroom practice. To foster this link, we ask readers to begin with their own theories, perspectives, and biographies relative to classroom management and adaptability, what Hunt (1987) calls "beginning with ourselves." Then throughout the book we help readers extend their personal views of management as they actively construct new meanings for managing classrooms in a pluralistic society. This book also extends and broadens existing textbooks on cultural diversity and multicultural education. Many of these books provide commendable discussions of cultural diversity in school classrooms from sociopolitical and theoretical perspectives but tend to skirt issues of classroom management.

Our extensive experience interacting with preservice and in-service teachers suggests that teacher education programs and their selected textbooks are effective in providing teachers with a view of traditional classroom management theory, but are mostly ineffective in helping teachers understand the limitations of traditional management strategies in contemporary culturally diverse classrooms. Moreover, these same programs, especially those that assume behavioristic approaches to classroom management, are misaligned with the demands on teachers in culturally diverse settings to establish and maintain effective classroom learning environments. Such demands include negotiating classroom interactions with students who represent many different cultures and nationalities. Teachers must also negotiate interactions with and manage learning environments for students with severe disabilities, who were once not a part of regular school classrooms and have not been included in mainstream education. To accommodate linguistic diversity, teachers must also know how to manage the information flow in classrooms where English is not the first language of many of their students.

Cultural pluralism in school classrooms requires new ways of viewing relationships between teachers and students and among students. Student apathy, increased delinquency, and high dropout rates attest to the need for viewing classroom relationships in new ways. This book holds potential to help preservice and in-service teachers understand the social curriculum in multicultural classrooms and to help them consider alternative ways of thinking about their classrooms, what we describe as *alternative metaphors*. Considering alternative metaphors is crucial in an age marked by a crisis of power and authority. Social models based on authoritarian power are untenable in a society that has become pluralistic and global, where multiple voices once silenced are no longer complacent with being marginalized from the mainstream culture. In this book readers will explore shared power and shared decisionmaking, which represent the sort of social negotiations that are needed in a pluralistic society.

With rapidly changing student demographics in schools everywhere, many classrooms that were once monocultural have become multicultural. Preservice and in-service teachers lacking in prior multicultural experiences both in and out of school may be unaware of how culture, ethnicity, and other social phenomena should be foremost considerations in contemporary schools and in managing classrooms. These monocultural teachers may therefore unknowingly implement management strategies based on their social class value systems, on their perspectives about teaching and learning, and on what may have worked for them as students in school. In culturally diverse settings, however, such unknowing implementation of monocultural management strategies undermines some students' learning.

FEATURES

Through ongoing activities that engage readers in reflective thinking, especially the kind of reflective thinking described by Dewey, Freire, and Rorty, users of this book will actively construct and refine their existing personal theories, philosophies, and metaphors for managing culturally diverse classrooms. Throughout the book readers will think about management in terms of a social curriculum. Consistent with constructivist principles, we hold the view that teachers are thinking persons who actively build personal knowledge for classroom social curricula as they interact with the classroom context, not necessarily as they discuss decontextualized theory in settings isolated from school classrooms. In this book we ask readers to rethink traditional metaphors for working in contemporary school classrooms, as presented in the book, and to organize their classroom context from new perspectives that align more suitably to culturally diverse schools.

The organizing principle for this book is metaphorical perspectives of classroom management in contemporary classrooms. Specifically, readers will consider various metaphors for classroom management, including traditional metaphors of industrial management and contemporary metaphors of negotiation and shared authority. Throughout the book readers are encouraged to rethink their personal perspectives of classroom management for culturally diverse classrooms and to reflect on their prior metaphors of management.

One central feature of this book is classroom-based action research (see chapter 11). A model for action research is provided. Using this model, readers are asked to conduct an action research project, or they can design other projects better suited to their personal needs and school contexts. This component of the book helps readers cultivate habits of reflection about management and helps them look closely and critically at traditional and contemporary views of working with classrooms of diverse learners.

Reflective and proactive learning activities in each chapter are intended to help readers explore the key elements of each chapter. Several activities are included in each chapter to engage readers actively in what is being discussed. Self-reflection and self-assessment are intended to help readers explore their knowledge, beliefs, and prior experiences related to organizational and instructional features of classroom life; therefore, conflict resolution issues are included. Readers explore their biographical predispositions for maintaining positive and productive social curricula. The human dimension of this book is intended to ground theoretical premises of classroom management and social curricula in the real life contexts of teachers and students.

ORGANIZATION OF THIS TEXT

Part I of this book includes information and activities that engage preservice teachers in thinking more deeply about how students and teachers live their school lives together. By completing the activities in this section, readers will be helped to reflect deeply and carefully on their views of the social curriculum in culturally diverse classrooms. Chapter 1 introduces readers to social changes that have profoundly influenced the cultural composition of most school classrooms. The purpose of this chapter is to establish a rationale for rethinking social interactions and the nature of management in contemporary classrooms. Chapter 2 introduces readers to traditional and alternative metaphors for thinking about the social curriculum. This chapter also encompasses historical antecedents to contemporary social curricula. Chapter 3 encourages readers to explore the relationship between classroom management and the labels that dominate school life. Chapter 3 also explores readers' prior schooling and nonschooling experiences (autobiography) about management and conflict resolution issues. One purpose of this chapter is to guide readers through a series of activities that help them become aware of their personal beliefs about and theories of classroom interactions. Chapter 4 helps readers come to terms with the everyday demands of classroom management.

Part II, which comprises chapters 5 and 6, focuses on two related themes. One theme addresses conflict and cooperation. Specifically, chapter 5 focuses on how to address cultural conflict in contemporary classrooms and raises questions about the so-called new demands placed on teachers in a pluralistic society. Comparisons are made between managing students in a traditional sense and working with students in a contemporary sense. Chapter 6 focuses on issues related to student behavior and discipline. This later theme is always a foremost concern of every pre-service teacher.

Part III introduces readers to visions of the possible regarding contemporary management. In chapters 8, 9, and 10 we report case studies of successful strategies of schools and teachers. These case studies are intended to help readers understand how selected schools and teachers have established successful learning environments for culturally diverse schools and classrooms. The studies were conducted specifically for this book, and focus on various dimensions of culturally diverse classrooms. They give readers a realistic view of how selected schools and individual teachers successfully negotiate their social curricula with students. Case studies of elementary, middle, and high schools are discussed, as well as vignettes of selected teachers.

Part IV helps readers explore classroom management from a personal perspective and guides readers in their development of a personal practical philosophy for classroom management. Readers engage in a series of reflective activities to develop this philosophy, determine how this philosophy is embodied in their classroom instruction, and develop action research projects associated with these issues.

ACKNOWLEDGMENTS

We are grateful to many persons who, in specific ways, contributed to the development and completion of this book. Various persons need to be acknowledged for helping us with the site visits we made to the three schools described in chapters 8–10. For John Tynes Elementary School in chapter 8, we are grateful to the principal and many teachers who allowed Tom Savage to explore the school openly and critically. For Brown-Barge Middle School (BBMS) in chapter 9, we are grateful to Camille Barr, who was principal of the school at the time this chapter was written and who gave Richard Powell opportunities to explore the school context from the perspective of classroom management. Thanks also goes to many BBMS teachers who rescheduled their class time to participate in interviews about management strategies in the school. For Estacado High School (EHS) in chapter 10, we are grateful to Jerry Lee and Ken Wallace who allowed us to make observations and to talk with those teachers who had time in their daily schedules. Moreover, Jerry Lee regularly spoke to education classes from a nearby university on management in schools with high levels of cultural, ethnic, and socioeconomic diversity. We thank Delores Martinez and Dave Dickerson, two teachers who were at EHS at the time this chapter was written, for allowing us to interview them openly and honestly about management at the school, and for permitting their classrooms to be observed on numerous occasions.

Our most sincere thanks also go to the untiring efforts of the critical reviewers of this book, including Frank D. Adams, Wayne State University; Karen Agne, Pittsburgh State University; Sandra L. DiGiaimo, University of Scranton; Joyce Lynn Garrett, Indiana University of Pennsylvania; Ray Gomez, Arizona State University; Jane McCarthy, University of Nevada at Las Vegas; Barbara McEwan, University of Redlands; Iris Nierenberg, Thomas College; Will Roy, University of

Wisconsin at Milwaukee; Robert Shearer, Miami University; Elizabeth Simons, Kansas State University; and Bruce Smith, Henderson State University. The painstaking work of these reviewers clearly strengthened the quality of our work.

Finally, we are deeply grateful to our editor, Debbie Stollenwerk, whose patience, advice, and emotional support permitted us to eventually reach completion of this work.

DISCOVER THE COMPANION WEBSITE ACCOMPANYING THIS BOOK

The Prentice Hall Companion Website: A Virtual Learning Environment

Technology is a constantly growing and changing aspect of our field that is creating a need for content and resources. To address this emerging need, Prentice Hall has developed an online learning environment for students and professors alike—Companion Websites—to support our textbooks.

In creating a Companion Website, our goal is to build on and enhance what the textbook already offers. For this reason, the content for each user-friendly website is organized by topic and provides the professor and student with a variety of meaningful resources. Common features of a Companion Website include:

For the Professor—

Every Companion Website integrates **Syllabus Manager**™, an online syllabus creation and management utility.

- **Syllabus Manager**™ provides you, the instructor, with an easy, step-by-step process to create and revise syllabi, with direct links into Companion Website and other online content without having to learn HTML.
- Students may logon to your syllabus during any study session. All they need to know is the web address for the Companion Website and the password you've assigned to your syllabus.
- After you have created a syllabus using **Syllabus Manager**™, students may enter the syllabus for their course section from any point in the Companion Website.
- Clicking on a date, the student is shown the list of activities for the assignment. The activities for each assignment are linked directly to actual content, saving time for students.
- Adding assignments consists of clicking on the desired due date, then filling in the details of the assignment—name of the assignment, instructions, and whether it is a one-time or repeating assignment.
- In addition, links to other activities can be created easily. If the activity is online, a URL can be entered in the space provided, and it will be linked automatically in the final syllabus.

- Your completed syllabus is hosted on our servers, allowing convenient updates from any computer on the Internet. Changes you make to your syllabus are immediately available to your students at their next logon.

For the Student—

- **Topic Overviews:** outline key concepts in topic areas
- **Electronic Blue Book:** send homework or essays directly to your instructor's email with this paperless form
- **Message Board:** serves as a virtual bulletin board to post—or respond to—questions or comments to/from a national audience
- **Chat:** real-time chat with anyone who is using the text anywhere in the country—ideal for discussion and study groups, class projects, etc.
- **Web Destinations:** links to www sites that relate to each topic area
- **Professional Organizations:** links to organizations that relate to topic areas
- **Additional Resources:** access to topic-specific content that enhances material found in the text

To take advantage of these and other resources, please visit the *Classroom Management: Perspectives on the Social Curriculum* Companion Website at

www.prenhall.com/powell

BRIEF CONTENTS

CONTENTS

CHAPTER 3: How cultural and personal labels influence teachers and students 48

CHAPTER 4:   Dealing with everyday classroom life: How to develop routines, promote responsibility, and respond to problems   68

CHAPTER 7:   Contemporary issues related to student behavior and discipline   144

PART III: DEVELOPING CULTURAL AND LOCAL UNDERSTANDINGS OF SOCIAL CURRICULA 169

CHAPTER 8: Coping with change at John Tynes Elementary School 174

CHAPTER 9:   The social curriculum of Brown-Barge Middle School: A case report of guidance and mediation   196

CHAPTER 12: Synthesizing your personal theories for management in contemporary classrooms   288

INDEX

P A R T

I

THINKING MORE DEEPLY ABOUT SCHOOL LIFE

CHAPTER

1

Toward Student-Centered Management

And I know
that in order for me to be a full human being
I cannot forever dwell in darkness
I cannot forever dwell in idea
of identifying with those like me
and understanding only me and mine.

(Smith, 1994, p. xxvi)

Almost every person who decides to become a teacher is very concerned about classroom management. In fact, few classroom issues concern preservice teachers more than effective management of classroom learning environments. In our many years of working with prospective teachers across the nation, we have discovered that classroom management is at first defined by prospective teachers as *controlling the behavior* of students so lessons might be taught more smoothly. Then when prospective teachers emerge as beginning teachers, and later when beginning teachers become more experienced, the idea of management broadens to other dimensions of the classroom. These other dimensions include, for example, making the most out of time allotted for each class, available resources, and student potential.

Another dimension of classroom life that is directly related to management in today's classrooms is *student diversity.* Once prospective educators move beyond the myth that management is mostly about controlling student behavior, they will be better prepared to see how knowing about and understanding student diversity, as defined by students' backgrounds and cultural abilities, is central to the successful operation of any classroom.

What we strive to do in this chapter, and throughout the book, is focus on the idea that student diversity makes the management of classrooms more student-centered and culture-centered than what we, as an educational community, have considered such management to be in the past. We do not wish to imply, however, that classroom management should only be viewed in terms of student diversity; there are simply too many other classroom factors that must also be considered. We nevertheless believe that student diversity should now become an important part of our educational conversation about how best to organize management practices in schools and classrooms.

Making student diversity an important part of classroom management gives rise to some pressing questions. For example, what is the relationship between management and student diversity? Can student diversity really be *managed?* How can student diversity and students' backgrounds be used in the classroom to strengthen instruction? Does a focus on student diversity require different approaches to classroom management than what has been used traditionally? These are just some of the questions, among many others, that you will find answers for in this book.

PURPOSE

By making diversity an important component of classroom management, educators must then strive to understand students who might very well be unlike them. This not only relates to what we said in the introduction above, but directly relates to the opening quote to this chapter by Smith (1994). Managing classrooms would be so much easier if all you had to do was teach students who are mostly like you—students who live in the same or a similar community as you, whose families make about the same annual income, who practice the same kind of religion, who eat basically similar kinds of foods, and who have the same language patterns. Just think for a moment about what this would mean for you as a teacher; you walk into a classroom of students whom you feel you already know. You share similar values, needs, and wants with them. And you probably have a work ethic like your students' parents. How convenient all of this would be for you as you plan for, implement, and manage your classroom learning environment. And think how much less taxing it would be for you to give students meaningful educational experiences if you intuitively know how your students learn best and if you know what examples, metaphors, and experiences have the most meaning for them.

As a classroom teacher in today's society, however, you probably *will not* have the opportunity of teaching students who are mostly like you in so many ways. In today's world you simply can't assume that, as a teacher, all you have to do to teach well in your school is to understand students who are like you. Neither can you assume that one model of instruction, for example, the Hunter (1994) model, or one model of behavior management, for example, the Canter model of assertive discipline or the Glasser model of noncoercive management, is suited to all of your students irrespective of their family and/or cultural backgrounds. As a teacher in contemporary society you must get used to the idea, certainly get used to the practice, of being around others, day in and day out, who are unlike you. Their parents' incomes could be much lower or higher, their ethnic community could be unlike any you have interacted with before, their language and English dialect might sound strange, and certainly their home life, with its values and needs, may vary from your own.

The purpose of this chapter is to help you understand that in order to be someone who is capable of teaching effectively in culturally diverse classrooms today, you must be able to identify with students who are very much unlike you, and you must be able to understand and accommodate many other backgrounds and life histories (Greene, 1993a). Unless you develop ways to create classroom environments that somehow are suited to all of your students and that help them feel a part of your classroom curriculum, you will most likely push some students to the margins of classroom life. At the margins they fall silent, feel unheard, become detached, and could learn little about what you are teaching (Greene, 1993b).

BROADENING YOUR PERSPECTIVE OF CLASSROOM MANAGEMENT

After reading this book you will better understand the value of organizing learning environments that pull all of your students to the center of classroom life, where they are given an authentic voice and feel heard, become engaged in your teaching, and can be successful. To help you build this kind of understanding we believe you must first explore various approaches to organizing classroom learning for students who, in most classrooms across the country, now represent many diverse cultural backgrounds, various socioeconomic groups, different religions, and multiple languages. While this kind of diversity appears to be mostly concentrated in urban areas, southwestern border schools, and coastal cities, sociologists report that this new wave of diversity exists even in remote rural areas (Stull, Broadway, & Erickson, 1992).

What is this kind of diversity that we mention above? And what are the student differences associated with this diversity that educators everywhere need to acknowledge, even in remote rural areas where students *seem* to be mostly alike? A few years ago diversity meant mostly ethnic diversity. However, a contemporary perspective of diversity is far more encompassing. For example, in today's terms the idea of diversity includes gender, ethnicity, socioeconomic status, religious beliefs, biographical experiences, parents' occupations and values, learning disabilities, and the list goes on. Amidst all of this diversity, however, you must search for common ground—school and classroom communities cannot thrive without shared understandings and commonly acknowledged goals. These tasks—to affirm diversity while finding common ground—are two of teachers' greatest challenges. This is true whether you teach in a remote, rural school in southern New Mexico, a suburban school in Colorado, or an urban school in Philadelphia.

If you truly affirm the many forms of diversity that your students represent, and if you successfully negotiate common ground and shared goals with your students, then you have no choice but to rethink your role as facilitator of student learning and as manager of student behavior. The recent transformations in classroom life, particularly the diversification of students in multiple ways, is requiring teachers everywhere to reconsider how they interact with every one of their students. Teachers must also consider how they organize instruction so that students are engaged with the content in culturally appropriate ways, and how they make students feel like they are part of school and classroom life (Ladson-Billings, 1994).

In order to effectively create meaningful learning experiences for students today, we believe that you must rethink entirely how you plan, implement, monitor, and maintain learning experiences. The practice of planning, implementing, and monitoring classroom learning experiences and of disciplining students commonly falls under the rubric of *classroom management.* Conventional classroom management, which will be discussed more in chapter 2, suggests that teachers are very much lone authority figures in the classroom, that management is top down, bureaucratic, hierarchical, and teacher centered. However, conventional classroom management, that which fosters a factorylike atmosphere in school, rarely considers what the student does outside of school or where the student is coming from culturally, linguistically, or biographically, among other traits (Erickson & Shultz, 1992).

Conventional classroom management has also been used for many decades as a model for motivating students extrinsically and for delivering content to learners in a prescribed manner (McLaughlin, 1994). Recently, however, conventional classroom management has been challenged.[1] One of our purposes for this book is to help you look closely at strengths and limitations of this kind of management, consider the challenges that have brought it under scrutiny, and consider alternative management strategies.

As you read this book and as you engage in the various activities we suggest, you will be encouraged to broaden your view of classroom management and to think of two alternative strategies—in addition to conventional notions of management—for interacting with students and creating learning experiences. These strategies, which provided us with a framework for writing this book and for rethinking conventional classroom practices, are classroom *mediation* and classroom *guidance.* To better relate these strategies to classroom experiences for learners, we provide you with three cases of teaching in the following section. These cases help you begin thinking about the challenges you face today in creating meaningful learning environments. The cases also help you begin thinking more critically about implementing culturally appropriate instruction.

CULTURAL CHALLENGES FOR TEACHERS AND STUDENTS

Classroom management practices that are culturally appropriate are able to connect specific students more directly to the content being taught (Ladson-Billings, 1994). A culturally appropriate context for learning, according to Au (1980), is "one which is comfortable for the [learners], comfortable for the teacher, and also productive of academic achievement" (p. 112). Surely not every student can be comfortable with every part of your classroom teaching all of the time. That is unreasonable to expect even in the very best of teaching conditions. However, when your classroom curriculum and instruction are culturally appropriate and sensitive to students' backgrounds, then students reportedly connect more with what you are teaching (e.g., Trueba, 1988). One assumption that underlies the movement toward a more culturally appropriate classroom is that all students will have similar opportunities for learning and for maintaining academic excellence throughout the school year (Gay, 1988). Below are cases that represent cultural challenges for teachers and students. These cases are taken from actual reports, and they reflect the kind of challenges you and your students might face.

The Case of the Hawaiian *Talk Story* [2]

After the introduction of a new reading program at the Kamehameha Early Education Program (KEEP), young learners who usually scored no better than the 20th percentile began scoring at or above the 50th percentile. The new program was de-

---

[1]Arguments for alternative educational approaches can be found, for example, in Apple & Beane, 1995; Bullough, 1994; Doll, 1993; McLaughlin, 1994; Perkinson, 1993.
[2]This case is based on the report by Au (1980). See also Jordan, 1985.

voted largely to teaching an understanding of what was read (i.e., teaching comprehension) while the old program emphasized the teaching of phonics (i.e., teaching sound-symbol relationships).

Au (1980) explored why the Hawaiian students' reading improved so dramatically when reading lessons moved from a conventional phonic orientation to a comprehension orientation. Although Au's study is several years old, we believe the study is still very relevant today. The study is certainly germane to our purpose in helping you think more critically about implementing culturally relevant instruction. The teacher in the Au study, who was also Hawaiian, created a type of instruction that melded students' informal communication patterns outside of the school with the teacher's more formal patterns in school. The informal communication patterns outside of the school were similar in many respects to *talk story*, which is a speech event in Hawaiian culture. Conventional reading instruction at the school would not have included talk story as a dimension of the lesson, but talk story was an important dimension of the new KEEP lessons that the teacher created. Tharp and Gillmore (1988) offer a more complete discussion of these lessons.

Au (1980) asserted that both the reading lesson in the classroom and talk story outside the classroom involved a high degree of joint performance. Au reported:

> Even given the controlling influence of the teacher, and sometimes because of it, the children engage in many forms of joint performance. . . . All involve cooperative production among different combinations of children. Speakers may assume a number of roles. . . .No single child takes the lead [and] although the children may divert the discussion somewhat, they never subvert it. (p. 109)

With only conventional teaching practices the Hawaiian students would have talked very little during the lesson. And they would have most likely talked only one at a time. This would have been culturally restrictive for the Hawaiian children. On the other hand, with only the talk story, the reading lesson would have likely turned into a free-for-all, with students all trying to talk at once. The teacher, however, created a lesson that was part conventional and part talk story, thus helping the students feel more culturally familiar with and comfortable in the KEEP learning context.

Also consistent with the KEEP reading program were two elements that the teacher implemented, namely breathing room and equal time. Breathing room occurred when the teacher permitted students to respond the best that they could at the moment, without undue criticism or correction. Equal time occurred when the teacher ensured that all students had equal time to read and to interact with the group. Breathing room, equal time, and talk story collectively provided an environment where there was no coercion on the part of the teacher, only of "continuing cooperation among teacher and children" (Au, 1980, p. 111). Consequently, students responded positively to the demands of learning in a context that was comfortable for them and with which they were partially familiar (i.e., talk story). This context was less restrictive for the Hawaiian students, and consequently engaged them more productively in the reading lesson.

The KEEP Program and Navajo Children

Because the KEEP program was deemed successful with Hawaiian children, the program was taken to the Navajo Reservation in Northern Arizona with the hope that KEEP could have similar results improving the reading skills of Navajo children. Tharp and Gillmore (1988) note how the KEEP program was expected to work on the reservation:

> In exploring the appropriateness for Navajo children of the KEEP systems, all program-team members predicted that the independent-centers activity settings would work in roughly the same way for Navajo children as for Hawaiians. Navajo children also are given a good deal of responsibility at an early age, are accustomed to operating independent of adults, and engage in high levels of sibling caretaking. (p. 182)

What researchers discovered, however, was that Navajo children reacted very differently to the KEEP program than Hawaiian children did. A closer examination of reasons underlying different reactions revealed the influence of local culture on childrens' predispositions to interact with KEEP. Unlike the Hawaiian children, the Navajo children did not function well in group-oriented independent centers. One reason for this is that Navajo children, who worked on their own papers and paid little attention to other students, demonstrated very little peer assistance. The Hawaiian children consistently sought the assistance of their peers whenever they met a problem they could not solve, but Navajo students preferred to approach such problems entirely by themselves, even if this meant not doing or learning much.

Also unlike the Hawaiian children who worked easily in groups that were of mixed sex and ability, Navajo children were accustomed at a very early age by their cultural context to working in same-sex groups. When Navajo children were put in mixed-sex groups in the KEEP program, the students were reluctant to do any of the work.

Clearly, the two cultures of Hawaiian children and Navajo children are extreme contrasts. By looking closely at how KEEP works in these two cultures, a better explanation is offered for how instructional management should be modified when moving from one culture to another, especially with the same instructional materials. What the KEEP experience with Hawaiian and Navajo children suggests is (a) the need to go into the community to find activities during which students are behaving cognitively and socio-emotionally in school-*appropriate* ways, and (b) exploring the knowledge base of teaching for best practices. Combining these *appropriate* ways of learning with knowledge of best practices is then an optimal approach for managing instruction.

The Case of Sioux Indian High School Students[3]

A mainstream high school just outside of a Canadian Indian reservation took considerable pride in maintaining conventional teaching practices. Students from the nearby reservation had to attend the mainstream high school since the reservation

---

[3]This case is based on the report by Wilson (1991).

school only went up to grade 9. So each year a new group of 10th grade Sioux Indian students would begin attending school off of their reservation. Annual reports from the school, however, were not in favor of the Sioux students. Each year approximately 80% of the 10th graders dropped out of the mainstream high school. Teachers at the mainstream school continuously blamed the reservation school for not adequately preparing Sioux students before sending them to the mainstream school. They also complained that the Sioux students lacked any motivation for learning, and they all had underdeveloped skills for studying. Wilson (1991) reported that "teachers said that Indian students could not speak proper English, could not read, would not mix with other students, and just did not fit into the system" (p. 373).

The mainstream high school teachers demonstrated conventional instructional management practices year after year. Rather than seeing their classrooms as socially and culturally organized learning environments, they chose to see their classrooms as behaviorally organized environments, where students compete with each other and where they master certain objectives required by the local district. It was this conventional schooling environment which the Sioux students continuously rejected.

While the teachers blamed the reservation schools and the Sioux students for their lack of success at the mainstream school, the Sioux students reportedly experienced high trauma as they moved from 9th grade at the reservation school to 10th grade at the mainstream high school. While they attended the reservation school Sioux students were observed having high levels of student-student interaction and instructional collaboration during lessons. Teachers in the Sioux school continuously worked in a culturally responsive way for the students. Teachers moved around the room, touching students whenever appropriate and possible and usually made some kind of personal contact with every student in the classrooms during class sessions. Moreover, Sioux students at the reservation school, as reported by Wilson (1991), were rarely asked to recite answers by themselves while in front of a classroom of peers. None of the classrooms in the reservation school were organized into straight rows of desks; rather they were arranged into groups and circles. Moreover, the halls were decorated with pictures of students in their native apparel. And there were many other cultural artifacts decorating all parts of the school.

The mainstream high school contained artifacts that were more representative of highly competitive school environments. For example, the trophy cases were filled with trophies of various competitions, and classrooms were arranged in straight rows reflective of an individualistic approach, rather than a group approach, to teaching. The high school teachers taught lessons using lecture and guided discussion. Students at the high school were expected to recite answers individually in front of their peers when they were called upon, and teachers made eye contact mostly with students who tended to volunteer more responses. The learning environment and corresponding instructional practices at the mainstream high school clearly contrasted those that Sioux students experienced at the reservation school.

Wilson (1991) describes what happened to the Sioux students she talked with at the mainstream school during her study:

> Because [Sioux students] felt unprepared and undervalued emotionally, they undervalued their academic ability and took undemanding courses and/or easy course loads either by choice or by allowing others to make choices for them. One student said that it took him a whole semester to get up the courage to say that he did not want to be in the welding class, "even though I hated every day of it and knew I was smart enough to be taking academic courses." (p. 377)

The mainstream school attended by the Sioux students, with its conventional management orientation, appeared to have been designed for their failure. The level at which the Sioux students appeared to perform at the high school had little to do with their native skills or inherent abilities. Rather, their level of performance was based on how they were perceived by mainstream teachers and students, and how the school was structured and managed. Little in the mainstream school suggested that it was a culturally appropriate place for the Sioux students. In their transition from the reservation school to the high school the Sioux students faced racism, rituals different from their own both institutionally and culturally, and instructional practices, including instructional and behavioral management, that they were fully unprepared to deal with.

The Case of Haitian Communication Patterns[4]

Ms. Ballenger, an experienced early childhood special education teacher, was teaching preschool in a Haitian community in Dorchester, Massachusetts. The school served children of Haitian immigrants, and Ms. Ballenger noticed that more and more Haitian students were being referred to her special education class. All kinds of concerns were given for referring students to Ms. Ballenger: Other educators at the school said the Haitian children were "wild," had "no language," and came from homes where their mothers were depressed. Ms. Ballenger, however, found that most of these newly immigrated Haitian children, after a brief period of adjustment, were responsive, intelligent children. She also discovered that their mothers felt unhappy in a strange country—they were homesick, not necessarily clinically depressed.

Ms. Ballenger became increasingly concerned over and interested in the relationship between Haitian culture and schools in the United States. She eventually took a position as a preschool teacher in a bilingual school where Haitian Creole and English languages were both spoken. Ms. Ballenger also understood that the Haitian culture was central to the school's culture. She was the only teacher at the school who was not Haitian. However, Ms. Ballenger was a fluent speaker of Haitian Creole.

Because of her many years of experience teaching in other early childhood positions, Ms. Ballenger expected to have virtually no problems when she began teaching at the Haitian bilingual school. Moreover, on a personal level Ms. Ballenger felt that she did not really need a lot of *control* over students. Early in the

---

[4]This case is based on the report by Ballenger (1995).

school year, however, she admitted that the children were running her ragged, and she was very uncomfortable with this. While she noticed that her own classroom had little order and control, the other teachers at the school (all Haitian) had orderly classrooms where children appeared affectionate and cheerful, and where they followed directions. Ms. Ballenger then began asking important questions about her classroom. Because she noticed that other classrooms were orderly and productive, she decided that the problem of control didn't really reside in the children. Ms. Ballenger asked herself, "Where, then, does the problem of control reside? What is it that the Haitian teachers are doing with the children that I am not doing?"

Finding answers for these questions was not an easy task. Yet Ms. Ballenger was committed to making her classroom more productive, certainly more orderly and respectful, for her Haitian students. In fact, Ms. Ballenger needed to find answers since the disorder she was experiencing with her students was giving her a lot of discomfort personally and professionally.

Ms. Ballenger was having difficulty with her Haitian students in giving them directions to do things. When she discussed this with some of her peers outside of school, she was told to explore what it was that the Haitian teachers *said* to the children when directions were given. So Ms. Ballenger decided to examine direction-giving behavior, language, and social interactions that Haitian teachers had with their students.

When she started this personal study on direction-giving behavior of Haitian early childhood teachers, Ms. Ballenger was unsure where this would take her. As she conducted the study, however, she soon came to realize the subtle yet powerful influence that cultural patterns of communication have on the interactions she was having with her Haitian students. And she discovered important differences between North American and Haitian teachers in their focus on student behaviors. The most significant difference appeared to be in the area of making connections with the children during control-talk (i.e., where teachers attempted to control students with commands, suggestions, and rules) and during direction-giving (i.e., where teachers gave directions to students to engage in certain activities and tasks). Ms. Ballenger noted that North American teachers sought to make connections with individual children during these times—specifically to make connections with individual students' feelings and problems.

On the other hand, Ms. Ballenger's observations and conversations with Haitian teachers suggested that these teachers emphasized *group values* related to Haitian culture during times of both control-talk and direction-giving, not the *individual values* that are an inherent part of North American culture. Consequently, when control-talk and direction-giving contexts were negotiated by Haitian teachers and their students, there existed a clear and explicit articulation of values and responsibilities of Haitian group membership. The success of the Haitian teachers in setting up an orderly, smooth functioning, and productive classroom rested partly upon their ability to talk to students in terms of group values, not individual values.

As Ms. Ballenger continued studying Haitian classroom practices, she discovered other important approaches to working with Haitian children. All of these approaches were based on differences between classroom practices of Haitian and

North American teachers. Ms. Ballenger gained much insight into some of the difficulties she had been experiencing with Haitian students in her classroom, and she began making changes in some of her interactions with students. For example, she changed the style of control-talk she had been using with the students—she assumed a style of control-talk that aligned more closely with the Haitian teachers. Ms. Ballenger reported this incident:

> I was struck by an experience I had the other day, when I was reprimanding one boy for pinching another. I was focusing, in the Haitian manner, on his prior, indisputable knowledge that pinching was simply no good. I also used my best approximation of the facial expression and tone of voice that I see the Haitian teachers use in these encounters. I can tell when I have it more or less right, because of the way the children pay attention. As I finished this particular time, the other children, who had been rapt, all solemnly thanked me. They were perhaps feeling in danger of being pinched and felt that I had at last been effective. (p. 205)

In coming to terms with the Haitian communication patterns, Ms. Ballenger was able to look beneath the many layers of North American instructional assumptions she was using when she began teaching Haitian children. She was able to question the efficacy of these assumptions for her teaching context. She began incorporating a new set of assumptions—a Haitian set of assumptions for communicating with students, for giving them directions, for organizing a meaningful learning environment, and for understanding how to make Haitian students more comfortable at school.

These changes for Ms. Ballenger, however, did not occur in only a few days. She worked diligently and continuously over time to discover alternative instructional strategies that were more culturally relevant for students. As she discovered alternative strategies, she came to realize the strengths of North American classroom management strategies. Perhaps most importantly she realized the limitations of such strategies for students who were more accustomed to communication patterns other than those associated North American mainstream culture.

ALTERNATIVE MANAGEMENT PRACTICES

The cases above provide a means to discuss how you can move toward alternative management practices. The cases also provide a glimpse at how culturally appropriate instruction relates directly to successful (or unsuccessful) learning strategies. The story of Sioux high school students represents a case of nonadaptation; that is, a case of how some students can be, and clearly are, marginalized from learning environments that are organized around traditional mainstream practices of managing curriculum and instruction. The other stories represent cases of adaptation—specifically of how instructional practices and teacher-student interactions can be adapted to make classroom teaching more sensitive to the cultural needs of students.

What then can we learn about organizing classroom learning environments from the successful experiences of the Hawaiian elementary schoolchildren, from the difficult experiences of the Sioux high school students, and from the transformative experiences of Ms. Ballenger as she worked with Haitian children? What do these stories tell us about conventional classroom management? To help answer these questions, we have identified key points from the case reports that are related to organizing productive learning environments.

- Moving beyond conventional instructional management
- Negotiating culturally appropriate instruction
- Becoming teacher as cultural negotiator
- Becoming teacher as guide
- Understanding school as a social curriculum

These points are briefly discussed below.

Moving Beyond Conventional Instructional Management

For Hawaiian, Navajo, Sioux, and Haitian students there was a clear need to move beyond conventional instructional management. The Hawaiian students made notable gains in their reading scores when instruction was organized differently: specifically, when *talk story* became a central feature of the new reading program. In the Haitian case report, Ms. Ballenger felt more successful in reaching the students when she began incorporating Haitian communication patterns in her classroom instruction. The students consequently felt more comfortable with Ms. Ballenger as they connected with her personally and culturally.

In the case of the Sioux students, mainstream high school teachers held to their conventional mainstream instructional strategies, and the Sioux students continued to drop out of school in high numbers. By believing that the Sioux students owned the problem of succeeding in school and by refusing to explore alternative strategies, teachers failed to move beyond conventional instructional management that had dominated the school learning environment for many years.

Negotiating Culturally Appropriate Instruction

The three cases further suggest that classroom instruction can be enhanced for some students when it is negotiated with students. Additionally, this negotiation can be implicit as well as explicit. For the Sioux 10th grade students there was little negotiation between mainstream teachers and students, and little between school and students. The Sioux students were expected to fit into the existing mainstream school and classroom cultures. And the school expected the Sioux students to do this from the first day they entered the school.

In the KEEP reading program, however, the use of talk story represented an alternative kind of instructional management, namely instructional negotiation. That is, by including talk story in the reading lesson, the Hawaiian teacher implicitly negotiated the learning environment with students; rather than using purely conventional reading practices, the teacher used a type of informal learning that the students experienced in their daily lives outside of school. The teacher didn't necessarily ask students how to change the lesson so they could improve their reading comprehension, but rather the teacher (and the developers of the new reading program) believed that talk story, when combined with some teacher-directed learning, might engage students more naturally, and certainly more meaningfully, in the reading lesson. This kind of implicit cultural negotiation benefited the children in helping them increase their reading skills and achievement levels.

Becoming Teacher as Cultural Negotiator

The cases further point to a very important phenomenon that occurred for the Hawaiian teacher and for Ms. Ballenger, but did not occur for the mainstream teachers of Sioux students. When the Hawaiian teacher incorporated talk story as a cultural dimension of the reading lesson, she moved beyond working only with students' classroom-based behaviors—she began working explicitly with students' cultural predispositions for informal learning. Ms. Ballenger did likewise for her Haitian students; that is, she worked explicitly with students' cultural predispositions when she began using Haitian patterns of communication to gain students' cooperation to do specified tasks and activities. Consequently, Ms. Ballenger became teacher as cultural negotiator, thus infusing dimensions of local culture into her classroom instruction. Similarly, the Hawaiian teacher did this when she used societal communication patterns in her reading lesson.

Becoming Teacher as Guide

In each of the cases the idea of teacher as guide, which will be discussed more fully in chapter 2, was salient. Consistent with the idea of being a guide, the Hawaiian teacher, as well as Ms. Ballenger, appeared more willing to try out different pathways to successful learning for her students. For example, rather than using only the conventional pathway (i.e., content-centered, phonics-centered), the Hawaiian teacher guided students on a learning pathway that intersected with their own cultural landscape. Students were able to relate to this landscape as they used talk story to enhance their reading skills. On the other hand, teachers in the high school were less willing to explore alternative pathways to learning. By remaining on the pathway of conventional instructional management they provided learning experiences that may have been comfortable for the mainstream students, but were mismatched with the personal and academic needs of the Sioux students. Throughout this book you will discover that effective teachers, when viewed as guides for student learning, know alternative pathways, know which routes pass through various cultural landscapes of learning,[5] and know which of these pathways may be most useful for helping students be successful in learning content.

---

[5]See Greene, 1978.

Understanding School as a Social Curriculum

Teachers who learn how to guide students along alternative pathways for learning, who adopt the perspective of cultural negotiator, view schools as having a social curriculum, not merely behavioral and academic curricula. When you view schools as having a social curriculum, then you begin to see more clearly how the cultural diversity of students pertains to your instructional decision making. And you begin to students as individuals with unique predispositions, subjectivities, and talents, rather than seeing them as groups of students labeled and tracked by the school system. More will be said about the social curriculum in chapter 2.

DIVERSITY IN THE CONTEMPORARY CLASSROOM

The key points we discussed above create a need to modify conventional views of classroom management. However, you might be thinking that a group of elementary children in Hawaii, a group of Sioux 10th graders in one mainstream high school in Canada, and a group of Haitian early childhood children in a Haitian community in Massachusetts do not relate to where you are teaching, or where you plan to teach. But the instructional and cultural conflicts that characterized the case reports above are the same kind of conflicts that are now occurring in schools everywhere. Ongoing societal transformations, particularly widespread cultural and linguistic diversity, are requiring educators everywhere to rethink the strategies they use to develop, implement, monitor, and manage their classroom learning environments. All you have to do is look carefully in your home communities to see these transformations. New immigrant students, for example, from Central America, China, Laos, Cambodia, and Vietnam are noticeably changing the composition of student populations in many locations, and they are bringing about new and exciting challenges for classroom teachers. Teachers who are unprepared to receive new immigrant students will do little to help these students connect with their classroom curriculum. On the other hand, teachers who realize the need for change will modify their classroom decision making and corresponding classroom strategies to accommodate these new students (Powell, 1996).

Newly emigrated students, however, are not the only transformation happening to student populations. Another transformation, for example, is the increasing number of Hispanic students attending schools in many locations (Arias, 1986). Some schools such as Hollibrook Elementary School, which is located in the Spring Branch Independent School District of north Houston, have over 80% native Spanish speakers attending school.[6] Conventional mainstream strategies for teaching students like those at Hollibrook Elementary School will fall short of meeting the educational needs of these students. Hollibrook is just one of hundreds of examples where rapidly changing student populations are literally transforming the face of American education.[7]

---

[6]Further information on Hollibrook Elementary School is provided by Powell, Zehm, & Garcia (1996).
[7]For an example of how diversity is influencing schools globally, see Kalantzis, Cope, Noble, & Poynting, 1990.

In addition to ethnic diversity, Jones (1995) explains what further changes you will deal with in today's classrooms:

> Managing classrooms in the 1990s and beyond will be a demanding task. Problems with school funding have, in many states, brought about increased class sizes. At the same time, teachers are being asked to include a wider range of students in their classrooms. This includes not only students with special needs previously served in "pull-out" programs, but an increasing number of students who come to school with personal, social, and emotional needs that negatively impact their ability to benefit from the learning environment. (p. 1)

The practice of placing students in regular classroom settings who have traditionally been placed in pull-out programs, as Jones notes above, and who have traditionally been located in special education self-contained classrooms, is becoming increasingly common. This practice, which is called *inclusion,* is creating yet another challenge for teachers: for general education and special education teachers to work together, in harmony, to maximize educational potential for students who have special needs for learning content and who might pose special challenges for interacting with other students. A common need has therefore emerged for general and special education teachers to increase their understanding and systematic use of inclusive practices (King-Sears, 1995). This means rethinking mainstream ways of organizing learning environments—and of managing classrooms—in terms of inclusion-oriented learning environments.

UNANSWERED QUESTIONS ABOUT CREATING LEARNING ENVIRONMENTS

Increased student diversity gives rise to several important questions related to classroom interaction. If you attended schools that practiced conventional instructional practices, how will you overcome the primacy of these experiences to broaden your perspective of classroom management? If your teachers negotiated little with you and your peers about instruction and about creating classroom curricula, you probably became habituated to conventional ways of thinking about classrooms. Then you, just like your former teachers, might easily fall into the singular role of teacher as content specialist and lone authority figure. How can you move beyond such roles to begin negotiating learning with your students? How will you share power and authority with your students, so their personal needs and interests become part of your classroom decision making? How can you expand your perspectives of conventional classroom management in order to accommodate alternative ways of organizing productive and meaningful learning environments? These may be some of the most important, and certainly the most pressing, questions you face as you move into classrooms that contain students whose backgrounds, and whose ways of understanding the world, differ from your own.

YOUR PERSONAL PRACTICAL PHILOSOPHY FOR ORGANIZING CLASSROOM LIFE

Exploring the questions in this chapter will help you think about the idea of classroom management from various perspectives. Exploring the questions will also help you think carefully, even critically, about your own views, perspectives, beliefs, and tendencies for maintaining positive classroom learning experiences for all of your students. Following the work of Connelly and Clandinin (1988), we use the notion of *personal practical philosophy* to describe your views, perspectives, and beliefs about classroom learning experiences. This kind of philosophy is not something you necessarily get from textbooks or other writings on educational theory, although such writings can certainly deepen and broaden your personal practical philosophy.[8] Nor is such a philosophy something that you can easily and automatically write down on paper, although you might be able to write out some of your beliefs about how students should be engaged in the learning process, how this process should be organized, and how students should behave while you teach a lesson. For the purposes of this book we will focus your attention on your personal practical philosophy for classroom interactions, and for organizing culturally appropriate and personally meaningful learning experiences for all of your students.

If you want to explore your personal practical philosophy for classroom management, and if you want to determine how well this philosophy serves students in the classrooms where you work, then you must explore personal biographical experiences related to education and you must think long about which of these experiences had the greatest influence on your beliefs and classroom actions. These biographical experiences, in addition to any professional teacher preparation you completed, provide you with a mental framework for planning, implementing, and maintaining culturally appropriate learning environments.

DEEPENING YOUR PERSONAL PRACTICAL PHILOSOPHY: AN EXPERIENTIAL APPROACH

Using an experiential approach, this book is intended to help you become more aware of your personal practical philosophy for creating culturally appropriate learning environments. The book is also intended to help you test the validity of your philosophy in the context of real world classrooms. To do this we have created a set of site-based experiences and action research projects that will help you look more deeply into both conventional and alternative strategies for teaching in today's classrooms.

---

[8]There is great likelihood that what you have read as well as what you have heard or discussed with peers have influenced your personal philosophy. This is because reading theoretical discourse about teaching and learning, and talking with peers about various approaches to classroom teaching, help you reflect on your own beliefs and either change or retain them based on new information.

In this first chapter we ask you to begin thinking more deeply about your personal practical philosophy for classroom management. We guide your thinking in exercise 1.1 below by asking you to focus on the salient points we discussed earlier in this chapter and to consider your beliefs about each of these points. In chapter 2 you explore a definition for social curriculum, and you examine three metaphorical frameworks for classroom management. In chapter 3 we ask you to examine the historical and biographical antecedents to your beliefs about teaching and learning.

In Part II you examine the concepts of conflict and compromise as they relate to organizing productive classroom learning environments. In chapter 4 we help you consider how to organize daily life in culturally diverse classrooms. In chapter 5 you consider different kinds of conflict and compromise in the classroom, and in chapter 6 you consider ways of dealing with the different kinds of conflict we describe in chapter 5. Chapter 7 introduces you to contemporary issues related to classroom management and behavior of students.

In Part III you learn how selected schools and teachers organize productive classroom learning environments using strategies and approaches other than those that are traditional and more conventional. By reading about selected schools and teachers, especially those that we call "visions of the possible" for maintaining culturally appropriate classrooms, you will be able to reflect on your ability and willingness to fit into these learning environments. This will further help you determine how your personal philosophy for management is suited to the social curricula in contemporary school classrooms.

In Part IV you reflect on your personal practical philosophy for organizing learning environments, particularly how this philosophy has changed, if at all, as you completed this book. We also ask you to develop a personal plan for implementing and maintaining a culturally appropriate social curriculum, and we engage you in an action research project.

EXERCISE 1.1   Beginning With Yourself

In this chapter we identified key points from the case reports of Hawaiian, Sioux, and Haitian students. The key points, which are listed below, relate to organizing productive and culturally responsive learning environments in today's classrooms.

- Moving beyond conventional instructional management
- Negotiating culturally appropriate instruction
- Becoming teacher as cultural negotiator
- Becoming teacher as guide
- Understanding school as a social curriculum

In this exercise we ask you to think more about each of these key points. This helps you get in touch with your personal philosophy for classroom management (Hunt, 1987). Remain mindful that these key points are grounded in real case reports of classroom teaching. Therefore, as you think about these points, try to determine the validity of your own beliefs about classroom teaching for the Hawaiian, Sioux, and Haitian learners.

Using as many of the key points in this chapter as needed, construct a report similar to one of the case reports described in this chapter. To do this, think back on your educational experiences in elementary, middle, or high school. Identify an event that occurred where issues of diversity and management were involved, either for you or for your peers. Develop a brief account of the event. In your account describe which key points in this chapter, if any, are part of your story. Compare and contrast your story with those developed by peers and colleagues.

EXERCISE 1.2   Building on Biography

Write a brief account of an incident you recall having to do with an issue of diversity in one of your former classroom settings. Relate the account to your idea of classroom management.

CONCLUSION

At the beginning of this chapter we noted that few issues provoke more concern in prospective and beginning teachers than classroom management and student discipline (Veenam, 1984). In our many experiences as teacher educators in various institutions we continuously hear prospective teachers ask for simple lock-step procedures and for fail-safe algorithms for managing classrooms of students and dealing with discipline problems. There are, of course, various theoretical models, including lock-step procedures and algorithms, to be considered and discussed in the safe corners of university campuses far away from the reality of classroom life. What we have found, and what you will probably find too, is that discussions which focus on theoretical models of management and discipline tend to have their roots embedded deeply in behavioral psychology. Consequently, prospective teachers come away from these discussions believing that one type of management (i.e., one model, one algorithm) could be generalizable to all students. However, in today's classrooms, where acknowledgment of diversity has reached its pinnacle and where pluralism has now become a prevailing theme for schools, the one-size-fits-all men-

tality for models of classroom management and student discipline is problematic. If there ever has been a time that we, as an educational community, need to look for alternative strategies for organizing meaningful and productive learning environments, and for working with students who represent so many diverse and interesting backgrounds, that time is now. This means that every one of us who is associated with schools must consider alternative ways for setting up classroom instruction, for interacting with learners, and for thinking about teacher-student relationships. This means rethinking the role of classroom manager.

Our purpose for writing this book, as we mentioned earlier in this chapter, is to help you consider alternative ways for thinking about and implementing culturally appropriate instruction in the midst of increasing student diversity. This does not mean you have to toss out everything that has already been written about classroom management. However, this does mean that you must look closely and carefully at existing theoretical models of management—to determine their level of appropriateness for today's classrooms and for today's students.

Societal transformations globally and locally, when combined with technological advancements, have put us at a crossroads. We can choose to stay on the same road of conventional classroom management. This is becoming increasingly bumpy and dangerous for some groups of students. Or we can choose an alternate road—one that will pass through various cultural landscapes of learning, and one that may be more appropriate for students who are now being marginalized from successful learning in hundreds of classrooms, such as the Sioux 10th graders described in this chapter. Because the social fabric of society has indeed changed, we believe that you have no option in today's classrooms other than to explore alternate roads; you must consider new ways of organizing and managing classroom experiences that provide interesting, engaging, and meaningful learning experiences for all students.

REFERENCES

Apple, M., & Beane, J. (1995). *Democratic schools.* Alexandria, VA: Association for Supervision and Curriculum Development.

Arias, B. (1986). The context of education for Hispanic students: An overview. *American Journal of Education, 95,* 26–57.

Au, K. H. (1980). Participation structures in a reading lesson with Hawaiian children: Analysis of a culturally appropriate instructional event. *Anthropology & Education Quarterly, 11*(2), 91–115.

Ballenger, C. (1995). Because you like us: The language of control. *Harvard Educational Review, 62*(2), 199–208.

Bullough, R. V. (1994). Digging at the roots: Discipline, management, and metaphor. *Action in Teacher Education, 16*(1), 1–10.

Connelly, F. M., & Clandinin, D. J. (1988). *Teachers as curriculum planners: Narratives of experience.* New York: Teachers College Press.

Doll, W. E. (1993). *A post-modern perspective on curriculum.* New York: Teachers College Press.

Erickson, F., & J. Shultz. (1992). Students' experience of the curriculum. In P. W. Jackson (Ed.), *Handbook of research on curriculum* (pp. 465–485). New York: Macmillan Publishing.

Gay, G. (1988). Designing relevant curricula for diverse learners. *Education and Urban Society, 29*(4), 327–340.

Greene, M. (1978). *Landscapes of learning.* New York: Teachers College Press.

Greene, M. (1993a). Diversity and inclusion: Toward a curriculum for human beings. *Teachers College Record, 95*(2), 211–221.

Greene, M. (1993b). The passions of pluralism: Multiculturalism and the expanding community. *Educational Researcher, 22*(1), 13–18.

Hunt, D. E. (1987). *Beginning with ourselves.* Cambridge, MA: Brookline Press.

Hunter, M. (1994). *Enhancing teaching.* New York: Macmillan.

Jones, V. (1995, April). *Classroom management: An expanded role for teachers.* Paper presented at the annual meeting of the American Educational Research Association, San Francisco.

Jordan, C. (1985). Translating culture: From ethnographic information to educational program. *Anthropology & Education Quarterly, 16,* 105–123.

Kalantzis, M., Cope, B., Noble, G., & Poynting, S. (1990). *Cultures of schooling: Pedagogies for cultural difference and social access.* New York: The Falmer Press.

King-Sears, M. E. (1995). Teamwork toward inclusion: A school system and university partnership for practicing educators. *Action in Teacher Education, 17*(3), 54–66.

Ladson-Billings, G. (1994). Like lightning in a bottle: Attempting to capture the pedagogical excellence of successful teachers of African American students. *Qualitative Studies in Education, 3*(4), 335–344.

McLaughlin, H. J. (1994). From negation to negotiation: Moving away from the management metaphor. *Action in Teacher Education, 16*(4), 75–84.

Perkinson, H. J. (1993). *Teachers without goals, students without purposes.* New York: McGraw-Hill.

Powell, R. R. (1996). The music is why I teach: Intuitive strategies of successful teachers in culturally diverse learning environments. *Teaching and Teacher Education, 12*(1), 49–61.

Powell, R. R., Zehm, S., & Garcia, J. (1996). *Field experience: Strategies for exploring diversity in schools.* Upper Saddle River, NJ: Merrill/Prentice Hall.

Smith, A. D. (1994). *Twilight.* New York: Anchor Books.

Stull, D., Broadway, M., & Erickson, K. (1992). The price of a good steak: Beef packing and its consequences for Garden City, Kansas. In L. Lamphere (Ed.), *Structuring diversity: Ethnographic perspectives on the new immigration* (pp. 35–63). Chicago: University of Chicago Press.

Tharp, R., & Gallimore, R. (1988). *Rousing minds to life: Teaching, learning, and schooling in social context.* New York: Cambridge University Press.

Trueba, H. (1988). Culturally based explanations of minority students' academic achievement. *Anthropology & Education Quarterly, 19*(3), 270–287.

Veenam, S. (1984). Perceived problems of beginning teachers. *Review of Educational Research, 54*(2), 143–178.

Wilson, P. (1991). Trauma of Sioux Indian high school students. *Anthropology & Education Quarterly, 22,* 367–383.

What Research Says to Practitioners

For additional reading that is related to this chapter, see the following items:

Hollins, E. (1996). *Culture in school learning: Revealing the deep meaning.* Jahwah, NJ: Lawrence Erlbaum Associates, Publishers.

Kozol, J. (1991). *Savage inequalities: Children in America's schools.* New York: Crown Publishers.

Ladson-Billings, G. (1994). *The dreamkeepers: Successful teachers of African American children.* San Francisco: Jossey Bass.

Lamphere, L. (Ed.). (1992). *Structuring diversity: Ethnographic perspectives on the new immigration.* Chicago: University of Chicago Press.

C H A P T E R

2

Managing Interpersonal Relationships in Your Classroom:

Historical and Metaphorical Perspectives

Texts place surprisingly little emphasis on assisting beginning teachers to learn how to think about and productively frame educational problems. In particular, little consideration is given to the interpersonal relationships teachers might desire to build with students or the social implications of implementing one or another discipline and management system.

(Bullough, 1994)

In chapter 2 we focus more specifically on the interpersonal relationships—what we call the *social curriculum*—that you might develop with your students. In the preceding chapter we focused more specifically on the cultural dimensions of management. After reading chapter 1 you should now realize that the professional framework in which you build the social curriculum is a *cultural framework*—the cultural backgrounds of your students meet and mingle with each other, and with your own cultural background, to make up the social curriculum. The social curriculum, as we view it throughout this chapter and throughout the remainder of this book, is central to teaching and learning. This is because this curriculum is comprised of the knowledge, skills, beliefs, emotions, and attitudes which are deemed necessary for people to work productively and live harmoniously together in the classroom. Consequently, the social curriculum is among the varied factors which either engage or disengage students from the content you teach throughout the school year. The purpose for this chapter is to help you understand the part that the social curriculum plays every moment of classroom life.

To achieve this purpose, we first discuss three metaphors that you can use to help you better understand the idea of social curriculum. These metaphors are *traditional management, guide,* and *mediation.* Second, we discuss historical antecedents to the traditional management metaphor, which we also refer to as the *factory model of management.* Because diversity, as a classroom reality, has historically not been an explicit dimension of management concerns, *diversity* is essentially lacking in the historicity of classroom management. Concurrently, the notion of diversity is not as explicit in this chapter as it is in other chapters in this book. The third section of this chapter focuses on the authority you have as a teacher. In this third section we connect teacher authority with the metaphors discussed earlier. In the fourth section of the chapter we compare the social curriculum to other forms of curricula.

METAPHORICAL THINKING ABOUT THE SOCIAL CURRICULUM

Managing Social Interactions

Because the traditional management metaphor—to *manage* as if in a factorylike or industriallike setting—is so prevalent in schools we will discuss it first. To *manage* can be interpreted to mean achieving a purpose. To manage can also mean to handle and to control (from the Italian *mano,* meaning "hand"). As conceived traditionally for schools, management had multiple purposes. Although discussed more fully later in this chapter, four of these purposes are to:

- *organize* and *control* what goes on in classrooms,
- enhance *predictability* of student behavior,
- promote *efficiency* in the school day,
- ensure students' *obedience* to a predetermined set of codes or rules.

As traditionally conceived, then, from a management perspective your authority as a teacher is based on your status as a teacher and adult. This is called *positional authority.* As a manager with positional authority you define what is appropriate and inappropriate classroom action and what constitutes a problem. Unlike culturally sensitive and democratic approaches to interacting with students in today's classrooms, students had little or no say-so in deciding appropriate classroom actions or in deciding what constitutes a problem. When students have little say-so in what happens in the classroom you exercise authority unilaterally. Consequently, in both explicit and implicit ways, you, the teacher, have ultimate decision-making power.

Traditional classroom management, as we have discussed it in the aforementioned paragraph, covers a lot of educational territory. A significant segment of this education literature has been rooted in behavioral psychology and consequently has focused on management in terms of *controlling* students' behavior. Teachers are viewed as successful managers when they *control* severe disruptions (e.g., fights) in the classroom or school by themselves without the assistance of administrators or other professionals; enforce laws; and fashion rules and procedures (as individuals or with a team). There are, however, broad definitions that entail:

- organizing, or keeping track of one's materials, establishing seating charts, and maintaining an accurate and up-to-date grading system,
- planning (using a variety of instructional techniques),
- knowing students,
- evaluating oneself, and
- shaping the physical environment.

The following excerpt serves to depict the complexity—and the potential positive power—of management as described above.

Pam's Classroom

Pam is a second-grade teacher with 25 years of experience in classrooms. In this vignette, George Noblit, a professor who observed and sometimes participated in Pam's classroom as part of a school oral history, describes one of the class rituals and analyzes its meaning.

> Discipline never really was an issue in Pam's class; rather, it was taken for granted. The children knew she expected them to behave, and largely they did. This was true even though Pam was likely to be given the children in the second grade with the major discipline problems. I counted four of her twenty-four students in this category (2 boys and girls, both races for each gender). . . . Pam's fundamental strategy with all the children (I noted in my field notes) was to lead the children to the right answers, to smile and praise their efforts. (Noblit, 1993, 30)

> The event as I saw it then was a "public testing event." I saw the event this way: it involved the teacher standing in front of the class, asking for answers to questions or problems that the children were to give for immediate and public evaluation. The students were competing to get the right answer for any single question, and the one who got the most right answers would get a chance to draw from the "surprise box" of prizes Pam and Sharon kept full of trinkets. A question was asked, and Pam usually called on someone who had raised a hand. Wrong answers were usually greeted with the response, "Can anyone help (the student's name)?" Children often raised their hands as soon as they recognized the wrong answer, and Pam would then call on one of them. . . . I repeatedly interpreted this as students' favorite time in the classroom. Pam's power made the collectivity stronger and each child stronger as a consequence. (Noblit, 1993, 32–33)

> There was, of course, much more to Pam's class each and every day, but I think you can get a sense of what it was like in our class. In educational jargon, the class was more teacher-centered than child-centered, and Pam saw this as appropriate. She felt it was her responsibility to set the agenda for the children to learn, and to teach them. The children were responsible for doing their work and for not interfering with others doing their work. . . . We were all responsible for looking after the collective good of the class, and I had to learn how I could participate appropriately in this. (Noblit, 1993, p. 30)

Noblit (1993) further highlights the difference between "power used for its own sake and power used for the service of others" (p. 35). Noblit believes that Pam used her power and her means of control in the service of continuity and community. Noblit's portrayal of Pam's moral authority adds depth to our understandings of authority and power. *Control* is one outgrowth of power: It represents the enacting of power in order to direct another person or to delimit the environment. Noblit shows us that control is not something totally negative in classrooms, but it is not the only end, either. Bowers and Flinders (1990) note that *solidarity* is another possible outcome of human interactions. *Solidarity* means that students, while being very diverse, have some shared interest, some shared power, and thus some cohesiveness.

During actual classroom events, the social curriculum is part and parcel of whatever academic tasks are taking place. Academic tasks that reflect the traditional management metaphor revolve around activities that are directly controlled by the teacher. This is reflected in the language of instruction: pedagogical terms such as *on-task, work sheets,* and *seat work* signify a teacher-controlled environment. Classroom activities such as *lecture, recitation,* and *closely monitored individual seat work* further exemplify the traditional management model.

As with all ways of viewing classroom and school life, management has its limitations. Criticisms of traditional management suggest that this approach forces obedience and thus may lead more often to confrontations with students. Other criticisms suggest that traditional management fails to teach students how to be responsible (Lickona, 1991). Proponents of Assertive Discipline, a well-known management program, have issued denials of the program's singular focus on obedience and have asserted that the approach encourages students to be "self-managers" (Canter, 1989).

The problem is that school management, when framed by factory and industry (not school) contexts, while requiring unquestioning obedience, incorporates a series of unexamined assumptions about the nature of power and control in classrooms and schools. The management metaphor excludes a consideration of consciousness and responsibility, which rely on actions related to our other two metaphors of *guiding* and *mediating.* Traditional forms of school management, because they are concerned with unilateral control, are limited in their ability to address these vital questions: What are the varied purposes of classroom and school relationships? What are different participants' interests, and whose interests are being served? How *should* we relate to students, and how *should* students relate to each other?

Guiding Social Interactions

The second metaphor we introduce in this chapter for managing interpersonal relations is a *guide.* A guide exhibits and explains points of interest; the word is akin to Old English *witan,* which means "to look after" or "to know." Guides tend to have very implicit knowledge of *the way* and of all its difficulties and dangers. The purpose of guiding is to enhance students' sense of individual responsibility and self-discipline. The metaphor of *teacher as guide* is based on personal and expert authority: who we are and what we know. When acting as a guide, we express expert authority but reject overt coercion. How successful we are depends on how much we develop mutual respect with students that is based on reasoned action.

Guidance is based on a teacher's (or other educator's) interpretation—sometimes an intuitive interpretation—of a positive direction for students. This requires understanding students' unique qualities (their talents and needs), their life contexts (classroom, school, family, community), and their diverse traits (ethnicity, culture, background, language). Guidance can be implicit and nonverbal. Often, we guide students by modeling and demonstrating how we hope they will act. For example, we may model a way of talking to students (our manner in classrooms) that expresses a language of acceptance or nonacceptance of others. We can model constant confrontation over seemingly small issues or react confrontively only when major situations occur. More explicitly, we can engage students in school tasks that involve caring for the environment, or we can conduct community service projects. Guiding is an everyday occurrence in many classrooms, although it may appear to be sometimes less explicit, as suggested in the following account of Mrs. Martin's classroom (see Jackson, 1992, pp. 51–52).

Elaine Martin's Classroom

Mrs. Martin is working with a reading group when she notices that Kevin and Judith, who are seated side by side at their desks, are talking with one another.

"Kevin and Judith, are you visiting or helping?" she asks.

"I'm working," says Kevin.

"Visiting," says Judith.

Mrs. Martin pauses for an instant, then asks, "Kevin, do you think you can sit there and work quietly without talking to yourself or to Judith?"

"I think so," says Kevin.

She then asks the exact same question of Judith, who says she thinks she needs to move. Mrs. Martin sends her to an empty desk on the opposite side of the room. Several minutes later Mrs. Martin notices the two of them together again at Kevin's desk and once again asks if they are visiting or helping.

"Helping," they both chorus.

From the standpoint of the pupils, what is common to all of these episodes is that the children being questioned are invited by the teacher to step outside their own skin, to see their actions from an external perspective and often to give them a name or label from that perspective. . . . Being questioned in this way encourages the children to become judges of their own actions. Yet the freedom to make those judgments, as the process also makes clear, is by no means unconstrained. The categories by which to judge are often set in advance and are usually few in number. There are other people present who are doing the judging as well—the teacher, one's classmates who are looking on, and sometimes an adult observer or two—which means that one's own judgment may not only be tested against those of others but may sometimes be contested, called into question, disagreed with. (Jackson, 1992, pp. 51–52)

What differentiates guidance from management in this instance is the commitment to allowing students to take responsibility as a part of the guidance process (which requires that they have some freedom to act). Choosing is central to guidance. Guidance is reflected in academic tasks such as demonstrations, experiments, and teacher-directed projects that incorporate student choice.

As with management, the limitations of the guidance metaphor relate to unexamined assumptions. Guiding students toward a predetermined way of acting that is simply assumed to be good but is not constantly reexamined may be detrimental to students' welfare. Acting as a guide, therefore, may not help us to answer these questions:

What part should students play in framing the purposes of education?

What should be negotiated?

Mediating Social Interactions

A third metaphor we introduce in this chapter for managing interpersonal relationships in the classroom is *mediation.* To mediate is to be in the middle of, to reconcile differences, to bring accord by action as an intermediary (from the Latin *medius,* meaning "middle"). Mediation is intended to resolve conflict and to enhance students' sense of social responsibility. Kohn (1991) argues that two of the approaches to changing students' behaviors and attitudes are "encouraging commitment to values" (to help that child see himself or herself as the kind of person who is responsible and caring) and "encouraging the group's commitment to values" (to help the child internalize the value of community) (p. 501). Schaps and Solomon (1990) talk about how children are motivated by "belonging and contributing" (p. 39) and Glasser (1990) talks of children's needs for "power and belonging" (p. 54). Those comments and others signal the need for schools to balance individual and social responsibility. In an ideal sense, the purpose is to create a community in the classroom or school.

Authority as a mediator in social interactions is based on our relationship with students. As a mediator you need to realize that you also become a *negotiator*—you negotiate authority with students, for example, nodding affirmatively on reciprocity. The purposes of negotiation should be to establish individual responsibility (self-caring and self-control) and cultural solidarity (social caring and social control). Negotiation cannot work without an individual commitment that incorporates a sense of responsibility for oneself. Nor can negotiation work without a sense of social responsibility which enables shared interests to be sought and conflicts to be directly faced.

Teachers mediate classroom and school social problems, some rules and procedures, and students' social responsibilities in the classroom. The process involves students and teachers working collaboratively, in democratic and culturally sensitive ways, to solve problems and make decisions. Both teachers and students need to exercise power for solidarity to be shaped. Mediation also concerns gaining *power with,* and not *power over* others. You have to be comfortable with and open to some uncertainty, which is especially difficult for new teachers. Mediation is built on a desire to determine shared interests, an ability to confer concerning decisions to be made and curricular ideas to be plumbed, and a willingness to face up to conflict and then effect compromise.

Academic tasks that require overt negotiation of purposes and processes and involve the collaborative resolution of problems are associated with mediation. We are mediating when we negotiate with students about the purposes of an academic portfolio, when we co-plan a community research project with them, and when we confer with a small group of students about what they are learning and what they want to learn, for example, in social studies. There is a distinction between choosing and negotiating authority in the ways just mentioned: "Choosing is not the same as actively negotiating the means and ends of one's education. Mere choosing embodies an individualistic, smorgasbord conception of freedom" (Nicholls & Hazzard, 1993, p. 102).

Lee Colsant's Classroom: A Case of Mediation

We now present an example of a teacher who, after many years of teaching, changed his conceptions of classroom authority. Lee Colsant had taught high school French for 17 years and was secure in his abilities as a teacher. One year, however, his students were resistant to the usual curriculum. At the time he was taking a graduate course that was intended to challenge the traditional norms of high school lecture-and-recitation teaching. Lee was determined to become more negotiatory, so he began to listen more closely to his students and to consider their interests. First he describes how he feels about the students, and then he tells a story about changing his grading system.

> Chandra is singing "rejoice, rejoice." I don't know why; I don't even care why. I'm just happy she's singing. The class is working on the reflexive verb *se coucher* (to go to bed). I decide to draw on how the absence of parents prevents children from being able to sleep; how a babysitter is no substitute for a mother's own security. The class reminisces silently, each one recalling memories evoking stories. I look out onto faces. They recollect quickly. Memories push their pens, testing their creativity as writers.[17]
>
> With midterm exams over, grades must be given. I decide to try something I've never done. They will give themselves their semester grade. They already know their exam grade. They know what effort they've made and the results of past tests. So, it seems to me they know where they stand in terms of an overall grade.
>
> "Would you all take out a sheet of paper?" I ask. "Put your names on them." ... "I'd like you to put your heads on your desks, close your eyes, and go deep into yourselves." ... "Imagine you are finishing your studies abroad; you are alone in the French Alps. There is just you and the surrounding beauty of the mountains." ... "You have just finished your short stint in learning French. You know how much effort you have given to this adventure. Now, alone on this mountain top, all alone, search your interior and give yourself a grade."
>
> Quietness reigns. It's still-life. Then heads begin to perk up. Pens and pencils move. Papers are passed in. Of the 24 who submitted a grade with its justification, I disagreed with only two students, who I thought inflated their grades and whose justifications also seemed inflated. Others were too harsh, and I pushed them up. I held private conferences with the two. We discussed what I thought were inconsistencies, and a new grade was agreed on. (Colsant, 1995, p. 79)

Lee Colsant's tale shows the connection between knowing students and moving away from a reliance on the traditional management metaphor, in social, cultural, and academic terms. His negotiation of semester grades was quite a risk for Lee, but taking that risk allowed him to learn what students really thought and what sort of responsibility they could handle.

Not everything needs to be mediated. On a schoolwide level, if one chooses to teach within a public school, such practices as grading, holding classes within certain periods, responding to bells, doing fire drills, and the like, are nearly inescapable aspects of school life. Some matters are best resolved by a traditional management decision; when you know of a student who brings a weapon to school, for example, you refer the student immediately to the principal's office. Mediation does not entail abrogating your power to make unilateral decisions or to demand certain actions of students. For example, we may not wish to negotiate with students about whether to perform community service as part of a unit on the environment, because we feel that community service is fundamental to our social curriculum in order to promote social involvement and responsibility.

In the classroom a teacher can ignore students, encourage them, mediate in one form or another, or try to directly control without negotiation. A common principle of classroom action is to ignore what appears to be peripheral and to control when a student is seriously disrupting the class or when the teacher believes that a certain direction must be taken. All else is grounds for mediation.

The questions we need to ask ourselves about mediation are: When will I *not* mediate? Why not mediate?

EXERCISE 2.1   How Do Teachers Manage, Guide, and Mediate?
Connecting the Ideas

How are these metaphors interconnected?

Why do we need to understand and act on all three metaphorical representations?

Connecting Your Experience

What examples of managing, guiding, and mediating can you remember from your experiences as a student?

Consider one particularly memorable situation when you were a precollege student. If you had been the teacher in that situation how might you have managed, guided, or mediated?

HISTORICAL PERSPECTIVES OF CONTEMPORARY MANAGEMENT TRENDS AND ISSUES

How educators have viewed interpersonal relationships in schools—especially relationships between students and teachers, and between students and the content to be learned—has changed over the years. More recently there has been an emphasis on interacting with students in ways that are more negotiable (Boomer, Lester, Onore, & Cook, 1992) and more culturally responsive (Ladson-Billings, 1994; Perry & Fraser, 1993). In this second part of chapter 2 we offer a brief historical overview of educational changes that have influenced managerial practices. To see where management is today you must first understand how it came to be what it is today. The overall purpose of this second part of the chapter, then, is to help you develop a fuller and broader understanding of the purposes and processes of social interactions in schools as they have unfolded over time and as they have given rise to the ideas we discussed in this chapter.

Earlier Views

Traditionally, teaching was viewed as a means of ensuring the transmission of a community's beliefs. In Greek and Roman societies, teachers promoted moral values and virtue. Harsh discipline, including beatings, was the rule (*paideuo*, the Greek root word of pedagogy which means "to teach," also means "I correct, I discipline"). Schools emphasized courage and self-control as the marks of character. Good behavior was more important than academic skills. In these and other traditional societies teachers also preserved the community's oral histories.

Relationships between teachers and students were usually quite formal, and teachers' authority came from their status as adults (positional authority) and not necessarily from their attributes (personal and expert authority). In Christian societies from medieval times forward, teachers were drawn from the clergy who maintained a rigid adherence to biblical text. Formal learning of the classics (Greek and Roman) was quite narrowly interpreted. Schools, for those few who attended them, emphasized hard work, routine, and a striving for excellence, not self-expression. With some exceptions, teachers relied on physical punishment to enforce order and on academic drill to ensure memorization.

Colonial Times

Puritan education in the New England colonies mirrored traditional education around the world in the 17th and 18th centuries. In early colonial societies education and religion were not necessarily separable. The limited education that existed was intended to strengthen children's belief in God and church and to ensure the survival of the community.

Colonial children of the 17th and 18th centuries were treated more like adults. At ages six to eight they began wearing adult clothing, engaging in the same family activities, and attending the same church services as adults. The child-rearing practices of Puritans were quite influential. Puritans practiced corporal punishment, and the word *Puritan* has today assumed a somewhat negative cast of one who is completely intolerant and who lives by the phrase "spare the rod and spoil the child." But much of the writing about how to raise children focused on providing an upbringing that was directed by love and consistency of response, not merely punishment. Discipline was a family and community affair, in addition to being an institutional imperative in schools. If you were a teacher during this time, then you assumed the mantle of authority provided by a restrictive, cohesive community.

In terms of classroom actions, teachers of the time were little different in the Middle Colonies and the South. However, two European writers, John Locke and Jean-Jacques Rousseau, challenged the prevailing 18th century beliefs about teaching and learning. Locke's ideal was a private education at home (for males only), with a parent and tutor presiding. Because he held that human nature was malleable and not fully determined by inborn inclinations, Locke was especially concerned with infancy and childhood. A classical training in weaponry, politics, and public speaking was to be de-emphasized, and children were to be taught to understand rationally the need for mental self-control.

Rousseau believed that learning discipline should not come through interactions in schools. The focus, like Locke's, was on self-control rather than societally imposed control. But Rousseau's idea of teaching differed from Locke's training in rationality. Teachers—according to Rousseau—were to act as guides, rather like advance scouts on a trek into the wilderness. Rousseau did not want the imprint of civilization on children before they had learned how to conduct themselves in the world. Until at least age 12, he felt that boys (girls were peripheral to his educational ideas) should be exploring the natural world. Rousseau's ideal curriculum, while hardly influential with regard to teachers' day-to-day actions, exerted tremendous influence among educational thinkers and writers.

The 19th Century

After the Revolutionary War, citizens in the new nation of the United States of America set out to conquer and settle the western lands. Part of that settlement involved constructing schools and ensuring the survival of the republic. In the 19th century there were actually two styles of teaching and two sorts of schooling taking place. You have already read about one style of teaching; the traditional way of strict teacher authority and student obedience. There were, however, 19th century educational innovators, such as Johann Pestalozzi, who challenged traditional ways that teachers and students interacted. Pestalozzi (1746–1827) was a schoolmaster who late in life achieved fame for his school at Yverdon in Switzerland, where he taught from 1805–1825. He has been called a disciple of Rousseau, who himself reacted to the ideas of Locke and other Enlightenment thinkers. Pestalozzi concurred with Rousseau that the child is innately good and that society can corrupt the child's nature. He frequently employed the metaphor of the child as a "bud not yet opened." Your job as a teacher was to help the bud to unfold, to allow the natural course of development to take place. Like Rousseau, Pestalozzi spoke of the importance of nurturance for young children during the process of unfolding. He perceived the school as a family, wherein there existed mutual love between teacher and student.

With regard to the nature of schooling, there was a gulf between life in rural and urban schools. The 19th century was marked by the continuing importance of one-room schools in rural areas, but the emergence of multiroom schools in urban areas became inevitable. There were many differences between rural and urban classrooms. One-room schools were situated in face-to-face communities with well-marked social patterns of life. Every day the children came to the teacher's desk to recite their lessons, returned to their benches shared with classmates, and quite possibly tutored or were tutored by another student. Children remained with the same teacher for many years (in what we now call *multiage classes*), and local parents retained control of their small schools. These schools, which seemed to be Pestalozzi-like in their orientation, still clung in part to the Puritan ethic.

In the growing cities, teachers taught in quite traditional ways, except that growing populations of school-age children and the effects of industrialization led to a push for greater efficiency in handling larger numbers of students. In the early part of the century there was an educational movement that would herald the coming changes, especially in school management. The movement was started by Joseph Lancaster (1778–1838), who was a major international figure in education during the first three decades of the 19th century. In 1798 Lancaster opened a school in London that featured economic, efficient instruction, inculcated discipline through routine, and induced motivation by competition. The crux of his systematic approach toward managing large groups of students (sometimes numbering in the hundreds) was the use of *student tutors* or *monitors. Qui docet, discit* ("He who teaches, learns!"), Lancaster proclaimed. This monitorial system utilized a rigid, bureaucratic process of instruction in which students held to an unbending schedule of individual seat work and recitation that was monitored by older students.

The monitorial system had ushered in the development of larger school systems, with their bureaucratic organization, detailed rules, standardized curriculum, and accountability procedures. In many locations the Lancaster school had initiated formal teacher preparation and had hastened support for mass education and tax-supported schools. A more hidden result was the infusion into education of business and factory ideologies and the enticing metaphorical language of the factory. Learning as a *product*, teachers as *managers*, and teaching as *science*; all of these metaphors that represent school life yet today can be traced to the ideas of the monitorial movement.

Pestalozzian models of teaching may have been popular among educational leaders, but most schools remained as they had long been: overcrowded, dependent on endless drill and practice exercises, and centered on monitorial control of students. During this time there were subtle yet powerful ways to control students. Instead of working at communal tables or benches, students sat at desks bolted to the floor, in rows, facing forward. Urban classrooms often contained 40 to 48 desks per room, accommodating as many as 60 students. Unlike the country schools, learning to read and write in urban schools was a private experience. Schools became graded by age groups, and ability grouping within classes was expanded. Texts were mandated and curriculum guidelines became formalized. Blackboards ultimately replaced the individual slates of students in country schools, and individual report cards replaced student performances and exhibits as a means of showing learning or achievement.

In both systems of schooling—rural and urban—the teacher's authority was absolute. Obedience was assumed, and inappropriate behavior, however defined, was punished severely. Some school reformers wanted to continue moral training but discontinue the physical coercion. Evidence suggests that corporal punishment diminished in the latter half of the century, although there may have been an increasing reliance on the fear of parental punishment.

Whatever the nature of punishment, the predominance of recitation and individual seat work as teaching methods and management models meant that learning was synonymous with rote imitation of skills and the reproduction of knowledge from standard texts. Finkelstein (1989) has proposed that there were three different styles of teaching actually taking place during the 19th century. Particularly in one-room schools, teachers acted as *overseers* who simply conducted the requisite recitations and closely monitored students' actions to ensure obedience. Teachers in urban schools could be characterized as *drillmasters* because they focused on the reproduction of increasingly complex texts and drilled large numbers of students as a whole group. Finkelstein also suggests that some teachers acted as *interpreters of culture*, who exposed children to a wider realm of literature or history and who tried to enable children to think more rationally about their world.

In the 18th and 19th centuries most children, especially if they were non-European or female, received little or no schooling. A small minority of these children attended high school by the end of the 19th century; most of them were apprenticing or laboring full-time in the home from an early age.

The 20th Century

The social curriculum in the 20th century has been influenced by changes in population, in the nature of the economy, in the effects of larger schools and centralized authority, and in adults' perceptions of children and adolescents. The huge influx of immigrants at the turn of the century was accompanied by a schooling boom. As the economy became more and more industrialized and urban centers proliferated, educators and societal leaders demanded lengthier schooling for all students. In 1890 there were 220,000 students attending 2,526 high schools in this country. That represented only 3.5% of the high-school age group. By 1900—only ten years later!—there were 519,251 students in greater than 6,000 high schools, and the number of students attending high schools would at least double every decade until the 1940s (Cuban, 1993).

Frameworks which consider how teachers have taught in light of the great changes in this century are helpful. Teaching patterns since the 1890s can be categorized as *teacher-centered and student-centered* (Cuban, 1993). Teacher-centered instruction largely entails whole-class interactions where you talk and students recite and where students participate during individual seat work sitting in rows of desks facing the teacher's desk and the chalkboard. This kind of management system tightly controls student movement and interaction. Bagley and other early 20th century educators, who were concerned with efficiency and economy in schooling, borrowed ideas and language from the new discipline of behaviorist science and from business. Bullough (1994, pp. 2–3) describes this influential view of education:

> The challenge faced by supervisors was to help teachers assume an "objective," "detached," and "impersonal" attitude, a supervisory attitude, toward the students, where "the element of personal feeling or animosity [is] rigorously excluded (1914, p. 52). . . . For Bagley, democracy qualified the metaphors of discipline and management in ways many other educators have since ignored; student conformity and compliance served the ultimate purpose of preserving "civilized society" (1914, p. 8). Bagley had a social theory, and this distinguishes him from some teacher educators of his time and ours for whom control often seems to be an end in itself. (see Bagley, 1932; 1934)

Cuban also describes two sorts of student-centered instruction: an *atheoretical, practical version,* and a *theoretical version* that mainly took root in certain private schools. Cuban's sketch of the *practical version* reflects some 19th century rural schools. Students helped one another, often across age groups, movement around the room was allowed, there was individual attention from the teacher, students could progress at different rates through the curriculum, and on occasion the content was related to community life (Cuban, p. 38).

The *theoretical version* was first practiced in experimental schools such as the Chicago Laboratory School begun by John Dewey and Marietta Johnson's Organic School in Alabama. Jane Addams's settlement house movement in the 1890s had brought attention to the plight of urban working-class adults and the limited educational opportunities for their children. Adhering to the ideals of Pestalozzi and Froebel (the 19th century originator of the kindergarten in Germany), among others, the new student-centered educators called for a curriculum that responded to children's interests, individual and small group learning, more freedom and creativity in the classroom, and a close connection with the community. They stood firmly in opposition to fixed grades in the schools, fixed rules for the children, and fixed furniture in the classroom (Cuban, 1993).

If you were teaching in the 1920s and 1930s you might have been part of more educational experiments. This was the time of *progressive schools* and *community schools serving rural areas.* Willard Elsbree (1939), in an influential book on teaching that was written in the 1930s, juxtaposed the traditional style of the *schoolmistress* with the then-current notion of teachers as *interpreters* and *guides.* Note how such metaphors fit nicely with Finkelstein's (1989) *interpreter of culture* and Cuban's (1993) *theoretical version* of student-centered instruction. Interpreters and guides were to model, to demonstrate, and to lead children toward greater responsibility for their own learning. But most teachers, then and perhaps now, continued to follow traditional patterns of teaching.

The 1960s witnessed three competing views of the *ideal* social curriculum in schools which were both repetitive of earlier approaches, yet represented the long-term emphasis on rationality and science. Behavior management, a technical approach derived from behavioral psychology and from the social efficiency movement of the early 20th century, was designed to shape and mold students' behavior so that it would be in compliance with efficiency models of school learning. Using reinforcement and contingency systems, which often included token systems (rewards for good behavior), behavioristic educators wished to rationalize *teachers'* behavior as an aid to reducing students' inappropriate behavior and enhancing academic achievement. Positional and expert authority were the key; personal relationships were secondary to a systematic approach to controlling learning.

Along with the numerous packaged programs to manage behavior, *values clarification* entered the educational scene. This approach blended ideas from the earlier child-centered perspectives and the idea of rational discussion of beliefs and values. With the growth of an ever more complex society, populated by diverse groups and divergent views on almost every matter, some educators argued that schools should stop imposing values on children. It would be better, the argument went, if students were given the chance to *clarify* what they believed—even if it ran counter to what their parents and most adults believed. Children could rationally determine their own socially responsible values.

Many of the 1960s experimental or alternative schools offered a different approach to classroom relationships. Free schools often let students participate in determining what they would learn and how they would learn it. Quite informal classroom relationships were the norm; adults' personal authority was more important then positional authority. This differed from both behavior management (which involved direct teacher control) and values clarification (which focused on rationality and objectivity, and was in that way similar to behaviorism).

The Present Day

In recent years there have been attempts to redefine *classroom management*, the most common term used to describe classroom interrelationships. Educators now try to use more varied forms of management of the old disciplinary tactics of public corporal punishment, rote recitation, and appeals to the fear of damnation. Strategies such as conflict resolution, peer mediation, cooperative learning, culturally responsive teaching, and other negotiatory initiatives in the 1980s and 1990s have centered on teaching children how to communicate and negotiate with others whose backgrounds are different from their own. The other approaches to the social curriculum have not disappeared, of course. The vestiges of traditional teacher control systems, behavior management, values clarification, and various child-centered approaches can be found in any school or teacher education program. We are teaching now in a very complex time, where no single approach is dominant, as we discuss more fully in chapter 12. This makes it difficult for you to consider how to act in classrooms, but it also frees you to consider from many angles what you believe is best for children.

Representing the Social Curriculum Through Metaphors

In order to determine what we can learn from the historical account just presented, we have already offered a discussion of the metaphorical representations of teaching. Metaphorical use of language can represent quite powerfully how we think. *Metaphora*, the Greek word of origin, means "to carry over, to transfer." Metaphors are figures of speech that allow us to understand something in terms of something else. They may help us to understand the new in terms of the familiar, the complex in terms of the simple, or the abstract in terms of the concrete. Metaphors provide us with a conceptual structure, a means of understanding our experience and perhaps imagining a new interpretation of a known situation.

Bowers and Flinders (1990) describe three kinds of metaphors: analogic, iconic, and generative. This last metaphor—generative—is also called a *root metaphor*. We are concerned here with exploring root metaphors because they "encode assumptions about reality deeply rooted in the mythologies and religious beliefs of the past" (Bowers & Flinders, 1990, p. 38). For instance, assumptions about reality are basic to the notion that classrooms are sites of classroom management, and that management is the primary metaphor to convey what happens in teaching. The triumph of this metaphor—management—as a way of describing classrooms has controlled the meaning of teaching to the extent that prospective teachers often list *classroom management* as the single most important thing to learn about teaching.

All metaphors about teaching and learning are related to philosophical beliefs and corresponding political stances, and they serve the interests of a particular group of people, living in a certain place, at a certain time in history. Why has classroom management become the predominant metaphor to represent relations of authority in schools? At a societal level, we attempted in this section of chapter 2 to explain how the modern management metaphor mirrors a centuries-old tradition of adult-child relations, while reflecting a more recent preoccupation with scientific efficiency and bureaucratic political control.

Management certainly represents one aspect of teaching, but it is part of a larger whole. Management is part of the social curriculum that is composed of ongoing interpersonal relationships that are constantly at work in your classroom. In the first part of this chapter we discussed three metaphors that encompass a wide territory in the social curriculum: teaching as *managing,* teaching as *guiding*, and teaching as *mediating.* Finkelstein's notions of the teacher as *overseer* and *drillmaster* and Cuban's concept of *teacher-centered* instruction represent the teacher as *manager*, one who controls the environment. When Finkelstein describes *the interpreter of culture* and Cuban notes the more *practical version* of student-centered instruction, we think of the teacher as *guide*, a term commonly used in teaching for hundreds of years. Cuban's more *theoretical version* of student-centered instruction has some characteristics of the teacher as *mediator.* To provide a summary of more up-to-date notions of the social curriculum, we view behavior modification as essentially a management approach, values clarification as a guidance approach, and the alternative schools movement as taking largely a mediational approach. The current emphasis on conflict resolution, peer mediation, and the like also represents a mediational approach.

By trying to understand these metaphors in their historical and current meanings we can consider the consequences of envisioning classrooms and schools through each metaphor's lens. Powerful metaphors such as management are difficult to challenge, and even more difficult to change, but such changes are necessary if we are to think broadly about social interactions in schools. We are trying to reconstruct or recast common usage—the taken-for-granted language that fills educational journals and conference presentations.

You can see from the descriptions of school life in prior centuries that certain patterns of interaction have prevailed, but that there have long been competing notions of how teachers and students ought to act. Based on our historical analysis, through the remainder of the book we will use these three metaphors to represent how teachers interact with students in schools and how you are viewed as an authoritarian figure by your students.

METAPHORS AND TEACHERS' CLASSROOM AUTHORITY

The previous section of this chapter focused on historical antecedents to modern-day management practices. Importantly, this previous section also alluded to how you, as a classroom teacher, get your authority. Different metaphors, of course, suggest varying kinds of teacher authority. *Traditional management* suggests legitimate authority; *guide* suggests expert authority; and *mediation* suggests negotiational authority. The guide and mediation metaphors, as processes and products of teaching and as discussed throughout this book, provide important potential for dealing with the many diversity issues that teachers face in today's classrooms. In this section of the chapter we want to deal more directly with the issue of your authority, especially with how this authority is related to power.

Deriving Your Authority as a Teacher

Power and *authority* are always involved in classroom decision-making. *Power* is a matter of how we act on our authority—on whether we act on our authority wisely and respectfully, or whether we act on it selfishly and disrespectfully. The idea of power represents an ability to affect others' and one's environment, which is enabled by certain resources. Teachers exercising power due to their authority are not completely autonomous, and they do not merely impose their desires on students if they want legitimate authority (later in the chapter we will discuss the issue of legitimacy).

That you understand how teachers gain authority to exercise their power is central to any discussion of classroom management. In general, authority can be assumed, conferred, or constructed. In premodern societies, the authority of top-level political rulers was usually granted by birth (the authority *assumed* by aristocrats), while the authority of religious figures often developed because some members of society followed and admired them (the authority *conferred* on cultural leaders). Authority in certain small communal groups was *constructed*; that is, group members decided together who was to lead and how they would deal with problems they faced. In modern schools authority is still assumed, conferred, and constructed, although within a different context than in a traditional society.

The Basis for Teacher Authority

We want here to describe three sorts of authority: *positional, personal,* and *expert.* We will explain each, and then ask you to analyze a description of students' ideas of classroom authority. In general, *positional authority* comes to someone as a result of their given social status: what job they do, what role they play on a committee, or perhaps what family or social group they represent. This sort of authority is defined by external contexts rather than by personal characteristics. It might be characterized to some degree as a reliance on who you know, not what you know, though more generally we would say it is about *what you represent.*

Expert authority is based on *what you know and can do,* that is, on your areas of expertise. Note that one's position need not always imply reliable expertise: Physicians may be titled "Dr." and yet make incorrect decisions about patients. Teachers can be considered experts in a subject area, experts in organizing large-scale school events, or experts in a number of other educational arenas, yet still make mistakes in the content they teach and in how students might best learn the content.

A teacher's *personal authority* (sometimes called *referent authority*) depends on students' interpretations of the teacher's personal characteristics. Is the teacher honest, fair, and consistent? Does the teacher care for students? Do the students admire and trust the teacher? Personal authority is concerned with *who you are.*

Susan Hazzard's Classroom

The following excerpt from *Education as Adventure,* by John Nicholls and Susan Hazzard (1993), is concerned with the major themes of this section: the meanings of power and authority and the nature of classroom authority. Sue Hazzard has taught for more than 20 years, and this account intersperses descriptions of conversations in her second-grade classroom with analytical comments. In the excerpt, Sue is talking with her students about why children should listen to adults. This was prompted by Sue asking Dan, a boy who has been physically aggressive with others on the playground, to listen in class. Except when noted, students are speaking.

> [Sue:] *"What if you meet a grown-up you don't know on the street, and he tells you to do something?"*
>
> *"No."*
>
> *"He's not your mother or father or even your friend, and he can't tell you."*
>
> [Sue:] *"What about a policeman? You wouldn't know him, but if he tells you to cross the street, do you do that?"*
>
> *"No, 'cause cars might be going along."*
>
> [Sue:] *"But isn't the policeman the law?"*
>
> *"So you look both ways."*
>
> *"You can run across."*
>
> *"The government is there to help you and the policeman wants to help you,"* says Evelyn.
>
> [Sue:] *"So do you mean,"* asks Sue, leading gently, *"that you can trust lawmakers and law enforcers? We learned to trust parents because we know they want to help you and make you healthy. So you know you can believe what they tell you?"*
>
> There are no objections so she asks, *"What about a classmate?"*
>
> There are lots of "no's," which is not surprising as Dan appears just to have done violence at a friend's insistence.
>
> *"Someone mentioned experience,"* [Sue recalls.] *"People want to stop you from making mistakes they made."*
>
> *"So when they say don't slug someone, they know why,"* adds Peter.
>
> [Sue:] *"OK, it's lunchtime now. We can talk more later, but in the meantime, I don't want anyone hitting."*[3]

EXERCISE 2.2   What Are Students' Ideas of Authority?

- Where in this transcript of Sue Hazzard's classroom do you find students discussing *positional authority?*
- At what point might they be talking about *personal authority*?
- Can you find mention of *expert authority?*
- What do you think are Miss Hazzard's purposes in this conversation?
- Would you ever engage students in this sort of discussion? Under what circumstances, and for what reasons, would you talk about these issues with students?
- What metaphors discussed earlier in this chapter represent the vignette of Sue above?

Teachers' Power and Legitimate Authority

In this book we will speak of *legitimate authority* as an ideal, a source of power that depends on shared interests. We pointed out earlier that as teachers we can assume authority because we are adults (a traditional position) and because we take on an officially sanctioned role within schools (a legal position). But positional authority is not sufficient if it is simply assumed, as any good teacher knows. The drill sergeant approach which demands respect and obedience and uses coercive power (including rewards and punishments) to maintain control over the classroom does not constitute legitimate authority. Legitimate authority depends not on coercion but on a belief that one's best interests are being taken into account. Legitimacy further requires a connection between a teacher's claims of authority and students' beliefs about the nature of the teacher's authority. Legitimate authority in classrooms, in summary, is based on a teacher's personal and expert authority, and it is both conferred *by* students and constructed *with* students.

POLITICAL DYNAMICS OF THE SOCIAL CURRICULUM

In every school, in every classroom, there is a constant give-and-take of authority and power. This giving and taking results in political dynamics that can be both explicit and implicit. Regardless of their explicit nature, the political dynamics in every classroom influence the personal interrelationships, or the social curriculum, that unfold over time. As the political dynamics change so does the social curriculum. The social curriculum consequently influences different students in different ways.

In this final section of the chapter we provide a brief overview of five types of classroom curricula. These curricula are a function of the kind of education that a school's community values, and thus the kind of social interrelations this same community values at school. The types of curricula we describe include the *ideal, formal, enacted, interpreted,* and *null* (see also such authors as Armstrong, 1989; Eisner, 1979, among others).

In short, you can view these forms of curricula this way:

- educators state how students should act and what they should learn from social interaction (an *ideal*);
- teachers, along with school or district personnel, determine specific policies intended to shape how students act (a *formal* curriculum);
- teachers and students together interact in the classroom and other school sites (the *enacted* curriculum);
- students develop conceptions about what they are learning from social interactions (the *hidden* curriculum); and
- teachers sometimes do not allow for certain sorts of interaction and thus limit what students can learn socially (the *null* curriculum).

There follows additional information about each type of curriculum. As you read the discussion remain mindful that each type of curriculum is a playing out of the political dynamics at work in the social curriculum.

The Ideal Curriculum

The *ideal curriculum* consists of beliefs about how students ought to act and what they ought to learn through social interactions. The *ideals* that predominate come from many sources.

- In our society there are many publications that express the author's philosophical and theoretical beliefs about school interactions. These may take the form of essays such as Philip Jackson's *Untaught Lessons,* compilations of different approaches to the social curriculum such as Thomas Lickona's *Educating for Character,* books about teaching that are coauthored by university and school faculty, such as *Education as Adventure* by Nicholls and Hazzard, and autobiographical accounts by teachers such as *My Country School Diary* by Julie Weber Gordon (see the section on Readings for Your Continuing Self-Education). These books are always influenced by societal conditions and prevailing beliefs of the time, but they can provide us with a coherent set of beliefs to weigh against our own.
- Texts about "classroom management"—like this one!—offer a summary of ideas about school interactions. Some of them simply present various classroom management approaches and ask you to make judgments about them, while other authors take a position and present their own approach.
- In-service workshops and conference presentations offer ideas about what ought to happen in school interactions.
- Packaged "discipline"programs or cooperative learning programs offer someone's beliefs about the best ways for teachers to act.
- *Your* interpretations of what you have experienced, read, and discussed create a set of ideals about school interactions. Your ideal social curriculum depends on your beliefs about teacher-student relationships and about the purposes of power and authority.

- Ideologies of religious groups can directly influence school curricula.
- Mainstream cultural values can influence what is taught and how it is taught.

The Formal Curriculum

The *formal curriculum* is composed of the written intentions, guidelines, plans, resources, and activities intended to further the social growth of individual students and the community life of the classroom and the school. As with the ideal curriculum, there are many sources for this form of the curriculum.

- Some of the formal curriculum is concerned with sanctions and not positive conditions. Governmental entities such as state legislatures and school boards determine laws that limit students' (and teachers') actions. For example, there are always state and district laws or procedures regulating the possession of weapons. There may, however, be different interpretations from district to district about what *weapon* means.
- School administrators and schoolwide committees determine policies about such matters as the nature of the in-school suspension program in the school. Schools also set policies about whether intramural sports programs will be developed, and such programs can certainly affect students' social interactions in the regular school day.
- Individual teachers and teacher teams develop formal classroom policies in the form of rules and procedures. Written discipline plans often lay out the steps that will be taken if students act in certain ways.
- Teachers also establish the classroom's physical environment, which may strongly affect students' actions.

The nature of the formal social curriculum depends on how a problem is defined, what actions are deemed appropriate and inappropriate, and one's understandings of research and theory on classroom interactions.

The Enacted Curriculum

The *enacted curriculum* consists of the social interactions that actually occur in classrooms and other school sites, regardless of the formal or ideal curriculum. Students' and teachers' actions are based in part on the customs and contexts of schools. Yet each classroom has its own culture of social interaction that differs in subtle or overt ways from other classrooms. Ideals or formal processes are constantly being reshaped by the teacher (and perhaps challenged or reinforced by the students) in the flux of classroom life.

Another reason why the enacted curriculum may not parallel what was intended by the teacher is that students embody the community's cultures as well. In any school, students have diverse ways of responding to adults and communicating with peers. If there is a mismatch between the cultural background of the teacher and some of the students, the discrepancy between a teacher's intentions and what actually occurs in the classroom may loom large. Cultural diversity can be a boon to social learning or a barrier to communication.

The Hidden Curriculum

The *hidden curriculum* is what is implicitly taught and learned in schools about how to act. We might think of this as the unwritten and implicit messages interpreted by students. Students may be affected by the physical environment of the school and classroom, for example, the arrangement of individual desks in rows. When teachers offer tangible rewards and assign negative consequences to good behavior, there may be implicit messages sent concerning the reasons to act right in life.

An example of a hidden curriculum is documented in Philip Jackson's depiction of veteran teacher Elaine Martin's first-grade classroom (Jackson, 1992). In this excerpt Jackson describes her means of handling student disagreements that arise on the playground.

> After recess on days when the teacher has no supervisory duty and thus has remained indoors, the children who have been outside return to the room in various states of readiness to resume their schoolwork. Some are excited, others are tired, a few quite matter-of-factly take their seats, and, almost invariably, one or two have stories to tell the teacher, sometimes tearfully, about what happened on the playground. Many of the stories are about injustice and cruelty. They often include accusations. Martha yanked Sarah's ball away. Freddy pushed Billy and then kicked him when he was down. . . .
>
> Mrs. Martin always takes these incidents seriously, but seldom deals with them privately. Even when she bends down to comfort a crying child, she rarely speaks in subdued tones. Instead, she discusses what happened in a voice that conveys sympathy and concern, and also usually can be heard several feet away, often across the room. . . .
>
> In addition to expressing the teacher's concern, something else seems to me to be conveyed to the class as a whole by the way these brief exchanges are conducted. Their semipublic nature announces to one and all that there are few secrets in this room, few subjects that cannot be talked about openly and loudly enough for everyone to hear. No need to go whispering behind people's backs, accusing them of this or that. Have a complaint? Then speak up and have it dealt with out in the open, the way one might discuss a difficulty one was having in arithmetic or reading. The voice of solace and the voice of instruction are practically indistinguishable. (pp. 44–45)

Jackson believes that Mrs. Martin's hidden curriculum has to do with settling disputes in public and with making the social curriculum an integral, apparent part of her instruction. By considering how other teachers act out a hidden curriculum, perhaps we can consciously consider aspects of teaching that may foster—or hinder—students' social growth.

The Null Curriculum

You can think of the *null curriculum* as what students do *not* get a chance to do, in terms of their social interactions. You can also think of the null curriculum as what students do not get a chance to learn, in terms of their academic interrelationships with each other and with the teacher. For example, when we do not allow students to interact in small groups within a classroom, we are not teaching them how to work cooperatively. When students take no part in keeping the school environment clean or when they are not involved in helping to resolve disputes among students, we are not teaching them how to be environmentally or socially responsible.

FURTHER THOUGHTS ON THE SOCIAL CURRICULUM

Classrooms in general tend not to be run at a slow pace. This means that your classroom assumes all these aforementioned curricula at any given point in time. As an example, a teacher is solving problems on an overhead projector in order to teach students how to divide fractions. During this whole-class activity, a student calls out a question without being recognized by the teacher. The formal social curriculum in this class includes a rule that calling out a question without being recognized is not allowed. The teacher then reminds the student of the rule about callouts and continues to write on the transparency. The teacher's ideal curriculum in situations like this may be that students will take responsibility for their own actions and consider how to change. The student, however, may feel frustrated or chagrined because she knows that the teacher often moves through mathematical problems too quickly, so that the only recourse is to slow down by interjecting questions during explanations. A hidden curriculum in this classroom may be the implicit message that mathematics is a subject with fixed answers, and that the best way to learn how to solve problems is through teacher demonstration or student seat work and not through group discussion. The entire episode constitutes the enacted social curriculum at that point.

To use more positive examples, teachers can also formally plan ways to negotiate classroom rules with students, they can use interviews and student journal writing to learn about the interpreted curriculum, and they can listen closely and respond respectfully to students as part of their hidden curriculum. You can see how complex the social curriculum is, because it involves teachers' and students' thoughts and actions.

EXERCISE 2.3   What Was Your Social Curriculum?

What is your *ideal curriculum?* (How should students act and what ought they to learn from social interactions in schools? What might they learn from each other as they bring their various cultural backgrounds to their interactions with each other?) Develop a set of ideals you hold about students' actions in school. Share your ideals with a peer, and see how you and your peer align in your views.

What was the *formal curriculum* of a teacher or a team of teachers in one of your former schools? (What was formally taught or expected of students with regard to their actions?)

What was the *enacted curriculum* in a school in which you have taught or have been a student? (In a particularly memorable situation, what occurred that was *not* part of the apparent ideal or formal social curriculum?)

What was the *hidden curriculum* in your school? (What was an implicit message that you or other students picked up?) How was this hidden curriculum conveyed? What was the *null curriculum* in your school? (What was *not* taught or expected of students, related to their social learning?)

REFERENCES

Armstrong, D. (1989). *Developing and documenting the curriculum.* Boston: Allyn & Bacon.

Bagley, W. C. (1932). *Education, crime, and social progress.* New York: Macmillan.

Bagley, W. C. (1934). *Education and emergent man.* New York: Thomas Nelson and Sons.

Boomer, G., Lester, N., Onore, C., & Cook, J. (1992). *Negotiating the curriculum: Educating for the 21st century.* Washington, DC: The Falmer Press.

Bowers, C. A., & Flinders, D. J. (1990). *Responsive teaching.* New York: Teachers College Press.

Bullough, R. V. (1994). Digging at the roots: Discipline, management, and metaphor. *Action in Teacher Education, 16*(1), 1–10.

Colsant, L. (1995). Hey man, why do we gotta take this? Learning to listen to students. In J. Nicholls & T. Thorkildsen, *Reasons for learning.* New York: Teachers College Press.

Cuban, L. (1993). *How teachers taught* (2nd ed.). New York: Teachers College Press.

Eisner, E. (1979). *The educational imagination: On the design and evaluation of school programs.* New York: Macmillan.

Finkelstein, B. (1989). *Governing the young.* New York: The Falmer Press.

Glasser, W. (1990). *The quality school.* New York: Harper & Row.

Jackson, P. W. (1992). *Untaught lesson.* New York: Teachers College Press.

Kohn, A. (1991). Caring kids: The role of the schools. *Phi Delta Kappan, 72*(7), 496–513.

Ladson-Billings, G. (1994). *The dreamkeepers: Successful teachers of African-American children.* San Francisco: Jossey Bass.

Nicholls, J., & Hazzard, S. (1993). *Education as adventure.* New York: Teachers College Press.

Noblit, G. (1993). Power and caring. *American Educational Research Journal, 30,*(1), 23–38.

Perry, T., & Fraser, J. (1993). *Freedom's plow: Teaching in the multicultural classroom.* New York: Routledge.

Schaps, E., & Solomon, D. (1990). Schools and classrooms as caring communities. *Educational Leadership, 48*(3).

What Research Says to Practitioners

Autobiography

Ashton-Warner, S. (1963). *Teacher.* New York: Simon & Schuster. [Story of a teacher learning how to work with Maori children in New Zealand]

Dennison, G. (1969). *The lives of children: The story of the First Street School.* New York: Random House. [The tale of an experimental school in New York City, from the perspective of a teacher there]

Gordon, J. W. (1946). *My country school diary.* New York: Dell Publishing. [Account of a teacher who tried to create a "community school" during the 1930s]

Rose, M. (1989). *Lives on the boundary.* New York: Free Press. [Written by a person who has taught "the slow, the remedial, and the unprepared," both children and adults, for 20 years]

Ethnography

Bullough, R. V., Jr. (1989). *First-year teacher.* New York: Teachers College Press. [Case study of a beginning teacher's first year]

Grant, G. (1988). *The world we created at Hamilton High.* Cambridge, MA: Harvard University Press. [A social history of an urban high school]

Jackson, P. W. (1992). *Untaught lessons.* New York: Teachers College Press. [See Chapter 3, Jackson's observations of a first-grade classroom]

Nicholls, J. G., & Hazzard, S. P. (1993). *Education as adventure*. New York: Teachers College Press. [Account of life in the second grade]

Nicholls, J. G., & Thorkildsen, T. (Eds.) (1995). *Reasons for learning*. New York: Teachers College Press. [Essays, autobiographies, and ethnographies on "student-teacher collaboration"]

Noblit, G. W. (1993). Power and caring. *American Educational Research Journal, 30*(1), 23–38. [Account of what a university researcher learned from a second grade teacher]

History

Beale, (1941). *A history of freedom of teaching in American schools*. New York: Charles Scribner's Sons. [An unusual history of the constraints teachers have faced]

Cuban, L. (1993). *How teachers taught* (2nd ed.). New York: Teachers College Press. [A history of teaching and school reform since 1890]

Finkelstein, B. (1989). *Governing the young*. New York: The Falmer Press. [A history of teaching during the 19th century]

McCaslin, M., & Good, T. L. (1992). Compliant cognition: The misalliance of management and instructional goals in current school reform. *Educational Researcher, 3,* 4–17.

General Texts

Bowers, C. A., & Flinders, D. J. (1990). *Responsive teaching*. New York: Teachers College Press. [See chapter 2 on metaphor and language, and chapters 5–6 on social control and power]

Bullough, R. V., Jr., & Gitlin, A. (1995). *Becoming a student of teaching*. New York: Garland. [See chapter 3 on "personal teaching metaphors"]

Lickona, T. (1991). *Educating for character*. New York: Bantam. [Accounts of what teachers across the country do to "educate for character"]

CHAPTER

3

How Cultural and Personal Labels Influence Teachers and Students

I've worked for twenty years with children and adults deemed slow or remedial or underprepared. And at one time in my own educational life, I was so labeled.

(Rose, 1989, p. xi)

Ignoring the past does not make it go away. It lingers, ever present and quietly insistent.

(Bullough & Gitlin, 1995, p. 40)

Our focus in the preceding chapter was to illuminate alternative ways of thinking about your school's social curriculum. In addition to *managing* students, we focused on *guiding* and *mediating* their learning. The preceding two chapters also revealed the powerful influence that culture has on the social curriculum of every school.

The purpose for chapter 3 is to help you develop a fuller understanding of how your personal history, both in and out of school, gives shape to your perspectives about how the social curriculum can be structured. A related purpose is to help you understand the relationship between your personal history and the perspectives and beliefs you have about the traditional notion of classroom management and student discipline.

UNDERSTANDING YOUR FORMER SCHOOL IMAGE

The notion of biography and personal history are expansive. Consequently, there are many ways to explore a biography relative to teachers' personal lives.[1] Rather than asking you to document your biography using a more general approach, such as the approach suggested by Bullough and Gitlin (1995), we ask you to explore and document your biography through the labels that are often given to students in school. Studying your educational history through the labels you carried through much of your school life seems most pertinent for the overarching framework of this book. This is because labels are a function of how schools are structured academically, socially, and culturally.[2] How schools are structured also reflects how schools are organized for learning. How schools are organized for learning further points to how schools are *managed*.

---

[1]For varying approaches to exploring teacher biography, see for example chapter two of Bullough and Gitlin (1995), and chapter nine of Goodson and Walker (1991). See also Knowles (1992).
[2]Evidence for this claim can be found in the work of Eckert (1989) and Fine (1991).

What might happen if you move headlong into the classroom as a teacher without first exploring, examining, and asking questions about the many labels you were given as a student, and the many labels you used to categorize your peers? The answer is simple: You continue using the same labels in a naive way. This kind of naiveté can lead to prejudice and misconceptions about learners. Bullough and Gitlin (1995) explain what can happen when these kind of naive prejudices become part of your classroom life:

> Preunderstandings about teaching and about self as teacher born of student experience and brought to teacher education are inevitably naive, perhaps misleading, and sometimes blatantly false. Prejudices blind. Prejudices cripple. Prejudgments —judgments lacking explicit justification—blind by cutting off other, perhaps more fruitful, sensitive and responsible ways of understanding and framing a problem or building a relationship; they cripple by unnecessarily constraining opportunities to learn and by truncating one's professional growth. (p. 42)

If the labels you know and use are helpful, that is, if they serve to build students' self-esteem and self-images as learners, then the labels are clearly educative. The corresponding social curriculum is likely to be both positive and productive for students. On the other hand, if the labels, such as the ones given to Mike Rose (1989) at the beginning of this chapter, serve to construct self-images of students as unsuccessful learners, as perhaps being academically underprepared, then they are miseducative, and certainly they are prejudicial. Without exploring your history through the labels you carried as a function of how your former schools were structured and organized, you could unintentionally structure, organize, and maintain classroom learning environments that are highly educative for some students, but less growthful for others.

The Labels You Carried

Think for a moment about your precollege years as a student. What was your life like in school? What self-image as a learner resulted from the schools you attended? What labels were associated with this image? What did these labels mean to you personally, socially, and academically? Were you ever able to change the school labels you received, or do you still carry them with you today? What was the relationship between school structure, student labels, and classroom learning environment?

The idea of relating school labels to the organizational structure of schools, and to how schools are managed, at first might seem remote to you. But think for a moment about labels such as *bilingual, gifted and talented, nonnative English speaker, fast learner, slow learner, learning disabled, advanced placement,* and the list goes on and on. Exploring both strengths and limitations of school labels such as these, especially those you adopted and possibly carried for many years, helps you better understand how schools are structured, and what specific schools, given this structure, expect from learners. Exploring labels also helps you gain insight into the values that society in general, and that local communities in particular, place on school achievement. That is why we are asking you in this chapter to look closely at *who you were* as a student, at what labels you received, and why you carried these labels for so many years.

Ordinarily, students carry their school-based labels for a very long time—and students often live out their lives at school in the ways that are prescribed by labels. At the beginning of this chapter, Rose (1989) says that he was labeled in school as a *slow learner;* he was viewed as being remedial and underprepared. Fortunately, at a later point in his life Rose moved beyond the low self-image that often comes with labels such as *slow learner, remedial*, and *underprepared*.

Not every person is as fortunate as Rose, however. Some students who are associated with a label that is less positive in school are unable to move beyond the negative stigma associated with it. This is because your past, which includes all of your life experiences, does not go away even if you try to ignore it. It is insistently there, as Bullough and Gitlin (1995) claim, however quiet and implicit, giving shape to your teaching perspectives, beliefs, actions, thoughts, and behaviors. It also gives shape to your self-image—to how you see yourself as a person, a teacher, a colleague, and a friend to others. Your past, particularly your prior educational experiences, helps to mold the classroom context you create with your students. All of this above results in part from the countless thousands of hours you spent as a student during the most formative years of your life, along with the many experiences you had outside of school.

THE PROCESS OF LABELING

In the very simplest of terms, labeling is a process that involves assigning a name to a person or to an object. Yet few things are sociologically more complex than this process, and few things have more lasting and more challenging implications for students than to be negatively labeled in schools and classrooms. Despite the inherent complexity of labeling, there is an important feature of labels you should remember: Labels are always context-specific—that is, labels are functional only in the context, and in the culture and society, for which they were created.

What comes to your mind when you hear some of the labels we listed above, such as *slow learner, fast learner, disabled learner, gifted and talented, bright, hyperactive,* and *attentive*? Each of these words is a label, a context-specific label, that has specific meaning in the context of schools and classrooms. If you consider the list above carefully, you will discover that these items also have meaning in factorylike contexts. Whether you are a teacher or a manager of a fast food restaurant, these words have similar value and meaning.

Labels are also structure-specific. Think for a moment about the structure of a factory setting, where there are many workers, and where each worker is expected to perform at a certain rate, be at work at a certain time, and follow rules and regulations as stated by factory guidelines. What labels might reflect high competency workers, and what labels might reflect low competency workers? Examples of labels that are associated with high competency workers include *efficient, effective, agreeable, collegial, supportive, productive, on time,* and so on. Examples of labels that are associated with low competency workers include *inefficient, slow, argumentative, disagreeable, low production, tardy, handicapped, inexperienced, lazy,* and so on.

That society in general endorses, and continues to endorse, the factory model of schooling and the factory model of managing students is clear (Bullough, 1994). That schools have likewise adopted a set of factory labels to describe student competency in school is also clear. What is not clear, however, is how well these labels, and the organizational structure they represent, serve highly diverse student populations in today's classrooms (Jones, 1995; McCaslin & Good, 1992).

As a microcosm of factory life in particular and of society in general, schools have labels for students, as we noted above. Factory-oriented labels tend to reflect competency-based outcomes of students. Moreover, as the domain of behavioral psychology became more commonplace in school reform, additional labels have been added over the years. Psychology-oriented labels tend to reflect the kind of thinking that students do, and how they might learn targeted concepts. We have organized factory-based and psychology-based labels into two groups: academic and social.

Academic Labels at School

Think for a moment about the academic labels associated with students, classrooms, and schools. For example, in Texas where state-mandated standardized testing predominates curriculum and instruction at all precollege levels, whole schools can be ranked as *low performing* or as *high performing.* These are powerful labels and they have a powerful effect on those who are forced to hold them.

Many low performing schools in Texas, for example, carry a negative stigma. Unless low performing schools improve their scores in a designated period of time, they are closely scrutinized, monitored, and evaluated. Principals and teachers can lose their jobs if the school remains at a low performing status over several years. High performing schools are also stigmatized; however, the stigma is positive and uplifting. Students in these schools get rewards, such as valuable field trips. Teachers in high performing schools often get special commendations; they are made to feel proud of their school.

The idea of *high performing* and *low performing* also pertains to individual students not only in Texas, but in schools everywhere. There are many other kinds of labels too. Every teacher wants to have a classroom of *upper stanine kids,* but few want classrooms of *lower stanine kids,* or those in lower academic tracks. Although some teachers enjoy teaching students regardless of their measured *academic ability,* there are many teachers who prefer to teach students who are labeled as *advanced placement, upper quartile, higher track,* and *upper stanine.* Teachers know these students all too well, since they are given labels such as *bright, quick, attentive, independent, self-starters*—attributes that are highly valued in factorylike schools, and, consequently, that carry positive connotations.

What about students on the other side of the academic coin? What about students who are labeled, for example, as *remedial, lower quartile, lower track, lower sta-*

nine, special education, disabled, limited English proficient, and *nonnative English speakers*? Teachers often assume that these students are *slow, dull witted, off task, dependent,* and unnecessarily *needy* (for example, see Langer & Chanowitz, 1988; Trueba, Jacobs, & Kirton, 1990).

Because of the structure of most schools, students know how they have been grouped, and they know which academic labels they have been given by the school. Nothing really needs to be said explicitly—everybody knows. Students know who is *smart* and who is *dumb,* who is *highly competent* and who is *incompetent.* Perhaps most problematic here is that students tend to see themselves as *smart* and *dumb,* as *competent* and *incompetent,* once they have been tested, categorized, sorted, and labeled.

An important attribute of these academic labels, as we noted above and as will be more fully addressed in a later section of this chapter, is that teachers seem to already know what students are going to be like, given the labels they receive. Why else might a teacher prefer to teach a class of *academically talented* students? Or why might a teacher think that he or she must "water down" the content for a class of *low ability* students, even before meeting them the first time? Whether you think labels are good or bad, the fact remains that you, as a classroom teacher, live in a world of labels, and these labels influence your lesson planning, classroom instruction, school curriculum, perspectives of students, social relations among students, and social relations between you and your students.

Social Labels at School

Like academic labels, social labels are powerful factors in influencing students' self-images in and out of school. Consider two extremes of social labels: One extreme is the school dropout, the other extreme is graduating at the top of the class.

When a student is unable to connect with school socially, personally, and academically, the student might be viewed as a school failure, although the student might be someone who is very capable in learning environments other than factorylike schools. Some students who are viewed as failures, and who feel pushed out of school, might eventually become part of the dropout phenomenon. *Dropout* is a powerful social label that can influence a person's image of self for an entire lifetime (Fine, 1991). On the other hand, when a student connects with the school academically and perhaps graduates with highest honors, the person might become known as being *top of the class.* This is a label that opens doors throughout life, including doors to colleges and universities that are looking for young persons who demonstrate potential to achieve at high levels. There is much social prestige that is associated with receiving scholarships from colleges and universities, just as there is much social denigration that comes from dropping out of school.

Being a *dropout* or being *top of the class* are only two of the dozens of labels that are bantered about daily in schools across the country. Eckert (1989) discusses two other labels, including *jocks,* or those who buy into ways of acting that are valued by the school system, and *burnouts,* or those who don't buy into valued ways of acting. The label of *jock,* however, is also linked to being a school athlete. In a discussion of high school sports, Bissinger (1991) discusses other kinds of social labels associated with school sports, including cheerleader, student athlete, hero, and so on.

As you reflect on your precollege school days, you can probably think of a social label for almost every student who attended your schools. There are so many labels that we cannot begin to list them all here. To exemplify the idea of social labels, we will list only a few that you will probably know, and perhaps have even used: *nerd, gangster, teacher's pet* or *teacher pleaser, druggie* (those who are part of drug-taking cultures), *class clown, know-it-all,* and *techy* (those associated most often with computer technology).

School Labels and Social Curricula

When you put together academic and social labels in the presence of a specific school culture, and when you consider that this school culture is further situated in a larger community, you begin to see how a school's social curriculum gains a certain definition. As noted in chapter 2, the social curriculum is concerned with how students ought to act and what they ought to learn from social interactions in school. This includes not only learning content, but also learning about themselves, their peers, and the community where they live. When you examine closely all the social and academic labels that make up a school context, then you begin to see more closely what the local school values, for example, in terms of learning or in terms of competitiveness. You also gain a better understanding of how the school explicitly structures learning and how it explicitly defines success. And you learn how it implicitly structures failure and inequity (Fine, 1991; Trueba et al., 1990).

In the next section is a biographical vignette of Richard Powell. The story represents the kind of social curriculum that is discussed above, namely a factory-oriented social curriculum. The story also demonstrates the powerful influence that labels have on our lives.

The Last to Be Called

On the first day of junior high school, all students were asked to report to the school auditorium before attending any classes. The school, which was one of two junior high schools in a rural Midwestern community, contained students from lower, middle and upper socioeconomic classes. Members of the town's various ethnic groups also attended the school. Most of the students were white, a much smaller percentage were African American, and only a few were Hispanic.

Just before going to the junior high school, I (Powell) attended an elementary school near my home. In contemporary terms, the elementary school I attended would have been classified "at risk," and most of the students were in the lower SES category. The mobile home that we lived in was on the edge of the town's African American community, and my parents had a lower socioeconomic class income.

As I think back on the junior high school I attended, it very clearly represented a traditional factorylike structure. This is because students were organized into an efficiency instructional model, with various academic tracks. I was placed in the lowest academic track, although I was fairly good in mathematics and science. School officials knew that I attended one of the lower SES elementary schools in town, and they believed that my elementary education was not as strong as students from other parts of town.

That I was put in a lower academic track in junior high school was something I had to accept. How I was put in the track, however, was problematic at the time, and in retrospect remains problematic for me. The first day of school I excitedly went to the school's auditorium. My friends from elementary school were there, and I began talking to students from other schools, although I had never seen any of them before that day. At 8:30 a.m. the school principal came into the auditorium with the school counselors. The principal asked us to get quiet, and then welcomed us to the school. He then explained that he and the school counselors had placed students into special groups. Each group contained, as he explained, students who had similar academic abilities. He then told us that he was going to call out students by name, and each set of names would represent a group. We remained in these groups not only for that entire school year, but for the remainder of the time we attended the school.

Names were called out, and groups of students began leaving the auditorium. Six groups of names were called out. After the second group of names everybody knew what was happening. The *smartest* kids, according to school records, were called first. Then the next *smartest,* and so on. I kept waiting for my name to be called, but my anxiety continued to grow, and I continued to wait. I was in the last group of names to be called, which meant I was in the lowest academic ability group in the school. I looked at the other students in my group, and many of them were my peers from elementary school. I, along with my peers, were the last to be called.

I knew who I was when I went to school that morning. I was an excited seventh grader who was eager to begin my junior high school years. I also knew who I was after being at the school only one hour. I was, according to the way my junior high school was structured, a slow learner, and a person who had low ability in school. I labeled myself *dumb,* which seemed to be what the school labeled me. My parents, who had only high school diplomas from a very small town in the Midwest, didn't know to question the school's practice of tracking students, and they didn't know to question how the school placed us into ability groups.

The final year of junior high school we met with counselors to schedule our high school classes. What began in the junior high school continued into high school. The counselors saw which junior high school ability group I was in, and they placed me in low ability classes in high school. Not until I completed and left high school did I begin seeing myself as someone capable of learning "book knowledge."

Being the last called in junior high school, which corresponded with the view I developed of myself that I was a less-capable learner than my peers, was a seriously debilitating experience for me, and in my judgment was a miseducative experience. I attended college after completing high school because of the sincere wishes of a close relative. Otherwise, I would not have attended college at all; the implicit message I received from both junior high school and high school experiences was that I simply was not college-level material. I distinctly remember one of my high school teachers telling me pointedly that I didn't have what it took, in his judgment, to be successful in college. He encouraged me to do anything else but go to college.

This story about "being called last" raises many important issues about the factorylike structure of schools, about efficiency models for tracking and managing student learning, and about the specific student labels that are an inherent part of this kind of system. It also is a powerful metaphor for how students label themselves as they get caught up in the cultural dimensions of their schools. I (Powell) labeled myself a slow learner, and I lived with that label for many years. Not until much later in college did I begin to see myself as something other than a slow learner.

I look back at my junior high school learning experiences with some resentment now. Perhaps more importantly, I look back with an informed view. I realize what a powerful influence specific labels, as a consequence of how my schools were structured and managed for efficiency, had on me—specifically what a negative effect they had on my self-image and on my self-confidence for learning school knowledge. After one hour at my junior high school those many years ago I was put into a specific academic passageway, and the school system I attended kept me in that passageway for the next five years. The labels I assumed in junior high school, which were the very labels that the school gave me, stayed with me along my five-year journey of low-ability classes and minimal expectations. While the labels were intended to make teaching more efficient for the schools I attended, they ultimately guided me into lower-level learning throughout all of my precollege years.

My precollege school experiences definitely predisposed me to teach certain ways when I became a teacher. I began teaching without ever questioning my former schooling experiences, or without ever critically assessing the labels I carried with me for so many years. I attended factorylike schools, I assimilated their management scheme into my beliefs about classroom life, I bought into their labels, I wore them continuously, and then I transferred all of this to my own classroom as a teacher. When I began teaching I grouped students together as *slow learners* and as *fast learners.* When I reflect on my years as a classroom teacher, and when I think of the way that I transferred my whole precollege years of schooling to my own classroom as a teacher, I often think about how many of the educational experiences I structured might have been miseducative, especially for students who need more time, or who need alternative learning activities. At that time I never questioned the many connotations surrounding the label *slow learner.* What I distinctly recall, however, was that I, like so many of my colleagues who also were socialized into factorylike perspectives of schooling, preferred to teach classes of other than slow learners—I preferred classrooms that were filled with the *bright* students, as I labeled them at that time in my teaching career.

EXERCISE 3.1   Getting in Touch With Your School Labels

In the vignette above, Richard Powell revealed how he labeled himself, as a function of the structure of the schools he attended, and as a function of how learning was *managed* in these schools. Powell attended schools that were traditional and factorylike in their orientation. We do not intend to suggest, however, that all schools that follow a factory model are inherently bad or denigrating to students. Clearly, this kind of suggestion would be false and misleading. However, in the story "The last to be called," the ability tracking of the school was problematic for Powell, and most likely for other students who also were placed in the lowest ability group with him in junior high school. Moreover, when Powell began a teaching career, he had never been asked in his teacher education program to think reflectively and critically about the schools he attended. Consequently, he carried the practices and problematic labels that he habituated in his precollege years to his own students.

To help you develop a better understanding of your own dispositions to structure school experiences for your students, based on your former experiences, and to help you determine the educational potential of your dispositions, we ask you to think carefully in this exercise about the school labels you adopted while a precollege student. We ask you to reflect on how these labels may have affected your self-image as a person and how they influenced your school experiences, particularly your learning experiences.

First, state whether you believe you were labeled at all. If so, then make a list of all the social and academic labels you adopted while in school. For each label, state when you acquired it, where and why you got it, and how it influenced your self-image. State whether or not you think the label was positive or negative.

Second, think about one of your former schoolmates. Pick one of your peers who perhaps had very different schooling experiences and who owned an alternative set of labels. What labels did this person have? Why did he or she get the labels, and how do you think they affected him or her?

Third, interview one of your peers in your teacher education program. The purpose of this interview should be to explore how she or he responded to the questions above. Compare and contrast your former experiences and labels with those of your peer.

After exploring personal labels you had, think about the relationship between these labels and the way your school was structured. How did the labels you acquired in school reflect the whole school context? What was the relationship between your labels (and the labels of your school peers) and the way the school was managed? How did the schools you attended group you, if at all, according to specific labels? What were the purposes of these groupings? For the schools you attended, which student groups may have been benefited more, or privileged, by the school's structure and by the labeling associated with the structure?

RETHINKING SCHOOL STRUCTURE FOR EQUITY AND EXCELLENCE

In the preceding section you began exploring how schools are structured by looking closely at the labels they use to categorize students and at the labels your former schools used for you. In this section we ask you to think more critically about school labels—specifically how they relate to the notions of equity and excellence in classroom learning. To help you do this we first discuss a few of the more general features of labeling. Second, borrowing from the work of Gay (1988), we connect the idea of labels to the notions of equity and excellence. In the final part of this section, we ask you to think about the kind of school and classroom organization that might best foster equity and excellence for all students. We also ask you to appraise your former schooling experiences according to Gay's perspective of educational equity and excellence.

Features of School Labels

If we didn't have labels, the world, including schools and classrooms, would be a very confusing place. Labels help you organize your thinking about teaching and learning, and in general, they help you make sense of things. The problem is therefore not the idea of labeling, rather the misuse of labeling—putting the wrong label on something, or using a word for a label that has a negative meaning. A greater problem is mislabeling unintentionally—that is, using labels for people that are harmful and not even knowing when you are doing this (Contreras & Lee, 1990).

Mislabeling can happen when you become socialized into ways of doing things and ways of thinking about things, and then you are never given cause to step back to think more critically and more deeply about the greater sociological effects of your actions. This is what Bullough and Gitlin (1995) mentioned in their quote earlier in the chapter. Out of naiveté we can teach in ways we were taught using the labels and organizational structure associated with these ways, and whether appropriate and educative, or inappropriate and miseducative, we carry on with the business of teaching, just as Richard Powell did in the story above, while thinking we are doing what any good teacher does.

This does not mean, however, that teachers are oblivious to students' feelings and that teachers in general are less than caring and aware people relative to their students. Teachers can indeed be very caring toward students and dedicated toward the teaching profession but still be less aware of the impact that labeling, whether positive or negative, can have on students' lives.

Habituations to ways of thinking, regardless of how well these ways served you as an individual in the past, may not be in the best interest of larger groups of students. To explore this idea further, consider the features of labels we briefly describe below (see the earlier work of Cardwell—Payne, 1973).

Labels Identify and Make Visible

Labeling students makes you, as a classroom teacher, get caught in a school paradox: When you label a student you make him or her more visible, while at the same time making that same student less visible. This is because labels help you to quickly identify students by a predetermined set of traits. However, by doing this you tend to objectify students; you put them into groups where their personal identity becomes overshadowed and lost by the identity of the group. This might be acceptable if the identity of the group provides students with some kind of positive self-image and helps connect them to the overall culture of the school in productive ways. However, objectifying students is unacceptable when the general image of the student group gives students some kind of negative self-image and serves to disconnect them from the overall culture of the school, thus minimizing opportunities for equitable learning. Some critics say this kind of objectification, which ultimately marginalizes some students from school-based learning, disenfranchises students from school culture and disempowers them from learning (Doll, 1993).

Labels Create Symbols

Labels create symbols, and symbols give students personal meaning. For example, think about labels such as star mathematician, star pianist, star writer, or star athlete. In many schools being a star of something is valued and honored by other members of the school culture. As such stars interact with the school culture over time, they take on many of the features that the label of *star* prescribes. Some of these features might include role model, hero, and leader. These features in turn give students who carry such labels personal meaning and enhanced self-worth. Regardless of the label you use for students, you help students create personal meaning for themselves, and personal meaning for being in school, as they interact over time with the school culture.

Organizational Labels Create Self-Labels

Labels are like looking glasses. This is because most students rely on their peers and on their teachers for an understanding of their identity at school. Students come to see themselves as they think others see them—and they give themselves labels and corresponding symbols that align with their self-perceptions. In the story above, Richard Powell was put in the lowest academic track of his junior high school; he labeled himself *dumb*. At the opening of this chapter Rose (1989) was labeled a remedial learner by the school, and this is how he viewed himself for many years. As another example, in the study conducted by Wilson (1991) that was described in chapter 1, Sioux students, who were new to a mainstream high school from a nearby reservation, were viewed by their teachers as apathetic and underprepared. Many of the Sioux students in Wilson's study soon viewed themselves this way, and most dropped out of school by the end of their first year in high school.

Labels Become Generalized

Traditional schools that depend on efficiency models of organization freely and frequently use labels in order to generalize certain student traits to whole groups of students. Academic tracking is one example of this. Once a school determines how students will be grouped according to ability levels, everyone in the school (i.e., teachers, counselors, administrators, students) generalizes a set of traits to each group—advanced placement, honors, average, remedial, and so on. This also pertains to physical differentiation in athletics, for example, first string, second string, sit-on-the-bench, and so on. Generalizing traits might make teaching more efficient, but it also leads to stereotypes. Stereotyping makes students both visible and invisible at the same time, as we explained above. Generalizing student behaviors and traits therefore causes us initially to lose sight of the unique subjectivities that students bring to school.

Labels Produce Subcultures and Specific Social Activity

As individual students are put into larger groups of students for specific reasons, they actually form a small community, or subculture, within the school. Implicit boundaries form around these subcultures. While students in a subculture may very well share traits with other students in the same subculture, these students may see themselves as being very different from other student groups in the school. Students in a gifted and talented subculture, for example, surely see themselves as different from other subcultures in the school. Similarly, students in a special education subculture see themselves as different from the non–special education part of the school. When we *see* students as gifted and talented and as in need of special education, and when we actually believe these groups should be identified and set apart in some manner, then we assume that these students are capable of participating in specific kinds of social and academic activities. Indeed, the school actually sets up different activities for each of its subcultures, thus striving ever more for efficient ways of engaging students in appropriate learning activities.

Proponents of academic tracking argue that higher achieving students and lower achieving students should be placed in separate subcultures. Educators who are against tracking obviously argue that it should be removed from schools. Removing it would place students from various subcultures of learning together in the same classroom for an entire school year. This debate about tracking is among the most pressing educational issues today, most especially in junior high and middle schools.

Labels Produce Mindfulness and Mindlessness

Mindfulness and *mindlessness* are two terms used by Langer and Chanowitz (1988) in order to understand the perception of and behavior toward disabled persons. The two terms are highly appropriate for our discussion of labels in this chapter.

According to Langer and Chanowitz, mindfulness is a positive attribute that involves active distinction. When applied to school settings, this active distinction means to actively be aware of important personal distinctions that teachers should make between and among students. If a teacher is mindful, then she or he is proactively constructing categories for students, that is, who they are, their personal strengths, assets, needs, and so on.

On the other hand, being *mindlessness* means to rely on categories that have already been constructed to describe students this way or that way. While there can be much mindfulness associated with students, there is also much mindlessness associated with school labels. That is, we can all fall too easily into the trap of using labels for grouping students together. Being in this trap, we then think that most students in a particular group are mostly alike; we don't look for mindful distinctions. This is how student stereotypes are born.

An important aspect of this mindfulness/mindlessness distinction is that teachers (and all educators), in order to be more responsive to personal and individual needs of students, must make more rather than fewer distinctions among students. This means that each of us must avoid the trap of unnecessarily labeling students if those labels cause us to see a student more as a member of a group and less as an individual.

The consequences of mindlessness can be seen in the following example. Consider the case of Ms. Thomas, who teaches only students who have been labeled *advanced placement (AP)*. These students are in the school's upper academic track, and many of them are in the honor roll and other prestigious academic organizations. Now that Ms. Thomas has worked with these students for several years she begins to mindlessly assume some uniformities and commonalities that very likely exceed those which really do exist for the AP students. The next school year Ms. Thomas is asked to teach one class of students who have been placed in a lower academic track. Because of Ms. Thomas' growing mindlessness for the AP students, she is clearly primed to look for extreme differences between her AP students and her lower track students. This can lead Ms. Thomas to have exaggerated perceptions of the differences between the upper track and lower track students, thus causing her to approach students in both groups with a mindless rather than a mindful attitude.

Toward Equity and Excellence

We all use labels loosely, and at times we use them carelessly and thoughtlessly. Using labels, we tend to generalize student behavior, create expectations, build self-fulfilling prophecies, create symbols, and establish subcultures for students. These phenomena would be fine if all labels for students had positive connotations; if all labels built strong self-esteem. But labels, and the school structure they represent, don't always do this. Studies in the anthropology of education reveal that cultural misunderstandings, which can be very subtle, unknowing, and implicit, cause teachers to mislabel students, and consequently generalize them into categories in which they do not belong (Ballenger, 1995; Erickson, 1987). This means that some students will likely be engaged in learning activities that are less academically suited to them than other students. Consequently, both equity and excellence become threatened when learning opportunities are unequally distributed.

Think about how the features of student labeling above relate to educational equity and excellence for all students. To do this first consider how Gay (1988) describes these two terms.

> Equity is a precondition and a means for achieving excellence. Whereas equity is a methodological input issue, excellence is an evaluative outcome measure. Excellence finds expression in common standards and expectations of high achievement for all students, and equity translates into appropriate methodologies and materials according to specific group or individual characteristics. Excellence occurs when individual students achieve to the best of their ability, and equity is accomplished when each student is provided with learning opportunities that make high level achievement possible. (p. 328)

Given the features of labeling described above, can educational excellence, as described by Gay, be attained in traditional schools and classrooms? This is not merely a rhetorical question; it is a pressing issue. Because of the methods that many schools use to organize students into academic ability groups, not to mention the many other types of formal and informal grouping that occur, and because of the stereotypical labeling that is associated with this grouping, excellence may be more of an idealistic than a realistic event. If, for example, you view a group of students as being *low ability* and you view another group of students as being *high ability,* you will also view these students with a set of assumptions commensurate with the labels they wear. This means you will most likely teach students labeled as *low ability* differently than you teach students labeled as *high ability.* Several important questions quickly surface: Will you teach the low ability and high ability students with comparable (but not necessarily the same) resources, facilities, instructional interactions, and academic expectations? If all of these things are comparable for the low and high ability students, as grouped and labeled by the school, then you will be striving, according to Gay (1988), for academic equity. Gay (1988) notes,

> If learners from different ethnic, social, and cultural groups do not have access to *comparable* quality resources, facilities, and instructional interactions as others who are succeeding in school, then their chances for achieving excellence are minimized. (p. 328)

What if, however, you teach students who have been labeled as *low ability* in an incomparable way to students who have been labeled as *high ability*? Will you "water down" your lessons for students who are labeled as *low ability* or *remedial*? Will the resources you use and the classroom interactions you have with students who are in different ability groups lead to learning experiences that are not necessarily comparable in quality and opportunity? Each of these questions points to the real challenge you have in attaining equity and excellence in schools that have adopted organizational structure, metaphors, labels, and procedures of traditional factory settings.

EXERCISE 3.2   Connecting Labels With Equity and Excellence

In the foregoing section we briefly described selected features of school labels. In this activity you consider how these features apply to your former experiences in school. You also consider how the features influenced the quality of education you received. Below are a set of questions that have been generated from the features we described earlier in this chapter. As you answer the questions, consider the notions of equity and excellence mentioned by Gay (1988).

- If you identified labels for yourself in Exercise 3.1, in what ways did the labels make you more visible in school? In what ways did the labels make you less visible?
- Did the labels you carried symbolize certain student attributes? What personal meaning, if any, did the symbolization create for you?
- As a consequence of the school labels you adopted, what self-labels did you give yourself? Were the self-labels positive or negative? How did these labels affect your relationship with school? with teachers? with peers?
- As a result of the labels you adopted and the corresponding groups you belonged to as a precollege student, do you think your teachers saw you more as an individual person, or more as part of a social, academic, or athletic group?

- What student subcultures did you belong to in school? What labels were associated with these subcultures? What specific activities were linked to your subcultures?
- As a member of a student subculture, do you think you received the same kind of educational opportunities as students in other subcultures? How did the social and academic opportunities you received compare to your peers' in the same subculture, and in other subcultures? Do you think you received equitable opportunities to learn, thus receiving the comparable opportunities to excel in school?

After answering these questions about yourself, use the same set of questions to interview a peer, an experienced teacher, and selected precollege students. Modify the questions to make them appropriate for each of these interviews. For your student interviews, try to talk with students who represent different ability groups, or other groups where student labels are a significant factor in forming students' self-images.

LABELS, SELF, AND BECOMING A TEACHER

Thus far we have talked mostly about the labeling associated with students and about your biographical experiences in school. In this section we want you to think about the labels associated with teachers in today's classrooms—specifically, to think about the labels you inherit when you become a teacher.

To begin thinking about inherited labels, consider how society in general views teachers. What roles and labels does society expect teachers to assume? And what kind of instructional perspectives do these roles and labels give you? We established earlier in this chapter that for many decades society has endorsed a factorylike orientation to schools. With this orientation come assumptions not only for students but also for teachers. Although the factorylike orientation has more recently been challenged as being culturally insensitive to some groups of students (Gay, 1988; Doll, 1993; Ladson-Billings, 1994; McLaughlin, 1994; Perkinson, 1993), this orientation continues to be the basis for creating and maintaining many school learning environments.

As we noted in chapter 2, the factory metaphor of management suggests certain roles for classroom teachers. These roles include classroom manager, authority figure, disciplinarian, and student behaviorist. The overarching metaphor here is control. That is, as a classroom manager in traditional school settings, you are expected by the school's administration and by the local community to *control* student behavior, to manage learning unilaterally, to be a subject-matter authority. Your responsibility is to transmit content to groups of students (most likely homogeneous groups) in the most efficient manner, given the limited time you have with them.

However, the cultural dimensions of school classrooms are causing us to rethink the traditional managerial roles of teachers, which include managing content, controlling student behavior, managing student learning, and managing paperwork and other daily duties associated with the job of teacher. We have become increasingly aware that classrooms are where a multitude of cultures meet and mingle; where teacher and student biographies are constantly interacting. These cultural and biographical views of classroom teaching suggest that a straightforward transmission of content that is performed by factorylike schools may be miseducative for students whose cultural backgrounds might not align well with mainstream schooling.

As the tradition of factory schooling interfaces with the kind of diversity that encompasses many classrooms, and some classrooms entirely, you are faced with the question: How can you redefine yourself as a teacher given cultural needs and cultural awareness of classroom dynamics? What new kinds of teacher roles and new kinds of corresponding instructional strategies might be better suited to highly diverse learning environments?

EXERCISE 3.3   Creating Alternative Passageways for Learning

Using the metaphor of *passageway* is one way you can begin thinking about new kinds of labels and new kinds of instructional strategies for diverse learning environments. This metaphor was used earlier to describe the course of learning that was set for Richard Powell in his junior high school and high school environments.

If you attended schools that were primarily traditional in orientation, you likely passed through a predesigned passageway for learning. Reflect carefully on the passageways for learning that you had in your elementary, junior high, and high schools. Which of the concepts suggested in chapter 2 best depict the relationship you had with your teachers as you traveled through your educational passageway? Were your learning and behavior managed? Were your learning and behavior guided? Or were your learning and behavior mediated?

As you consider these questions, you might think about times that you were guided as a learner, and times when teachers negotiated learning with you. What you should look for here, and what will have the greatest impact on your perspectives of classroom structure, will be the general tendency of your former schools over time to organize learning for you in a certain way.

Most prospective teachers we have worked with have been socialized into traditional management models, and have traveled through highly managed educational passageways. We have found that these same prospective teachers often have difficulty thinking of other ways they can interact with students and other passageways they can create for learning. The following questions will suggest the breadth of your perspective for organizing alternative educational passageways.

- What are key passageways for learning in schools that are framed by the traditional metaphors of *manage* and *control*?
- What are key passageways for learning in schools that are framed by the alternative metaphors of *guide* and *facilitate*?
- What are key passageways for learning in schools that are framed by the alternative metaphors of *mediate* and *negotiate*?

With these questions we do not mean to imply that a school should be entirely ruled by only one of the metaphors (i.e., *manage, guide, mediate*). Every school continuously demonstrates variations of these metaphors. However, most schools tend to follow one metaphor slightly more than the others, and because of this each school has its own orientation to learning, its own environment, and its own culture. For example, schools that tend to follow the metaphor of *guide,* and structure learning experiences and social interactions around this metaphor, will differ in tone and in student expectations from schools that tend to follow traditional management metaphors. Unless you attended a school that was more reflective of the *guide* and *mediation* metaphors, you might have had more difficulty answering the questions above about passageways.

In a later chapter we describe a school culture that based its student learning and its teacher and student interactions primarily on the *guide* and *mediation* metaphors. As you will see, this kind of school creates very different passageways for management than the kind of school that is more traditional in orientation.

CONCLUSION

What we attempted to do in this chapter was to sensitize you to how the structure of schools, and the organization of classroom learning environments, give rise to specific student subcultures (and labels), and to specific expectations for teachers. Of importance here is to realize how your biographical experiences in school have predisposed you to view student subcultures a certain way, given the school culture and school structure that you assimilated and internalized throughout your educational history. We agree with Bullough and Gitlin (1995) that your past is always with you as a teacher. Following this logic we believe that to know yourself as a teacher means first to closely explore your past in and out of school—particularly exploring how your prior experiences have influenced your present perspectives of students and, consequently, have influenced the labels you are disposed to use—labels that associate students with a certain set of prescribed traits. Knowing how labels are used in both educative and miseducative ways, and knowing why they are used, is the key to creating culturally relevant passageways for learning where all students can be engaged in meaningful learning experiences.

REFERENCES

Ballenger, C. (1995). Because you like us: The language of control. *Harvard Educational Review, 62*(2), 199–208.

Bissinger, H. G. (1990). *Friday night lights: A town, a team, and a dream.* New York: Addison-Wesley.

Bullough, R. V., & Gitlin, A. (1995). *Becoming a student of teaching.* New York: Garland Publishers, Inc.

Contreras, A., & Lee, O. (1990). Differential treatment of students by middle school science teachers: Unintended cultural bias. *Science Education, 74*(4), 433–444.

Doll, W. E. (1993). *A post-modern perspective on curriculum.* New York: Teachers College Press.

Eckert, P. (1989). *Jocks & burnouts: Social categories and identity in the high school.* New York: Teachers College Press.

Erickson, F. (1987). Transformation and school success: The politics and culture of educational achievement. *Anthropology and Education Quarterly, 18,* 335–356.

Fine, M. (1991). *Framing dropouts.* Albany, NY: SUNY.

Gay, G. (1988). Designing relevant curricula for diverse learners. *Education and Urban Society, 29*(4), 327–340.

Goodson, I. F., & Walker, R. (1991). *Biography, identity and schooling: Episodes in educational research.* New York: The Falmer Press.

Jones, V. (1995, April). *Classroom management: An expanded role for teachers.* Paper presented at the Annual Meeting of the American Educational Research Association, San Francisco.

Knowles, J. G. (1992). Models for understanding pre-service and beginning teachers' biographies: Illustrations for case studies. In I. F. Goodson (Ed.), *Studying teachers' lives* (pp. 99–152). New York: Teachers College Press.

Ladson-Billings, G. (1994). *The dreamkeepers: Successful teachers of African American children.* San Francisco: Jossey Bass.

Langer, E., & Chanowitz, B. (1988). Mindfulness/mindlessness: A new perspective for the study of disability. In H. Yuker (Ed.), *Attitudes toward persons with disabilities* (pp. 68–81). New York: Springer Publishing.

McCaslin, M., & Good, T. L. (1992). Compliant cognition: The misalliance of management and instructional goals in current school reform. *Educational Researcher, 21*(3), 4–17.

McLaughlin, H. J. (1994). From negation to negotiation: Moving away from the management metaphor. *Action in Teacher Education, 16*(4), 75–84.

Payne, W. D. (1973). Negative labels: Passageways and prisons. In J. D. Cardwell (Ed.), *Readings in social psychology: A symbolic interaction perspective.* Philadelphia: F. A. Davis Company.

Perkinson, H. J. (1993). *Teachers without goals, students without purposes.* New York: McGraw Hill.

Rose, M. (1989). *Lives on the boundary.* New York: Penquin.

Trueba, H. T., Jacobs, L., & Kirton, E. (1990). *Cultural conflict and adaptation: The case of Hmong children in American society.* New York: The Falmer Press.

Wilson, P. (1991). Trauma of Sioux Indian high school students. *Anthropology & Education Quarterly, 22,* 367–383.

4

Dealing with Everyday Classroom Life: How to Develop Routines, Promote Responsibility, and Respond to Problems

Maintaining high standards around the central goal of children taking responsibility ensures that my classroom will be the opposite of permissive. I ally with children around their needs, not just their wants. I listen to children to help them figure out how to solve a problem, not how to evade the hardest part. I expect that the children in my care will think through hard equations, turn in beautiful work, learn to stop themselves from hitting, work quietly while I am having a conference with a child, work through their quarrels with each other, and figure out a way both to wait and to use energy inside during March. I am constantly trying both to expect the best from children and to accept them for who they are, to be in the middle but not in the way.

(Strachota, 1996, pp. 13–14)

The quote above from Bob Strachota, an elementary schoolteacher, captures some of the central goals—and quandaries—we face as teachers. Strachota knows that we must balance high expectations and acceptance, that we must direct students and yet let them figure out things for themselves. He also knows that the problems which arise in classrooms are at once academic and social. The purpose of chapter 4 is to help you consider how to think about the everyday challenges and issues that occur in classroom life and how to be "in the middle but not in the way" of students' learning. We believe that you should initially *plan procedures* and *develop routines* for your classroom social curriculum. What do you want to happen before, during, and at the end of class? How will you plan and work with students to help it happen? We want you to consider what routines and student responsibilities are necessary to create positive classroom interactions.

Then, once you have planned the procedures, how will you *respond to problems* when they inevitably arise? We will not try to convince you that a particular approach to classroom problems is the correct one, but instead will provide you with numerous examples of how teachers might think about and respond to the difficulties they face. The examples in this chapter come from three sources: descriptions of classroom situations written by practicing teachers, proposals for ways to act taken from various texts, and case studies written by preservice teachers.

PLANNING FOR PROCEDURES AND ROUTINES

Harry and Rosemary Wong (1991) give us a useful distinction between *procedures* and *routines.* A procedure is "how you want something done," while a routine is "what the student does automatically without prompting or supervision" (p. 172). Routines, then, result from establishing and reinforcing the procedures that guide classroom actions. For example, you may want to show students a certain way to pass their homework in—that is, the procedure. When they have consistently followed the procedure and don't have to ask questions about how to do it, the procedure has become a routine.

We think there are four questions that teachers should ask themselves when considering their classroom procedures, and the routines they wish to develop. Those questions relate to *purposes, participants, processes,* and *patterns.*

What are the *purposes* of each procedure? Some classroom procedures are a form of management that is intended to enhance order and efficiency (e.g., keeping track of absences and tardies and the schoolwork due as a result of them). The purpose of other procedures is to guide students to become more responsive and respectful (e.g., learning how to get the teacher's attention). Still other procedures are negotiatory because they are meant to develop students' sense of responsibility (e.g., learning how to take care of the physical environment).

Who will be the *participants* in decision-making? Often, individual teachers simply determine the procedures before the school year starts or develop procedures as the need for them arises during the year. Teachers can also collaborate with other teaching faculty on their team, their wing of the school, or even a grade level to decide on common approaches to certain procedures. Frequently, teachers agree on particular times when students can visit their lockers or go to the bathroom, because constant noise in the halls may disturb other classes.

What will be the *process* of developing and maintaining classroom procedures? Teachers need to create procedures for many tasks before school begins and then begin to use the procedures on the very first day of school. We think there are three phases to the process of making these procedures into routines that operate throughout the school year. You must first *manage* by explaining the procedure and explaining why the procedure is needed. Then, you will need to *guide* by demonstrating how the procedure will work and by consistently using the procedure over time. Finally, you will sometimes feel the need to *negotiate* with students when developing the original procedure or changing a procedure when the original plan is not working well.

What sort of *patterns* might a teacher create to maintain consistent procedures? The teacher could decide, for example, to do something at the start or end of class on a regular basis, or perhaps on a certain day of the week. In the following sections, we will give examples of how teachers can help students to develop routines related to starting class, interacting and acting during the class session, and ending the class.

Starting Class

At the start of class, you need to be most concerned about developing relationships with students, keeping up with administrative procedures, and enabling students to begin learning. The essential part of starting class has to do with how *you* establish the tone of interaction. Will you be sitting at your desk hurriedly searching for a handout, or engaged in conversation with a student in the back of the room, or standing at the door to greet students as they enter the classroom? Your job is to interact with students, and a few words said to certain students as they enter the room can often make a positive difference in what happens later. You might ask how Jonathan's soccer team is doing, how Maria's sister is doing after her surgery, or how much you liked Jerushia's science fiction story written yesterday. By greeting students at the door, you signal that you are organized and responsive to your students.

Now, what should students do after they enter the room, but before you have formally started class? If one of your social goals is to enhance students' sense of responsibility and you want worthwhile learning to occur from the time class starts, then have a *warm-up* or *opener* ready. Your students must know that this activity is one of the everyday classroom routines. An opener might consist of three vocabulary words from last night to include in a written paragraph for language arts, or a *puzzler of the day* in mathematics, or a photograph of a family scene from Senegal to provoke a written response in social studies. Students also need to know that tomorrow's assignment will be on the board in the same place every day, although you may choose to change the assignment at the end of class, based on what has been dealt with during the session. For many students, there is great security in having an assignment book and in knowing when and where to get the assignment copied down.

There are also administrative tasks to take care of at the beginning of class, in order to maintain order and efficiency. As students work on the opener, you may have to take attendance, collect and return homework, take up money for lunch and school activities, deal with absences and tardies, and talk with students about missed assignments. For example, if students are already working on the warm-up activity, there is no need to call out names or ask students to respond. Wong and Wong (1991) describe three ways to take roll:

(1) "Look at your class and refer to your seating chart. Mark whoever is absent."

(2) "Have folders . . . in a box at the door. When students come in, they are to take their folders, go to their seats, and get to work on the posted assignment. After the students are at work . . . you see three folders left, note the names, and mark these students absent."

(3) "When the students come in, they are to take their pencil [from a paper loop placed on a bulletin board beneath each student's name] and go to their seats to work. After the students are at work, you note the pencils remaining on the bulletin board and mark these students absent" (p. 131).

Remember: No matter which approach you choose to take roll, pass back homework, or collect school forms from students and other daily tasks, the focus should be on your responsiveness to students and students' responsibility for learning. A good beginning to class sets the stage for the rest of your time together that day.

Interacting and Acting During Class

Once class is under way, one primary issue to consider is *how you can get students' attention* when you need to provide information or ask questions, and *how they will get your attention* when they wish to ask a question or make a comment. This is related to your purposes of responsiveness and respect. Here are several ideas for how to gain students' attention, a matter of special importance to newer teachers.

- Use an environmental cue such as turning off the lights or ringing a bell. Such cues probably work better in lower grades because some students will think you are *babying* them if you do this in middle or high school classes.
- Have the students choose a new cue phrase each month or two. In elementary school, they might decide on " 'Boo' for October, 'Gobble Gobble' for November, and 'Ho Ho Ho' for December" (Jones & Jones, 1995, p. 232). In middle school or even high school, students might choose a phrase associated with what you're studying, or you could give them a choice of three phrases you have devised. Students may be more likely to listen to a catchy phrase than to a well-worn line such as "let's start now."
- Many teachers count down from 10 to 1, assuming that when they get to 1 the students will stop talking. This can be effective, although we do wonder what happens when the count arrives at 1 and the students are still talking. Wong and Wong (1991) described a variation on this counting approach that seems promising. In the incident, the teacher has quieted a large room filled with sixth-grade students and their parents in just five seconds, by utilizing a five-step procedure:

My five steps are these:
1. Eyes on speaker
2. Quiet
3. Be still
4. Hands free (put things down)
5. Listen

The way it works is, I say, "Give me five." They go through each of the five steps in their mind. I have rehearsed them in this procedure, so when I say, "Give me five," it takes them no more than five seconds before I have their attention. (p. 186)

There are numerous other ways to get attention, ranging from simply stopping whatever you are saying or doing and being completely still (which may work better in higher grade levels), to raising your hand and having students who are listening follow suit (perhaps more workable with younger students), to quite politely asking for attention and verbally praising students who are listening. You will have to experiment to see what works best for you and be prepared to change your approach from time to time when it is taking longer for students to tune in to you.

Students also need to get your attention when they wish to ask a question or make a comment. Teachers tend merely to require that students raise their hands (rather than call out from across the room), but the best idea we have seen uses finger signals:

In this system the students signal the teacher with a predetermined number of fingers. The number of fingers raised corresponds to a predetermined request established by the teacher. Post a sign on the wall with your hand signal chart. Then train your students to use the system.

- If they wish to speak, they are to raise the index finger.
- If they wish to leave their seat, they are to raise two fingers.
- If they need your help, they are to raise three fingers.
- When you see a signal, silently respond to the signal with a nod of the head or a gesture of the hand.

The important thing is that the class is not disturbed. (Wong & Wong, 1991, p. 189)

We would offer a fourth signal to this list. When students have completed a task and they need direction or when you have asked students whether they are done, they can raise their thumbs (a universal gesture signaling "okay" or completion of a task).

It is also vital to think about *what sort of talk and interaction patterns you want* during different class activities. For example, during whole group lecture, recitation, or discussion, be clear about how you want students to respond. Will they have to raise their hands to be recognized to speak? Under what circumstances can they call out a response, and how will you alert them that they must gain recognition or speak when they wish? Many new teachers struggle as they try to balance their desire to encourage students to respond with their desire to have an orderly demonstration or a worthwhile discussion with students.

Independent seat work may require another set of procedures than a whole group activity. We have already spoken about students getting the teacher's attention. What should students do when they have finished their assignment? A common approach is to have them automatically take out their favorite reading book (*not* a textbook) and read silently until the teacher signals that independent seat work time is over.

Small group work also needs clearly understood procedures. When students are using computers or working in learning centers, how much freedom to talk should they have? How will they know when the room is getting too loud for productive work? When you have students work in pairs in the computer lab, for example, be clear about what sort of "voice" you expect. There are also special circumstances, such as taking and retaking tests, in which you will need to clarify the expectations for interaction and the voice level desired. Independent seat work, group work, and work in learning centers are all connected to the purpose of engendering greater student responsibility, so it may be helpful to talk early in the year with students about what conditions they believe foster learning in these different contexts.

Movement in the classroom is another potentially troublesome issue for teachers and students. What will be the procedures for sharpening pencils, going to the bathroom, visiting a locker, going to the library, or getting a drink of water? Your major decision concerns whether or not students will take some responsibility for their actions apart from your directives. Many teachers and teams of teachers have a procedure that students may not move during the class period unless directed or approved to do so by the teacher. Other teachers may set different guidelines, depending on the sort of movement. For example, you could have the following three procedures:

- students may not visit the library or their locker during the period unless the whole class is going;
- students may sharpen their pencils, at the sharpener in the room, whenever no one else is doing so;
- students may take the hall pass to go to the bathroom or get a drink of water if no one else has the pass.

The key point here is that there is a trade-off between your desire to maintain order and your desire to deepen students' sense of responsibility for their actions. Before school starts, make a conscious determination of how you will handle that trade-off.

There are also procedures related to *classroom materials.* Students may fail to bring materials such as pencils or paper, or their materials may be insufficient. In these situations, teachers can opt to punish the student by having them go through class without the materials to write, but that essentially defeats the purpose of fostering learning *and* responsibility. Also, students who are disengaged from the class activities tend to cause trouble more often (isn't that also true with disengaged adults?). Many teachers have developed interesting ways to deal positively with such situations. For example, the teacher may require that a student who failed to bring notepaper "trade" something of value for the class period (commonly, an object such as a shoe) in exchange for getting paper from the teacher. Perhaps you will ask students to sign up on a "repayment" sheet, and notify the parents about what needs to be brought in at the end of each grading period. Some teachers develop a monetary system (perhaps asking students to pay 5¢ in order to use several sheets of paper). Teachers may also incorporate this issue into a larger system for student responsibility, in which there could be positive points for being responsible (bringing paper every day each week).

End of Class

At the conclusion of class there are many things for teachers and students to remember. The end of class can be a confusing time and you can easily forget important matters unless you have established clear procedures. Some of the procedures have to do with order and efficiency, such as making sure the students have the assignment for tomorrow and having the teacher (not the bell) dismiss the class. This is closely related to the purpose of being responsive and respectful, which is met by asking whether students have any remaining questions or confusion about the day's lesson. Finally, you must also require that students take care of the environment by having them pick up the room. We will have more to say about students' responsibilities in the next section.

Here is one final note about classroom procedures related to maintaining order. Some procedures are not done in any preset pattern, but occur in a patchwork throughout the year. For example, you should maintain a well-organized record book that keeps an account of students' attendance, their current and cumulative grades for the marking period, and any formal actions you have taken in response to a problem with the student. This sort of management becomes especially crucial when you have to talk with other teachers, school administrators, and the family about what the student is accomplishing and how they are acting in school. Being well-organized is important for keeping track of students' achievement, and it is also connected with your responsibility to demonstrate and model how to act every day. If a teacher constantly loses students' papers or speaks to students in a rude manner, students will wonder why they are held accountable for not losing papers or for speaking respectfully to peers and adults.

Student Responsibilities

We have spoken already about how the sorts of procedures and routines that are established in your classroom can foster students' sense of responsibility. Responsibility is also enhanced when students assume different jobs in the classroom and the school. Barbara Brodhagen (1995), like many other teachers, has developed a start-of-the-year activity where she works with middle school students to write a *class constitution* comprised of the rights and responsibilities that will form the foundation for classroom actions during the year. Ruth Charney (1991) constructed a constitution with her fifth-graders as part of a unit on the American Revolution (pp. 58–62). Both teachers involved students in determining what classroom responsibilities should be part of the constitution. Here is a lovely description of how another teacher, Sue Hazzard, works with second-grade students to assign classroom responsibilities.

> Students' input is again requested and again they are all pillars of the emerging community.
>
> [Teacher]: "We could do more learning if you could help me do my job. Would you do that?
>
> [Students]: "Yes." "Yes." Hands wave. Suggestions abound.
>
> "How could you help?"
>
> "Keep the calendar."
>
> "Pass out the books."
>
> "Erase the board."
>
> "When you come in, get to work right away."
>
> "Put chairs down when you come in."
>
> "Pick up trash."
>
> "Help other kids."
>
> "Push chairs in under the desks if someone forgets. . . ."
>
> Sue explains that she has written the names of these jobs and some other ones on small disks. Included are the roles of color guard, pledge-leader, calendar-keeper, and roll-taker. A lottery ensues, with Sue picking jobs out of a bowl. These are to be reassigned weekly. . . . The class begins to fall into routines for dealing with everyday necessities. The children look more relaxed, as if they belong here, are part of whatever is evolving. (Nicholls & Hazzard, 1993, pp. 22–23)

One more example of focusing on student responsibility comes from a particularly inventive student teacher we worked with (named John). John created a set of student jobs and he would act out what every student was supposed to do in every task. The jobs included the *Homework Hound,* whose task was to collect student homework. When he portrayed the Homework Hound, to show what the job entailed, John went up and down the aisles between student desks, sniffing loudly and telling students he could "just smell that homework cooking." Being a clever teacher, John asked Kevin, a student with a good attitude but a poor record of turning in homework, to be the first Homework Hound. Sure enough, Kevin would shuffle around the room at the start of each class during the warm-up, sniffing out the homework. Not only did John see a large improvement in the number of students turning in their work, but Kevin became one of the most conscientious homework finishers in the class!

Another important routine of classroom life in every grade level is taking care of plants and animals that live in the room. How much responsibility will students have for watering and fertilizing the plants, or feeding and taking care of any classroom animals? In what ways will they be responsible for cleaning and beautifying the environment, even in middle and high schools?

The aforementioned stories of Sue and John, and the questions about caring for the environment, are worth pondering. Being well-organized and using time efficiently is important, but you should never lose sight of the *big picture* purposes: how can you enhance students' responsiveness and respect for others and their sense of personal and social responsibility?

EXERCISE 4.1   Developing Routines and Responsibility

1. Develop responses to the following procedural question individually, and then corroborate your responses with one or two peers. Then generate a whole-class chart summarizing what procedures may be workable, and assign priority to those procedures that seem the best choice. Be prepared to discuss *why* a certain procedure might be good.

WHAT IDEAS DO YOU HAVE FOR PROCEDURES TO HANDLE THESE MATTERS?

Start of Class
Returning homework to students
Taking up students' money for lunch and other school activities
Dealing with students who have missed assignments (because of being absent or because of choosing not to do them)

During Class
Collecting work and distributing materials
Students sharpening pencils
Students going to the water fountain or going to the bathroom
Students lacking materials

End of Class
Cleaning up the room
A pattern for giving assignments
A pattern for dismissing students

2. Consider the following two questions about student responsibility:

   • What responsibilities should students have in your classroom? In the school?
   • How should each of these responsibilities be determined?

RESPONDING TO PROBLEMS

No matter how carefully we plan for and try to implement rules and routines, life in classrooms can be unpredictable. Problems surface, conflicts arise, and teachers have to respond to the problems and mediate the conflicts. We are well aware of the emotional aspects of teaching, and we know that situations occur in which teachers react quickly. Something *sets us off* and we raise our voice or say something we later regret. This happens to everyone at some point, but the goal should be to act in the best way we can, which means in a manner that shows you are a responsive, respectful, and responsible teacher. To prepare yourself to act in these ways, you must ask some basic questions about a range of problems:

What is the problem?

What do you know about the student(s) and families involved in an incident?

For whom is this incident a problem?

What should you do in response to the problem?

What Is the Problem?

Many psychologists have written about why students act as they do, and about what motivates or does not motivate students. How you define what constitutes *a problem* depends on your beliefs about students' actions. Our use of metaphorical language often indicates what we believe. You will hear teachers and certain purveyors of classroom management systems talk about *problem children* or about students *being a problem.* This language defines classroom problems as individual matters that somehow reside within children. We also speak of children *having problems,* which assigns ownership of the problem to the child. All of these phrases fail to convey the social underpinnings of the difficult situations we face in classrooms, and the teacher's role in helping to create and mediate problems. We believe that teachers and students *experience* problems that develop as part of the day-to-day social interactions at home and in school. When a child acts out by yelling across a room, everyone experiences the situation and the teacher is directly involved in defining whether or not the yelling is a problem, and how to deal with the problem.

What Do You Know About the Student(s) and the Family Involved?

Every problem that arises has a personal context related to the student and his or her family. The age of the students can affect how you define and respond to a classroom problem. You may think differently about a 6-year-old child who blurts out comments and fails to listen to instructions than you may about a 16-year-old doing the same thing in a high school classroom. Unfortunately, our stereotypes of children at different ages may sometimes get in the way of a reasonable response to a problem. Some teachers, for example, think of young adolescents (10–14 year olds) as overly emotional and largely controlled by their hormones. Given that sort of belief, a teacher may think that negotiating or reasoning with the student will be of little value, and that the student needs merely to be directed and controlled to do what is right. It is our responsibility to challenge *our own* preconceived notions of children's capabilities.

The cultural background of the students is another contextual factor to take into account. Directness and assertiveness may be valued more in some cultural groups, while tact and acceptance of adult authority may be emphasized in other groups. Culture is not just a matter of ethnicity, of course. Ways of interacting in rural communities and in inner-city neighborhoods may differ quite radically, and girls may respond differently than boys to some of your actions.

The context also includes your current relationship with the student and the family. If you have developed a bond of trust with the student in past encounters and have consistently communicated with the family, it may be easier to deal with a current problem. Conversely, if an incident is the latest in a string of misunderstandings or hostile acts toward the teacher, you may have to get help from another teacher or an administrator. It is crucial to know when you need outside help, even though you will try to handle problems "within the room."

All of these contextual issues influence the amount of time and effort that might be needed to deal with a problem. If you do not know the student or the family well, and you come from a somewhat different cultural background, you should take the time to confer with the family and learn more about what they do to handle problems that occur.

For Whom Is It a Problem?

Part of defining what constitutes a problem is deciding who is most affected by an incident. Sometimes, a student's actions cause a problem for the teacher, but other students are not really disturbed by the situation. In other cases, the student's actions reflect a problem he or she is experiencing, or affect other students' opportunities to learn.

Problem for the Teacher

You might think more clearly about how you define a problem if you ask yourself two questions:

What are five things you do not want *students to do in the classroom?*

There will be a variety of responses to this question, but we believe all of you may agree that you do not want fighting or bullying to occur in your classroom. In many cases, though, teachers are also bothered by relatively minor incidents, especially if they occur frequently. When students pass notes, whisper to a neighbor, stare out the window, or doodle on their paper, are they really bothering other students? Should you even assume that the student's learning is being impeded?

Although a student who is often distracted may be experiencing a serious problem in his or her learning, be wary of making assumptions about the mind-wanderers and doodlers. Sometimes, a small word to them will bring them back into the classroom activity—and you may be surprised at what they actually paid attention to!

What are five things you do want *students to do?*

This question concerns the ways in which you want students to be responsive, respectful, and responsible. Thinking in terms of *positive* actions (those you see already from students and those you hope to see) will help you to stay away from possible negative comments about students that pervade some teachers' conversations in hallways and work rooms.

Problem for a Student

We could argue that any time a student acts in a way that leads to classroom disruptions, the incident indicates that the student is experiencing a problem. A student who teases others is often experiencing a sense of doubt about his or her own attributes or abilities. Some problems, however, do not directly affect other students but do affect the individual student's social or academic development. One common example is that a student may choose to remain apart from others in the room (see also chapter 7). This *isolation* from the teacher or other students can be related to a basic way of interacting with others, as with shy students, or to a conscious decision about not being connected with adults in the school. Jere Brophy (1996) has analyzed how teachers can work with shy students, and he offers many good ideas for how to respond (pp. 376–401).

Boredom is also a problem for some students who may be either academically advanced or far behind. Some students who *act out* in class are seeking attention or bringing frustrations from other parts of their life into your class, but other students may simply be uninterested in what is happening in class. You need to be honest enough and brave enough to examine the depth and interest of your own curriculum and the activities in class. Alfie Kohn (1996) urges us first to ask "What's the task?" when problems arise. Says Kohn: "One of my own . . . revelations as a teacher was that behavior problems in my classroom were not due to students' unnatural need for attention or power. The students were acting up mostly to make the time pass faster. . . . Back then, I was thinking about a new approach to discipline. What I really needed was a new curriculum" (p. 19).

Social Problems

There are numerous social problems that affect students. Some students seem constantly to seek attention and to change the direction of class activities. They may, for example, interrupt others, make disruptive noises, or ask questions designed to divert a discussion.

You may also perceive that there is conflict among students in the class. Perhaps several students are bullying and teasing others, or there is a more general inability to get along during group work activities. Cathy Jacques (1997, pp. 83–86), a fourth- and fifth-grade teacher, has written a particularly good description of name-calling and how to deal with that problem.

Problems may arise outside of your classroom that you still have to deal with. On occasion, your students may disturb students in other classes by yelling in the hall or peeking in classroom windows and making faces. Nearly every teacher has had an unpleasant experience on a field trip when students acted obnoxiously and engaged in dangerous or even illegal acts.

There could also be a social problem associated with students' attitudes toward authority, including yours. An individual or a small group of students may openly or privately challenge your authority by offering what some have termed *student resistance*. Some students have a history of defying adult authority and getting in trouble for insubordination. While some students may simply be trying to assert their power, others may be rejecting the curriculum or the experience of life in school. Herb Kohl (1994) has written eloquently about students who choose to *not-learn:*

> In the course of my teaching career I have seen children choose to not-learn many different skills, ideas, attitudes, opinions, and values. At first I confused not-learning with failing. When I had youngsters in my classes who were substantially "behind" in reading, I assumed that they had failed to learn how to read. Therefore, I looked for the sources of their failure in the reading programs they were exposed to, in their relationships with teachers and other adults in authority, and in the social and economic conditions of their lives. . . . Sometimes I was correct, and then it was easy to figure out a strategy to help them avoid old errors and learn, free of failure. But there were many cases I came upon where obviously intelligent students were beyond success or failure when it came to reading or other school-related learning. They had consciously placed themselves outside the entire system that was trying to coerce or seduce them into learning and spent all their time and energy in the classroom devising ways of not-learning, short-circuiting the business of failure altogether. . . . In rethinking my teaching experience in the light of not-learning, I realize that many youngsters who ask impertinent questions, listen to their teachers in order to contradict them, and do not take homework or tests seriously are practiced not-learners. (pp. 7, 28)

The children Kohl described are not low ability and may not have hostile relationships with adults in school, but they do not accept that the curriculum and perhaps the instructional methods are of value in their lives. Appealing to failing grades or imposing negative consequences may matter little to such students, but understanding their way of thinking and offering them intellectual or social challenges may make a difference.

In every one of these examples of a social problem, you will need to determine whether to address the problem as a whole class or with a small group of students. Whatever approach you take, it is absolutely essential that you think carefully about what you know about the students and their families, about the context of the problem, and about who seems to be affected by the problem.

▨▨▨▨▨▨▨▨   **EXERCISE 4.2   Defining the Problem**

Here is a case study of a classroom situation experienced by a student teacher working in seventh grade. Some questions for you to consider follow the reading.

> The lesson I was presenting in health class that day was on air pollution. I had not prepared a detailed lesson plan because (as most new teachers), I was overworked from other classes. I figured that I already knew a lot about air pollution. I planned to ask some general questions about local air pollution and then read from the textbook. . . . I asked for volunteers to name sources of air pollution, expecting to hear answers about automobiles, factories, cigarettes, buses, airplanes, fires, and sewage. Richard, the most notorious troublemaker and leader of the pack, raised his hand and wisecracked, "I know, teacher! Farts!" This response caused a round of boisterous, exaggerated and lengthy laughter and farting sounds from the class, and it gave Richard a feeling of personal satisfaction as a successful comedian. . . .
>
> I called the class to order and cautioned Richard on his behavior. I could feel the students eagerly awaiting another excuse for an outburst. (Shearer, 1988, p. 39)

1. What might you want to know about the student and his or her family or life experiences?
2. Describe the characteristics of the problem. In what ways might it be both individual and social?
3. Who seems to be affected by the problem?
4. What factors might make this problem difficult to handle?

What Should I Do?

To answer the question of what actions to take, you must ask yourself what your choices of action are and decide what sorts of consequences you will promote or enforce. Then, you can decide whether to take immediate action, ignore the incident, or respond to it at a later time. Given your choices and your decision about immediate action, what seems the best course to follow? We know that the press of classroom life usually does not allow for a slow, measured response which takes into account answers to all these questions. We do think, however, that giving serious thought ahead of time to how you want to respond to problems will help you consider what to do when a difficult situation occurs. You ought to consider the level of seriousness, and then your understanding of the nature of consequences.

THE LEVEL OF SERIOUSNESS

Depending on how you define the problem, you will assign varying levels of seriousness to it. The first key question to ask is: *How disruptive is the incident?* To keep matters simple, you could consider three *ripples of disruption.* Maybe you and the student are the only two people being disrupted (there is only a small disturbance or ripple in the waters of classroom life). A larger ripple would involve a group of students being disturbed, and a larger ripple yet would touch the entire class. For example, if a student repeatedly taps a pencil on her desk or fails to pay attention when you give directions, it could be that only you and she are being disturbed by the action. Blurting out responses or interrupting others during a small group activity might disrupt this group but not other groups. Calling a greeting to students across the room or making fun of someone when they answer a question posed by the teacher, however, will disrupt the entire class.

You should also ask yourself: *How frequently does the problem occur?* For simplicity's sake, you could assign three rates of frequency to a problem: *rare, occasional,* and *persistent*. A rare problem occurs at most a few times a year. In most classrooms, fights are rare. There are also occasional problems that occur no more than once a week. An example of this may be students passing notes in class. You will also face persistent problems that take place almost daily, and certainly weekly. For example, you may find that students in a class frequently interrupt or fail to listen to each other.

THE NATURE OF CONSEQUENCES

As you think about how disruptive and frequent certain classroom incidents are, you also need to consider the nature of possible consequences and your views on the best approach to use consequences in the classroom. We define a *consequence,* simply, as what occurs after some action. The word is not synonymous with *punishment* because there are also positive consequences, what we could call *rewards* or *incentives*. We may think of consequences as *given, natural, logical,* and *negotiated.*

With *given* consequences, you have no real choice of action, especially when the problem relates to the safety of others. For example, you must abide by given laws governing students who carry a weapon into the school. Often, schools have policies regarding other dangerous acts such as fighting. When you have seen a student with a weapon or you have been able to separate the combatants in a fight, you are required to send them to the office where a formal set of negative consequences will be enacted.

Educational writers have claimed that consequences can be *natural* or *logical*. A natural consequence is said to occur when there is no direct adult intervention. If a student teases and bullies others, the consequence may be that the other students won't want to play with the person who teases. While there are some occasions when the teacher might let natural consequences take their course, if there is danger or a disruption of learning for others, we should probably intervene in some way.

A logical consequence is an adult intervention that is appropriately linked to the original action. Charney (1991, pp. 69–73) writes about three types of logical consequences. The first type is called a *reparation,* which requires students to take care of what they have done. For example, if a group of students leaves a mess in the back of your classroom, then they should clean it up and perhaps pick up the entire room. A second logical consequence is *a breach of contract and loss of trust*. If a student is given freedom to go to the bathroom on his own and he stays away too long or gets into trouble outside the room, Charney suggests that the teacher say: "You're not able to take care of yourself in the bathroom, so I guess you won't be able to go by yourself for the next two days." Trust is breached also when students tell lies or disregard others' rights. The third type of logical consequence, which is called *time-out,* will be dealt with in a subsequent section.

Wong and Wong (1991) have tried to distinguish between *logical* and *illogical* consequences. While their approach is predominantly nonnegotiatory, the authors do pose some helpful principles for determining logical consequences.

(1) Avoid consequences that are related to the academic grade, such as deducting a grade or points for that day.
(2) A consequence is reasonable when the student sees that it is reasonable and logical and in the student's best interest.
(3) The consequence should be suitable and proportional to the violation. . . .
(4) Do not stop instruction when giving out the consequence. (p. 158)

As we mentioned earlier, there may also be natural or logical consequences that are *positive*, in the form of rewards and incentives. There are any number of possible incentives, ranging from *smiley face* stamps on an assignment, to verbal praise and encouragement, to having the chance to do something interesting outside of school. Thomas Lickona (1991) has included many examples of how creating a *moral community* and *caring beyond the classroom by helping others* can be quite an incentive for students to act responsibly and to learn.

All of the consequences discussed thus far were predetermined by adults, whether in the courthouse or the schoolhouse. Teachers may also *negotiate* the consequences in certain situations. Kohn (1996) has issued a passionate challenge to the prevailing ideas of consequences. Kohn asserts that most approaches to discipline and classroom management favor overt control over discussing problems with students:

. . . [C]onflict is regarded as comparable to dandruff: something unsightly to be eliminated as rapidly as possible by using whatever seems to work. . . . Such contempt for rational discourse with children—and indeed for children themselves, whose points of view are just so much "hot air"—follows naturally from the fact that a respectful dialogue may interfere with one's attempt to control them. (pp. 27–28)

Kohn also describes how a choice we offer to students may actually be a pseudochoice. A pseudochoice entails giving students options that are severely limited or based on veiled threats. (See Kohn, 1996, pp. 48–52, for the full text of his argument.) Real choices, however, are generated through negotiation with students and are not predicated on an impending punishment.

Consequences are a normal part of human interaction; if we act, then something will happen as a result. As teachers, however, we must be clear how we think about the consequences we create with and for students. No matter how you conceive of choices and consequences, Kohn's critique should give you pause before you launch into a preplanned or even prepackaged system of teacher-generated consequences.

THE LEVELS OF INTERVENTION

Once you have thought about the seriousness of an incident and the possible consequences for different incidents, you are ready to think concretely about how to intervene in the situation. You may choose no immediate intervention or may choose to respond with a low-level, medium-level, or high-level intervention. We will explain each sort of intervention by providing specific examples of possible actions to take.

No Immediate Intervention

When you desire not to disturb the class in any way, you make no immediate intervention. Here are some choices:

1. At the most noninterventionary level, you can simply *ignore* the incident. If you were to respond to every whisper, every sidelong glance from one student to another, every momentarily distracted student, all you would do for the entire time would be to monitor and control students. More importantly, you bring attention, thus reward the wrong attention.
2. If you do have concerns about what may happen if something continues, try to *monitor* what is happening. For example, in a small group where one student is talking loudly and telling other students what to do, you may watch and listen carefully so that you can intervene if needed later. See if the students themselves can sort out the problem before intervening.
3. You may *document* students' tardies or their inability to work with a group. Quantitative information may be put in your record book, while you may want to keep a journal that details your thinking over time about certain students, and what you have tried to do in response to problems that surfaced.
4. As part of your role as a guide, you can *model* speaking respectfully with others. For example, if a student does not say "excuse me" when bumping into you, say "excuse me" to him, although not sarcastically, which would interfere with what you are trying to accomplish.

Low-Level Intervention

Low-level intervention results in little or no disturbance of classroom life. *Proximity* is a simple but often effective response to certain situations. Move near students who are tuned out and they will quite often tune back in. Merely establishing eye contact with students lets them know that you want them involved. You also need to cultivate *a look,* which is a facial demeanor and even a posture that signals your seriousness. (See Bowers & Flinders, 1990, pp. 77–78, 84–86, and Wong & Wong, 1991, p. 167, for further information on these issues.) This sort of intervention can be effective when responding to students who are engaged in minor activity, such as whispering to one another.

Sometimes, you will want to *alter the class activity* or the curriculum focus. When students have their heads on their desks or when you detect increased whispering, consider whether students are confused or bored. Don't let inflexibility or false pride get in the way of changing something to improve the chances of learning.

In certain cases you will want to *ask a student some question about a topic related to a class activity,* after alerting them that you will soon call on them to speak. You can say quietly to the student: "Letisha, I really want to hear from you, so I'll ask you a question within a minute or so." This works well with some students when they are staring out a window or seem distracted. Your objective is to get them engaged in learning, not to *stick them* with a tough question so that they will be embarrassed into paying attention.

Medium-Level Intervention

A medium-level intervention involves directly talking with the student and his or her family, or deciding on a negative consequence related to the student's actions. One fundamental response is to *ask a question* in order to determine the student's interpretation of what is happening. Rather than asking "what happened?" try to ask "what are you doing?" and then "why are you doing this?" This puts the focus on the student's responsibility in a situation, enables her to give her interpretation of the incident, and yet does not allow her simply to blame someone else. Be clear about your purposes for asking a question. If the question is intended to demean a student, *don't do it!* Questions should be intended to gain a greater understanding of the situation and to encourage the student's sense of personal and social responsibility. Sometimes, you will straightforwardly *demand that a student act differently.* You may at the same time remind the student about the rule, procedure, or classroom expectation that you talked about (or worked out as a class). For example, when a student throws some wadded-up paper across the room, you can walk over to him, quietly remind him of his responsibility to keep the environment clean, and tell him he must pick up the piece of paper at the end of class. (If you require him to pick it up right away, more class time is taken up with the incident than it warrants.)

You may also choose to *move the student* within the room. This may involve placing a student with another group of students, if he or she is talking too much or if there is a low-level tension among the students. If you seek to separate a particular student from the entire class, this is referred to as a *time-out.* Time-outs are a common response to students who seek attention or disrupt the class in ways that you find unacceptable. You move the student to a place in the room that may be specially designated for this purpose, and you tell the student clearly what he or she will need to do in order to return to his or her regular place with the class.

Lickona (1991) describes two kinds of time-outs. The *fixed-interval time-out* sets up a specific time period (5 or 10 minutes, for example) when the student must be away from the group. In a *conditional time-out* the student returns to the group when he believes he is ready. Lickona also thinks there might be a two-step system. "With the first time-out, you can come back when you're ready; but if you repeat the offense within the next 30 minutes, you're out for a fixed length of time. It's also good to help prepare kids for reentry by asking, 'Are you ready to go back?' " (Lickona, 1991, p. 121). Charney (1991) devotes an entire chapter to setting guidelines for time-outs (pp. 93–110).

Sometimes, teachers on a team or a wing of the school will make an agreement that a student who is causing a problem can be moved to another teacher's room, usually with a work assignment in hand. This is really a different form of a time-out, which requires explicit communication between teachers.

Not everyone is enamored of time-outs. Bob Strachota (1996) used this method for years and then, after reading Vivian Paley's critique of it, he decided to handle the disruptions during class meetings in another way:

> First, I became more resourceful about what to do about this unwanted behavior. I soon found myself able to distinguish between different kinds of talkers: the impulsive, the silly, those who were chatting with their neighbor, those who were showing off. I was able to adopt different responses for different types of talkers. I might talk with an impulsive recidivist outside of meeting and together we'd brainstorm what could help: perhaps sitting next to me for a while, perhaps a signal, maybe a system for keeping track. . . . I now have to deal with behavior that I had been ignoring; and I have changed my expectations and come to tolerate a little more disorder as a fair exchange for greater connection and understanding. There is also a third benefit: giving up time out has made me deal more with my emotional responses to misbehavior. Where I often used to use time out to sweep an offense under the rug, I now ask myself, *Why is this bugging me?* (pp. 115–116, 118–119)

Strachota exhibits the sort of observational skills, willingness to ask difficult questions, and honesty about one's own motives and actions that we hope for all teachers. He writes elsewhere about how he still chooses to direct students' actions in certain circumstances, but he does not assume that teacher direction or methods such as time-outs should be a frequent recourse when everyday problems surface.

You may also decide on a relatively minor negative consequence in response to the incident. Three possibilities are to: (a) *assign students to silent lunch* or some other medium-term consequence; (b) *require students to clean up or to perform a task* if it is associated with the problem; or (c) *decrease the student's free time or remove privileges and rewards.*

In addition, there are medium-level interventions that involve the student's family. This involves three steps, although all three are not always necessary. The first thing to do is to *call or send a letter home.* A brief call will suffice to alert the parents about the situation and ask how you can all work together to help the student improve in some way. Step two is to send a letter which relates in more detail what happened in the incident from your perspective, and what you and the student have agreed to do. The student needs to know about calls and letters home so she can be prepared to talk with her parents about the *action plan* you have developed. If requested by the parents or determined by you, the third step can then be a *conference with the student or family,* in an informal or formal manner.

High-Level Intervention

A high-level intervention should be saved for an incident that presents a risk to others or that disrupts the class in a serious way. Such interventions are dealt with in other chapters in this book, so we will just mention a few possibilities here. You can hold, on a regular basis or for special issues, a *class meeting* (see chapter 6). These meetings are for social problems that affect the entire group, in which a number of students are involved. Charney (1991) and Lickona (1991) have extensive chapters describing how to conduct effective class meetings. Gathercoal (1993) remarks about this idea: "Class meetings are important because they create among students a sense of enfranchisement. They have the effect of giving students a sense of significance as well as having some control over what happens to them in school. . . . The success of class meetings is related directly to the ability of teachers to help students see all sides of the issues presented, by asking the relevant questions and then listening" (p. 99).

For individuals, you can *make a contract* with the student and family. Contracts may be open or closed. A *closed contract* is one in which the consequence has already been decided by you, either alone or in conjunction with other teachers or administrators. In *open contract*, the agreement about what needs to happen next is negotiated with the student and the family, and all parties must concur in order for the contract to work.

When more serious incidents take place, you will feel compelled to quickly remove the student to the main office. If the incident is severe enough, the student may then be assigned to in-school suspension or suspended from school. When you send a student to the office in most schools, the decision about what to do is taken out of your hands. Depending on the laws that govern your school district, *corporal punishment* may be an option for the principal to consider. Corporal punishment is *not* your decision to make. Usually, a series of procedures is carried out and parents are notified before striking a child. We are adamantly opposed to corporal punishment because we believe there is insufficient evidence of its effectiveness in changing children's actions, and because we believe school officials have no right to hit a child. Still, it is legal in some places in the United States, so you should find out the procedures and the legal boundaries associated with this punishment.

EXERCISE 4.3   Responding to a Problem

Here is a case study of a classroom situation experienced by a first-year Spanish teacher who took over a high school class in midyear. Some questions for you to consider follow the reading.

> . . . Karen felt that they regarded her as only another substitute, and she constantly struggled for control. At first, the problems seemed relatively minor: side-bar conversations, off-task activities, minor disruptions. But gradually the students' inattention increased, and whenever she demanded their focus, they would chatter about a football or basketball game or about the upcoming ski season or anything else that was unrelated to the material.
>
> During the first day of her second week, Karen was caught in a crossfire of coins being flung around the room behind her as she tried to conjugate a verb on the chalkboard. . . . She held the brief hope that the disruption would subside on its own if she ignored it. She continued writing on the board, reciting the verb as she conjugated it and pushing dutifully ahead with the lesson plan.
>
> A sudden loud CRACK! shattered Karen's concentration and her sense of safety. Instinctively, she jumped back from the board and swerved to face the class. A Kennedy half-dollar, which had ricocheted off the chalkboard only a few inches from her ear, fell to the floor and rolled to the back of the room, accompanied by a chorus of chuckles from her students.

That was the last time Karen turned her back on the students. From then on, she used the overhead projector rather than the chalkboard whenever she needed to illustrate something to the whole class.

After the coin-tossing incident, Karen tried a variety of the assertive discipline techniques she had learned in her college education courses, but few seemed to have any effect. For example, each time a student acted up, she placed a check next to his or her name on the chalkboard. If a student received five checks, he or she was assigned an hour of detention. But it became a game before long as students competed for the checks and ignored the detention assignments. (Silverman, Welty, & Lyon, 1996, p. 10)

1. Describe the problem. What questions should you ask about this situation?
2. What did the teacher try to do, and what were the effects?
3. What would be your choices of action?
4. What might be the best thing to do in the situation? Why is it the best course to take?

DEVELOPING A VISION OF YOUR ACTIONS

When we talk about all the possible procedures and ways of responding to problems in the classroom, it is easy to "not see the forest for the trees." The fundamental word here is *see*, because you should try to *see* your students and yourself as clearly as possible (see also chapter 7). You need a vision of what you want to do and not do with students, and of the sort of classroom community you want.

What Should You Do and Not Do?

We have written a great deal in this chapter about what actions you might take—how you can establish routines, promote responsibility, and be responsive to classroom problems. You also ought to think about what you *won't* do. Obviously, you should not depart from district or school-level policies unless you have talked about it with one of your administrators. That would be an unusual circumstance, but there are many things you should not do that are part of your basic vision of teaching. Forrest Gathercoal (1993) has developed a list of *nevers* that addresses this issue. Here is a selected list of them:

1. Never demean students.
2. Never judge or lecture students on their behavior. Instead, ask questions and listen to the student's side of the story in order to learn more about the problem.
3. Never compare students. . . . Students simply want to be judged on their own merits and not be thrust into the shadow of others.
4. Never give students constructive criticism; always give them reflective feedback.
5. Never demand respect; give it to your students. By giving it away, it is usually returned many times over.
6. Never fear an apology.

7. Never accuse students of not trying or ask them to try harder; always help them try again.
8. Never get into a power struggle.
9. Never become defensive or lose control of your feelings.
10. Never use fear or intimidation to control students.
11. Never punish the group for the misbehavior of one of its members.
12. Never say "you will thank me someday" as a rationale for a decision that students perceive as not making sense or having any immediate purpose.
13. Never think that being consistent means treating all students alike. . . . Students know they have different personalities and abilities that require various educational strategies in order to meet their many needs and goals. (pp. 40–45)

Gathercoal's *nevers* can be a useful resource as you develop your vision of who you want to be—as a teacher and as a person.

WHAT KIND OF CLASSROOM SOCIAL CURRICULUM DO YOU WANT?

In the end, how you will act and not act depends on your vision of the classroom. What routines will help to keep everyone organized? Will this be a place where conflict is denied, controlled, or perhaps negotiated as a part of everyday life? In what ways will your classroom social curriculum be a community in which people act responsively, respectfully, and responsibly? These questions are answered in the small, everyday interactions in your classroom, the interactions that are the backbone of classroom life.

REFERENCES

Bowers, C. A., & Flinders, D. J. (1990). *Responsive teaching: An ecological approach to classroom patterns of language, culture, and thought.* New York: Teachers College Press.

Brodhagen, B. L. (1995). The situation made us special. In M. W. Apple, & J. A. Beane (Eds.), *Democratic schools* (pp. 83–100). Alexandria, VA: Association for Supervision and Curriculum Development.

Brophy, J. (1996). *Teaching problem students.* New York: The Guilford Press.

Charney, R. S. (1991). *Teaching children to care: Management in the responsive classroom.* Greenfield, MA: Northeast Foundation for Children.

Gathercoal, F. (1993). *Judicious discipline* (3rd ed.). San Francisco, CA: Caddo Gap Press.

Jacques, C. (1997). Outer structures, inner supports: Teaching respect to fourth and fifth graders. In R. S. Charney (Ed.), *Habits of goodness: Case studies in the social curriculum* (pp. 77–93). Greenfield, MA: Northeast Foundation for Children.

Jones, V. F., & Jones, L. S. (1995). *Comprehensive classroom management.* Boston: Allyn and Bacon.

Kohl, H. (1994). *"I won't learn from you" and other thoughts on creative maladjustment.* New York: The New Press.

Kohn, A. (1996). *Beyond discipline.* Alexandria, VA: Association for Supervision and Curriculum Development.

Lickona, T. (1991). *Educating for character: How our schools can teach respect and responsibility.* New York: Bantam Books.

Nicholls, J. G., & Hazzard, S. P. (1993). *Education as adventure: Lessons from the second grade.* New York: Teachers College Press.

Shearer, J. (1988). Foul language. In J. H. Shulman, & J. A. Colbert (Eds.), *The intern teacher casebook* (pp. 39–41). San Francisco, CA: Far West Laboratory for Educational Research.

Silverman, R., Welty, W. M., & Lyon, S. (1996). *Case studies for teacher problem solving* (2nd ed.). New York: McGraw-Hill.

Strachota, B. (1996). *On their side: Helping children take charge of their learning.* Greenfield, MA: Northeast Foundation for Children.

Wong, H. K., & Wong, R. T. (1991). *The first days of school.* Sunnyvale, CA: Harry K. Wong Publications.

II

UNDERSTANDING CONFLICT AND COOPERATION IN TODAY'S CLASSROOMS

C H A P T E R

5

Conflict and Cooperation in the Social Curriculum

It was the beginning of another typical day in the middle school for teacher Juan Molina. He was a bit frustrated because unexpected interruptions over the past few days had slowed class progress significantly. As the class entered for the first period he urged the students to quickly find their seats so that they could get started. The normal social interaction and talking began to subside as he asked students to begin correcting their homework from the previous evening. He was using this time to check attendance when he noticed a disturbance in the center of the room. One boy, Hector, seemed to be having difficulty. First he broke his pencil, which he promptly threw on the floor, and then he wadded his homework into a ball and threw that in the direction of the waste basket. Hector came from a low income family that frequently moved from one location to another as they sought work. As a result, he was considerably behind in his academic progress. This, plus the fact that he had few friends in the classroom, caused him considerable frustration and a lot of anger.

Juan's first reaction was to severely reprimand Hector and insist that he pick up the pencil and paper and quit disturbing the class. However, he resisted this impulse and instead told Hector that he would like to see him for a minute outside of the classroom. As Hector made his way to the classroom door, he pushed a couple of students out of his way. This brought about some angry complaints.

When they were both outside of the classroom, Juan said, "Hector, you seem to be having some difficulty getting started today. What seems to be the problem?" Downcast eyes and a shrug of the shoulders met the inquiry. "Hector, I need to understand what is going on." After a minute Hector replied, "Mr. Molina, you know that bike I got that I've been fixing up? Well, last night it was stolen."

UNDERSTANDING THE IDEA OF CONFLICT

Conflicts occur when an activity interferes with the ability of a person to satisfy wants, needs, or interests. Because individuals have different wants, needs, and interests, conflict between individuals is inevitable. In the opening vignette, there was a clear conflict between the wants and needs of Mr. Molina and those of Hector.

The presence of relatively large numbers of individuals in a classroom creates social curricula where conflict is inevitable. The concern then, is not the avoidance of conflict, but how to respond when conflict does occur. Johnson and Johnson (1995) point out that conflict can be healthy and valuable when it is used to create interest and excitement. They define schools that use conflict in constructive ways as "conflict positive" schools. These schools use conflict as a basis for building cooperation and teamwork.

The task of the teacher is to recognize the various types of conflict that are possible in the classroom and to use this conflict to accomplish constructive outcomes. Conflicts become destructive when they are denied, suppressed, or avoided (Johnson & Johnson, 1995). Denied appropriate techniques for expressing their concerns and conflicts, students will become frustrated, angry, and hostile. The overt responses can range from minor disruptions, which are little more than symbolic protests, to verbal abuse and physical violence. Dealing with the conflict that occurs in classrooms so that it is used to a positive rather than a destructive end, which is the overall purpose of this chapter, requires considerable thought and attention. The three metaphors that we use in this book for creating a constructive framework for dealing with conflict are management, mediation, and guidance. These metaphors were more fully described in chapter 2.

In the case of Hector's bicycle, the traditional view of classroom management would encourage Mr. Molina to exercise his power and authority when dealing with Hector. He would be urged to deal with this inappropriate behavior swiftly by implementing a punishing consequence so that the class could quickly be focused on the academic task that needed to be accomplished. The concerns and needs of Hector would have been avoided or suppressed. Indeed, the first reaction of Mr. Molina in a traditional classroom might have been to make an example of Hector in order to send a message that he was in charge and he would not tolerate disturbance. What do you think Hector's response would have been to that kind of display of teacher power? Rather, Mr. Molina's actions created the possibility for helping Hector learn how to cope with frustration and anger. Such an outcome in the long range would have important consequences for Mr. Molina's social curriculum.

As we noted in chapter 2, the traditional view of management emphasizes the authority and power of the teacher. The traditional perspective, as McLaughlin (1994) suggests:

- places time-on-task and efficiency of curriculum coverage as the priorities,
- views learning as independent of student concerns,
- assumes that students learn self-control and social responsibility by unyielding obedience to adult rules and consequences,
- assumes that power is nonnegotiable because it is inherent in the role of the teacher rather than conferred by students,
- places the blame for problems with the students,
- eliminates the need for student input, and
- treats all students the same regardless of cultural or family backgrounds.

These assumptions need to be challenged in order to build a foundation for a *conflict positive* classroom where conflict is used constructively, where cooperation blossoms, and where meaningful learning takes place. One way to challenge these assumptions is to consider three dimensions of classroom contexts. *The first dimension* relates to viewing management not as just the exercise of teacher authority but as involving mediation and guidance as companion metaphors. Management involves creating an environment with the students so that students' needs are met as constructive learning occurs. The first dimension is not the exercise of *power over students* but, rather *power with students.* This sharing of power with students then requires considerable mediation with students and guidance to help them learn self-discipline and social responsibility.

In order for teaching and learning to take place, the cooperation of the students is essential. Making a connection between the students, the teacher, and the curriculum is a necessary ingredient in any productive learning environment. This possibility is reduced if the students, the major players in the process, feel that they have little power or input into their own learning. In fact, if they feel manipulated and oppressed by the educational environment, as we discussed in chapter three, they will resist and create an opposition culture that openly defies school authorities (Spring, 1994). Unfortunately, this opposition culture can be readily observed in all too many schools across America. Viewed in this context, disruption of the school is an understandable and rational response to strains and tensions created by the structure of the school and the classroom (Slee, 1995).

A second dimension of the classroom context that needs attention is the identification of the causes of conflict within the educational environment. Schools and students are both very complex. Contemporary classrooms are more complex and include a wider range of diversity than ever before. A classroom may contain students from a wide variety of cultural and religious backgrounds, students from homes where the primary language is not English, as well as students who once would have been removed and placed in what is commonly called *special education.* They may well be experiencing conflicts in the home concerning their roles and expectations that will influence how they respond in the educational environment.

Many conflicts arise from student-to-student interactions that are based on a lack of understanding or acceptance of diversity. In fact, cultural and ethnic ignorance was cited in a California report as one of the primary causes of violence in the classroom (Dear, 1995). This lack of understanding and acceptance may lead to verbal abuse and teasing that can quickly escalate into major incidents.

Student responses to the curriculum are yet another aspect of the educational environment that needs to be considered. Students may not see the importance of what they are studying in the school and perceive little connection between their needs and concerns and what the school is requiring of them. Those who have a history of school difficulty may actually view the curriculum as a threat to their emotional well-being. It is a place where they expect to fail and their self-concept to further erode unless students are placed in and learning at the level they need with the teacher they need.

The diversity that is now common in schools requires that teachers rethink the assumptions they have about their role in the classroom. Some teachers may be unaware of how many of the conflicts that arise in the classroom have their roots in diversity issues. You must realize that your classroom is a culturally rich and charged environment, not a neutral environment where everything is left outside the classroom door.

A third dimension of the classroom context that requires attention is that of defining what is acceptable and unacceptable classroom behavior. While many prospective teachers immediately respond, based on their earlier experiences as students in schools, that they know exactly what is acceptable and unacceptable in the classroom, deeper analysis often reveals that their expectations are rooted in tradition and culture. These expectations may not be appropriate for all students regardless of gender, ethnicity, disability, or cultural background or may not be appropriate for the activities taking place in the classroom. This is a very difficult area for most teachers to address because of their past experiences as students. They bring with them a set of beliefs that are so deeply ingrained that they are subconsciously accepted as *the right* set of beliefs and practices. These ideas and practices need to be brought to the level of conscious discourse so that appropriate ones can be supported and inappropriate ones challenged.

This chapter addresses the three concerns above. The first section below identifies the sources of conflict so that you can understand the dynamics of the classroom and use conflict in a positive manner rather than letting it become destructive. The second section focuses upon the nature of classroom cooperation and conflict. The final section challenges you to identify the foundations that can be used to build interactional models that will respond to the needs of the students and the diversity they bring to the classroom.

SOURCES OF CLASSROOM CONFLICT

Understanding the sources of classroom conflict is an important step toward understanding factors that influence constructive cooperation in the classroom. There are a number of sources of conflict in the classroom which will vary from class to class.

Interpersonal Conflict

Interpersonal Conflict and the Teacher

Teaching is an intensely personal act. With every lesson you—the teacher—put your ideas, values, and beliefs in the open for all to see. Because of this, teaching is not quite like other occupations. In most fields, a product can be rejected apart from the person who produced it. When the act of teaching is rejected, it is also easy for the person who is teaching to feel rejected.

The impact of difficulty in teaching on teacher behavior is related to the motivations, self-concept, expectations, and prior experiences of the teacher. For example, teachers who are motivated by a need to be liked by all students will be very sensitive to any negative student comments. Similarly, teachers with a positive self-concept are less likely to respond to lesson failures with hostility and defensiveness.

Teachers with realistic expectations about student performance and conduct are less likely to create conditions where students are bound to fail and therefore increase conflict. Many beginning secondary teachers assume that the students they teach will be like them. They will have the same motivations, the same aspirations, the same points of view. This is simply not the case. Most individuals entering the teaching force were not typical students. They generally have experienced more enjoyment and satisfaction for school than many other students. Or, like the vignette by Richard Powell in chapter 3, some were not happy with their experiences and assumed they could do better, so they became teachers.

As we discussed in chapter 3, the prior experiences you bring to the classroom will dispose you to view student behavior in a particular way and influence the way you respond to disruption. Individuals tend to teach the way they have been taught and that might mean responding to perceived challenges to authority with traditional teacher power actions. This usually results in unproductive power struggles between teachers and students.

Interpersonal Conflict and the Student

Learning is also an intensely personal act. Unlike some of the conventional beliefs about teaching that we discussed in chapter 2, schools do not have to be factories where the students can be viewed as raw material that can be molded and stamped into a particular form or product. Using this analogy, failure is attributed to faulty production. However, if learning is to take place, the student must take an active role in the process and must choose to learn. Learning cannot take place without their personal commitment or without capability for motivation to learn.

Thus, failure to learn is not a fault of production mistakes but a personal failure of the student. Being labeled as a learning failure is one of the deepest personal failures a person can experience, as we noted in chapter 3. Being labeled a failure cuts to the very core of one's being and one's potential for classroom success. Individuals who feel they have failed as learners often feel as if they are somehow less worthy and valuable than those who have succeeded. Learning failure also leads to a feeling of being rejected by mainstream society. It is no wonder that individuals who have a history of school failure often band together to form antisocial gangs.

When the personal nature of teaching and the personal stake in learning are combined, the potential for interpersonal conflict is high. We are all striving to satisfy our needs in an environment where others can easily interfere with this effort. You are the key actor in solving interpersonal conflicts and in building interpersonal cooperation. There are several things that you need to do.

Teacher Actions in Response to Interpersonal Conflict

The first step is for you to examine your own interpersonal relationships. How do you relate to others? Do you feel like you need to always be right? How do you react to failure and difficulty? All of us have observed people who have such power needs that they must always be in charge and must be right. When this occurs with teachers, some may respond to lesson failure by blaming students and becoming overly hostile or defensive.

Not all lessons will be successful and not all students will be as interested in the lesson as you would like. However, these seemingly uninterested students must not be rejected or blamed. They need to be respected as individuals and allowed to express their concerns. This type of open communication allows you the opportunity to help students clarify their feelings and seek meaning in the classroom activities.

One useful way of viewing lesson difficulty is recognizing that teaching is hypothesis testing. Each lesson is essentially a hypothesis where the teacher predicts that a particular strategy will achieve desired results. However, like all other hypothesis testing activities, sometimes inappropriate variables are considered and inappropriate strategies implemented so that the predicted results are not achieved. Thus an individual can learn from failure by learning to more accurately identify the factors that need to be considered when planning an instructional strategy.

Meeting Interpersonal Needs of Students

All students, like teachers, have interpersonal needs that must be met. These interpersonal needs include love, respect, success, belongingness, power, and fun. If you ignore these needs, or even unintentionally overlook them, students will seek other ways of meeting them. Unfortunately, these alternative ways of meeting them are detrimental to a productive learning climate. Return for a moment to the bicycle story at the beginning of the chapter. Hector had some very important interpersonal needs that had to be met before he could be expected to make a positive contribution to the classroom. His sense of powerlessness and his anger clearly superseded his need to learn academic content. The need to consider the interpersonal needs of students implies that students should be given a voice in the classroom and treated with kindness and respect.

Mediation is an important method in helping understand interpersonal conflict. Individuals are often unaware of how their words and actions are interpreted by others. Through mediation and sharing, misunderstandings and faulty interpretations can be corrected.

Interpersonal Conflict and the Self-Concept

Another major consideration in dealing with interpersonal conflict is recognizing the importance of the self-concept. As a classroom teacher, you greatly influence the self-concept of students. All individuals learn their self-concept in part by seeing themselves through the eyes of others. In other words, the way people respond to you can greatly influence the way you view your self-worth.

This has some powerful implications for teachers. Teachers are significant others in the lives of students. Acceptance or rejection by you as a teacher has a powerful influence on students. Although many students will proclaim that they don't care whether they are accepted by a teacher, a little probing reveals that they usually care a great deal. Students want to be accepted and be successful. Some are just convinced that they cannot be successful and that you don't care about them.

A major step in enhancing the self-concept of students is the reduction of student failure. This does not mean that you abandon standards and give students praise and success when it is not deserved. Quite the contrary, standards need to be kept high so that students feel a sense of accomplishment and pride when success is achieved. What this implies is avoiding placing students in highly competitive situations with each other, labeling students, putting students down, or placing demands on students that are unrealistic.

This requires classrooms where teachers have a healthy self-concept and are not easily threatened by lesson failures. It also means that you need to respect the dignity and the potential of every student in the classroom. In these classrooms, interpersonal cooperation becomes the norm and interpersonal conflicts are solved in productive ways.

Understanding and enhancing the self-concept is extremely important in dealing with interpersonal conflict that arises because of *inclusion.* Inclusion, which is discussed more in chapter 7, refers to the practice of placing in regular classrooms students who have been previously isolated in special education classrooms. Inclusion ensures that students will feel competitiveness of the situation whether or not labelling occurs and regardless of the teacher's level of respect and kindness. This means that the diversity of the classroom population is being expanded in yet another way, that of ableness. Therefore, teachers are likely to have students in the classroom with various levels of physical, emotional and educational ability. These students may have a negative self-concept because they need assistance and may not be able to participate in all classroom activities. They are especially sensitive to actions that further diminish their feelings of self-worth. This can create feelings of failure and frustration that easily lead to disruptive outburst.

Academic Conflict

Because of the centrality of academic content to the mission of the schools, the possibilities of conflict over academic issues are great. These conflicts tend to relate to what is taught and how it is taught.

The Curriculum

An increasing number of students see little connection between what they are taught in school and life outside the classroom. They often fail to see a connection between the curriculum of the school and their concern for a productive life. They see widespread unemployment and a lowering standard of living even among those who have attained fairly high levels of education. In addition, they constantly hear critics of education claim that the schools are failing to produce well-prepared graduates. In many cases, this is a true assumption. Recent political changes have led to a lessening of opportunities for individuals to move on into higher education. Thus, the incentives to behave and to study the prescribed curriculum because it will have a future "payoff" are shrinking. It is little wonder then that many seem to view school as little more than a custodial institution designed by adults to keep students busy and entertained. This view of the lack of importance of school then provides one set of excuses for disruption and defiance. Students do not see that they have anything to gain by putting forth the time and effort required to learn the prescribed curriculum.

In traditional school settings, students are virtually powerless over what they will learn and how they will learn it. Academic conflict is a natural byproduct of this situation, and acts of disruption and defiance become a protest over this lack of power.

Teachers who encounter this attitude become frustrated and discouraged because they see their job as essentially tied to the delivery of the content prescribed by the state and the school district. If students fail to learn the content, teachers are frequently blamed and held accountable. Discipline then becomes a means of forcing students to learn something to which they attach no importance. They perceive that the most effective means of doing this is through the exercise of teacher power.

This can lead to a phenomenon that we call *defensive teaching*. With this kind of teaching, you assume that students do not want to learn and cooperate, and they reject your efforts if given the opportunity. You are then quick to interpret any misbehavior as an overt challenge to your institutional authority that must be met with a display of teacher power. The result is a power struggle between you and the students; needless conflict is created. Teachers and students become adversaries rather than partners in the learning process. Students create a strong subculture where disruption is encouraged and rewarded.

Testing Procedures

To further compound academic conflict, students are then subjected to standardized tests over a prescribed curriculum—test scores are used to compare and label students. Some students not only attach little significance to these tests, they often see them as personally demeaning. They feel that the scores they earn on tests which they view as being of little importance are being used to manipulate them within the system. Their response is often one of passive resistance. If they refuse to take the tests seriously, then they have a basis for rationalizing low scores as meaningless and thus preserve their self-concept. Since many of the other students view these testing practices in the same way, there is an abundance of support for their actions in the subculture of resistance that they have developed.

Other students may choose to deliberately protest this imposition. For example, a number of high-achieving high school students in a California school district purposefully did poorly on required statewide tests to protest the amount of time the school devoted to an activity that they saw as meaningless. They claimed that the tests wasted school time that could better be spent on learning something that was of importance.

Teaching Methods

Another source of potential academic conflict is found in the way students are taught. Frequently they are asked to learn content for which they see little relevance using approaches that call for little or no opportunity to search for personal meaning. Student involvement is discouraged because it can lead to off-task behaviors and noisy classrooms. Too much student involvement means that the prescribed curriculum cannot be *covered;* this may ultimately result in lower standardized test scores.

The methods used in most classrooms tend to isolate the students from each other, discourage interaction and discovery, and focus on competitive goal structures that pit students against each other. Traditional approaches of grading based on a normal distribution mean that it is to a personal advantage that others in the group do poorly. This pitting of students against students creates unneeded peer pressure and can cause students to be underachievers. Those who choose to play the academic game successfully are often ostracized and labeled as *nerds* by other students. This conflict between students creates an environment where mediocrity is reinforced and those who do poorly in school receive as much, if not more, support and attention than do those who do well. The classroom now becomes a tense environment where academic conflict between students is ever-present.

Individual Differences

In recent years there has been increased discussion over multiple intelligences. This means that the traditional notion that there is some general factor known as intelligence that individuals have in varying degrees is being replaced by some educators with the view that there are numerous types of intelligences. Thus while a person may not be talented in something such as logical-mathematical skills, that same person might be talented in another area such as interpersonal communication. However, traditional school curriculum tends to reinforce and support those who are talented only in a very narrow range of abilities. Those students who might be gifted in other intelligences become frustrated in their attempts to achieve success and recognition. This sense of frustration translates easily to either passive or active resistance and resentment, another potential source of conflict in the classroom.

Another individual difference that has an impact on student success relates to learning styles. Learning style theory indicates that different people learn best in different ways. Some individuals learn best through visual means, others through verbal means, and others through kinesthetic means. However, traditional classrooms are very verbal environments with most of the instruction being delivered either verbally by the teacher or through information read out of textbooks. Those individuals who learn best through this abstract verbal style then have the best chance for success. Those who have other preferred learning styles find success more difficult to attain. Those who are frustrated in using their preferred learning style obviously become potential disrupters.

In summary, there are a number of ways that the content of the curriculum and the way it is delivered can cause conflict and disruption. In fact, it sometimes seems to be a miracle that anything gets accomplished. As a sensitive teacher you need to be aware of these potential areas of conflict and learn how to address them so that the amount of frustration, anxiety, and anger is reduced. You need to find ways to help students discover the importance of what they are learning and to work together toward the solution of academic problems. Skillful mediation and guidance can be the means of accomplishing these outcomes rather than through the implementation of power and coercion.

Cultural Conflict

That schools serve some groups of learners better than others is clear. Teaching methods, the curriculum, disciplinary policies, and the phenomenon of student labeling can favor certain groups. Nieto (1992) contends that the closer students approach the preferred ideal of European American, male, English-speaking, middle-class, heterosexual, able-bodied, competitive individuals, the more likely school will serve them.

Discrimination like that mentioned by Nieto (1992) may well be unintentional by well-meaning teachers. This is because you might not be accustomed to thinking about the cultural, social, and gender backgrounds of your students (Nieto, 1992). Lack of reflection on the elements of culture can lead to discrimination and be a component of the hidden curriculum discussed in chapter 2.

Culture and Gender Differences

All of us are products of our cultural and social backgrounds. We make certain assumptions and have attitudes that are deeply ingrained. We are all subject to unintentional and intentional discrimination against others. This discrimination can be based on social status, culture, or gender. Some of this can be prevented through education and by becoming aware of different social, gender, and cultural perspectives. However, to be responsive to every nuance of culture and gender is just not humanly possible. Because total prevention is not possible, what is needed is a process that allows individuals to freely express their feelings and a commitment to resolve conflicts in a productive manner.

Conflicts will arise when individuals believe they are being discriminated against or treated unfairly. Denials of discrimination and the inevitable conflict will only magnify the issue and lead to more serious problems. Systematically investigating the sources of cultural conflict in the classroom is a beginning step in helping teachers become responsive to diverse learners in the classroom.

The Culturally Appropriate Curriculum

An investigation of cultural conflict must include the curriculum. Research on the appropriateness of school curricula reveals that some curricula alienate students (Nieto, 1992). Although there have been great strides in recent years to move toward more of a multicultural curriculum, the curriculum still pretty much reflects the white European American perspective. One study of textbooks found that white males still dominate textbooks, still receive more attention, and are given credit for most of the accomplishments. Very little is included about contemporary race relations; consequently, the impression is given that there is harmony between diverse cultures and contentment with the status quo. However, what is often depicted in textbooks and what is then studied in school, are often at odds with the reality experienced by students outside the classroom.

Social studies, for example, still tends to present the European American interpretation of history. The culture and the interpretations of women, Native Americans, African Americans, or Mexican Americans are rarely given more than cursory attention. Events such as Black History Month seldom address issues of diversity and are inadequate attempts to seriously address the need for multicultural education. In fact, because such events are routinely included in the school year, there is a tendency for many teachers to think that nothing more needs to be done.

Culturally Sensitive Teaching Approaches

Another important topic that needs attention in identifying the way discrimination in the classroom leads to cultural conflict is that of the methods of instruction. Most teachers have experienced schooling where competition and individual accomplishments are highly valued. Standardized tests were a regular feature and ability grouping was common. Since teachers tend to teach the way they have been taught, they tend to assume that these are the natural processes of education. However, these practices often conflict with cultures that emphasize cooperation and the values of community. The case of the Hawaiian talk story cited in chapter 1 is an example of the relationship between instructional practices and culture.

Culturally Biased Testing

Testing, a common feature in most classrooms, is another feature that can lead to cultural conflict. Tests often have biases that discriminate between different cultural groups, social classes, and genders. For example, one of us (Savage) reviewed a standardized test given to students living in southwest Texas. One item asked the students to identify the season of the year when the leaves fell off of the trees. It is little wonder that students living in a region where there are few seasonal changes and few trees that lose their leaves would have trouble with this item. Students living in other regions might also have trouble with this item if they received a most cursory level of geography, meteorology, or seasonal-related curriculum.

Students have a keen awareness of fairness in the classroom. Violations of fairness, as interpreted by students, can lead to conflict (Gillborn, Nixon, & Ruddock, 1993). If they believe that they or other students are being unfairly labeled through the use of biased testing procedures, they can lose confidence in school and may be unable to find reasons to cooperate with teachers.

Teacher Expectations

Research has revealed that ethnicity, gender, ableness, and social class influence the expectations that you have for your students. These expectations then influence the amount of attention you give to particular students; the types of questions they ask; the amount of time you give students to respond; the types of clues you provide; the type of feedback you give students; the amount of criticism you give; and in general the intellectual demands you place on students (Good & Brophy, 1994). This can result in instruction that emphasizes rote memorization and that is fragmented, repetitive, and less intellectually stimulating.

There are numerous ways that students may react to these factors. Boredom alone may stimulate some students to seek relief; others will be angered by the inference they receive that they are less capable; and others may respond by becoming passive learners with little apparent motivation for school tasks. All of these states establish fertile grounds for teacher-student conflict.

Behavioral Expectations and Discipline Procedures

Another aspect of the classroom that leads to conflict is the establishment of discipline expectations and procedures. A key ingredient here is identifying what is considered to be appropriate and inappropriate behavior.

For example, a high school principal tells the story of a time when he was hired to be the principal of an inner-city high school beset with problems. He quickly became aware that many students and teachers seemed to be in constant conflict with each other. As he sought to find out the sources of the conflict he found some school policies that appeared to have no relationship to the central purpose of school. One of those forbade the wearing of caps and hats in class. This became clear to him one day as he observed a confrontation between a teacher and a student over the wearing of the cap. He noted that the cap was not interfering with the ability of any of the students to learn and was not making any statement about gang affiliation. He asked himself, "Why do we have this rule? Is this a serious problem?" His investigation led him to conclude that the rule was established based on definitions of how the administration and faculty felt students ought to look rather than what was important for learning. Students viewed this rule as one that infringed on their rights and was designed to diminish their power. This had led to the creation of a subculture within the school that emphasized defying authority rather than cooperating to create a healthy and positive school climate.

The principal met with the faculty and discussed this, and other rules, with the faculty. He attributed the beginning of the turnaround from a strife-torn school to one with few problems and high achievement to the abolishment of the "hat" rule.

By telling this story we are not suggesting that there need to be no rules in school. Such a suggestion would be absurd. An orderly environment with an emphasis on academic pursuits is essential for a smoothly functioning school (Nieto, 1992). However, the rules that are established need to be based on a clear set of shared values and principles. Focusing on the principle behind a rule rather than a strict enforcement of the rule helps avoid conflict (Gillborn, Nixon, & Ruddock, 1993). Students will more likely commit to rules when they have an understanding of the principle behind the rule and when they do not feel they are being treated in a cold and uncaring manner. A commitment from the students is essential if any disciplinary plan is to succeed.

Religious Diversity

Religious diversity is a cultural dimension that can also lead to conflict. Public schools across the nation have been relatively insensitive to the importance of the religious dimensions of life. Religion has been largely ignored in the curriculum and most teachers have little understanding of the varieties of religious experiences. They tend to assume that most people believe pretty much as they do. The growing awareness of the impact of diversity on student behavior and learning has led to a growing awareness of the importance of understanding religious diversity. You need to understand the various religious backgrounds that your students represent. In some locations, the variation might be slight; however, in other locations the variation might be highly variable. This understanding can help you avoid conflicts, such as serving food at a class party that might be offensive to a particular religious belief. When this happens, the student is placed on the spot and made to feel different. What had been considered as an occasion to build solidarity may turn into something totally different.

Sociopolitical Conflict

The school and the classroom are a part of society, not separate from it. Teachers cannot ignore the social and political reality of the world outside of the classroom. Thus, the social and political currents in society will be reflected in school. If there are crime and violence in society, there will be crime and violence in school. If there are prejudice and racism in society, they will be present in school. Social conditions such as unemployment, economic stress, alienation, powerlessness, and family disintegration will have an impact on the behavior of students in school.

The Political Influence on Educational Practice

You must realize that schools are very much influenced by politics. The potential power of education and schools to shape the destiny of a nation has long been recognized. It is no accident that one of the first institutions seized when a government is overthrown is education. This has been recognized, and attempts have been made in America to separate the schools from political influence. To assume however, that schools in America are somehow insulated from political influence is naive. Apple (1990) contends that schools are not neutral but are connected to the forms of domination and subordination found in a society. Others contend that the schools are places where the expected behaviors, expected language competencies, the implicit and explicit values, and knowledge and attitude required for success are all competencies that favor one class or one group of students (Slee, 1995). It is interesting to view current political arguments relating to educational reform from this reference point.

   To place this in the context of this chapter, we can ask, to what extent do expectations for student learning and behavior depend upon cultural and social class distinctions? Do our expectations and practices favor some groups? Perhaps some of the disruption and resistance in school reflects a frustration as students try to cope with school practices that discriminate between students based on factors such as social class, ethnicity, and gender. As teachers, we need to examine even our basic assumptions about our educational expectations and invite the perspectives of all students as we seek to connect schools with student concerns.

Education as a Campaign Issue

Dealing with political influences in the schools will not be easy. Politicians have discovered education as a political issue and one of the important planks is to create "safe" schools. While there is no disagreement concerning the need for safe educational environments, many of the proposals merely reinforce the notion of "getting tough" with students and enforcing teacher and administrator power and ignore the need to determine the basic causes of student alienation and frustration. Thus teachers who rely on power methods of control are likely to be reinforced while those who seek ways of including student voices and student perspectives are likely to be labeled as "soft." However, schools cannot buy enough metal detectors, hire enough guards, and teachers cannot be taught to be "tough" enough to eliminate violence in the schools if the students do not cooperate. Fruitful cooperation cannot be based on coercion and fear. Making the school safe requires intense and meaningful involvement of students.

Student Powerlessness

One of the sociopolitical factors that relates to conflict in the schools is powerlessness. Students find themselves in a society that does not seem to care about them. There are few places where they can openly express their concerns and feel that they can make a difference. This sense of powerlessness extends to school. They are given practically no voice in the operation of the school. Because schools and teachers are convenient targets, they vent their frustrations on them. They develop subcultures that support the challenge of school officials through overt and passive resistance.

It is a sad fact that school is one of the few places in society where students can achieve power. Glasser (1986) states that the need for power in young people is one of the most difficult to fulfill. He further states that few teachers and administrators recognize the extent to which the need for power is on the mind of secondary students. Students are frustrated as they begin to experience an increased need for power and are denied fruitful opportunities for fulfilling this need.

This need for power offers important opportunities for teachers who understand this need and are willing to guide students in the constructive use of it. We are not advocating the abdication of teacher responsibility. Rather, through mediation teachers and students can identify those areas where students can exercise real and meaningful power. They can then be guided to exercise their need for power in socially responsible ways. This is the essence of citizenship in a democratic society and ought to be a priority goal for schools.

Student Hopelessness

Another sociopolitical factor that influences conflict in the schools is a sense of hopelessness. No matter what political party is in control, few substantive changes ever really seem to occur. As future job opportunities narrow and as higher education opportunities constrict, a great many students begin to question the purpose of school. To them the future looks hopeless and bleak. Is it not better to live for the here and now, experience the momentary highs induced by alcohol and drugs, and not worry about the consequences of pregnancy because there is no hope for tomorrow?

Students who have a sense of hopelessness and see little connection between school and a productive life have little to lose by disrupting school. Goals of immediate pleasure and feelings of power take precedence over hard work and delayed gratification.

It is clear that many of the challenges in schools are related to fundamental societal issues. This is not meant to provide an excuse for teachers to give up and develop their own sense of hopelessness when confronting serious problems of disruption. There are numerous instances of teachers who are accomplishing a great deal even in the most difficult environments. Part of their solution is to develop an understanding of the students, their motivations, and frustrations.

CLASSROOM COOPERATION AND CONFLICT

An important step in moving toward a productive classroom social curriculum based on mediation and guidance is an understanding of the many sources of potential conflict within the classroom. Many problems are created when a single classroom culture is reinforced and dominates the classroom.

Slee (1995) suggests that disruptions in the classroom might be indicative of fundamental social issues related to the structure of the school, definitions of normality, status deprivation, labeling, and class, ethnicity, and gender conflict (p. 94). The behaviors expected in school, the values to be learned, and the things to be learned in order to achieve success tend to be competencies that one culture or one social class, usually the mainstream culture and/or class, brings to school. Classroom challenges often result from rational student responses as they attempt to cope with a culture that is unfamiliar to them.

A Matter of Perspective

Understanding conflict and potential responses to conflict requires an understanding of self and the perspectives and biases that are brought to the situation. All of us are a product of the culture in which we have spent much of our lives. This includes our ethnicity, socioeconomic level, religious background, geographic origin, and cultural traditions. These factors exert powerful and subtle influences on the way we view the world around us and what we identify as *right* or *appropriate behavior.* In fact, the influences of these factors are so subtle that few of us think about how they impact our expectations and behavior. They have simply become a *part of us* to the extent that we just assume that our views are the *natural* views. This is what is termed *ethnocentrism.* Ethnocentrism is the belief that one's own culture is the natural or superior one.

The issue of ethnocentrism becomes a concern when individuals come into contact with people from other cultural backgrounds. Individuals from other cultures are viewed as strange, even primitive and backward. Ethnocentric individuals fail to understand or appreciate the perspectives and the actions of the others. Their behavior just doesn't make sense to them. When this happens, misunderstanding and conflict between the groups can be great.

This is precisely the situation faced by numerous teachers. The majority of teachers in the United States are drawn from generally the same social class and are predominantly white and female. These individuals have developed a sense of what it means to be a teacher and what is appropriate behavior for both the teacher and the student. However, there is a tremendous diversity of students in the typical classroom. This diversity includes individuals from a variety of socioeconomic, religious, ethnic, and cultural groups.

Throughout American history there has been an assumption that through this mixing in the classroom, individuals from these other groups would come to understand, appreciate, and accept *the American way.* Thus, the school was a major ingredient in the melting pot where all groups are put together and out of it emerged a unified American culture. However, some cultures resisted this attempt to have them lose their cultural identity. More and more individuals began to realize that not only was the melting pot idea not working, it was the cause of a considerable amount of conflict and divisiveness within society.

In the classroom, the ethnocentrism of the teacher can be a cause of management and discipline problems. The expectations that teachers have for students, their cultural interpretation of student behavior, the types of behaviors that are defined as acceptable, and the responses to these behaviors are all rooted in the background of the teacher and in the job she is hired to perform. Because these values are not shared by all of the students (perhaps not by a majority of them), needless conflict can arise that interferes with the ability of the school to fulfill its mission, which is to enhance the ultimate level of learning for each student.

Reflecting on Your Ethnocentrism

At this point you need to try to make explicit your ethnocentrism and how it influences your expectations as a teacher. A useful technique for this is to reflect on your biography that you explored in chapter 3 and answer the following questions.

- What do you see as the major purposes of education?
- How do your background and culture influence what you expect of students?
- What do you see as the most effective conditions for learning?
- What should motivate students to do well in school?
- What types of behaviors would you view as inappropriate?
- What types of student action do you consider disrespectful?
- What might your immediate reaction be if a student said, "I don't have to do what you say!"

As you seek answers to these questions, and as you compare your answers to those given by your peers, you can begin to understand the ethnocentric roots of many classroom conflicts. This understanding is essential in moving toward a solution.

The next step is in understanding specific areas of potential conflict. This means being aware of the social context of the learners, their cognitive and personal development, and your own ethnocentrism. Then the foundation for mediation and understanding will be established and a classroom organization plan can be instituted that respects the dignity of all students and helps them move toward the goal of self-control and social responsibility.

BUILDING NEW MODELS FOR MANAGING DIVERSE CLASSROOMS

For this final section, you must recognize that management and discipline in the diverse classrooms of contemporary America are challenging and complex dimensions of teaching. If this were not so, lack of classroom order would not be a leading cause of teacher failure and a major concern of parents and students. Simplistic responses to complex challenges seldom work. Thus it is not likely that one model of school organization will fit all. The bracing truth is that each teacher needs to construct a classroom context that is based on the social curriculum of her or his classroom. Our purpose is to provide a few broad goals that can help you engage in this challenging yet crucial task.

A beginning point for building new models that will respond to the realities of contemporary teaching is the identification of clear goals. Having a clear set of goals in mind helps you search for solutions and evaluate alternatives. Unfortunately, many educators do not stop to consider how the classroom organization fits in the overall social education of students. They assume that the goal is to handle disruptions quickly so that curriculum content can be *covered.* Therefore, there is a great deal of interest in management models that promise a *quick fix* to the challenges of disruptive behavior in the classroom. These tend to be power-based and lead to simplistic responses that interfere with the search for productive, long-term solutions.

There are several important reasons for identifying goals for the social curriculum. One major reason is that understanding the purposes for any activity provides a foundation for developing a personal theory that influences the decisions about the organization and management of the classroom interaction and about appropriate responses when problems do occur.

Another important reason is the establishment of a basis for self-evaluation. Becoming a reflective teacher requires self-evaluation. Evaluation requires a set of criteria that can be used to determine growth. A clear set of social curriculum goals provides this criteria.

GOALS FOR ESTABLISHING A PRODUCTIVE LEARNING ENVIRONMENT

There is an overall goal in education under which all else can be subsumed. That basic goal is the development of productive and active citizens in a democratic society. It matters very little if individuals attain high levels of scientific and technological literacy and then do not choose to use their knowledge to constructive ends. Consistent with this over-arching goal, several goals for the social curriculum begin to emerge:

- The social curriculum should be consistent with the educational goals of the school and classroom
- Creating a productive learning environment requires a consideration of the social curriculum and cognitive and personal development of the students
- A basic goal of the social curriculum is the development of student self-control and social responsibility
- Responses to discipline and management challenges need to focus on the causes of the problems not just on the symptoms

The Social Curriculum Should Be Consistent With the Educational Goals of the School and Classroom

A primary goal of the social curriculum is to further the learning of the students. The social curriculum needs to be considered as an important part of the instructional process. The social curriculum should not be divorced from the central purposes of education but should be considered as related to the central core of educational outcomes. This integral linkage between social curriculum and academic outcomes is apparent in the case of the Sioux students mentioned in chapter one.

The social curriculum must support and be consistent with the goals of the school and the classroom (Slee, 1995). For example, if the goals of the school and the classroom are to help students become problem-solvers and critical thinkers, then the social curriculum should somehow be organized to help them do this—it must help them critically think about individual behavior. Personal behavior is one of the most important and meaningful dimensions of education. Learning should begin with personal behavior and social responsibility rather than considering them as secondary to other educational goals such as content coverage.

This means replacing the view of management and discipline as a form of control that is decided by the teacher for the good of the students, with the primary goal of ensuring curriculum content. Students must be involved in discussing, reflecting, and making decisions about personal and social behavior just as they ought to be involved in discussing and reflecting on curricular content. The outcomes of the social curriculum need to be considered alongside the academic outcomes.

Creating a Productive Learning Environment Requires a Consideration of the Social Curriculum and Cognitive and Personal Development of the Students

A common mistake made by many educators as they search for ways to create a productive learning environment is that they do not consider the social context of the classroom. Some discipline and management programs are extrapolations from concepts that were developed in relationship to working with individuals in a one-to-one situation in a laboratory or counseling setting. While these might work well in these settings, they are often ineffective when applied to a classroom inhabited by a relatively large number of individuals, each playing a cultural role and trying to find a place in the social order. In other words, the classroom is not just a collection of individuals, it is a group that exists in a given setting at a given time. The members of that group bring with them into the classroom their prior experiences with schools and teachers, cultural heritage, family norms and expectations, unique abilities and interests, and past and present relationships to the peer group. This is what makes teaching both fascinating and frustrating. No two groups or two classes are alike. What works first period may not work fifth period. What works in Chicago may not work in Atlanta or Los Angeles. What works in third grade may not work with high school seniors. Anyone who has attended teacher workshops is familiar with the response of one or more teachers who respond to suggestions with, "I tried that, it didn't work," or, "That's not realistic, my class is not like that." These teachers are not just being negative—they are expressing an important principle. There are multiple realities of teaching. Each teacher must seek understanding and take into account the social context of his or her own classroom. There are no simple solutions or pat answers that will work in all situations. Teachers need to understand that simplistic solutions cannot be applied to all situations. Teaching is primarily a decision-making process and teachers must learn which factors to take into account when making a decision.

This is related to a key point made in chapter 1, that of establishing culturally appropriate instruction. Culturally appropriate classroom structure also needs to be established. An important way of accomplishing this is through mediation. Through the process of mediation teachers learn about students and students learn about the teachers. This is essential for building the foundation for cooperation. Mediation helps clarify the interpersonal goals of individuals and helps make assumptions public. Although many teachers think they understand the social context within which students live, the fact is that few really do. Teachers need to talk with students and allow them to share their insights and frustrations. This is where mediation is especially useful—in providing an opportunity for students to participate in decision making and helping prevent situations where the goals of the student and the goals of the school are diametrically opposed.

Teacher guidance can then be used to help students make sense out of their social environment and consider the consequences of their decisions. You must realize that the amount and the type of guidance provided will vary according to the social and personal development of the student.

Similarly, the cognitive and personal development of the students is an important consideration. Young children are not just miniature adults. They think in significantly different ways than do adolescents or adults. Thus, specific plans for management and discipline need to take into account these differences. Students who demonstrate considerable self-control and social responsibility can be responded to differently than those who demonstrate little self-control. This implies that teachers should have a range of options available when responding to classroom disruption. The options chosen should be related to the seriousness of the disruption, the causes of the disruption, and the cognitive and personal development of the student, especially the ability to exercise self-control and social responsibility.

A Basic Goal of the Social Curriculum Is the Development of Student Self-Control and Social Responsibility

This goal places the welfare of the student as a priority. Given this context, student behavior problems need not be viewed in a negative light. Rather they need to be viewed as opportunities to help the students accomplish some important life goals.

Self-control is not something that just happens—it is learned. Therefore, when considering how to manage a classroom or when responding to classroom disruption, the teacher should ask, "What will help the students move toward greater self-control and social responsibility?" This is where the importance of the teacher as a guide is readily seen. Teachers must help students see the consequences of their own actions and develop a values base that highlights the importance of self-control and social responsibility. As teachers discuss and mediate conflict with students, they are able to gain insights into the behavior of students.

Mediation helps students develop a sense of ownership and responsibility for their behavior. Guidance is then provided so that the teacher assists students in their development toward self-control. A management plan can then be established so that conditions are created that make self-control possible.

Responses to Discipline and Management Challenges Need to Focus on the Causes of the Problems Not Just on the Symptoms

Moving toward a healthy and productive classroom atmosphere requires that those issues causing problems be acknowledged and addressed. It is all too easy to take care of an immediate disruption and then feel successful if the behavior is at least momentarily stopped. However, if the cause is not addressed, it is highly likely that future disruptions will occur. Because they may be different than the original problem, some teachers fail to make the connection between the behavior and the underlying causes.

This is where an understanding of the sources of conflict is important. Unless the source of the conflict is addressed, the problem will not be solved. As you begin to work with students toward solutions, you need to understand the impact of the social curriculum. This understanding of the mix of unique personalities, backgrounds, and culture of the students is essential in building a successful classroom conflict.

When taken together the principles above form a foundation for helping teachers build a constructive and humane learning environment. The principles imply that students must be deeply involved in planning and in maintaining school and classroom learning environments. This also implies that the diagnosis of problems is shifted from blaming individual students and labeling them as deviant or dysfunctional to an understanding that human behavior has deeper causes imbedded in a conflict between the culture of the school and the culture of the students. This results in a shift of understanding management as something in which students must be involved and must support.

It is through student involvement that the basis for learning self-control and social responsibility is developed. This involvement helps build a sense of respect for the dignity of the students and helps teachers understand and build on the diversity that exists in every classroom.

This is not an easy process and does not provide neat prescriptions for discipline problems. Teachers must have a clear understanding of the limits of their power and must understand what is negotiable and what is not (McLaughlin, 1994). There are some students who will view this as an opportunity to be irresponsible (Gillborn, Nixon, & Ruddock, 1994). In the face of this irresponsibility some teachers abdicate their legitimate authority while others reject the idea of mediation and resort to power methods of control.

Mediation does not mean that the teacher gives up all authority, rather, it is exercising the authority of the teacher in the context of caring and concern for the growth and development of all students. The development of self-control in students requires the creation of a classroom where students feel affirmed and respected while at the same time forced to evaluate their behavior and sometimes facing sanctions.

EXERCISE 5.1   Identifying Sources of Conflict

As stated in the opening of this chapter, an important step in meeting the challenges of the classroom is identifying the types of conflict that are present in the classroom. Once this is done, systematic attempts to use that conflict in constructive ways can then be constructed.

In this chapter, four types of conflict were identified. Those included interpersonal conflict, academic conflict, cultural conflict, and sociopolitical conflict. In this exercise we want you to begin identifying these types of conflict by doing some research. The sources of information for your research are teachers, current students, and peers. Use the following questions as a focus for interviewing each of these groups.

Peer Interview

1. Describe the school you attended. What was the social, cultural, and ethnic composition?
2. What sorts of extracurricular activities were there in the school? How many were related to cultural events?
3. Did your school have bilingual programs, full inclusion of special education, etc.?
4. What do you think were the most serious problems in the school?
5. Can you give some examples of the types of conflict you observed?
6. How did the school deal with conflict?
7. Can you give examples of how cooperation was implemented in the school?
8. How did this experience shape your expectations of schools?

Student Interview

1. Describe the school you attend. What is the student population like?
2. What extracurricular programs does your school have? Are there any programs or clubs that focus on cultural events of cultural groups?
3. Does your school have any special services available to students such as bilingual programs, help for students with problems, etc?
4. What do you see as the most serious problems that occur in your school?
5. Can you give some examples of the types of conflicts you see in school? How often do you see conflict?
6. How does the school deal with conflict situations?
7. To what extent do the teachers and administrators involve the students in helping solve some of the school problems?
8. Can you give examples of where cooperation is implemented in your school?

Teacher Interview

1. Describe your school. What is the student body composition?
2. What are the special programs in your school (full inclusion, bilingual, ESL, etc.)?
3. What extracurricular activities are available? How many of them focus on cultural events of specific cultural groups?

4. What do you see as the most serious problems in your school?
5. Can you give some examples of the type of conflict you have experienced?
6. What do you do when you experience conflict?
7. To what extent are students involved in the resolution of conflict?
8. To what extent is cooperation emphasized in your school?

Once you have gathered data from these three sources, begin to analyze it. Categorize the types of conflicts that were mentioned according to the four types described in the chapter. What types seem to be most common? Are there some types of conflict that do not seem to fit into the four categories? To what extent is cooperation used? To what extent are students allowed a voice in the schools? To what extent are the schools trying to accommodate diversity? Do you see any patterns emerging from your interview data? How do students and teachers differ in their views of the school? How are your experiences and those of your peers similar to and different from those reported by current students? How do you account for this difference?

CONCLUSION

Classrooms are complex social environments. It is inevitable that conflicts will arise. Rather than meet these conflicts with displays of teacher power that further alienate students, you need to rethink the sources of conflict and their responses to them. This makes it possible for you to use these conflicts constructively so that students learn self-control and social responsibility.

These are educational goals that are at least as important as academic ones. When you accept the social curriculum as an important part of education and when you address the sources of conflict in diverse classrooms, then you make a positive and productive beginning toward creating a classroom that is engaging, rewarding, and meaningful for you and your students.

REFERENCES

Apple, M. (1990). *Ideology and curriculum.* New York: Routledge and Kegan Paul.

Dear, J. (1995). *Creating caring relationships to foster academic excellence: Recommendations for reducing violence in California schools.* Sacramento, CA: Commission on Teacher Credentialing.

Gillborn, D., Nixon, J., & Ruddock, J. (1993). *Dimensions of discipline: Rethinking practice in secondary schools.* London: HMSO.

Glasser, W. (1986). *Control theory in the classroom.* New York: Harper and Row.

Good, T., and Brophy, J. (1994). *Looking in classrooms* (6th ed.). New York: HarperCollins College Publishers.

Johnson, D., and Johnson, R. (1995). *Reducing school violence through conflict resolution.* Alexandria, VA: Association for Supervision and Curriculum Development.

Nieto, S. (1992). *Affirming diversity: The sociopolitical context of multicultural education.* New York: Longman.

McLaughlin, H. J. (1994). From negation to negotiation: Moving away from the management metaphor. *Action in Teacher Education, 26*(1), 75–84.

Slee, R. (1995). *Changing theories and practices of discipline.* Washington, DC: The Falmer Press.

Spring, J. (1994). *Wheels in the mind: Educational philosophies of authority, freedom and culture from Socrates to Paulo Friere.* New York: McGraw-Hill.

6

Promoting Cooperation and Dealing with Conflict: Classroom Strategies

If you want one year of prosperity, grow grain.
If you want ten years of prosperity, grow trees.
If you want one hundred years of prosperity, grow people.

—Ancient Proverb

Growing people, as the proverb says above, in personal, social, and academic ways is a foremost concern of all educators. Few jobs, however, are more demanding, more challenging, and more important than growing people. This is particularly true for young people—students in today's schools—who will be molding and shaping future society. Helping these young people understand the value of interpersonal and intercultural cooperation as they live their lives in a pluralistic society, and helping them understand how to deal with interpersonal and intercultural conflict, must be central concerns, and consequently central instructional issues, for all teachers.

Recall that at the beginning of this book we pointed out that schools, on a nationwide scale, are more culturally diverse than at any previous time in history. This diversity requires you to rethink traditional educational practices, especially traditional classroom management. Traditional teaching practices rooted in assumptions that the present student population is mostly homogenous—that all students are cut from the same mold—with similar interests, goals, needs, and wants, will impede your ability to promote an effective education for all of your students, and will keep you from understanding how cultural diversity, while adding important dimensions to your classroom, can also be a source of conflict: instructional conflict, curricular conflict, and interpersonal conflict. The case studies in chapter 1 illustrated this point very clearly. We suggest that an important aspect of being a teacher in today's classrooms is that of becoming a cultural negotiator, where you know how to meld together students' backgrounds with your classroom curriculum and with your classroom management plan.

This chapter presents you with suggestions on how cooperation can be promoted and how conflicts can be resolved in the classroom. In the discussion below, we first build on the three metaphors that have already been presented and show how those can be used to deal with the issues of conflict and cooperation. Second, we describe specific classroom approaches in order to move from metaphorical abstraction to classroom reality. The specific approaches that we review are fostering conditions for learning, using social contracts, resolving conflicts through communication, using classroom meetings, and resolving classroom conflict.

BUILDING ON THE METAPHORS

Our search for culturally appropriate ways of dealing with conflict and cooperation led us to consider some root metaphors that exert a powerful influence on your thinking. The metaphors of *management, guidance,* and *mediation* were introduced in chapter 2. Descriptions of those metaphors were provided, and you were challenged to think of how your understanding of these metaphors impacts your decisions as a teacher. In fact, each of us may have a slightly different understanding of each metaphor based on our personal history and experience. At this point, we need to reestablish some common understandings of these metaphors in order to provide a context for designing strategies that can help deal with conflict and cooperation in the classroom.

The Management Metaphor

Traditional classroom management was defined as a method to help you *organize* and *control* student learning, to promote *efficiency* in your teaching, and to ensure *student obedience.* We want to emphasize a different and broader definition of management that we think will be more useful when you think about classroom management. We want to emphasize the definition of management as a *tool,* or a *means,* to help individuals achieve a purpose. Good classroom management should be able to foster academic success for all students.

Hoover and Kindsvatter (1997) identify one of the problems in classrooms as that of defining teacher and student roles as *choosers* and *learners.* Teachers are the ones that choose, and therefore they have the power that is related to the act of choosing. The role of the student is to follow the choices of the teachers and therefore learn what is appropriate. Contemporary trends, however, emphasize a different set of classroom roles by focusing on sharing power with students, fostering cooperation among students, and fostering cooperation between students and teacher (Kouzes & Posner, 1987). Glasser (1990) uses the notion of *lead management* to describe the process that teachers use to share power with students and to foster an atmosphere of cooperation in the classroom. You should not be surprised, then, that Glasser believes that teacher-as-leader of students, not teacher-as-boss of students, is a more appropriate way of getting students engaged in noncoercive ways in your classroom activities, thus enhancing potential for students' success at school.

Some classroom teachers, to follow the teacher-as-leader idea of Glasser (1990), recognize that motivating students by coercion is not an effective way, and certainly not a respectful way, to encourage and motivate students to learn content, and to be engaged in your lessons in personally meaningful ways. In elementary schools, teachers often use coercion by threatening students with loss of privileges or activities, for example, loss of recess or loss of a favorite class time, in order to extrinsically motivate them. Some secondary teachers may use a form of psychological coercion by using ridicule, shame, or put-downs. Interestingly, secondary students frequently cite assaults on their dignity as reasons for their classroom misbehavior. Often these uses of power and coercion become so subtly ingrained in the teaching style that teachers are unaware of them.

Strategies and techniques such as these above tend to create adversarial relationships between you and your students, which tends to keep you from creating a classroom environment where cooperation can flourish and where successful learning can take place. Yet Glasser believes that by the end of seventh grade, more than half of the students feel that teachers and administrators are their adversaries (Glasser, 1990).

Glasser (1990) identifies four characteristics that, when applied to classroom teaching, typify teachers-as-leaders:

- engaging students in discussions of the work to be done and providing an opportunity for their input,
- modeling what needs to be done and continually asking for input on better ways to perform the task,
- asking students to evaluate their own work and listening to what they say,
- performing as a facilitator, providing a nonadversarial, noncoercive atmosphere in the classroom.

Teachers who demonstrate teacher-as-leader qualities—that is, teachers who reflect Glasser's lead management ideas—tend to have a different perspective on the nature of power in the classroom. Traditional management practices promote the idea that power is a fixed sum commodity (Kouzes & Posner, 1987). Viewing power in the classroom as a fixed sum commodity means that if students have *more power*, then you—the classroom teacher—have *less power*. For example, teachers may resist allowing students too much input in classroom rules out of a fear that this will diminish their authority as a teacher. Teachers who don't like students to have more power often set up autocratic classrooms where these teachers try to guard their power and limit student choices.

An alternative view, however, and a view that we hold in this book, is that power is not a fixed sum, but rather is expandable (Kouzes & Posner, 1987). Thus, sharing power doesn't mean taking legitimate power away from you. Theoretically, when you share with students the legitimate power you have as a teacher, you will find that students often become more committed to carrying out their responsibilities. This is because students who share power with you develop a sense of ownership in the classroom, which gives them more stake in making sure that the classroom is a worthwhile place to be. Surprisingly, this makes your role as a classroom teacher even more important and powerful. You become more important because as a manager your power is used as *power in service to others* rather than *power in service to self*. Power in service to others, when used respectfully and trustfully, is the kind of power used to grow people, as the proverb suggests at the beginning of this chapter.

The Guidance Metaphor

In order to expand the role of teacher beyond a purely traditional management role, we include the metaphor of *guidance* as a way of understanding and organizing classroom life. Although guidance, like management, conveys the image of someone with greater amounts of knowledge, wisdom, and insight assisting those with lesser amounts of knowledge, wisdom, and insight, our use of guidance is intended, however, to elicit a different image of teacher than does traditional management. Specifically, with the notion of guidance we convey the image of teacher as being a more experienced or knowledgeable person helping younger, less-experienced persons navigate through challenging educational territory. Using this notion of guidance for teaching, we further suggest that such guides, as teachers, understand how to make challenging territory exciting, even adventuresome. This view of guidance implies that teachers have more of a caring, consultative relationship with students; traditional management, on the other hand, implies that teachers have more of a dominating, authoritarian relationship with students.

Guidance also implies that there are positive pathways that students can take in their learning, and that you, as the classroom teacher, are familiar with these pathways and likewise familiar with students' backgrounds, and are thus able to successfully connect selected pathways with certain backgrounds. However, for teacher-as-guide and student-as-guided to work in classroom settings, you must work toward a classroom environment that has mutual respect and shared decision-making. You must also understand that applying the metaphor of guide to classroom teaching creates new roles and responsibilities for you and for students. As a guide, you have the responsibility of providing advice about which pathways might be best for students to take as they engage in various learning activities. Students will generally take the pathways you suggest. When you provide students with several pathways, or when you negotiate pathways with students when they suggest pathways for their own course of learning, then students must decide which path they will follow among the paths you provide or negotiate. For example, when confronted with a conflict in the classroom, a tendency of many teachers is to prescribe for the students what they must do. The guidance metaphor suggests that the teacher should help provide alternative ways to solve the conflict with careful consideration of the consequences of the alternatives.

The Mediation Metaphor

From the discussion above on teacher as guide, we assume that questions will surface about what learning path to take. Students may ask: "Why do we have to read this material?" "I'm not interested in this stuff, why can't I just learn what I want to learn?" Other students may say: "I don't understand why we waste our time working in groups. I can learn it faster by myself." "It isn't fair that some of us do more in our group." This is where the metaphor of *mediation* further enriches the role of teacher. One way you can understand mediation is to view yourself as being in the middle of the classroom context, and as being continuously available for reconciling differences. Mediation requires negotiation, and in the process of negotiation, you learn about students: their wants, personal needs, educational needs, backgrounds, biographies, and individual strengths. While moving you toward a greater awareness of your students, negotiation enhances solidarity, as we noted above, and provides you with a basis for developing your legitimate authority as a teacher. *Note that you must become aware of your legitimate authority—that you must know this authority well—before you can actually share it with students.*

Viewed collectively, management, guidance, and mediation provide a set of powerful ideas that form the basis for creating a positive classroom environment. These same ideas also form the basis for fostering conditions of cooperation in the classroom, which we discuss in the next section of this chapter. The *manager* organizes and creates a noncoercive environment seeking the cooperation and input of everyone in the classroom so that you and your students can embark on an educational journey together. The *guide* provides advice and suggestions to keep everyone moving in a positive direction. The *mediator* provides a method for solving inevitable conflicts that will arise without jeopardizing the group solidarity.

FOSTERING CONDITIONS FOR COOPERATION

A good beginning place in developing classroom strategies for dealing with conflict and cooperation is that of considering how conditions can be created that facilitate cooperation and solidarity. Cooperation among students and between you and your students are essential elements for applying the three metaphors above. Cooperative approaches in the classroom require guidance and mediation. Such approaches also suggest the need for a teacher-as-leader management style, and thus are useful in promoting both the social and the academic curriculum.

The conditions that foster classroom cooperation need to be addressed especially because people cannot be forced to cooperate. Conditions must be created so that everyone in your class has an opportunity to explore advantages of cooperation and of working together. One example of such conditions includes positive, trustful, and caring relationships with peers (Jones & Jones, 1986). The conditions that are discussed below can help you foster cooperative approaches to learning in your classroom. These conditions include:

- understanding peer relationships
- implementing cooperative goal structures
- communicating respect and trust
- developing group cohesion
- decreasing risk factors

Understanding Peer Relationships

Understanding peer relationships in classrooms also means understanding group dynamics. Such group dynamics depends upon how students know each other, and how each individual feels accepted or rejected. Group dynamics also include norms of the classroom and include the roles that different individuals in the class see themselves playing as class members. Unfortunately, given the continuously busy pace of classroom life, teachers sometimes are limited in the time they can focus more specifically on group dynamics and peer relationships in the classroom. This oversight can lead to increased conflict in the classroom and an unproductive classroom environment.

The dynamics of the group will very likely change during the academic year. Some students may achieve success, while others experience failure. Some students may leave the classroom and new students will be added. As the students begin to know each other better and get to know you better, the dynamics obviously will change. These changes can lead to a positive and highly engaging classroom climate. However, if the changes are not conducive to the development of a positive classroom climate, then steps need to be taken to try to create a positive one.

Implementing Cooperative Goal Structures

Another aspect of classroom life that relates to increased cooperation is classroom goal structures. A goal structure refers to the way students relate to each other in order to accomplish a particular goal (Woolfolk, 1995). There are three types of goal structures: *competitive, cooperative,* and *individualistic.* Competitive goal structures are present when students perceive that the only way for them to achieve success in attaining a particular goal is to *beat,* or finish ahead of, other students in the class. The competitive goal structure has long been the dominant one in education. Grading on the curve is just one example of how the competitive goal structure is applied in the classroom. Contests, ranking of students, and labeling are other forms of competitive goal structures.

Part of the reason that competitive goal structures are so pervasive in education has been the belief that competition has strong motivational value. Following this belief is the conception that competition can motivate students to work harder. However, competition as a motivator generally works only for those individuals who think they have a chance to win. Individuals who do not believe they have a chance to win are not necessarily motivated; these persons can easily become discouraged as learners. Studies suggest that continuous competition among students in the classroom tends to interfere with positive and successful achievement (Kouzes & Posner, 1987). Therefore, the popular notion that competition enhances performance is a misconception. Surprisingly, the misconception still has a powerful hold on classroom teaching.

There exist some widely held assumptions about goal structures in culturally diverse classrooms. For example, some students who represent ethnic or racial minority groups in schools from other cultural backgrounds may believe that they lack the prerequisite knowledge and experience to be competitive with students from the mainstream culture. Their response is not one of increased effort. Rather, it is one of discouragement, frustration, and withdrawal. Another problem is that some students, such as those in the Sioux Indian high school case study discussed in chapter 1, have cultural values that actually discourage competition. A classroom environment where competition is stressed puts them in cultural conflict. They must either ignore what they have been taught as appropriate and respectful in their culture, or they must moderate their success in the classroom.

Competitive goal structures have the potential to create tension in the classroom and to divide the individuals. If, for example, you assign a classroom task that is competitive, some students will ultimately think this about other students:

It is to my advantage that you do not do well, so any success you have will be a threat to me. The result of this kind of thinking leads to factors such as frustration, hostility, and low productivity (Kouzes & Posner, 1987). These factors clearly get in the way of reaching social and academic goals in most classrooms.

An individualistic goal structure, as a condition for success, is an alternative to a competitive goal structure. Individual goal structures maintain that the way to achieve a goal is through individual effort; this effort, however, is not in the context of intragroup or intergroup competition. While individual goal structures avoid the negative and destructive elements that can be introduced by competition, these goal structures tend not to build upon the fact that some of the most significant accomplishments are team efforts. This is also true for society in general. We do not live in isolation but are extremely interdependent in all that we do. Undue and wholesale emphases on individualization isolate individuals from each other and ignore the human need for socialization and belonging. Such emphases can also isolate students from each other, thus causing students to overlook valuable resources they can build upon and learn about from their peers.

Cooperative goal structures are those where the cooperation of all students in a group are necessary in order for the goals to be attained. Cooperative goal structures mean that everyone in the classroom must work together as a team (i.e., your success is important for my success). Cooperative goal structures capitalize on the need for students to socialize and on the reduced threat that students feel when they are working together as a team to accomplish goals.

To be sure, there are times when individualistic goal structures are useful, and there are times when competitive goal structures are useful. For example, some of your learning activities might require students to rely on themselves and not on others. Similarly, there are times when competition is useful. For example, some students enjoy the challenge of fair athletic competition, while others enjoy the challenge of fair academic competition. Consequently, there are situations when competition adds a certain type of excitement to school life. However, we believe that in contemporary classrooms, cooperative goal structures should receive a high priority.

Communicating Respect and Trust

Respect and trust are important ingredients in creating classroom conditions for cooperation. Respect means that we trust students enough to give them some power and responsibility. Without respect or trust, there will likely be an unwillingness to share power, and students will be unlikely to trust whatever power and decision making you give them; very little cooperation is then possible. Mutual respect is what sustains extraordinary group efforts (Kouzes & Posner, 1987).

Respect and trust, which are key ingredients for cooperation, must be developed in a genuine manner if these two ingredients are to become a classroom reality. Students seem to have a built-in radar that detects insincerity in teachers. As a classroom teacher, you cannot simply walk into the classroom the first day and say to students, "You can trust me because I respect and trust you." That will not work. You must genuinely have and demonstrate these qualities over time for students.

If, in a classroom of students, you discover that you are unable to respect and trust a few students, then you should explore your feelings for these students very carefully, closely, and honestly. And you must work to resolve these feelings if at all possible, or you run the risk of alienating some students from your classroom, and consequently alienating them from the content you teach, thus contributing to their possible lack of success at school.

Allowing students to have opportunities to make decisions about how the classroom operates, what is taught, and how they learn are other aspects of communicating respect for the students. This willingness to share decision making, and hence power, with students is an application of the *lead management* and *guidance* metaphors we have been discussing in this chapter.

Developing Group Cohesion

The development of *group cohesion*, which can also be viewed as *solidarity* among students in the classroom, is often overlooked as an important feature in developing cooperation. Importantly, both group cohesion and solidarity are related to students' need for belonging. Glasser (1990) identifies belonging as one of the most powerful of human needs. Individuals want to be accepted and belong to a significant group. Street gang membership, which has a very powerful cohesion and solidarity among members, for example, is often an expression of the individual need to belong to a supportive group. In building a classroom climate conducive for cooperation, you must consider how to develop group solidarity and cohesion.

Group pride and *espirit de corps* are important ingredients for building cohesion in any group. Each group needs some sort of identity and wants to feel unique or special. Teachers need to consider what can be done to give each group a sense of identity or specialness. One method that is often successful is to embark on a class project where all students are involved in some sort of service activity for the school or the community. Students who feel like they are doing something worthwhile, which can happen during successful service activities, can work toward building group spirit and cohesion. Too often, we communicate to students that worthwhile contributions need to be put off until later in life. Students, however, need to feel significant in the here and now. Importantly, group projects can also further the school curriculum. For example, cleaning up the neighborhood, teachers can connect students with science and the environment, recycling, the needs of plants and wildlife, decomposition and composting. Using any of these topics, students can read about them; write newspaper articles and letters to the editor; and measure, weight, and graph what was collected, among other activities.

Providing students with opportunities to make decisions about classroom activities and events—that is, when you give students power to change or negotiate some aspects of classroom life—contributes to classroom cohesion and solidarity. Individuals, most especially students in your classroom, rarely want to be a part of a powerless group. They want to make a difference. Even small changes brought about by a group can result in powerful feelings of group identity and pride among your students.

An important part of your role as a teacher is to build group cohesion. Teachers, as lead managers, bring students together, and help them organize so that they can accomplish important tasks and goals. Guidance is used to help the students as they work through group tasks and make decisions. Mediation is used to solve interpersonal conflicts without destroying group unity and spirit.

For example, a group might be brought together to work on a specific project or task. The teacher can help foster group cohesion and pride by helping the group see how the various abilities of the group members might be utilized in order to produce a product of which they might be proud. Suggestions on specific responsibilities of group members can be provided so that each individual understands what is expected. Providing assistance to individual team members in helping them fulfill their responsibilities then reduces some of the anxiety and allows each individual to feel successful. The success of each individual within the group builds positive interdependence and a sense of cohesion.

As the group is faced with decisions, the guidance function emerges as you help students explore alternative solutions and their possible consequences. You point out alternative choices that might not have occurred to the group. You might need to provide assistance to the group in helping them reach consensus and compromise.

Intragroup conflicts and disagreements will arise. Your role as a mediator is to help students solve these conflicts so that the work of the group is not harmed and so that everyone can complete the task with a sense of pride and accomplishment. You might need to meet with individuals who are having an interpersonal conflict and work as a mediator in order to help them solve their differences so that they can return to work.

You should also be alert for tasks or projects that groups could do that would foster cohesion and solidarity. For example, some high school teachers have found that community projects, such as organizing a Special Olympics, provide them with a sense of pride that they are doing something worthwhile. Elementary students may engage in providing a service that might be needed at the school, such as assisting in the care of the school grounds. However, remember that students, whether working alone or in groups, need to have input regarding the tasks they undertake. As noted above, input should also be about the classroom curriculum, which provides students with opportunities to apply the knowledge and skills they are learning.

Another important task you need to perform is to organize groups within the class, if possible, so that a diversity of skills is present in each group. Some students in the class may have artistic abilities while others have more highly developed writing and language skills. Still others might enjoy the process of organizing and keeping track of materials and tasks. These students can be grouped so that each is contributing a special ability to a task and so that the final product is better than had it been produced by any one individual. The greater the diversity within the group, the greater the possibilities of interesting and creative group responses.

However, the group project approach is only one way that group solidarity and cohesion can be developed in your classroom. Another way is to create and emphasize memorable events. Sometimes what appears to be a relatively minor or insignificant event can actually be turned into something that builds class cohesion and solidarity. Unplanned, humorous occurrences are good candidates for this. A key element here is enjoyment. Students need to enjoy being a part of the group. Teachers who build on special times often discover growth toward solidarity and a renewed commitment to the class.

Giving students opportunities to do their best and to share their strengths with you, and with each other, is yet another way to build cohesion and solidarity. Every student needs to feel competent at something. Feeling competent helps students feel confident, and helps to build their self-esteem. Unfortunately, we sometimes structure classes in ways that tend to emphasize shortcomings rather than strengths. However, if we choose to take the concepts of multiple intelligences and learning styles seriously, this would infer that students have different strengths and preferred ways of learning (Gardner, 1993). Transforming the notion of multiple intelligences into classroom instruction, you would then consider how group tasks can be structured so that every person in the class is able to build on the strengths they have and be recognized for what they do well. Reducing the competitive goal structures and celebrating the growth that individuals make toward important goals is an important aspect of building pride in group membership.

Decreasing Risk Factors

Decreasing *risk factors* is another fundamental condition for fostering classroom cooperation. When you decrease risk factors, you then begin moving toward a safe classroom environment. By a safe classroom, we are referring to a classroom where there is psychological and emotional safety as well as physical safety. This means that individuals feel safe in expressing their opinions, attitudes, and emotions. In such classrooms, there is no ridicule and no put downs. In short, the classroom needs to be a comfortable and inviting human environment.

One of the greatest risk factors for students is the fear of failure. In general, students are reluctant to get involved or to take chances when they have a great fear of failure. Such fear can often be overcome when individual students feel supported in their efforts to achieve success (Kouzes & Posner, 1987).

Some strategies for reducing risk factors have already been mentioned in the chapter. For additional strategies, students need to feel as if their perspectives, values, and personal needs have a place in the classroom. They also need to believe that they have a fair opportunity for success and that there are people who can help them achieve their goals. This means that you might need to rethink aspects of the classroom environment, including homework assignments, tests, and grading procedures. Students often view these aspects of schooling as posing threats to their success rather than as necessary challenges for their academic growth.

An example of how one teacher tried to reduce risk factors through changing grading is found in the story of the French teacher in chapter 2. More recent efforts, for example *authentic assessment*, and the use of alternative assessment procedures such as portfolios, are examples of strategies that can help to minimize, if not reduce, risk factors. Many alternative assessment procedures allow students much more input in the assessment process. Students can determine the items that are presented as evidence that learning has taken place rather than worry about their performance on a test. The use of alternative assessment where clear rubrics are presented to the students concerning the assessment procedure helps each student know what needs to be done in order to achieve success. It is not left to guesswork and chance. These kinds of assessments help students see that it is their effort that leads to success.

EXERCISE 6.1   Enhancing Cooperation

We have made several claims above about creating a classroom climate that fosters cooperation. In this exercise we ask you to gather practical information about conditions that enhance cooperation in real classrooms.

As a first step, consider each of the dimensions related to creating a cooperative climate:

- peer relationships
- cooperative goal structures
- respect and trust—group cohesion
- decreased risk factors

Brainstorm indicators or specific things you think you would see in a classroom that would indicate the presence or absence of each of these factors. Refine your list, then observe a classroom where you record notes on what you see. Develop a summary report of your observations of the climate in the classroom. To validate your conclusions, seek permission to interview a few students to see how they view the same classroom you observed. For example, do they feel they have any power to make decisions that influence the classroom curriculum? Do they believe they have input in how the class is operated? Do they feel comfortable speaking in class, or are they afraid of ridicule? Does the classroom climate help them enjoy working with their peers? If you find a discrepancy between what you thought and what the students report, how might you explain this discrepancy?

DEVELOPING SOCIAL CONTRACTS

Changing your metaphor of traditional classroom management to an alternative metaphor that emphasizes power sharing and cooperation can be done by using the strategy of the *social contract* (Curwin & Mendler, 1980). The social contract is a strategy that involves students in establishing rules and consequences that will guide their activities and interactions together. The social contract makes the issue of power sharing very real by involving students in making rules not only for themselves, but for the whole class. Interestingly and importantly, one rule that can be involved in making social contracts is about sharing power.

Defining the Social Contract

A social contract, in very simple terms, is based on the premise that law and government rely on the consent of the governed, or on a social contract between the governed and the government. Successful teachers have learned that you can apply this premise to the classroom. Any form of classroom organization, and any form of classroom discipline, will be effective only to the extent that it is accepted in some valid way by students. The social contract is a way of addressing this need by having you and your students agree on a list of classroom expectations that will lead to respectful and trustful communication. When these expectations have been discussed and evaluated by everyone in the class, and when an agreement is reached, a list of expectations is developed into a social contract.

Developing a Social Contract

There are several steps involved in developing a social contract with your students. Although these steps take up class time, the time spent settling these issues when a class first meets will be relatively minor compared to the time that can be saved later on by preventing many problems. The basic steps to the process are the following:

- implicit rules are identified
- you propose some rules and consequences regarding student classroom behavior
- students propose rules and consequences regarding your classroom behavior
- students propose rules and consequences for each other
- the rules and consequences are discussed
- the rules and consequences are adopted (Adapted from Curwin and Mendler, 1980)

Implicit Rules Are Identified

In all social situations there are certain understood rules and protocols that govern social interactions. In other words, there are just some things we know that we are not supposed to do in some situations, and just some things we know that we are supposed to do in other situations. We call these things *implicit rules*. One example of this comes from the personal experience of one of us (Tom Savage). "When our family moved from a northern state to a southern state, our junior high school–aged son had some difficulty because he was unaware of the implicit rule in many areas of the south that teachers are to be addressed with 'Yes, ma'am' or 'Yes, sir.' Our son was viewed as not respecting the teacher and not being polite. The problem occurred in reverse when we moved to a northern region of the country. Students there were viewed as being a "smart-aleck" when they responded to their teachers with 'Yes, ma'am' or 'Yes, sir.' " We share this example with you to show that problems can arise when students with differing understandings of implicit rules come together in the same classroom. This frequently happens in classrooms that are richly diverse in student culture, background, nationality, and family. What is accepted as normal by one student might be interpreted as offensive or demeaning to another. Therefore, implicit rules, to the extent possible, need to be made explicit in order to avoid misunderstanding and conflict among students and between teachers and students.

An important point to make here is that some teachers approach the classroom as if all students have a clear understanding of the implicit rules and customs that govern social interactions. This assumption can lead to difficulties as students, and certainly teachers, unknowingly violate these unwritten rules and are confused when difficulties arise. This is why we believe that you should address the implicit rules, customs, traditions, or unwritten rules that govern social interactions in your classroom when learners first come together as a class.

One way we can do this is to ask your students the following question: *Suppose you learned that a friend or relative of the same age and gender was going to be coming to live with you. What rules and expectations would you have for them while they are living in your house?* At this point your students can write down the rules that they would expect the other person to follow. When this is done you can then ask students to identify rules that they would explicitly talk about and rules that you would just expect them to know. Students are often surprised to note that many of their rules are implicit or ones they would expect others to know. A discussion of the consequences of not telling a person some of the expectations usually leads to the conclusion that this can lead to anger and a breakdown of communications. At this point you can shift the discussion to the importance of clarifying the implicit rules for the classroom. A discussion of these implicit or unwritten rules can help to prevent many misinterpretations and can help to establish a firm foundation for moving into a more formal social contract. This same discussion can also help students understand each others' backgrounds.

Teacher Proposals

The next step in the development of a social contract is for you to clarify what you expect in the classroom. There are two types of classroom expectations that you need to identify. One set are those that you feel are absolutely necessary to establish a safe and productive classroom environment. As the teacher, you need to develop a list of these expectations, and develop rationales as to why each one is necessary and important. You will probably be less flexible in altering these expectations since, in your professional judgment, they are crucial to a safe and respectful classroom for all students. The second set of expectations are those that you would like to see implemented, but can also be altered as you discuss this second set with students. You will need to list some of the consequences that might be applied when students violate this second set of expectations.

Try to keep both sets of expectations very short, concise, and positive. The expectations need to be specific enough so that students know very well when an expectation is violated. The first set of expectations, the ones that are less flexible, should be presented to the group and the rationales provided for why they are necessary. Make sure that the students are clear about each of the rules. Perhaps most importantly, help students understand why the first set of expectations is less flexible for students to alter. Let students express concerns about the expectations, and respond in a caring and respectful manner to their concerns. The second set of rules, which are more flexible and thus more negotiable by students, will be dealt with later in the process.

Student Proposals for the Teacher

After the first set of expectations is presented and discussed, allow students to develop some rules for you. While allowing students to make these expectations might be disconcerting for you, allowing them to do this is an important response to presenting them with your first set of less-flexible expectations that you developed for them.

As students begin developing expectations for you, explain to them that your primary goal is to be a fair and supportive teacher, and to help every student in the classroom be successful. Have them think about things they have seen teachers do that they do not believe is either fair or supportive of a comfortable, safe, and engaging classroom. Then think of an expectation that they would have liked that teacher to follow. Examples of these expectations might include:

- the dignity of the student is to be respected, and teacher sarcasm or put-downs are not allowed,
- personal property of students is not to be used without permission,
- the class is to be released on time,
- homework papers are to be returned promptly,
- the grades and scores of class members are not to be shared with others unless permission is granted, and
- teachers must get permission to enter a student's desk.

Explain to students that there are some guidelines for establishing teacher expectations. These guidelines include complying with federal, state, or local laws, the educational code, or school rules over which the teacher has no control. Rules concerning the enforcement of weapons, for example, or controlled substances are laws that are beyond the control of the teacher. For such laws there can be little or no negotiation. This helps prevent proposals that are clearly unreasonable. A sense of seriousness needs to be communicated so that students don't view this as some sort of frivolous activity. Be sure to remind students that at this time, these are only proposals and not every proposal will be adopted.

As expectations are proposed for you by students, they should be recorded where everyone in the classroom can see them. Once student expectations for you have been made and a reason given for each one, then you respond. Any proposals that would violate laws, the education code, or school rules should be identified and discussed. If you identify an expectation that is in violation of a school rule, help students understand how the expectation violates the rule before removing it from the list. Be sure to discuss each expectation the students have developed for you, honoring and respecting each item.

The entire class needs to be involved in discussing each proposed expectation made for you by the students. Following each discussion, a vote can be taken on whether or not to adopt each expectation. Once a set of expectations has been adopted, it should be posted in the classroom. One way to do this is to write out the rules on a page that contains your signature, if students request this, to indicate that you accept and commit to them. Importantly, this can be an event that can build group solidarity in your classroom.

Although this process can create anxiety for some teachers, most discover that students take this activity seriously and will respond to suggestions from you when you respond to their set of expectations in a caring, respectful, and honorable way. One of the significant outcomes of this process is that teachers discover things that students find offensive. For example, one expectation for teachers that students tend to state is that teachers are to respect the privacy of students, and teachers must gain permission before going through students' desks or personal belongings. Knowing what the students find offensive helps you avoid these things and builds more trust and respect. Other common rules often include the teacher not eating in front of the class, not humiliating or putting down students in front of others, not keeping the class past the bell, and allowing students an opportunity to state their side when accused of a rule violation.

The next step is for students to discuss a set of consequences for you if you happen to violate one of the students' expectations. Typical consequences students tend to develop include teacher apologies, free time for the class or an individual, canceling homework assignments, or allowing the students a choice of activities.

Student Proposals for Each Other

At this point in the contract process, your students need to discuss classroom expectations they have for each other. A good approach to this is to ask them to follow the procedure they used for making expectations for you. Ask students to meet in groups to identify what they think are essential, and respectful, expectations for each other. Working in groups, students can discuss and vote on these expectations. This is a good time for you to present the second set of proposed expectations that you have developed. Often the students have already identified many of the expectations you have on your list. Allowing them to propose and vote on these expectations, however, gives them more ownership of the classroom, and allows their perspectives, as a group of students, to be involved in decision making. Once there is a consensus regarding all expectations, students can discuss consequences for varying from adopted expectations. Some consequences can be general and will apply to several expectations, while others may need to be more specific. Allowing students considerable input on the consequences shifts much of the responsibility for student behavior, and consequently student discipline, to students. Students may then be less likely to blame you for being unfair when consequences are applied.

RESOLVING CONFLICTS THROUGH COMMUNICATION

Many conflicts in the classroom arise because of poor communication. You should not be surprised, then, to read that effective communication is among the most important elements for preventing and dealing with conflict in the classroom

(Alschuler, 1980; Charles & Senter, 1995; Ginott, 1972; Gordon, 1974; Johnson & Johnson, 1995; Kohn, 1996; Savage, 1990). An important first step in fostering effective communication among students, and between you and students, is to *decide who owns the problem* (Gordon, 1974). Different responses to communication problems are required based on who owns the problem. Moreover, ownership is determined by who is experiencing the tangible, concrete effects of the problem. Suppose, for example, that a student is daydreaming and not paying attention as you teach the lesson. Who is experiencing the tangible effects of this action? The student will experience the tangible effects by not knowing what to do. Therefore, the student owns the problem. If, however, a student is talking to a friend in such a manner that you are unable to effectively teach the lesson, then you are experiencing the tangible effects and you own the problem.

When you communicate with students, you engage in two obvious processes: you *send* messages and you *receive* them. While the ideas of sending and receiving messages might sound rather simple, in reality the process is exceedingly complex, particularly when you consider the many different backgrounds represented by your students. As an example, at Mark Keppel High School (MKHS) in Alhambra, California, students speak over 35 first languages other than English (Powell, Zehm, & Garcia, 1996). Schools like MKHS certainly pose special challenges for teachers to effectively send messages to and receive them from students.

Teachers often focus more on the *sending* component, or on how to be clear in their personal and academic communications with students and other teachers. Because of this undue focus on effectively *sending* messages, the listening or receiving component is sometimes overlooked by teachers. As a classroom teacher, how will you keep from overlooking the receiving component? Of what value will this component be to you and to your students?

Student-Owned Problems

Gordon (1974) emphasized both the sending and the receiving dimensions of communication. When something blocks communication when dealing with a student-owned problem, then you have what Gordon (1974) calls a *roadblock.* Examples of these roadblocks that both students *and* teachers might demonstrate are ordering, directing, warning, threatening, moralizing, lecturing, and providing solutions; judging or putting down others, blaming, name-calling, or labeling; attempting to make the problem go away through praise, reassurance, sympathy, distractions, and diversions or withdrawal; and creating defensiveness by questioning, interrogating, and using sarcasm. Edwards (1997) points out that these responses tend to cause students to feel and experience anger, increased resistance to behavioral change, defensiveness, embarrassment, and lower self-esteem.

Keep in mind that these responses are roadblocks to communication when students own the problem. There are times when questioning, probing, reassuring, praising, and so on, would be appropriate. For example, probing and questioning are appropriate when you are dealing with content issues. Similarly, reassuring and praising are appropriate when a student is struggling to learn a new concept or skill. However, they become roadblocks when, for example, a student is wrestling with a personal problem and you respond, "You're a bright student, you should be able to figure it out." This is clearly a roadblock to problem resolution because it is carrying the message that the student should be ashamed to even have a problem like this and the teacher doesn't want to be bothered with personal problems.

Edwards (1997) notes that many teachers have difficulty understanding that one of the important ingredients in problem resolution is listening. Listening might be categorized as passive listening, where you remain silent and allow students to do all of the talking. However, most teachers feel compelled to participate. Gordon (1974) coined the phrase *active listening* to describe the type of listening where teachers actively encourage student talk. Active listening involves an interaction where you listen carefully to what a student is saying. Then you provide a nonjudgmental interpretation of the message to the student. This feedback usually involves paraphrasing what the student has said. For example, you might respond to a statement with, "I hear you saying that you are bored. . . ." or "Are you saying that. . . ?"

Edwards (1997) states that when students attempt to communicate, they may not be portraying their feelings accurately. They may have difficulty expressing how they feel, or they might be trying to avoid incrimination. Active listening communicates acceptance and an openness for additional communication and clarification. Students are then more likely to share their true feelings. The intent of active listening is to let students know that having a problem is OK, and that you are willing to listen and to assist in finding a solution if possible. Many teachers incorrectly identify a student problem as one of their own and try to seek the solution. This makes some students distrust their own feelings, which can cause these students to depend on others to tell them how to feel and behave (Edwards, 1997).

Teacher-Owned Problems

For those problems where you, the classroom teacher, have more ownership, a different communication process needs to be used. The process used in this instance is what is called *I-messages.* I-messages are intended to communicate what you are feeling and are characterized by the use of "I" rather than "you" (Gordon, 1974). Although I-messages are common and widely known, we think they are sufficiently important to classroom communication to include a brief discussion of them here.

There are three parts to the I-message. The first part involves identifying what is creating the problem in a nonblaming and nonthreatening manner. This might be phrased as "When individuals do not pay attention when I'm giving directions . . ." or "When students are late coming to class . . ." The second part of the message identifies the tangible effect, and uses "I" as a reference. For example, "When individuals do not pay attention when I'm giving directions, I have to stop and repeat them." The third part of the I-message is stating feelings. Examples might include: "The way you respond to the lesson makes me feel like other students are interested," or "I feel really frustrated when students fall asleep in class." Note that the message is delivering a statement that is not demanding a change. Rather, the message is simply communicating your feelings to specific behaviors.

Let us take a concrete example. Suppose you have started giving instructions to the class at the beginning of a class period. You are well into the discussion about your expectations when the door bangs open and in strides Joe. This is a teacher-owned problem because the behavior is interfering with the ability of the teacher to teach. An "I" message response might be, "Joe, when people come in late and make noise (nonjudgmental description), it distracts the attention of the classes and wastes important classroom time (tangible effect). When this happens I feel very frustrated (feelings)." This type of message is less likely to result in hostile responses that generally occur when teachers take a more confrontational approach. The "I" message leaves the door open for further communication with Joe in order to reach a resolution and prevent further occurrences.

CLASSROOM MEETINGS

Another strategy that is consistent with our views of management, guidance, and mediation is the *classroom meeting* approach (Glasser, 1969; see also Charles, 1992). The classroom meeting is a time when the entire class of students discusses concerns and issues and works toward the resolution of these things. This needs to take place, of course, in an open, accepting, and trusting environment. You have the responsibility to focus the discussion, keep the discussion on track, and clarify points. As you do this you should seek to become a nonjudgmental member of the classroom rather than a dominant leader. Plans for action about concerns and issues need to come from the students. Group-oriented plans for action are likely to be more successful since students will have more ownership in the plan. Students can then see that their opinions and shared decision making can make a difference in how classroom life unfolds.

The classroom meeting can focus on two things: *identifying the problem or conflict* and *seeking workable solutions*. The classroom meeting is not a time for blaming, name-calling, or disciplining (Charles, 1992). Try to keep classroom meetings brief, perhaps no more than 30 minutes (Glasser, 1969). Meetings that are brief will keep students from getting bored with proceedings.

Glasser (1969) identified three different types of classroom meetings, which are called *social problem-solving, educational-diagnostic,* and *open-ended.* Social problem-solving meetings are those that focus on a social problem at school or in the classroom. This can include, for example, issues of interpersonal conflict, cultural conflict, and sociopolitical conflict. Educational-diagnostic meetings are those that focus on curriculum and educational practice. Issues that are addressed in these meetings, for example, can include appropriateness of the curriculum, teaching methods, testing procedures, and so on. For example, students might not appear to be interested in a particular topic that is being studied in the classroom. A classroom meeting allows the students to share their feelings and help the teacher diagnose what is needed in order to increase interest in the topic. Open-ended meetings are those that provide an open forum for students to discuss or share concerns.

These meetings can be started with a thought-provoking question designed to get the students to think. In the example above, you might begin the classroom meeting with the following: *There are times when all of us find ourselves engaged in doing things that are not really personally interesting. Who could share some examples with us?* As the discussion begins the teacher can probe for clarification and ask students how they respond to these situations. Then you might ask: *I sense that some of you feel that way about the topic we are studying in class. Am I right?* The goal here is not only to get an answer to a problem or to defend the curriculum. The goal is also to provide an opportunity for students to share their feelings and perspectives in order to form a basis for seeking mutually satisfying solutions.

Social Problem-Solving Meetings

The focus of these meetings can be on topics that are related to the social curriculum. Most schools, however, lack a systematic approach for teaching students social problem-solving skills. Consequently, students tend to avoid discussing social problems with teachers. If social problem-solving meetings are to be successful, then you must be willing to trust and affirm students' insights about the issues that are discussed. Unfortunate circumstances occur when you formulate a solution, and when you then try to get students to accept it. However, students often consider points that you might overlook. Students are very capable of suggesting creative solutions to concerns, issues, and problems. The fact that students, rather than teachers, have proposed the solution often makes it more acceptable to other students. For example, personality conflicts often occur between students in the classroom. This might be the topic of a classroom meeting. The teacher might begin the meeting as follows: *Throughout life we will find ourselves encountering people with whom we don't seem to get along. Sometimes we can simply avoid these people but there are times when we cannot. For example, you can't always avoid a fellow worker and you certainly can't avoid your boss. What are some ways that we can deal with these situations?*

Social problem-solving meetings are usually held when there is a concern that is exerting an influence in the classroom. One of us (Tom Savage) found a classroom meeting to be extremely helpful in dealing with a group of fourth-grade pupils who witnessed an act of violence on the way to school. Their attention was not focused on learning mathematics, and they needed an opportunity to discuss violence in society before they were ready to focus on the curriculum. Another instance when the approach was useful was with teacher education students whose focus on the content of the class was being overwhelmed by a concern that local financial problems might mean that there would be no jobs for them at completion of the program.

In a social problem-solving meeting, you begin with an open discussion that first focuses on *exposing the concern or problem*. In the next step, students are involved in *proposing solutions* to concerns or problems that are expressed by students. The final step involves *getting a commitment* from the students regarding a solution they are willing to try. One classroom meeting might not be sufficient to solve some problems. A series of meetings might be needed to adequately and appropriately propose solutions, agree on the solutions, and get a commitment.

Your role in the meeting is to provide guidance to students as they negotiate solutions with each other. Your role is not to solve the problem for the students. While you need to remain somewhat neutral and nonjudgmental, this does not mean that the teacher is uninvolved or just listening. You might need to probe for clarification, challenge some of the proposed solutions, thus playing the devil's advocate in order to help students think about an issue more deeply.

Educational-Diagnostic Meetings

The focus of educational-diagnostic meetings is on the written curriculum that students are studying. The focus can also be on the teaching methods that are being used. These meetings are very valuable in helping you determine the level of success, or the degree of appropriateness, of your teaching methods. You might begin these meetings by stating the issue to be discussed. For example, students might groan when they are asked to do a particular assignment. Teachers who are willing to improve their practice, and create a more engaging classroom curriculum, will ask themselves questions about why students are responding in this manner.

Some students will be brutally honest and state that they simply do not see why the topic is important for them to learn. They may not have the needed prerequisite knowledge to complete the task or they may not even know what to do. For example, social studies is a topic that elicited signs of disinterest when introduced to a group of sixth-grade pupils. A classroom meeting revealed that while some were interested in the topic (Ancient Egypt), most did not understand how learning about that topic had any relevance to their lives today. Although ancient Egyptians might be rather interesting to read about, the topic did not seem to provide them with any information on topics that were of concern to them. As they discussed the things that worried them, possible connections between the world of the ancient Egyptians and 20th century Americans could be identified. This information could then be used by the teacher to capture student interest in this state-mandated curriculum topic.

Our experience suggests that most teachers want their students to succeed. The problem is that they are often teaching using erroneous assumptions about students' interests, backgrounds, or understandings of the importance of certain curricular topics that lead to inappropriate educational practices.

Any topic related to the school and classroom experiences of students can be used as a focus for educational-diagnostic meetings. Such meetings can be conducted using the format described for the social problem-solving meetings. As the teacher of the class, you must sincerely try to follow through on suggestions and possible solutions provided by students. This communicates to them that you are listening and that you are willing to change in order to accommodate their needs and feelings.

Open-Ended Meetings

Unlike the meetings above that are held only when there is an obvious problem, concern, or issue, *open-ended meetings* focus on topics that can encompass almost any topic. Consequently, open-ended meetings might be the most frequently used type of meeting. As an example of this kind of meeting, some students may be confused or concerned about how some of the political issues of the day impact them. They may feel powerless in getting their views across to policymakers and those in power. Others may have questions about what college is really like or how they go about getting a job. Other topics that might arise in open-ended meetings are those that deal with values and ethics.

The value of open-ended meetings is that many students see the school as divorced from reality and not really addressing their concerns. They seldom have school experiences that focus on contemporary issues and problems that concern them. School experiences tend to focus on academic issues identified as important by adults. Thus, students often see the school as just some sort of ritual imposed by adults on all school-aged students. Open-ended meetings are one way of breaking down the barriers between concerns students have about connections in their lives inside and outside school.

Because of the broad scope of open-ended meetings and because of their open nature, they may be held on a regular schedule. One approach is to set aside a time once a month for an open-ended meeting. We must offer you a word of caution at this point about holding classroom meetings like we have described above: the first few meetings may not seem to be very productive. When students begin to feel that you are genuinely interested in their points of view and when they feel that you will seriously listen to them—that they can participate openly and share their concerns and insights without criticism and ridicule—then meetings will become more productive.

TEACHING CONFLICT RESOLUTION THROUGH NEGOTIATION AND MEDIATION

Another approach for dealing with conflict that is consistent with the major thrust of this book is conflict resolution. Conflict resolution programs focus on the idea that students of all ages need to learn how to negotiate and mediate conflict. Perhaps one of the most important things any of us learn is how to deal with conflict. Johnson and Johnson (1995) have proposed a conflict resolution program that contains three parts. These parts involve creating a cooperative context, instituting conflict resolution/peer mediation training, and using academic controversy to learn conflict resolution skills and to improve instruction. Since this chapter has already dealt in depth with creating a cooperative context, we will focus on the last two components. However, we must emphasize the importance of cooperation because all parties of a conflict must be willing to cooperate and engage in negotiation in order for the process to work. That is why establishing a cooperative climate is so vital to success.

Conflict resolution programs for schools generally follow one of two different approaches (Johnson & Johnson, 1995). They usually focus on training a group of students who will serve as negotiators or mediators when conflicts arise, or they focus on training all students to manage conflicts. We believe that training all students in conflict management is an approach that holds much potential. There are three phases to conflict resolution programs (Johnson & Johnson, 1995). Those three phases are negotiation, mediation, and arbitration. The discussion below applies these phases to school settings.

Negotiation

Negotiation is defined as a process where students who are in conflict with each other attempt to work out an agreement. The goal of negotiation should be to arrive at a solution that benefits both students, or both groups of students, who are in conflict. This is generally called a *win-win* negotiation, where everyone involved is somehow made to feel like a winner, as opposed to a *win-lose* negotiation, where at least one person involved (if not more) feels like he or she has lost something.

The steps of the negotiation process should be taught to members of the class directly so that they can learn to solve their own problems. There are several programs that have been developed to teach students this process. These include the Teaching Students to Be Peacemakers program at the University of Minnesota (Johnson & Johnson, 1995) and the Conflict Resolution Curriculum developed by The Mediation Center in Irvine, California. Johnson and Johnson (1995) identify six steps in the negotiation process:

- describe what each student wants,
- describe what each student feels,
- exchange reasons for specifying positions that have created the conflict,
- understand each other's position,
- invent options for mutual benefit, and
- reach an agreement that is mutually beneficial.

Describing the Wants of Each Student

This is an important first step in the process. It involves communicating clearly the wants or needs of each student. Making progress toward the resolution of any conflict requires a clear understanding of each position. This step requires that those involved in the negotiation be good listeners. One of the ground rules should be that there is no interrupting when a student states his or her position. Each student gets to state what is desired. When students are finished with their statements, then active listening can be used to clarify positions. A simple paraphrasing rule, which requires students to restate the position of another before replying, can assist in avoiding interruptions and in focusing attention on the active listening process.

Describing Feelings

This can be one of the most difficult parts of the negotiation process because students are rarely encouraged to openly share feelings. This is especially the case when someone feels angry, fearful, or humiliated. Students often fear that sharing feelings puts them at risk of ridicule or rejection. In addition, when students are hurt or angry, they often have difficulty communicating clearly. For this reason, all of us have a tendency to downplay our feelings in conflict situations. Sharing feelings is encouraged if a cooperative classroom climate has been developed and a sense of trust and solidarity developed. If necessary, you may need to intervene in the process and serve as a guide to help students learn how to share their feelings. This might involve teaching them how to use active listening and I-messages.

Exchanging Reasons for Positions

Merely stating what is wanted, and what students are feeling, may not be enough. Each person needs to provide some reasons for his or her wants and feelings. This step is crucial because understanding the reasons often establishes a basis for working out a resolution. For example, two students—Dan and Amy—are having a conflict concerning the use of a computer. When reasons are presented, Dan states that he has to leave the room early today and will not be able to complete the assignment unless he is allowed to use the computer first. Amy might counter that her reason for wanting the computer first is that when other students go first, they tend to monopolize the computer and don't allow others a chance to use it. An understanding of these reasons provides a solid foundation for working out a solution that will be mutually beneficial for both Amy and Dan.

During this step you must ensure that the conflict is clearly defined. To do this you might ask yourself, "What exactly is the conflict?" Global statements such as "Dan is just a rude person" aren't specific enough to lead to a resolution. To really get to a resolution, you must find out what Dan was doing that has led to the possibility of his acting rude toward Amy.

As with sharing feelings, sharing reasons can also be difficult for some. Students may be afraid to reveal their reasons for fear that others may take advantage of them. Students are sometimes unable to clearly state their reasons, or they will share a secondary reason rather than the major reason for their position. For example, when asked for a reason, an elementary student might respond with, "I don't know." This is another situation where you will need to help students learn how to identify and state the reasons for their actions.

Understand the Perspective of Others

Perspective taking is one of the important aspects of negotiation. Unfortunately, many students have difficulty understanding the world through the eyes of another. Because of students' varying backgrounds, and because of specific circumstances at the time, students tend to view events very differently. In a conflict situation, understanding the perspective of the other is critical in moving toward an acceptable solution. One strategy for doing this is to have students switch places or reverse perspectives through role-playing. You can also ask students to respond to proposed solutions from the perspective of the other person.

Students can participate in simulated activities in order to help them learn how to take a different perspective. For example, students might explore the reactions of other students to some occurrence in the classroom. Younger students are often surprised to learn that not everyone views an event as they do. One program (Mediation Program in the Schools) poses situations to the class such as how they would respond to receiving a new bicycle. After the initial response, the conditions are altered such as the student being sick, living in an area where there were few places to ride a bicycle, and so on. This helps students learn that there are important reasons for why people have different perspectives.

Inventing Options for Mutual Gain

This is the step where potential solutions are proposed. An important criterion in posing solutions should be that there are win-win solutions that benefit both students. Johnson and Johnson (1995) contend that this step is often ineffective because students are often too quick to accept the first reasonable solution. They suggest that at least three solutions must be generated before a choice is made. If the negotiation process has been successful in identifying the needs, feelings, reasons, and perspectives of students who are in conflict, the search for mutually beneficial options is much easier. Give students sufficient time to think about proposed options and to brainstorm other possible solutions before moving to the next step.

Reaching a Wise Agreement

The step, *reaching a wise agreement,* is where an actual decision is made. Before an agreement is implemented, it must meet the criterion of being one that meets the needs of all students and must be viewed as fair to all students. If this is successful, then reaching a wise and fair agreement will strengthen the ability of the students to resolve future conflicts constructively and cooperatively (Johnson & Johnson, 1995).

If the process breaks down and a wise agreement is not reached, discussion should continue. The teacher might want to refocus attention on one or more of the steps. For example, you might say, "An agreement wasn't reached and I wonder if it was because feelings or reasons were not shared honestly. Why don't you start at one of those steps and work through the process again."

Mediation

When students are unable to reach an agreement by themselves, mediation becomes the next step. Mediation is the application of the negotiation process and requires the addition of a third party to facilitate the process. Initially, you may need to serve as mediator until students begin to learn to mediate conflicts between others. The basic goals of the mediation process is to help students resolve conflicts constructively and to teach them how to negotiate (Johnson & Johnson, 1995).

Mediation is often required when emotions are high and when students have been fighting or are angry with each other. A prerequisite for mediation is to allow some time for *each party* to cool off and lower his or her emotional level. Another requirement for mediation is that it must be the choice of the participants and they must commit to their involvement. A lack of commitment will doom the mediation process. First attempts at mediation may be met with some reluctance. However, some persistence and success with the program will generally lead to more enthusiasm and commitment.

Some programs make the mediation phase more formal than the negotiation phase. Students who serve as mediators are given forms and guidelines to follow as they mediate conflict. Following suggestions offered by Johnson and Johnson (1995), each student who is involved must answer some specific questions prior to becoming engaged in the mediation. These questions ask each student to identify with whom they were in conflict, what they want, and what they think the other student wants. The form also asks for students' proposals for resolving the conflict. This form gives the mediator some foundation for proceeding.

The mediator introduces him or herself and establishes the ground rules. Both sides must agree to the ground rules. They are often presented in the following manner:

- Do you agree not to interrupt each other?
- Do you agree not to use put-downs or name calling?
- Do you agree to be as honest as you can and to tell the truth?
- There will be no physical fighting, do you agree?
- Do you agree you want to solve the problem?

Once this has been established the mediator guides students through the steps identified in the negotiation process. The goal of the mediator is to facilitate the process so that students can learn how to use it on their own. One of the harder tasks of the mediator is to keep the discussion focused on the conflict at hand and not to allow students to go off on tangents or to address other issues. The goal of the mediator is not to solve problems for the students, just to assist them in finding a solution. Once an agreement is reached, it is written on paper and each student, including the mediator, signs it. Mediators keep the agreement to verify that students are doing what was agreed. If there is a breakdown, the mediator may call the students back together. If the mediator has been a peer mediator, this mediator notifies the teacher that an agreement has been or has not been reached. If agreements are not reached during mediation, the teacher may take over the role of mediator or the issue may be submitted to the teacher for arbitration.

Arbitration

Arbitration is a process in which a disinterested student makes a final judgment on how to resolve a conflict (Johnson & Johnson, 1995). Because it is imposed from the outside, the resolution tends to be less effective than if both students mutually agree and commit to a solution.

Some teachers combine mediation and arbitration. They hear both sides of the dispute and then make a decision about a solution. At this point a variation of arbitration called *final offer arbitration* may be used. In this form of arbitration, each student submits what he or she thinks is a final, best solution. The arbitrator then chooses one offer (Johnson & Johnson, 1995). This can be effective in getting students to be as open and fair as possible in proposing a solution because they recognize that unreasonable or unworkable solutions will be rejected by the arbitrator and the opposing proposal will be chosen. If teacher arbitration fails to resolve the conflict, the next step might be to include the school administrator as an arbitrator. The majority of the conflicts will be resolved before they reach this point.

ACADEMIC CONFLICT

One way of introducing conflict resolution to the classroom is by engaging students in the study of conflict situations that occur in the academic curriculum (Johnson & Johnson, 1995). This has the dual benefit of not only teaching students about conflict resolution; it has the benefit of making the curriculum more interesting. Almost any subject has numerous instances of conflict that can become the focus, including the kind of conflict where a student's background and ethnic heritage is not made either an explicit or implicit part of the classroom curriculum. A series of steps that can be used in an academic controversy is as follows:

- Divide the class into groups and have each group develop a position and how to present the position on the issue to the rest of the class. If more than one group is taking the same position, the groups may compare their notes.
- Each group makes a presentation to the class on its position.
- Group members then discuss the issue and the points that were made by the opposing side. They reexamine the evidence supporting both sides.
- The groups reverse positions and make a case for the position opposite to the one they initially took. Then all advocacy is dropped and the class develops a class report that synthesizes the best thinking from both sides. (Adapted from Johnson & Johnson, 1995)

The advantage of this approach is that it models the negotiation process for the students while dealing with content that is not as emotionally charged. Thus they can learn to apply the process in a nonthreatening environment and can be more objective in applying it.

CONCLUSION

This chapter suggests some significant changes in the way you view yourself, the students, and your role in the classroom. It requires that you rethink the uses of power in the classroom and focus on ways to share that power with the students. This is not easy to do because it requires most of us to move beyond the conventional wisdom that we have acquired through our own personal experiences as students. Because we have experienced teachers who tend to use power methods of responding to incidents of misbehavior, we come to think they are the right methods.

In this chapter we challenged you to engage in some reflection and to challenge some of those unstated assumptions that you may have regarding the role of the teacher in the classroom. We challenged you to consider your actions as a teacher as the result of reflective thought that is grounded in solid principles of teaching and learning.

As you develop your view of the roles of teachers and students, consider the implications of helping students become empowered through having choices in the classroom. These choices may extend far beyond that of choosing the rules for the classroom. Perhaps they can also be engaged in choosing what they will study and how they will study it.

The approaches suggested in this chapter for dealing with conflict and cooperation have application beyond that of responding to incidents of misbehavior. Consider how the basic principles outlined in this chapter relate to your philosophy of teaching and learning as well as to your interpersonal relationships outside the classroom. We believe that this effort can have a significant impact on many aspects of your professional life.

REFERENCES

Alschuler, A. (1980). *School discipline: A socially literate solution.* New York: McGraw-Hill.

Charles, C. M. (1992). *Building classroom discipline* (4th ed.). New York: Longman.

Charles, C. M., and Senter, G. W. (1995). *Elementary classroom management* (2nd ed.). White Plains, NY: Longman.

Curwin, R., and Mendler, A. (1980). *The discipline book: A complete guide to school and classroom management.* Reston, VA: Reston Publishing Co.

Edwards, C. H. (1997). *Classroom discipline and management* (2nd ed.). Columbus, OH: Merrill/Prentice-Hall.

Gardner, H. (1993). *Multiple intelligences: The theory in practice.* New York: Basic Books.

Ginott, H. (1972). *Teacher and child.* New York: Avon Books.

Gordon, T. (1974). *Teacher effectiveness training.* New York: David McKay.

Glasser, W. (1969). *Schools without failure.* New York: Harper and Row.

Glasser, W. (1990). *The quality school: Managing students without coercion.* New York: Harper and Row.

Hoover, R. L., and Kindsvatter, R. (1997). *Democratic discipline: Foundation and practice.* Columbus, OH: Merrill/Prentice Hall.

Johnson, D., and Johnson, R. (1995). *Reducing school violence through conflict resolution.* Alexandria, VA: Association for Supervision and Curriculum Development.

Jones, V., and Jones, L. (1986). *Comprehensive classroom management* (2nd ed.). Boston: Allyn and Bacon.

Kohn, A. (1996). *Beyond discipline: From compliance to community.* Alexandria, VA: Association for Supervision and Curriculum Development.

Kouzes, J., and Posner, B. (1987). *The leadership challenge.* San Francisco: Jossey-Bass.

Powell, R. R., Zehm, S., & Garcia, J. (1996). *Field experience: Strategies for exploring diversity in schools.* Columbus, OH: Merrill.

Savage, T. (1990). *Discipline for self-control.* Englewood Cliffs, NJ: Prentice Hall.

Woolfolk, A. (1995). *Educational psychology* (6th ed.). Boston: Allyn and Bacon.

Contemporary Issues Related to Student Behavior and Discipline

144

To make the most out of your classroom time you first must learn to deal successfully with student behavior. This means you must also learn how best to approach all kinds of student discipline issues. If you are like so many other prospective teachers, few things concern you more than issues pertaining to student behavior and discipline. Many prospective teachers have an underlying fear that they will not be successful in working with students who are viewed by professional educators as being more challenging than other students.

Contrary to the widespread fear demonstrated by prospective teachers over student behavior and discipline, we believe that you can be successful in working with all students. A primary means to achieve this kind of success is to first develop an understanding of the personal, social, cultural, and familial backgrounds of your students. We do not mean to suggest that you must know every student in deeply personal ways. This would be an arduous task for some teachers who meet and mingle with hundreds of students every day. What we mean to suggest is that you, in some way, must understand students whose personal lives out of school differ from yours, and thus whose personal and social behavior in school will have a different out-of-school framework from which it is constructed. The purpose of this chapter is to help you more clearly understand how students' personal lives out of school profoundly influence their in-school behavior. Related to this purpose is our intention to help you realize that *guiding* and *mediating* student behavior are more feasible classroom approaches to working with students than *controlling* and *manipulating* student behavior.

STUDENT BEHAVIOR IN TODAY'S CLASSROOMS

If you have not recognized it by this time, you will likely be in for a bold awakening when you begin your first teaching assignment. The students who populate your elementary and secondary schools are greatly different than those who walked the halls of schools a generation ago (Bauer, 1993). Consider for example the vignette of a first year teacher which follows. Regardless of grade level, what happened to her could also happen to you.

Joanne's Story

Joanne, a first-year teacher in a southwestern urban school, recently learned the reality about what students from diverse backgrounds bring to contemporary classrooms when she received her first teaching assignment. This bright, enthusiastic teacher completed her undergraduate course work with the highest grades. She was recognized by her professors as an outstanding student with a bright future awaiting her as an elementary teacher. In the middle of her highly successful student teaching experience, her master teacher was so impressed with her instructional skills that she invited the principal to come to her second-grade classroom to observe Joanne's extraordinary work with children.

The principal was impressed by the competent and caring instruction she saw this young student teacher providing her students. The principal was especially impressed with Joanne's ability to actively involve all her students in cooperative learning experiences in which students demonstrated a mutual esteem for each other. A short time later, after Joanne had completed her student teaching at the end of the fall semester, her graduation coincided with an increased enrollment in the very school where she had starred as a student teacher. The principal received special permission to offer Joanne a contract to fill this new position. Joanne, of course, immediately accepted this dream position in her dream school.

Come the first Monday of her new assignment Joanne met some serious challenges. The new second-grade class was formed by taking a number of students from the other second-grade classes overcrowded by the increased enrollments. Students who were most likely to be reassigned to Joanne's new class were the students who already wore the indelible labels of school failure: learning disabled, developmentally delayed, at risk, emotionally and physically challenged, attention-deficit disordered, and attention-deficit hyperactive disordered (see a discussion of labeling in chapter 3). Joanne had many of these challenging students infused into her *regular* classroom.

Although these students were not the ones she had prepared herself to teach, Joanne tried everything she could think of to reach, motivate, and engage these students in genuine learning. Nothing seemed to work for Joanne. They resisted her attempts to establish a caring relationship with them; they demonstrated no caring for her or for each other. When Joanne wanted them to participate verbally in a classroom activity they greeted her requests with silence. When she asked them to quietly complete their seat work, they were rebelliously loud and boisterous. By Wednesday of her first week, Joanne had exhausted her entire instructional repertoire. Come Thursday, she began to panic and spent all of Thursday night in a full-blown panic attack. On Friday morning, amid uncontrollable sobs, Joanne called her principal and resigned.

Joanne's short-lived professional life may not be typical of the experience that awaits you as a beginning teacher, but it is a fact that even many of our experienced teachers are calling an early end to their classroom careers because of the taxing realities resulting from the infusion of students into their classrooms whose labels excuse them from the responsibility of making academic progress and displaying acceptable classroom behavior (Bullough, 1995). If you are to survive these harsh realities of today's schools, you must prepare yourself as fully as possible to know, understand, and be ready to reach students who need teachers in ways students of the past have not. In the activity that follows, we ask you to begin now to prepare yourself for the taxing realities teachers must face today, arising from students who comprise today's classrooms. More specifically, we ask you to walk in Joanne's shoes to see what alternative you might find that would make your walk less difficult than hers.

EXERCISE 7.1   Putting Yourself in Joanne's Shoes

Throughout your readings of the chapters of this book, you have been asked to reflect on ways you can prepare yourself to make decisions for assisting your students to improve their individual, social, and academic performance. You have just read the story of a beginning teacher who was so unprepared to face the realities presented by the diversity of today's students that she made the emotion-charged decision to walk out on her students. In this exercise, we ask you to put yourself in Joanne's shoes and to reflect about what you would have done in similar circumstances. Consider the following questions:

- What was the real cause of Joanne's problem?
- Did Joanne do anything to create this problem?
- What alternative decision might Joanne have made to solve this problem?
- What would likely be the consequences of this alternative decision?
- In order to make use of this alternative course of action, what would be the first task Joanne would have to do to implement this decision?

As you consider the aforementioned questions, write a letter to Joanne, who is considering a return to teaching. In this letter explain the alternative courses of action contained in the items above which Joanne might want to consider when confronted with a similar classroom challenge in the future.

GETTING READY FOR GENERATION X

Now that you have considered some alternative decisions and courses of action for beginning to deal with challenging classroom situations, you must focus more closely on the students who will most frequently present you with these challenges. Today's young people are often lumped together under the unflattering label of *Generation X* because of their tendencies to consider their own needs first. Many of these students discover to their dismay that they are shackled with an *at risk* label, another convenient diagnostic tag that pretends to explain the causes of their less-desirable classroom behaviors. Before you buy into this labeling of contemporary youth who will be or already are your students, we ask you to do once more what we have repeatedly urged you to do throughout this book: Check out the reality of these labels (see especially chapter 3). Who are these young people? Why do they behave the way they do? If they are self-centered, what is motivating this widespread behavior? If they are at risk, what are the underlying causes of this risk? Are there any societal antecedents that might be contributing to their negative classroom behaviors?

We want you to prepare yourself as completely as you can before you sign your first teaching contract to be ready to negotiate the learning of students who wear the *tough kid* labels. As our previous chapters and the opening quote of this chapter indicate, we want to assist you in helping students with a history of emotional, social, and academic problems find school success. We want to assist you in establishing in your classroom a supportive, safe environment where all students can learn to manage their own behaviors and make genuine social and academic progress. This is the ideal classroom situation which many beginning teachers seldom attain.

Many idealistic beginning teachers, like Joanne, are not prepared to negotiate the realities of classroom behaviors displayed by students that many teachers today unfalteringly refer to as *students from hell.* Not prepared for the behaviors they find displayed in today's classrooms, they soon scuttle their idealism. They turn from warm, caring, empathetic individuals into hallway wardens and classroom police who clamp the tightest controls on students who display any deviance from their strict codes of classroom behavior. They punish mistaken behaviors as misbehaviors (Gartrell, 1995).

This loss of idealism soon takes its toll on beginning teachers. Veteran teachers with similar dwindling idealism clean out their desks and seek work in other professions. They too cite the increasing difficulty of classroom control resulting from the inclusion of students with serious learning and behavioral problems as one of the primary reasons for leaving their classrooms.

How will you prepare yourself to weather the storm presented by students who will challenge your authority and your idealism? This will be the real test of your professional dedication and preparation. To begin to prepare yourself you must fully understand the realities with which your challenging students will present you in your first years of teaching. In the section that follows, we ask you to examine the realities that are shaping the contemporary classroom behaviors of students in our elementary, middle, and high schools. Balancing idealism with realism can help you get yourself ready to be successful in your experience with special need students. Finding this balance can also prepare you to find effective approaches for helping them discover the life and school successes they really deserve (Farner, 1996).

CONTEMPORARY INFLUENCES ON STUDENTS' BEHAVIOR

There are a number of contemporary issues that are influencing the lives of all students in our public and private schools. Although many of these influences have been known to classroom teachers in previous generations, you could not have made in past times the sweeping generalization we just made that all contemporary students, whether located in public or in private schools, in urban or in rural settings, are being negatively influenced by a number of debilitating sociopolitical pressures. These influences place all students at risk of behaviors and attitudes that will not only lead many to academic failure, but also to personal lives marked by suffering and tragedy. In this section, we ask you to forearm yourself with the knowledge of these influences on students' behavior. Without an understanding of the realities that shape students' destructive perceptions of self and the world they live in, we cannot hope to help students to improve their classroom performance and behavior.

Alienated Students

One of the first realities you will notice among many of your students in today's classrooms is the chilling lack of caring that many contemporary students display. "Nobody cares about us," you will likely hear them assert, "so why should we care about anyone else?" These are students who have been tagged with the label of *the aliens* for the primary behavior they display in the classroom of total apathy toward anything that has to do with learning. They appear to be highly self-centered and will resist attempts to make them into something they don't desire to be (Brophy, 1998).

When you take the time to check out the underlying realities and implications of a label like the tag of *self-centered* that many alienated students find hung around their necks, you might soon discover a more pressing underlying cause for these behaviors. The basic skills required of students in today's schools do not begin with the 3-Rs—they begin with survival. Kids, whether in Los Angeles or in Laredo, must first learn how to get to school safely, how to avoid getting their lunch money stolen, and how to protect themselves from drive-by gangbangers on their way back home. Survival means learning how to take care of one's self. This is not a narcissistic form of self-centeredness. The ability to survive, to take care of one's self, is becoming the essential skill on which all of the other academic skills depend.

Children and adolescents cannot really care about others until they learn how to take care of themselves. An understanding of this reality is critical if you are to learn how to negotiate appropriate classroom behaviors with your students. Learning how to survive inside and outside of school is the key to genuine self-esteem. Your efforts in helping your students to acquire this important skill will eliminate many of the student-made barriers to a classroom community in which students mutually esteem, support, and care for each other. We will help you build on this critical understanding later in this chapter with an action plan to promote students' ability to take care of themselves.

Permeable Families

Consider another contemporary reality that is shaping the lives of children and young people in their homes. Social psychologist David Elkind describes the families that the majority of our young people come from as *permeable* families to distinguish them from the nuclear families of the past (Elkind, 1984). The permeable family is comprised of a variety of features that prevent children from getting essential caring and nurturing.

Permeable families come in many patterns. Since approximately one half of today's marriages end in divorce, many are single-parent families in which one parent strives to support and nurture his/her children. Many two-parent families may appear to be traditional, nuclear families, but if you looked more closely, you would find they are not. More often than not, both parents are required to work to earn the increasing amounts of money it takes to provide a contemporary family with a comfortable lifestyle. This demand for both parents to work has transformed the traditional nuclear family from close-knit social units of people who care for one another into camps of individuals who pass each other like people in speeding automobiles moving fast, with engines running at maximum stress levels. The stresses encountered by contemporary families lead to regular disconnections that find many children warehoused after school in latch-key situations well into the evening. There is little time for meaningful family talk or for consistent parental supervision of their children's home behavior. For some families, there is absolutely no parental involvement in their children's formal education.

When you look at the realities of contemporary family living, you may be inclined to be cynical. Don't feel alone: Many veteran teachers openly express a similar cynical view you may hear uttered in one form or another in faculty lounges. "My students' parents don't care about their children's school work or classroom behavior anymore!" is not untypical of these cynical views.

These kinds of cynical responses, however, are not going to help you know how to help students behave, learn, and care for one another. Regardless of the realities of contemporary families, once you sign your contract as a classroom teacher, your moral obligation is to search for positive ways to help students learn and behave. Cynical excuses will not help you in this search. How can you then possibly manage to find ways to counteract the contemporary realities of permeable families who do not find time to consistently supervise their children's academic and social behaviors at home?

One of the most dangerous aspects of educational and social labels, as we discussed in chapter 3, is that they often create realities that inhibit further thinking and problem solving. The realities that these labels create are like half-truths that are often worse than whole lies. Look at Elkind's label of the *permeable family* again. We can see this as a scientific descriptor that excuses us from our professional search for answers. This approach, however, would fail to encourage teachers from looking more deeply into this reification. Although Elkind was simply describing the emerging pattern of contemporary family life, his later discussions of the *permeable family* suggest an alternative approach you can use to begin dealing with this influence in your classroom.

Elkind has noticed in his studies of the *permeable family* that the parent(s) of these families are expecting more responsible behaviors from their children. Parents expect their children to take care of themselves and their younger siblings. They expect them to do family jobs that were previously done by parents: housecleaning, grocery shopping, laundry, cooking, etcetera. Herein lies another avenue for you to pursue in negotiating more successful classroom behaviors with your students, connecting with parents in establishing the highest expectations for responsible academic and social behaviors in your classroom.

Contemporary Victims

Your classroom will come under the influence of another set of realities that we have chosen to cluster here under the heading of contemporary victims. Students who are forced to wear a victim label will bring ready-made excuses for their many and varied negative classroom behaviors. They are negatively motivated by what psychologists call *learned helplessness*, a condition which robs many of them of what they need most to succeed in school and life: personal responsibility, high expectations, and consistent boundaries (Seligman, 1991; Powell, Zehm, & Kottler, 1995). The four most common types of students who wear the labels of victims are:

- the children of toxic families, where parents or children are connected directly to some kind of addiction,
- the children of economically deprived families,
- children/adolescents who have suffered from physical abuse and other forms of violence (Baines, 1995), and
- students with learning disabilities (Gefland, Jenson, & Drew, 1997; Singh, 1997).

Knowing how to recognize these contemporary victims whose behaviors can negatively impact the culture and deportment of your entire class is your first challenge in learning to effectively negotiate acceptable levels of classroom conduct. The following snapshots will provide you with concrete examples of each of these four types.

Children From Toxic Families

In our book, *Classrooms Under the Influence,* we describe four types of students who come from dysfunctional families where one or both parents are addicted to alcohol or drugs (Powell, Zehm, & Kottler, 1995). The first type is frequently identified as the *family hero.* This child is usually the oldest child and early on is designated as the family member who has the responsibility for restoring the family's damaged image by achieving high grades in schoolwork. This child's classroom behavior is generally exemplary. Teachers usually are not even aware of this student's home situation because of his/her adeptness in maintaining the family secret and in selecting only those classroom behaviors that will please the teacher. This child is the teacher pleaser, *par excellence,* and will only betray his dependence on his parents' addiction when he loses control after receiving an A− grade rather than an A+ grade. Teachers who fail to recognize these achievement-driven, perfectionist students further abet the underlying anxiety that will ultimately end in personal, social, and academic disasters for the family hero.

Lost children may also go unrecognized in classrooms because they isolate themselves in their classrooms and on the playground. Keeping to themselves, they mask their pain from others by pretending to be super-independent. Frequently they mask their pain from themselves by medicating their feelings of loneliness and inadequacy with eating disorders.

There are two toxic family types you will not be able to miss or ignore in your classroom; both will try your patience to the breaking. The *family scapegoat* acts out his/her rage for the treatment he gets from his parents by rebelling against them at home and against his teachers at school. The scapegoat's behavior is defiant and rebellious. He will dare you to get close enough to teach him anything. The *family mascot* attempts to recover the attention she fails to get at home by becoming recognized by teachers and students for her outstanding performances as the resident class clown. The clowning facade is a feeble mask for the real insecurity this student feels because of daily shame she must live with as a daughter of an alcoholic or drug addict.

Recognizing the symptoms these children of toxic families bring into your classroom is important, but not so you can label them and write yourself a dispensation for trying to reach them. These additional labels would become just another batch of stereotypes that would do more harm than good if that were your purpose. We want you to recognize these students through the behaviors they present in your classroom so that you can be ready to help them take charge of their fears, anxieties, and anger and negotiate behaviors that will improve their academic, personal, and social behaviors in your class. Once you recognize their needs, you can employ the helping strategies we will share with you later in this chapter to assist them to find the personal, social, and academic success they long to possess.

Children of Poverty

Children who come from families with fewer economic resources—who fall into the economic bracket of lower socioeconomic status (SES)—bear some resemblances to the children from toxic families we have just described. In fact many may bear a double curse when their parents seek to assuage the pain their poverty-stricken condition forces them to endure by using drugs or alcohol to medicate this condition. Children from poor families are frequently misidentified by teachers as less-able learners. These students, as early as kindergarten age, may find themselves locked into rigid classrooms where they fall further and further behind in their academic skills.

Andy was one such student born of a very poor family. He was retained twice for his complete lack of academic progress. He was regularly pulled out of his assigned classroom and given extra doses of remedial assistance. And even on those days when he did make some progress with his remedial teacher, he never had a chance to apply what he had learned to his regular classroom activities. Andy lacked the ability to read at grade level, a fact which his more academically able seventh-grade classmates never let him forget.

A victim of *academic status disorder*, Andy's academic and social behaviors are not unlike the behaviors of many children who come to school from lower SES families only to find a classroom environment that imposes limits on their academic achievements (Rist, 1970; Cohen & Lotan, 1997). Andy's noncompliant and aggressive behaviors were unknowingly being encouraged by the low academic status he had been locked into by teachers and students who lacked the understanding of what prompted his rage and rebellion and what could be done to change his self-destructive behavior.

EXERCISE 7.2   Contemporary Influences on Students' Behavior

In this section of the chapter, we have provided you with snapshots of students who bring to school a variety of difficult life experiences that will create obstacles to successful learning and conduct in your classroom. Look once again at the following list of *at risk* students we have identified:

- alienated students
- children of poverty
- students with disabilities
- children from toxic families

- abused children
- children from disintegrated families
- violent students
- victims of learned helplessness

In order to learn more about students who come from these diverse situations which place them at risk of school and life failures, complete the following tasks:

1. Select one category of students at risk of school failure and find more information in books and journals.
2. Use the information you gather to write a descriptive definition of this student which replaces the label he/she wears with a set of specific symptoms and causes of the behaviors that prevent him/her from finding school success.
3. Share a draft of your definition with an experienced teacher and revise your definition where needed.
4. Compare and contrast your descriptive definition with those of your peers.

Your Reality Check

The definitions of *at risk* students that you and your peers have compiled will help you begin to make your own reality checks regarding the likely composition of your future classes of students. Your classroom will contain students like Andy who come from low SES families.

This is another depressing reality of our times. Children make up the largest percentage of our citizens who live in poverty and this number keeps growing each day. Only about half of these children who qualify for Head Start programs are receiving the opportunity to participate. Similarly, only about half of those children from poor families who are eligible to receive free meals at school are being fed. The greatest number of these children from poor families are white children; children of color represent the highest percentage of our population living in poverty.

Such children and the children that come from the variety of dysfunctional families we have examined in this section will present you with one of the greatest challenges you will face as a classroom teacher. Knowing how to recognize the causes of the complex behaviors that these students will bring into your classroom will help you to accomplish two important tasks:

- avoiding unnecessary labeling of the symptoms of their behaviors that will generate excuses for their failure
- beginning to prepare the approaches, expectations, and interventions that will help these tough cases become responsible, effective learners

If you are not ready to begin addressing these two tasks that will assist you in providing a safe and supportive learning environment even for the *tough students,* you will unwittingly continue to propagate the myths of classroom management. These myths prevent kids from finding what they want most in your classroom: a place where they can really belong and can find personal, social, and academic success.

THE MYTHS OF MANAGING BEHAVIOR IN TODAY'S CLASSROOMS

You will face many obstacles to creating a classroom culture that removes the victim labels from students and nurtures their active participation in a community of learners. Before you begin to acquire the tools to negotiate the positive classroom behaviors of the special need students you are learning to recognize, we need to assist you with the task of clearing away a number of classroom management myths that may be barriers to your success. We ask you to consider each of the myths we have identified, examine how they fit with your own observations, and reflect on the implications they may have for the approaches you plan to use for handling classroom discipline problems as they arise.

Myth 1: "Just Be Consistent!"

If you have not heard it by now, you soon will. It is the simplicity theory of classroom management that says: "It doesn't matter what action you take, just be consistent!" When you press these givers of advice to clarify what they mean by "just be consistent," they'll likely respond that you must treat every student the same, demonstrate the same teacher demeanor toward each, and impose the same consequences for each of their violations of specific rules.

Upon first hearing this you might think it sounds logical, even democratic. Unfortunately, with all the diversity students are bringing into today's classroom, few teachers could consistently treat these different students in the same ways. Moreover, it is not advisable for you to try to treat your special needs students in the same way. "Consistency is the hobgoblin of small minds," Emerson reminded us. Although we cannot treat all students with the same, simple disciplinary plan, we must treat all students fairly. The disciplinary actions you negotiate with each one of your more challenging kids will be as complex as the causes that motivate his or her misbehaviors. Your success in negotiating acceptable classroom behavior will depend largely on your ability to identify and affirm the needs of your students.

Myth 2: "I can out-tough them!"

This is another myth you frequently hear from the macho type of teacher. "I am an assertive teacher," he or she maintains; "I keep all my students in line by being tougher than they are!" While it is true that you can use firm and assertive approaches to maintain classroom routines of acceptable behavior, aggressive tactics may silence unruly students for a while. But watch out, your tough behavior will surely backfire in many possible ways. First of all, you are not diffusing your classroom learning environment of the hostile and negative influences presented by your tough students. You are merely putting a temporary lid over this volatile situation that will soon be blown off by the anger, rage, hostility, and even violent behavior of students who have already experienced similar heavy-handed treatment in other classes and at home. The previous tough tactics they received from their teachers simply made them more rebellious and determined not to be easily subjected to similar humiliations in subsequent classes.

Gentle teaching is an alternative that Haberman (1994) wisely prescribes to address the ills of the violence which surrounds our students. "Beyond kindergarten and the first two grades," he asserts, "teachers can no longer physically control their students with external sanctions or fear. For teachers to pretend they have the means which can force students to learn or even comply is a dangerous myth which can make the social curriculum of poverty schools as coercive and violent as the neighborhood outside the school." Be firm, be fair, maintain high expectations for all your students. But when you try to play it tough with the tough kids, you'll not only lose them, you'll create a hostile learning environment for every student who enters your classroom.

Myth 3: "All They Need Is Love!"

Reflect for a moment about the old adage: "You catch more flies with honey!" This adage is related to another myth that on first blush appears to be just the opposite of the "out-tough-'em" option. It says that if you want to bring the unruly around, don't just use honey, use love. You may hear it put another way by beginning teachers, "I am not going to have major problems with any of my students; I'm just going to love them and they'll respond." We know many naive beginning teachers who uttered these words only to be devoured by the tough kids who do not easily respond to caring attitudes. The sad thing is that many teachers who find their genuine sentiments rebuffed by the apparently hard-hearted tough kids end up by reversing their controlling behaviors from love to fear-based tactics similar to those we examined above.

We want you to nurture feelings of love and affection for all your students and display this affection in professional ways. However, we don't want you to fall into another simplicity trap of thinking that these genuine feelings of affection will be reciprocated by your tough students and returned in kind by angelic classroom behavior. Your heart will always be an important element in your successful relationships with your students. Nevertheless, you will need more. The causes of the diverse problems that prompt all the negative personal, social, and academic behaviors of the tough students will require your mental energy, your practical intuition, your precious time, and your daily renewal of commitment.

Myth 4: "Grades Will Motivate the At-Risk to Change Their Behaviors!"

"You'd better behave," a frustrated teacher threatens an apathetic student whose insolent, noncaring attitude is a real threat to his teacher's authority, "or you'll get an *F* in this class!" The student utters a sardonic laugh and his response keys similar knowing laughs from his classmates who know something that this naive teacher has yet to learn. Grades will never motivate positive behaviors of the apathetic students who simply have ceased to care about learning or anything related to school.

Grades can have chilling effects on the behaviors of another type of at risk student we described above. Give the student who is forced to assume the perfectionist role of the toxic family hero an *A*− or less and be prepared for another negative response you could not have anticipated. This achievement-driven student will react to this less than perfect grade with resentment and will try to make you feel that you have betrayed him or her. It is not unlikely that this student will become depressed by this grade. Teachers who are startled by this kind of response may alter their own assessment practice and refrain from ever giving these "model" teacher-pleasing students any grade but *A* for fear that these students may react by contemplating suicide. These students effectively control the behaviors of their teachers and place their classroom under the influence of toxic family tactics (see Powell, Zehm, & Kottler, 1995).

Myth 5: "Somewhere There's Prepackaged Magic Available!"

One of the prevailing myths that circulates among beginning teachers is the vain hope that somewhere there exists a special program with training and materials that will give the teacher the exact behavioral tool he or she needs for fixing every one of the negative classroom behaviors the tough kids display. Maybe you have heard stories of these mythical tools. One such myth involves a jar of marbles and an ice cream party. You just put marbles in a jar when you catch students exhibiting positive behaviors and take them out when you catch them in negative behaviors. When the jar is full, everybody gets an ice cream party. If you believe this is the magical road you can follow as a teacher, then you indeed are myth taken.

There is no magical road, no single strategy, leading to the instantaneous cure of the causes of the serious breaches of behavior of some of the at risk students who will be infused into your classroom. To think otherwise would be a naive buy-into the simplicity myths we described above.

Myth 6: "These Are Not My Students!"

This is a myth that veteran teachers frequently pull out of a hat to explain their frustration in dealing with increasing levels of student diversity they find complicating their classroom routines. The teacher utterances vary, but they have some common features. "These are not my students . . . I am a fourth grade teacher and these students belong to special ed." "These are not my students . . . I am a junior high English teacher and these students don't even speak English." Finally, "These are not my students . . . I am a high school math teacher and these students belong in a third-grade arithmetic class!"

This disowning myth is not, however, a modern myth. It is rooted in the myth of the homogeneous classroom where all the kids are at grade level. The fact is that you will never have a fully homogeneous classroom. They don't exist! The students assigned to you next year will likely demonstrate increasing levels of intellectual, linguistic, cultural, social, and academic diversity than the class you had last year. The fact also remains that they are all your students and that once you sign your contract, it is your moral duty to help them become responsible for their own learning.

Myth 7: "Don't Ask Your Principal for Help With the Tough Kids!"

This myth, like many of the others, contains a half-truth. You will likely receive the kernel of truth lodged in this myth from a number of sources. The instructor of your undergraduate course in classroom management, the master teacher supervising your student teaching, and the principal of the school in which you receive your first contract are three of the most likely sources. The advice they will share with you is a part of the conventional wisdom that governs the effective management of a classroom. It can be expressed in a variety of forms, but it usually is offered as advice similar to the following: "Be ready to handle most of your classroom discipline problems yourself." This is good advice. This is what this book is attempting to help you ready yourself to accomplish.

The myth under present consideration goes beyond the conventional wisdom expressed in this advice. The myth changes the word *most* to *all*. It directs you to be ready to handle all the tough cases by yourself. It cautions you, especially during your probationary period as a teacher, never to take your tough cases to the principal lest you reveal your weakness in this highly sensitive area of classroom control.

Remember Joanne, the beginning teacher with a class of tough kids whose unfortunate story we told you about at the beginning of this chapter? She was a victim of this myth that requires beginning teachers to survive the tough kids on their own. What makes this story genuinely sad is that Joanne not only had the potential to be a most effective teacher, she also possessed a principal who would have gladly come to her assistance if Joanne had only asked. Principals do not want teachers to refer steady streams of students to their offices for corrective actions that could readily be handled in the teachers' classrooms. Today's principals, however, are most aware that all teachers are going to have some kids who will require special interventions from school administrators.

Alternatives to the Management Myths

As we argued in chapter 2, schools are not meant to be factories with assembly lines in which students are managed to produce canned, homogeneous commodities of the same texture, weight, and quality. The myths you have just examined are remnants of this old management model that restricts the freedom, initiative, and potential of all of our students to begin making the responsible choices that will govern their own classroom conduct. In the sections that follow, we ask you to enhance your repertoire of understandings and strategies that will enable you to assist even your toughest of students in negotiating acceptable individual, social, and academic performance in your classroom.

EXERCISE 7.3   Myths You Have Discovered

In this activity, we ask you to respond to the seven classroom management myths we have described on pages 154–157 by inventing your own myth. Working with a group of peers, think of another myth that pretends to have *the answer* that will explain a foolproof system for ensuring the positive, angelic behaviors of all your students. If possible, base your myth on your own experience as a student.

BUILDING EFFECTIVE RELATIONSHIPS WITH SPECIAL NEED STUDENTS

All of the tactics, strategies, plans, and policies that aim at helping teachers maintain order in the classroom are doomed to ultimate failure without an essential prerequisite: a teacher who genuinely cares about all of his or her students. This caring is not a simple intellectual affirmation, nor is it commensurate with the myth, "all you need is love"; it must be a conscious, intentional stance. As a teacher, you stand for the individual, social, and academic success of each and every student assigned to you. Moreover, it is your moral obligation to do everything in your power to reach out to each of your students and negotiate goals for conduct and learning based on the highest of civic and academic expectations.

How, then, are you to display this pervasive caring for all your students in a way that will encourage even the tough kids to respond? We are not suggesting that you employ a caring response as an intervention to repair the negative classroom behaviors of the tough kids. Interventions are important strategies you must be ready to use when needed. Interventions, however, are designed to restore order in your social curriculum, not to build order. The first step we recommend to you—to become a relationship specialist—is designed to help you build caring, trusting relationships based on open communication with all your students (Reichle & Wacker, 1993).

On Becoming a Relationship Specialist

Think of those teachers who brought magic into your own elementary and secondary classrooms. Recall those teachers whose classes you eagerly looked forward to attending. Remember that special teacher who really made you feel welcome in her class and prompted you to respond to her daily roll call with an enthusiastic, "Present!" What did all these teachers have in common? Most likely it was the human capacity to build positive, warm relationships with you, relationships that encourage you to use your freedom in a responsible way that encourage your learning. They may not have been the most brilliant of teachers. In fact, they may have not been regarded by their teacher peers as experts in their respective fields. Nevertheless, they were effective teachers in your eyes and in the eyes of your classmates because they really cared about each of you and maintained a classroom environment that encouraged students to care about each other.

We are confident that your capacity to build effective relationships with your students will be your key to unlocking the padlocks that shackle the personal, social, and academic success of your most difficult and challenging students (Zehm & Kottler, 1993). Deep down these students want a teacher who will give them chances, believe in them, and recognize their uniqueness, talents, and voices. When you learn how to become a relationship specialist, you can join the ranks of those special teachers who are the best hope of many a troubled and lost student who may turn to gangs or the street if they don't find your classroom an inviting place in which to belong, learn, and reconnect.

Characteristics of Helping Relationships

Before you can establish positive helping relationships with your students, you must build a classroom environment grounded on trust. Moustakas (1986) describes three key elements we urge you to cultivate for maintaining effective helping relationships with your students. The first key element is called *being in*. Being in your student's pain, disappointments, and negative life experiences means that you can genuinely empathize with them. It means that you understand their feelings of abandonment, depression, and loss. When your students recognize your empathy, they realize that you really care about them and are not judging their failures and disappointment.

The second key element, *being for*, adds another crucial dimension you must cultivate in your relationships with students. Being for means that you are committed to be an advocate for your students. This will be an especially important dimension of your relationships with those alienated *students from hell* who will find in school few adults who are willing to be their advocates. When you become their advocates, they will reciprocate at first with unbelief. No teacher has ever cared anything about them in the past, so why should they expect any different treatment from you. Don't let this initial distrust put you off; just continue to let them know that you genuinely care about them and will do everything you can to help them. This kind of genuine warmth will ultimately melt the icebergs of emotion and abuse that prevent many students from enjoying your advocacy. In the security of caring relationships that are manifested in your classroom social curriculum students will begin to open up, begin to remove their masks, and begin to take the risks required of success in school and success in life.

The third key element in building a helping relationship of mutual trust is the component of *being with* your student. Being with is an acknowledgment of support, "I am with you to help, Sue," but it is also a recognition of separateness, "you are a bright person Sue; you have the ability to find your own success." Both of these dimensions are important elements of the relationships you forge with students. When a troubled or discouraged student knows you are with them to support their first feeble efforts, they will begin to find the confidence they need for taking the risks required of genuine learning. But the separateness dimension of the *being with* component of your professional relationships with students must not be forgotten by either students or teachers.

You will always remain the teacher and students will always remain the students. You are not their buddy, big sister, or big brother. You are genuinely respectful of the students placed in your charge; your students, in turn, look up to you as their trusted teacher. On your part, being with your students does not mean that you are controlling their classroom behaviors. On your students' part, being with you does not mean that they are not responsible for their conduct and the high academic expectation you maintain for all your students. Finally, being with your students means that you both don't have to worry about exposing the fact that you have bad days, say hurtful things without thinking, or blow your stack from time to time. Genuine relationships are built on a firm foundation of trust which accepts and excuses these momentary slips.

NEGOTIATING CLASSROOM BEHAVIOR WITH SPECIAL NEEDS STUDENTS

Even with a class where you have been successful in building strong teacher-student relationships built on genuine trust, you must be ready to negotiate the challenges presented by the diversity of special needs students assigned to your class. Be conscious of the metaphor we are using to describe the approach we recommend you use in facing these challenges. We are using the terms *negotiate, mediate,* and *guide* in addition to *manage* because the major purpose of this new text is not just to present the same old approaches to classroom management, but to offer you a more effective lens for viewing student behaviors, understanding them, and building an approach that is more adaptable to the student diversity we find in today's schools.

We believe classroom negotiation is a particularly useful metaphor that suggests several effective ways to deal with the challenges of needs, behaviors, multiple abilities, and cultural diversities that complicate both student learning and student conduct in contemporary classrooms. The only way you are going to be effective in supporting successful learning and conduct of your students in your heterogeneous classroom is by knowing and appreciating the background of knowledge, skills, and attitudes of each student. Knowing the capabilities of each will enable you to negotiate a path leading to the successful learning and deportment for each student. You will not be able to remove these students from abusive homes.* You cannot end the poverty into which they may have been born. You cannot find a magical cure for their disabilities. You can, however, begin to reach all of these students by your willingness to negotiate and renegotiate the classroom learning and conduct of your special needs students. They will become even more successful when you learn to use a helping process like the one described below.

Using A Helping Process for Special Needs Students

Figure 7.1 outlines a suggested helping process we have described in another book (Zehm & Kottler, 1993). Many of your special needs students who display behaviors of disruption, hostility, or alienation will benefit from your help to become responsible for their conduct at school. To make your helping intentional and effective, we recommend that you learn and reflect on this helping process. We are convinced it will make your relationships with special needs students, who are in most need of your help, more effective.

---

*In most states, teachers are required to report suspected abuse.

FIGURE 7.1
The Helping Process

(From Zehm & Kottler, 1993)

Stage	Skills
Assessment	Attending
	Listening
	Focusing
	Observing
Exploration	Reflecting feelings
	Responding in content
	Probing, questioning
	Showing empathy
Understanding	Interpreting
	Confronting
	Challenging
	Giving information
	Self-disclosing
Action	Goal-setting
	Role-playing
	Reinforcing
	Making decisions

Assessment

Assessment, the first task of effective instruction, is also the first stage of the helping process. Assessment means the systematic collection of information about the needs of your students. If you do not systematically collect information about the knowledge, skills, and attitudinal levels of your special needs students, you will not be able to negotiate successful learning and resocialization. Likewise, if you do not collect information about their individual, social, and behavioral needs and limitations, you will not be able to provide them with the intentional help they will need to negotiate successful school lives.

Indirectly, you assess special needs students by carefully observing them in the context of their social interactions and academic performances. When these students get off task or display unacceptable behaviors, you try to assess the circumstances that may have keyed these behaviors. You use a direct assessment helping strategy when you find the right opportunity to conference with special needs students. Of importance during the conference is for you to set aside your agenda and give your full attention to these students. This will be the critical point in building a helping relationship by communicating in word and body language how special these students are to you. You also demonstrate your nonjudgmental caring by attentively listening to their explanations for their difficulties, failures, and misbehaviors. Sometimes you will have to look past their hostile responses and listen to what is going on inside these troubled students.

Exploration

When you gain the trust of your special needs students through the strategies you use to assess and attend to their needs, they will be more ready to have you help them explore and understand what is going on in their lives. You can facilitate this process of helping your students gain the self-understanding they need to become more responsible in their school lives with several strategies (see also chapter 6). One is to reflect the feelings by restating the emotions you hear the students express. For example:

> Student: *Why should I try? Every time I study hard I never pass the test anyway.*
>
> Teacher: *You feel frustrated. You don't want to try hard anymore because you think you're going to fail again anyway?*

This strategy is an effective tool to help students more clearly see and explore their own feelings and motivations. It helps them understand better what is going on inside; it also convinces them that you are really listening to them.

Reflecting a student's comment is a related helping strategy you can use to assist a student in beginning to find self-understanding. Consider this response:

> Student: *Yeah, I'm the dumb one in my family. My sister gets all the A's. My dad comes after me with the strap 'cause all I bring home is big, red F's.*
>
> Teacher: *I can tell you're sick of being compared to your brainy sister all the time.*

When you restate a student's comment, you help him or her give words to what is really bothering that student. This helps them get closer to the issues that stand as obstacles to their individual, social, and academic successes.

Understanding

When you have been successful in your attempts to help your special needs students explore their feelings and frustrations, you also help them begin to understand why they feel and react the way they do. Not infrequently will these initial glimmerings of understanding help your depressed, abused, and/or angry students begin to interpret what is happening to them and what are the real sources of their conflicts and anxieties. This process will take time and it may be advisable for you, with the permission of the student, to seek the assistance of the school counselor who possesses the training to help students recognize the pattern of their behaviors and the underlying causes of their self-destructive actions.

When you have established a helping relationship of trust with your students, you may be able to use two more approaches to help them understand their own behaviors. You may feel comfortable in disclosing aspects of your own personal life that reveal how you faced similar obstacles and found the help to overcome them. You may also employ a caring confrontational approach that can help your students to understand that their words are not matching their actions. At all times during your attempts to help your students understand their fears, frustrations, and feelings, you must remember that you are not trying to solve your students' problems. This would only make them more dependent on you. Your goal is to help them understand their own hearts and minds so they can become more in control of their own lives.

Action

When people learn how to understand the real causes of their negative attitudes and behaviors, they are ready to begin assuming responsibility for making changes in their dysfunctional lives. Your students may not be able to mend their parents' wrecked marriage. They will not likely be able to rescue their family from the uncertainties of economic insecurity. Nor will they be able to bring an end to a parent's addiction to alcohol (or other substances). But when they understand that they are not responsible for any of these harsh conditions that complicate their young lives, they are ready to detach themselves from their self-destructive behaviors. With the help of an understanding teacher, they are ready to take action to change the only thing they can change, namely, themselves.

When you become aware of this readiness, your responsibility is not to give your students advice about what course of action to take. They probably wouldn't follow it anyway. Your responsibility is to help your students establish a course of action with realistic goals to which they can commit with confidence and enthusiasm. They must own these goals for making changes they want to see in their own personal, social, and academic lives. Your role is to be encouraging and to help them make the most suitable decisions. You might role-play a situation with them to help them better understand what choices are available to them. You must also assist them to formulate a contingency plan to help them get back on track if and when the old behaviors begin to reassert themselves. Finally, you must be there to reinforce by words of praise and support the efforts your special needs students make to become more responsible for their own behavior. When you see them trying to put their plans into action, you will be justifiably proud of them and proud that your classroom is becoming a real haven for understanding, support, and sanity in their chaotic lives.

THE DYNAMICS OF ENFORCING DISCIPLINE: IMPLICATIONS FOR STUDENTS' SCHOOL LIVES

Beginning teachers are treated no differently in regard to the principal's high expectations that all teachers know how to enforce discipline in their classrooms. Nevertheless, beginning teachers without the protection of continuing contracts and tenure will be scrutinized by the principal more carefully to make sure they have the skills to effectively enforce school expectations for student conduct. We expect that when you enter your classroom ready to teach lessons that are relevant and engaging, you will find 85 to 90% of your students ready to participate in meaningful learning (Teasley, 1996).

The difficult cases, the remaining 10 to 15% of those whose negative behaviors we have charted earlier in this chapter, will require you to ready yourself with alternatives to deal effectively with their daily challenges to your authority, ingenuity, and patience (Farner, 1996). In the long run, your success in reaching these distressed and distressing students and preventing their disruptive classroom behaviors will depend on the efficacy of your determination to build the kind of trusting relationships and to utilize the helping process you were introduced to in the last section. In the short run, however, you will need to begin now to build your skills of practical intuition that will provide you with effective interventions for handling the classroom brush fires caused by the complicated behaviors of some students (Tipton, 1995).

Nurturing Your Practical Intuition

The dynamics of enforcing classroom discipline are not governed by hard and fast rules that you can apply in a mechanical way to address and solve the disruptive and confrontational behaviors of difficult students. The worst thing you can choose to do in these situations is react to the heated students' emotions with equally incendiary emotional responses of your own. The best thing you can do is quietly maintain your composure and activate your practical intuition in search of the most suitable tactic to address the negative behavior of the students and to maintain control of your classroom. Tactics are those present-oriented tools you prepare in advance for dealing with the potentially disruptive behaviors. Strategies are your future-oriented plans for helping students overcome the emotional and social obstacles that prevent them from being more responsible for their own conduct. The following vignette will provide you with an example of the difference between these important approaches available for enforcing student discipline.

Donovan is a first-year teacher in a school serving a population of students who come from low-income families. When he began his assignment as a high school teacher, his principal made him aware of the fact that his classroom would have several students with disabilities whom he would find challenging. This fact was confirmed by Mrs. Dixon, a veteran 10th-grade teacher in the classroom adjoining his. "Donovan," she confided in him prior to the beginning of school, "I don't want to prejudice your attitudes toward your students, but you're going to find out soon enough that one of your inclusionary students, Derek, will make you question your decision to become a teacher. I had him last year and he nearly drove me crazy until I began to learn how to handle his outbursts." She then shared with her new teaching colleague what was to become Donovan's first tactic for handling Derek's tantrums.

But before he used the tactic, Donovan reflected on the practice as we urge you to do to prevent tactics from becoming negative forms of teacher control. He agreed that it fit his own intuitive criteria for a disciplinary action. It was not too harsh. It was more instructive than punitive. It was not intended to intimidate the student or the rest of the class into making their behaviors compliant, teacher-pleasing actions. It was not a shame-based reaction. Finally it was a response aimed at helping the student become responsible for his own behavior.

School started the next week and the second day of school had hardly begun before Derek began to paralyze the entire class with wordless, rage-filled outbursts. Donovan recalled the advice of his teaching colleague, Mrs. Dixon, and quickly removed Derek to a quiet corner of the classroom. "Derek, I can tell you're upset and I don't know what you're upset about, so I need you to help me. Mrs. Dixon tells me that you are excellent at drawing and that when you got upset in her class you drew her a picture about what made you upset. So here is what I want you to do." He gave Derek a sheet of paper divided into four quadrants and asked him to draw pictures of the things that made him mad in three of the quadrants. "Leave the last one blank, Derek," his teacher directed him. "When I finish reading the story to the class, I'll come back and you and I will begin to write in the words in the last blank, words you need to know to make word pictures of the things that upset you so that we can talk about them." Donovan's tactic effectively quieted the behaviors of an enraged, out-of-control student, but the tactic which was designed to resolve a present conflict, also contained a strategy for future intervention and possible solution based on an effective relationship-building response.

EXERCISE 7.4   Exploring Practical Intuition

In this exercise we ask you to use your intuition for addressing a classroom conflict. Read and reflect on the challenging scenario below and identify the following actions you would take to address the unacceptable classroom/school behavior.

1. What tactic(s) would you employ to resolve the conflicts and end the behavior(s) that threaten the safe climate of your classroom?
2. What strategy would you employ as an intervention to resocialize the student(s) whose behaviors threaten the safety of your students and the solidarity of your class?

THE CLASS BULLY

In your first year of teaching, you have been presented with a number of difficult students who have challenged your authority. You have begun to develop the intuitive understanding for dealing successfully with most of these, but there is one student who presents a behavior that has you stumped. This fifth-grade student is female and she is the class bully. You didn't realize this for a long time because you thought female students were immune to bullying behaviors. Sally does not act like you expected a bully to act. In your classroom, she does not physically bully any other student. When you began to observe her more closely in your assessment of her behavior, you saw her pass covert threats by gestures, whispers, and glares designed to intimidate other boys and girls in your class.

Her behavior is not all that disruptive, but you are concerned because you believe that she is dividing the class and preventing a sense of solidarity. When you ask an experienced teacher for advice, she tells you to ignore her and save your energy for the really tough cases. You decide this teacher is right; you decide to overlook her quiet intimidating behaviors.

Not long after this decision, you are walking across the playground to the library during the lunch break, when you see Sally harassing another student in your class. This time she is using more than quiet intimidation. She is pushing Jennifer, pulling her hair, and hurling verbal threats and obscenities. You start to intervene, but another teacher who is serving as the playground monitor stops you and tells you that kids have to learn to protect themselves and resolve their own problems. You return to your classroom, upset with the inaction of the adult monitor. You are also concerned because you saw a number of what you thought were docile, cooperative students encouraging Sally's bullying actions.

KNOWING YOUR SCHOOL'S BEHAVIOR AND DISCIPLINE POLICIES

By now you know that you will be expected to take care of your routine classroom discipline problems by yourself. School principals will not tolerate the referral of students whose discipline problems could have been effectively addressed by the classroom teacher. Unfortunately, the majority of beginning teachers whose contracts were not renewed after their probationary periods were let go because of their inability to successfully negotiate and mediate the routine disciplinary problems of their students.

We urge you to be mindful of this caveat; but we also want to assure you that most states and school districts have policies and procedures for assisting you in handling student behaviors that are deemed serious disruptions of classroom learning or threats to the safety of students and teacher. In this section we will review typical policies of the kind you will likely find in your school district. As you review these sample policies from an urban school district in a southwestern state, be sure you can identify those serious behaviors that demand the immediate referral of the offending student to your school supervisors.

Regulations and Procedures

The following list of serious cases has been identified by a school board and placed in their legal document of school policies as serious student behaviors which administrators should provide "strong and direct support" to teachers in handling:

1. students in possession of weapons or dangerous implements
2. students in possession of drugs and/or alcohol
3. students who display immoral conduct
4. students caught stealing
5. students who destroy property
6. students who physically or verbally assault others

With the six serious behaviors identified above, your responsibility, if you were under contract in this district, would be to seek the assistance of your building administrators in applying the prescribed corrective actions in response to these serious violations of acceptable student behavior. Students who possess weapons, sell drugs, or physically assault others will be removed from your class.

They will most likely be referred to the appropriate law enforcement agencies and hearings will be scheduled to determine whether suspension, expulsion, or some other corrective disciplinary action will be taken.

In most of these serious cases, your principal will ask you to document what happened in each instance. Since these serious cases will involve the intervention of police and other legal officials, you must be prepared to provide additional documentation if such documentation is required. These cases may also result in litigation against the school by disgruntled parents who maintain the innocence of their children and seek legal redress against the school district. Since you may also be named as a defendant in these lawsuits, you must know ahead of time what the legally binding policies of your school district require you to do as a participant in handling these serious violations of school policies.

EXERCISE 7.5   Examining Your School District's Policies

Prepare yourself for referring serious violations of school district policy and for protecting yourself from litigation that may result from your participation in the handling of these serious cases by completing the following tasks:

- Locate and make copies of the policies of the school district where you will student teach or where you currently teach that require you to refer students to school administrators for serious violations of student conduct.
- Make a list of the serious cases identified in these policies and brainstorm strategies you might use to prevent students from being involved in these serious behaviors in your classroom.
- Check with the building representatives of the local association (e.g., National Education Association; American Federation of Teachers) to find out what kind of legal protection you can count on from your district in the event that you will be named in a lawsuit connected with a serious disciplinary action involving your principal.

CONCLUSION

The alternative classroom management strategies we are sharing with you in this book will help you establish a classroom order focused on maintaining a safe and inviting environment. Your classroom must be a haven that supports the learning of *all* students. You will be confronted with the challenging realities and serious problems of discipline that many students, like the ones we have examined in this chapter, will bring into your classroom. The more serious the discipline problem you face, the more emotionally charged it is likely to be. Moreover, the more serious discipline problems you face may be complicated by legal and moral issues that have the potential for testing the resolve and endurance of even the hardiest veteran of the teaching ranks.

You cannot prevent students with serious behavior problems from being assigned to your classroom. You will get your share of these serious cases. You cannot hope to pack a suitcase filled with ready-to-wear remedies you can use to remediate these serious discipline problems. Nor will your success in establishing classroom order from day one or in preparing a proactive plan to handle classroom misbehaviors liberate your classroom from the challenges of the *students from hell.* If you are to find the resources that will empower you to deal effectively with all the serious behavior problems students will bring into your classroom, you will need alternative approaches to traditional school discipline practice. We are confident that the relationship-building and helping strategies we have shared with you in this chapter will provide you with approaches that will assist you in helping your most challenging students find the personal, social, and academic success they long to achieve.

REFERENCES

Baines, L. (1995). Violence in our schools. *English Journal, 84*(5), 59–64.

Bauer, A. M. (Ed.). (1993). *Children who challenge the system.* Norwood, NJ: Ablex Publishing Corporation.

Brophy, J. E. (1998). *Motivating students to learn.* Boston: McGraw-Hill.

Bullough, R. V., with Baughman, K. (1995). Inclusion: A view from inside the classroom. *Journal of Teacher Education, 46*(2), 85–93.

Cohen, E., & Lotan, R. (Eds.). *Working for equity in heterogeneous classrooms: Sociological theory in practice.* New York: Teachers College Press.

Elkind, D. (1984). *All grown up and no place to go: Teenagers in crisis.* Reading, MA: Addison Wesley.

Farner, C. (1996). Discipline alternatives: Mending the broken circle. *Learning, 25*(1), 27–29.

Gartrell, D. (1995). Misbehavior or mistaken behavior? *Young Children, 50*(5), 27–34.

Gefland, D. M., Jenson, W. R., & Drew, C. J. (1997). *Understanding child behavior disorders.* (3rd ed.). Fort Worth, TX: Harcourt Brace.

Haberman, M. (1994). Gentle teaching in a violent society. *Educational Horizons, 72–73,* 131–136.

Moustakas, C. (1986). Being in, being for, and being with. *Humanistic Psychologist, 14*(2), 100–104.

Powell, R. R., Zehm, S. J., & Kottler, J. A. (1995). *Classrooms under the influence.* Newbury Park, CA: Corwin Press.

Reichle, J., & Wacker, D. P. (Eds.). (1993). *Communicative alternatives to challenging behavior.* Baltimore, MD: Paul H. Brookes Publishing Co.

Rist, R. (1970). Student, social class and teacher expectations. *Harvard Educational Review, 40,* 411–451.

Seligman, M. E. (1991). *Learned optimism.* New York: Knoph.

Singh, N. N. (Ed.). (1997). *Prevention and treatment of severe behavior problems: Models and methods in developmental disabilities.* Pacific Grove, CA: Brooks/Cole Publishing Co.

Teasley, A. B. (1996). New teachers: Dealing effectively with student behavior. *English Journal, 84*(4), 80–81.

Tipton, C. (1995). Minor changes/major results: Three small steps to better discipline. *English Journal, 84*(5), 56–58.

Zehm, S., & Kottler, J. (1993). *On being a teacher: The human dimension.* Newberry Park, CA: Corwin Press.

P A R T

III

DEVELOPING CULTURAL AND LOCAL UNDERSTANDINGS OF SOCIAL CURRICULA

The right thing would have been to focus on the realities themselves as the true standard and to measure your success by the degree of psychological robustness you have given your students to sustain them through life. That's what they need most of all, no doubt about it.

(C. Wolf, 1984, p. 112)

Part III focuses on the practical realities of the social curriculum. Specifically, part III focuses on the cultural realities of three selected schools as a way of helping you apply the concepts and ideas we have discussed in the first two sections of the book. Following the thinking of Christa Wolf (1984) in the quote above, we believe that by focusing on realities, you can think more broadly and deeply about how the idea of a social curriculum in real schools can better sustain you as you attempt to create, implement, and manage lessons that engage your students in meaningful, positive, and culturally responsive teaching.

By focusing your attention on the realities of three selected schools, we are holding to a very important assumption. We assume that the curriculum and corresponding instruction of any school creates a specific school culture. This culture in turn predisposes you, in certain predictable ways, to interact with your students, to engage them with the content, and to expect students to behave a certain way. This means that the more alike two schools might be in their curriculum and instruction—that is, the more alike they are in the specific knowledge and skills that they expect students to acquire and in how they expect students to acquire them—then the more alike these schools will be in how they expect you to interact with students instructionally, personally, socially, and academically.

Of course, we are not suggesting that schools which are very similar in their formal written curriculum and instruction have exactly the same social curriculum, exactly the same routines, exactly the same discipline policies, exactly the same management plans, exactly the same contexts for guiding and mediating learning, and so on. While schools can have similar curricula for their students, and have similar instructional goals, schools do not necessarily have exactly the same *feel* for students given local variations in how teachers and administrators actually deliver instruction.

More generally, however, if two schools tend to follow, for example, the traditional management model described in chapter 2, then educators in these schools will also adopt very similar kinds of thinking about teaching, learning, and management. Clearly, there exists a strong and viable connection between the overall curricular and instructional goals that a school has for students, and the way that teachers and students interact in the presence of content to be learned (Jones, 1995). This kind of connection is mentioned by McCaslin and Good (1992), who argue: "A curriculum that seeks to promote problem solving and meaningful learning must be aligned with [a school] system that increasingly allows students to operate as self-regulated and risk-taking learners (p. 4)." Schools and classrooms where self-regulation and risk-taking are goals for learners create a very different culture for learning than schools and classrooms where obedience and compliance are goals of learners. **Central to part III of this book is, therefore, the idea that schools and classrooms, *as cultural contexts*, give shape to the daily reality of how you manage, guide, and mediate student learning.**

Self-regulated and risk-taking learning, and the social curriculum that fosters these kinds of learning, is very different from obedient and compliant learning, and the social curriculum that fosters it. The social curriculum and its goals for student learning are central factors in determining how you, as a classroom teacher, plan, implement, monitor, and sustain a specific way of teaching and learning and a specific way of interacting with students. *In simplified terms, the social curriculum determines how you carry out teaching and learning.*

What emerges from the discussion above, and what will unfold in the chapters in part III, is the idea that the social curriculum is a cultural phenomenon (Bruner, 1996; Gay, 1988). Consequently, any interactions you have with students within a specific social curriculum, or within a specific school, are embedded in cultural phenomena. Thus, *traditional classroom management*, which has historically been aligned with behavioral psychology and has given rise to behavioral-like perspectives on learning, is very different from that which we call *culturally responsive education*. This later kind of education, which aligns with Bruner's (1996) description of cultural psychology and with Ladson-Billings' (1995) notion of culturally responsive teaching, has given rise to cultural-like perspectives for learning. The notion of *social curriculum* aligns closely with the notion of *culturally responsive education.*

By using culturally responsive education as a framework for this book, we challenge the assumptions which underlie traditional classroom management. These assumptions include: the teacher is the sole authority in the classroom; the curriculum is linear and hierarchical; the curriculum is predetermined; information to be learned is transmitted from knowing teacher to unknowing student; and classroom instruction is embedded in a behavioral-like context. These assumptions are collectively misaligned with many goals of current school reform (see McCaslin & Good, 1992; Quartz, 1995). Such goals call for classroom instruction which helps students become self-regulated and risk-taking learners and thinkers. Students who become self-regulated and risk-taking learners have minds that function differently in society than others who have been taught to be obedient and compliant learners and thinkers (Powell & Skoog, 1995). In order to fully understand the social curriculum of any school context, and in order to understand why teachers and students interact in certain ways in a specific school or classroom situation, you therefore must look first at the kind of *mind* that the school is trying to create for each of its students. Developing a student's mind, of course, is central to any educational endeavor. How the mind is developed reflects the nature of a set of learning experiences, and reflects the nature of the interactions that teachers have with their students during learning experiences.

Although *mind* is something that schools try to develop for students, not just any mind will do. Rather, a specific kind of mind is usually sought—the kind that will serve society well and in somewhat of an obedient way. When you view schooling as a place to develop minds in a certain way, for example, in an obedient and compliant way, or in a critical, questioning, and risk-taking way, then school curricula and corresponding management practices become political contexts, and the shaping of minds with school curricula becomes as much political work as educational work.

One means for understanding how *traditional classroom management*, and how *culturally responsive education*, work in a particular school is to study, explore, and observe the experiences of students and teachers at schools as they live out their educational experiences together in the presence of prescribed knowledge and skills. The means by which knowledge and skills become translated into *mind*— that is, the means by which schools cause students to become specific types of *thinkers* and *doers*—is the overarching framework for all social curricula. Understanding how teachers and students are expected to live their school lives in predictable ways, therefore, depends first on understanding the nature of the curriculum and corresponding instruction.

The primary purpose of part III is to help you better understand the relationship between a school's curriculum and instruction, and the kind of educative experiences it creates for and with students. Embedded within these experiences are such things as creating instruction, implementing instruction, interacting with students, translating curriculum into learning experiences, fostering certain academic behaviors in students, fostering certain social behaviors in students, and so on. Also embedded in these experiences are certain ways of thinking about teaching and learning—that is, certain metaphorical ways of thinking about how students acquire certain knowledge and skills and about how they develop a certain kind of *mind.*

To develop the chapters in part III we visited three schools across the country. We made extensive site visits to a traditional elementary school in California, a nontraditional middle school in Florida, and a traditional low socioeconomic high school in Texas. Each of the schools represented a different cultural context for learning, each represented a unique social curriculum, and each had a unique way of organizing and implementing instruction. We explored these schools' curricula and instruction, and how teachers in the schools interacted with students. We also looked very closely at what kinds of skills and knowledge the schools wanted their students to develop, and at the nature of the social and academic interactions that were put into place at the schools to help students acquire certain skills and knowledge and, consequently, a certain kind of mind.

After you read about the schools and teachers in part III, you should be able to answer these questions:

- What is the relationship between the educational goals that a school has for its students and the type of social and academic interactions teachers in the school have with students?
- How do schools that vary significantly in the skills and knowledge that they impart to students differ in the way they create, implement, and maintain classroom instruction?
- How do schools that vary significantly in the skills and knowledge that they impart to students differ in the way they establish and maintain relationships between teachers and students and among students?

- What managerial roles do teachers who work in nontraditional curriculum frameworks view themselves as filling?
- What managerial roles do teachers who work in traditional curriculum frameworks view themselves as filling?
- What is the relationship between a student's *mind* and the kind of classroom management that a school strives to maintain?
- What is the relationship between a school's social curriculum and the teacher metaphors of manager, mediator, guide, and facilitator?
- How would you interact and interrelate with students in each of the school contexts described in part III?
- How would you solve conflicts that arise in each of the school contexts described in part III?
- What would you foresee as a problem in each of the schools?
- How would you foster cooperation among students, and between you and the students, in each of the school contexts described in part III?

REFERENCES

Bruner, J. (1996). *The culture of education.* Cambridge, MA: Harvard University Press.

Gay, G. (1988). Designing relevant curricula for diverse learners. *Education and Urban Society, 20*(4), 327–340.

Jones, V. (1995, April). *Classroom management: An expanded role for teachers.* Paper presented at the annual meeting of the American Educational Research Association, San Francisco.

Ladson-Billings, G. (1995). Toward a theory of culturally relevant pedagogy. *American Educational Research Journal, 32*(3), 465–491.

McCaslin, M., & Good, T. (1992). Compliant cognition: The misalliance of management and instructional goals in current school reform. *Educational Researcher, 21*(3), 4–17.

Powell, R., & Skoog, G. (1995). Students' perspectives on integrative curricula: The case of Brown Barge Middle School. *Research in Middle Level Education Quarterly, 19*(1), 85–114.

Quartz, K. (1995). Sustaining new educational communities: Toward a new culture of school reform. In J. Oakes & K. Quartz (Eds.), *Creating New Educational Communities* (pp. 240–252). Chicago: University of Chicago Press.

Wolf, C. (1984). *Cassandra: A novel and four essays.* New York: Farrar, Straus, Giroux.

8

Coping With Change in John Tynes Elementary School

by Tom Savage

The only way to help students become ethical people, as opposed to people who merely do what they are told, is to have them construct moral meaning. It is to help them figure out—for themselves and with each other—how one ought to act.

(Kohn, 1996, p. 67)

The overall purpose of this chapter is to describe how an elementary school developed a social curriculum that was intended to help its culturally diverse students "figure out for themselves," as noted by Kohn (1996) above, how to act toward school, toward learning, and toward each other. Consistent with this purpose are the following goals:

- Introduce you to a contemporary, real-world example of one school's social curriculum—namely John Tynes Elementary School (JTES)—and corresponding management practices at the school
- Introduce you to the reality of student diversity at JTES and to the educational challenges that this diversity created for the school
- Describe a school context where social class, as well as ethnicity and nationality, impact how teachers interact with students and how students relate to each other
- Engage you in reflective thinking about how you, as a prospective teacher, might be suited to teach in a school such as JTES, and suited to interacting with students in such a way that your classroom social curriculum is sensitive to the backgrounds of all students

To achieve these goals, we first offer a more general discussion of change in schools as this change relates to various kinds of student diversity. Second, we provide a detailed case report of John Tynes Elementary School. This report serves to provide a context for better understanding of how changes in diversity are bringing about new challenges for teachers. We then relate the discussion of JTES to the idea of school and classroom management and to the ideas of teacher as guide, negotiator, and facilitator.

COPING WITH CHANGE

In recent decades there has been a profound change in the composition of the student population in the schools of our nation, as described elsewhere in this book. This has been a shift from a largely white population of students to one that is predominantly nonwhite. For example, just between the two decades of 1980 to the year 2000 the nonwhite student population will increase from 25% to 42% (Gonzalez, 1990). These individuals are culturally, linguistically, and racially very different from many of the teachers who will be teaching them.

However, there has been another population shift taking place. Not long ago, much of the diversity that existed in school was found in urban schools. Now schools in every part of the nation, including rural and suburban schools, have faced an increasingly diverse student population. As this chapter and the two chapters that follow reveal, teachers preparing to teach in the schools of our nation must be prepared to teach students who are very different from themselves. This change requires that all of us rethink our assumptions and our educational practices. We need to find ways of not only accommodating this diversity but for finding ways of using it to build even better schools.

This increased diversity creates a number of challenges for a number of different constituencies. Policymakers and state agencies, local school boards, parents, administrators, and teachers all have issues that must be faced and decisions to be made in response to these challenges.

The response to these challenges has been varied. In some instances, the response has been a declaration of an educational crisis with solutions found in a return to school practices of the past. Under the label of *educational reform* some individuals advocate more standardization by emphasizing a common curriculum based on Western civilization, more standardized testing in order to guarantee that all students have learned this body of knowledge, an emphasis on "power" methods to control student behavior and make sure they learn, and increased teacher accountability for student achievement. Proponents for this kind of school reform include, for example, Allan Bloom, E. D. Hirsch, Jr., William Bennett, Diane Ravitch, and Lynne Cheney.

Others, however, have had a different response. They see the changes in the school populations as a challenge, not a crisis. They believe that educational reform requires an acceptance of the fact of diversity and a search for new ways of meeting the needs of this more diverse population. They reject the notion that the traditional practices were the best for all students, and they question the idea that merely emulating the past is an adequate solution. Proponents of this kind of school reform include, for example, David Berliner, James Banks, Stephen Arons, and James Moffett, among various others.

This chapter is about an elementary school that has faced such challenges, and how they have sought to respond to the challenges posed by an increasingly diverse student population. John Tynes Elementary School is a rather conventional school in a suburban community in southern California. JTES has faced the issue of change in a community context that is relatively conservative and in a school district that is very sensitive to student achievement test scores.

THE CHALLENGE

Few regions have experienced a more dramatic change in population than southern California. Many sections of this region have undergone dramatic population shifts. Over the past few years there has been not only an increase in the student population in the schools, but also a shift in the population of people within the region. These changes are related to a number of factors. The region has long been the recipient of migration from other parts of the nation. However, the most significant change in recent years has been the immigration of people to the region from around the world. Southern California's location on the Pacific Rim has made it an accessible entry point for many southeast Asians who have been displaced because of the political turmoil in their native lands. Pacific Islanders have sought employment and economic opportunity in the United States. Proximity to Mexico and the third world countries of Latin and South America has resulted in growth from these parts of the Western Hemisphere. The result has been the creation of a region with tremendous diversity. The diversity of the population continues to expand. For example, I recently heard a principal of one of the schools where I have been working say that one of her most immediate challenges has been communicating with a large number of Romanian immigrants who have recently settled in the school attendance area.

Consistent with previous settlement patterns, many of the new immigrants have settled in the older housing areas. This in turn created a demand for housing that has fueled large-scale housing development. Areas that were once orange groves have been converted into suburban housing tracts. Mostly dry hillsides are now covered with homes. Residential areas that a few years ago had been predominantly white, middle-class, have now changed and are the places of residence for a very diverse population.

Certainly a formidable task related to the growth of diversity has been that of changing the schools to meet the educational needs of this population. In many communities this change has led to serious political and social unrest. Schools are often caught in the middle. On the one hand they often face tremendous pressures from some segments of the community to retain the familiar pattern of education that served the earlier generation; while on the other hand, the reality of a changed student population confronts them daily.

Teachers and schools have varied tremendously in their adaptation to these changing demographic realities. Some have been successful in meeting these challenges, others have not. This chapter is the story of one school that has faced rapid change in the composition of their student body and how they have dealt with the challenges for school management that this has created.

THE CONTEXT OF JOHN TYNES ELEMENTARY SCHOOL

John Tynes Elementary School is part of the Placentia-Yorba Linda School District located in the communities of Placentia and Yorba Linda in Orange County, California. The community is just a few short miles from the well-known tourist attraction, Disneyland. The region has some historical significance as the birthplace and original home of President Richard Nixon. The Nixon Library is located in the school district and is just a couple of miles from the school.

The region still maintains a strongly conservative, Republican image. As late as the early 1960s the area was predominantly orange groves. In fact, when Walt Disney built Disneyland in nearby Anaheim in the mid 1950s, many thought he was foolish for building so far out in the orange groves. At about the same time a branch of the California State University System was established nearby on the boundary between Placentia and Fullerton, about 2 miles from Tynes Elementary School. Original pictures of the new campus show a couple of buildings engulfed by a forest of orange trees.

In the early 1960s industry started moving into the region from the more urbanized Los Angeles area. New freeways increased accessibility and the undeveloped land was a prime target for builders and speculators. Aerospace industries built some large plants in the Placentia and Fullerton areas. Although the large orange groves are gone, traces of them can still be found. Across the street from the playground at Tynes, the remnants of an orange grove are being replaced by some new homes. A few trees have been left to mask some oil wells pumping along the fairways of a nearby golf course. Backyards of many of the homes still contain orange trees.

Some of the aerospace industries in the area have now been closed. However, a substantial mixture of industry exists within the boundary of the school district. Continued growth of the community is evident. In addition to the new homes being constructed across the street from the school, other housing developments and a new strip shopping center have been built less than a mile from the school.

The Placentia-Yorba Linda area is typical of much of Orange County, thus containing relatively new homes, businesses, and shopping centers. The community has the appearance and feel of a relatively affluent suburban community; most of the housing is in the upper-middle-class price range and above. Some of the newer areas contain what would be considered luxury homes. The streets are wide, clean, and tree lined. There is little evidence of graffiti on buildings or signs. Some parts of the community contain lots that are large enough to permit horses. Consequently, bridle paths wander through sections of the community.

The Placentia-Yorba Linda School District has 19 elementary schools. Several new schools have been built in the past few years on the east end of the district as new housing has emerged on the hills of the Santa Ana Canyon. These schools are attractive, with state-of-the-art technology. The schools are sprawling, one-story buildings with ample playground space and attractive landscaping.

The area immediately surrounding JTES has not only new, relatively expensive housing but also older homes that have been built within the past 20 to 30 years. A block away from the school is a private country club and golf course. A couple of blocks away in the opposite direction of the country club are apartment buildings. The impression that you get when driving through the school's community is that the student population of JTES is predominantly white, upper-middle-class children who are economically advantaged. That conclusion, however, is wrong.

The student population of Tynes Elementary School is 68% Hispanic and 28% Anglo. Nearly 50% of the students in the school are either non-English or limited English speaking. The school has grown rapidly over the past decade from a population of about 490 students to a population of 850 regular students and 50 special education students. JTES is a special education center and students with a variety of challenging conditions are bussed to the school. Interestingly, only about 25% of the students who attend the school reside in the community surrounding the school. Nearly 75% of the students are bussed to the school, some from as far away as seven miles. Not surprising, then, is the fact that JTES is one of five schools in the district impacted with large numbers of limited–English-speaking students.

About a mile from the school is the old central core area of Placentia. This area is a transition zone that includes smaller, older homes and apartments that have become low-income housing. This region stretches several miles to the west. These are homes that were once the inexpensive housing for the workers who migrated to the area to work in new industries in the 1960s. The families of this initial wave of growth have grown and many of the people have moved away. Subsidized housing in this region has attracted a large number of low-income families. Many of these families are immigrants and a large percentage of them speak Spanish as their primary language. These immigrants have led to a significant increase in population density. The result has been that the district has experienced significant population growth from two sources, the large homes of the affluent community in the hills to the east and the increased population density in the older parts of the community to the west. The schools in the west end of the district have reached an exceeded capacity, and there is no space left for building new schools. Therefore, students have been bussed past crowded schools in their neighborhood to other schools such as JTES.

The bussing predictably has met with some resistance throughout the school district. Parents at one school, faced with the prospect of having students from this region bussed to their school, agreed to do volunteer work at one of the impacted schools in order to prevent the bussing. Every week parents leave their neighborhood and do volunteer work at a school their children do not attend.

In attempting to meet the challenges posed by this changing population, Tynes Elementary School has also changed. There is a total staff of 27 teachers at Tynes. Eighteen of the teachers have some Spanish fluency and 12 are Spanish-English bilingual teachers. Eight of the teachers in the school are Hispanic. The age range for the teachers is from 23 to 63. The school has a full bilingual program of English and Spanish. English-speaking students are learning Spanish, and Spanish-speaking students are learning English. Spanish-speaking students begin in classrooms where they are taught in their primary language along with a structured transition program to English so that by the sixth grade they attain English fluency. A problem does occur, however, in meeting the needs of older students who move into the region who have not been in a transition program and therefore have limited English proficiency.

The school, like most other schools in the district, is a sprawling, single-story building with a large grassy playground. Some portable buildings have been added to accommodate the growth. The interior of the school was designed with movable walls. Thus, classroom space can be reconfigured easily to meet the needs and desires of teachers. This provides for a variety of small and large group learning spaces throughout the building. Some teachers do quite a lot of teaming and others are primarily self-contained.

The school principal during this time of change was energetic and professionally involved. She worked tirelessly in finding creative ways of meeting the needs created by the changes occurring in the school. She refused to accept the notion that the changing demographics meant that the quality of the school would decline. For example, she developed numerous linkages with the nearby university. As a result of her involvement, JTES became one of the first Professional Development Schools established in a cooperative relationship between the school district and the university. The school serves as a site for numerous observers and student teachers. The school has hosted meetings for other principals and teachers interested in the Professional Development School idea. The Professional Development School concept has evolved slowly in the school. Most of the focus has been on the preservice component with only small steps being taken in establishing the school as a center for continued professional development.

GETTING TO KNOW JOHN TYNES ELEMENTARY SCHOOL

Because of my (Savage) involvement with JTES, I have become very familiar with the school and its functions. In various ways I have been involved with JTES for over seven years. About one-third of the current teachers at Tynes are former university students of mine who have completed the Professional Development Program. Consequently, I have developed valuable rapport and trust with many JTES teachers. They continuously speak openly to me about their thoughts, ideas, and professional feelings for teaching at the school. In addition to the various forms of involvement that I have had with the school through the years, I conducted extensive informal interviews with several of the teachers and the principal specifically for this chapter. Those interviews were spaced over a period of several months and lasted an average of two hours. Individuals were asked to respond to the same basic set of questions. Those questions included:

- Tell me about the biggest challenges you face.
- What challenges are created by having a diverse student population?
- What do you see as the advantages of having a diverse student population?
- What have you altered in order to accommodate this diversity and achieve success?
- Have you changed the curriculum in order to accommodate a diverse student population?
- What do you see as your most serious problems?
- What type of management do you use?
- How do you deal with difficult students?
- What is your role as a teacher in decision making?
- How are parents and students involved in decision making?

Notes were taken on the interviews and an interview summary was written shortly after the conclusion of each interview. Additional visits were conducted to clarify any questions that arose as the interviews were reviewed and the chapter written.

MEETING THE CHALLENGES

Doubling of the school population within a decade is a significant challenge by itself. However, couple that growth with a change in the composition of the student population from one dominant culture to another and the challenge is an awesome one that could easily overwhelm a school. These changes created a number of issues at JTES that had to be addressed.

The parents who reside in the area immediately around the school had concerns as did the parents of those students who were bussed to the school. Teachers who had been at the school were faced with a new managerial challenge for which many did not feel prepared. The needs and the interests of the students had to be addressed and the issue of managing culturally responsive classrooms had to be resolved. The curriculum needed to be adapted in order to be responsive to the needs of the students. None of these issues could be ignored. Indeed, the issues needed immediate attention.

BUILDING COMMUNITY SUPPORT

To say that schools exist within community contexts is axiomatic. The attitudes, values, and beliefs of the surrounding community have a strong impact on the social curriculum of a school. The local community offers both opportunities and limitations to teachers and administrators as they develop and implement their program. The attitude of the local community will impact the attitudes of the students and their view of the role of the school. Similarly, the attitudes and beliefs of the local community have a profound impact on the attitudes and corresponding actions of the teachers. Teachers will be reluctant to make changes if they believe that they face resistance from members of the local community. The community can create support for the mission of the school or they can create an apathetic, nonsupportive, even adversarial context within which the school must operate.

The potential for a nonsupportive community—even for a hostile one—for JTES certainly exists. The school is located in a county that has a long legacy of conservatism. Not surprising, then, is the fact that the school district emphasizes traditional measures of academic achievement despite local cultural diversity that suggests other forms of achievement measures might be better suited to the school. Clearly, there is great potential for cultural conflict over the nature of achievement in place at the school.

As the school population began to change, the neighborhood surrounding the school became suspicious and fearful because the school did not reflect their ethnic and socioeconomic composition. One of the expressed fears of people living in the neighborhood was that there would be an increase in gangs. They worried about school-related issues such as violence, graffiti, and theft. Some community members believed that the quality of education provided at the school would decline as the addition of students from the low socioeconomic area would mean an influx of low-ability students that would hinder the possibilities of academic excellence.

These community concerns above were addressed by the principal very early in the school's transformation to a multicultural student body. Community meetings were held where the principal focused not on the challenges posed by the changes, but rather on the opportunities that would be provided by the increased diversity. She convinced community members that a wider range of programs could be implemented. These programs, according to the principal, would be to the advantage of *all* students who attended the school, not just those coming from the low socioeconomic neighborhoods. She argued that increased social, national, and linguistic diversity brought about a need for all students to be bilingual, thus providing JTES with an opportunity to have a bilingual program where all students could learn a second language. The principal was quick to note that a bilingual curriculum did not mean a "watered-down" curriculum.

The principal further argued that changes in student demographics would bring opportunities for additional funding. Such funding would help the school to add new programs that would benefit *all*, not just some of the students. For example, some additional funds could be used to lower class size in the primary grades. Lowering class size enhances the possibility for early diagnosis and intervention for any student experiencing academic or other difficulties in school. Other funds could allow for the development of after-school and enrichment programs. She emphasized that academic talent crossed cultural and socioeconomic boundaries, and there would still be many opportunities for gifted and talented students and in providing an environment where academic excellence was prized.

Another strategy that seemed to ease some of the fears of local community members was that the Drug Abuse Resistance Education (DARE) officer who conducts drug education programs throughout the school district was given an office at the school. The presence of this officer in the school has been viewed as a positive one for both the school and the community.

A number of opportunities were created for community members to give input into JTES affairs. School Site Councils, a Bilingual Advisory Board, as well as the traditional PTA were created to maximize opportunities for community input. Regular surveys of community members' attitudes were conducted. And recently a community conference was held about school issues. At this conference small groups of teachers, administrators, parents, and other community members discussed and evaluated how well the school was doing in meeting seven guiding principles established by the school district and in meeting the goals of the school. Areas of strength as well as areas of additional work were identified.

Indications are that these efforts have helped to create a positive community climate where the school is still highly respected. However, the principal worries that the unwillingness of other schools in the district to accept low SES and ethnically diverse students poses a threat to JTES. She would like to see a balance of about 50% of the students coming from the local neighborhood and about 50% bussed in. Her concern is that as the percentage of students being bussed to the school increases, the surrounding neighborhood will begin to lose its sense of identity and attachment to the school. This could lead to a loss of the community support that the school has enjoyed.

PARENTS OF JTES STUDENTS

Typical of most schools, parent involvement and support are viewed as a major concern by the administration and faculty at Tynes. Relationships with parents are cited as the major challenge by the teachers. There are a number of factors that appear to make this such a major concern. One factor is related to the location of the school relative to the homes of the students. The homes of the majority of the students are located at a considerable distance from the school. These are the homes of the lowest socioeconomic group, and public transportation is poor. Many of the parents simply have difficulty getting to the school.

Another factor is that well over one-third of the parents do not read or speak English. All notes, assignments, and communications sent home must be translated. Everything is done in both English and Spanish. The presence of families in the attendance areas with primary languages other than Spanish and English further complicates teacher-parent communication. This means that some tasks which teachers in other schools take for granted are difficult and time consuming. Notes home have to be translated, teachers can't simply call home and speak to a parent, and many parent conferences require a translator. Teachers report that parent-teacher communication is their biggest frustration.

The teachers state that basically the parents are very supportive of the school and want to help. However, language differences often limit their ability to do so. Many of the parents are struggling with problems related to survival and as some teachers reported, parents are *"on the edge."*

JTES teachers indicated their concern over being sensitive to students' home and community environments. Some students come to school with very different ideas about what is appropriate behavior. One of the issues identified by teachers concerned the use of appropriate language. Some parents use language generally not seen as appropriate for school. Thus, some children use language that many consider to be inappropriate. This takes a concerted effort on the part of the teachers to not overreact and to teach students what is considered appropriate and inappropriate in the school setting.

Another area where the teachers report a need to be sensitive is in making assumptions about what students can bring from home. For example, in the primary grades teachers need to be careful about the *sharing time* activity since differences between students' SES backgrounds can be extensive. Many of the children do not have much to bring to school for sharing time whereas others have an abundance. On field trips, teachers cannot assume that all students will be able to bring a sack lunch from home. Donations from home for extra events are not possible. Any extra funds needed must be raised in ways other than by asking parents. The unequal distribution of resources in the homes must be taken into account when giving homework assignments. Some homes have an abundance of materials and resources and others have almost nothing.

Teachers have attempted to address the inequalities of their students in several ways. One teacher has taken her class to the public library and helped all the class members get library cards so that they obtain support materials. Other teachers send material home with students. This creates additional burdens of making sure that everyone gets the needed material and keeping records to make sure that material is returned. Homework projects need to be assigned carefully so that success is not determined by the socioeconomic status of the home.

Teachers indicate that cultural differences in terms of ownership of property also create potential problems. Some students have a more communal view of property ownership and therefore do not see using materials owned by someone else as a problem. However, other students get upset when someone uses their property without permission. The potential conflict that this can create needs to be dealt with very early in the school year so that everyone understands what is appropriate behavior.

The administration attempted to address the problems of diversity in the parent population by creating a Bilingual Advisory Board designed to provide an avenue of involvement for non–English-speaking parents. This board meets on a regular basis and frequently has as many as 80 parents in attendance.

Although the advisory board has had a positive impact, there is a negative dimension. English-speaking parents generally attend the regular PTA and non–English-speaking parents attend the Bilingual Advisory Board meetings. This fragmentation serves to reduce the contact between the two groups of parents.

Parents have expressed a desire to be involved and kept informed. For example, parents have indicated that they are concerned about problems at two places, bus stops and in the rest rooms. Rest rooms were identified as an area of concern because the structure of school makes it possible for individuals from the outside to enter some of the rest rooms unobserved. Parents believe that the times when the students are waiting for the bus is the time when many of the problems occur.

Parent volunteers are involved in the daily operation of the school by being present on a daily basis to help in the classrooms. Parents are also included as tutors for some of the students who need extra assistance. When problems occur in the school, groups of parents are brought into the school to help solve the problems. These efforts have been successful in increasing parental involvement and in building community support for the school.

Teachers indicate that their concern about parental involvement and support has little to do with cultural diversity. They see the problem as increased parent apathy and lack of parental support that cuts across ethnic and socioeconomic groups. The frustration that parents do not support efforts of the teachers was voiced by one teacher who stated that "regardless of what you have done at school, the kids still go home to parents who just don't seem to care."

THE TEACHERS

Teachers are obviously a critical element in the success of any school program, especially that part of the program that relates to management. One of the first issues addressed by the principal was that of positive teacher attitudes. The principal believed that in order to develop a school where success for both teachers and students was possible, she first had to cultivate teachers with positive attitudes toward teaching such a diverse student population. The principal insisted that all teachers communicate a respect for all the children and all the parents. She believed that the teachers must avoid the perspective that "our students are so economically and academically low."

The need to deal with teachers' attitudes was facilitated by the presence of a variety of schools within the school district. The presence of new, attractive schools in affluent areas on the east end of the school district—the same schools which contained mostly middle- and upper-middle-class Anglo students—provided alternative placements for those teachers who had a negative attitude toward teaching diverse students. The principal assisted these teachers in moving to another school.

New teachers were then chosen for their positive attitudes and their willingness to work hard to keep the focus on positive attributes. The goal of the principal was to create a warm, positive, and supportive professional environment so that teachers would want to be a member of the faculty. One result of the principal's efforts is that teachers uniformly are proud of the school and most indicate they are not interested in transferring to other schools.

One important dimension of building this positive professional culture was the sharing of power. A great deal of power usually held and maintained by the administration is shared with the teachers at JTES. The teachers are involved in the selection of new faculty for the school, all teachers in the building are involved in staff development activities, and many of the staff development programs are conducted by the teachers. In addition, teachers have considerable freedom in the classroom in teaching and in establishing their own classroom management approach. The teachers generally view the principal and vice principal as supportive of them.

The teachers were challenged to consider how the curriculum and the methods of instruction needed to be altered in order to help the students achieve success. One way that the effort to consider new approaches was facilitated was by giving groups of four to five teachers some released time to visit other innovative schools in the region. These groups then return to share their observations with the rest of the faculty and to conduct staff development workshops where they adapt what they have learned to the unique requirements of the school.

Another staff development activity that was included to help the teacher understand the issues related to diversity was a staff development workshop conducted by the Anti-Defamation League. The workshop was designed to help the staff develop a sensitivity for what it feels like to be on the outside. Other staff development workshops have focused on conflict resolution and on building community.

Building a sense of community and facilitating cooperation between teachers is an important component of the school climate. The physical structure of the school building facilitates that effort. Most of the interior walls of the school are movable and can be moved to create different types of learning spaces. If desired, space can be arranged to make it easy for teachers to work together and to team-teach students. One teacher stated that she thought one of the most important features of the school was the establishment of relationships between teachers, so that challenges and concerns could be shared.

Teaching in a school like Tynes is not easy. There is a lot demanded of the teachers and they have high expectations for themselves and for the school. Both teachers and administrators indicated that the heavy involvement of teachers creates a great deal of stress, and many feel "burned-out" by the end of the academic year.

Although a number of outstanding teachers teach at JTES, there is one factor that could limit their success in meeting the needs of the students. This factor—one that is discussed again in chapter 10, is the apparent differences between the social and cultural backgrounds of the teachers and the students they teach. Many teachers at JTES come from totally different social class and cultural backgrounds than the students. When interviewing the teachers regarding what they viewed as problems, several of them mentioned that they thought most of the problems had their origins in social class differences. They perceived that the parents of the low SES students were less concerned and supportive of the school. They also mentioned issues such as ownership of property and appropriate use of language. These teachers' perceptions, however, were likely to be misconceptions. Although teachers perceived parents this way, they had no concrete evidence that parent apathy was indeed a reality.

THE CURRICULUM

There are several ways that the curriculum has been changed at Tynes in order to accommodate the needs of diverse learners who attend the school. These changes have been done within the context of a rather traditional elementary curriculum where there are state frameworks to follow and traditional expectations of a school board to meet. These changes, however, communicate important messages to the parents and students regarding the importance the school places on accepting and accommodating diversity and on maintaining high standards. These messages form an important component of the social curriculum of the school and the kind of management that takes place.

As the school attempted to develop a culturally appropriate curriculum, the faculty believed that there was simply too much content to be appropriately and adequately taught. One way to solve that problem was by choosing some basic themes that would guide both the academic and social curriculum decisions. The themes they chose were *problem solving* and *critical thinking*. A third theme that influenced instructional decision making focused on *individual differences*. The faculty also decided to place strong emphasis on providing success for all students and on teaching students to exercise self-responsibility.

The aforementioned basic themes and perspectives are applied to the curriculum of the school in several ways. One way is to build upon a framework of fine arts. Teachers felt that the fine arts provided a vehicle for including cultural perspectives and for maximizing student success while increasing student responsibility and problem solving. Every afternoon the entire school in some way focuses on the fine arts. English-speaking and non–English-speaking students are grouped together. Some instruction is provided in both English and Spanish, and students are teamed together so that they can provide each other with language support. The curricular topics include lots of cultural expressions of artistic work such as ethnic dancing and Folklorica. These topics allow students to develop a sense of pride in their own culture as well as respect and appreciation for cultures other than their own.

The nature of fine arts is seen as one that facilitates an interaction between students and between teacher and students in spite of primary language differences.

There are many concrete ways that students can communicate while working on a project together. While doing so, each student is gaining practice in learning to use a second language.

Fine arts is also an area where success can be provided for a wide range of students. The threats normally associated with content areas such as reading or math are simply not present. Effort and creativity can be reinforced and rewarded regardless of ethnic or socioeconomic background. Teachers believe that the success provided in this area of the curriculum has a positive impact on the attitude and the motivation of the students toward school and, therefore, influences achievement in other areas of the curriculum.

Self-Responsibility

There are some additional ways that the school provides students with opportunities to develop self-responsibility. One example is in the planning and presentation of a talent show. One month each year is devoted to planning this show. The students have the major responsibility for planning and performing in the show. Not only does planning the show require students to interact and solve problems together, it also impacts how students respond to the diversity that exists within the school. Because of the success of the talent show, the students have developed a sense of pride in the school. The show is also important in demonstrating to the parents one of the basic points the principal made: giftedness crosses cultural and socioeconomic boundaries.

Another example of how focusing on self-responsibility has been implemented is the self-esteem project. This project emphasizes teaching students coping skills so that they can accept responsibility for dealing with problems and issues that they might confront. Tied to this was some in-service conducted for teachers to help them implement conflict resolution approaches with the students. Peer mediation was also included as an element of this program. However, some teachers reported that the peer mediation component was de-emphasized because the students were reluctant to serve as peer mediators. They felt that this role was uncomfortable for them and they believed that it interfered with the establishment of friendships with other students.

Many teachers at the school note that one of their primary goals is to build a sense of solidarity and community in their classrooms. They state that they want the students to have a sense of belonging so that they "feel like a family." One way that some teachers attempt to build this sense of community as well as emphasize self-responsibility is through the use of classroom meetings. During classroom meetings problems and issues are brought up and students are encouraged to share their feelings and to provide suggestions on how problems might be solved.

Emphasis on Success

In addition to building positive attitudes of teachers in order to promote success, numerous programs have been put into place to facilitate student success. In the primary grades, class size was reduced and some fully certified teachers were hired and used as tutors. A phonics-based small-group, pull-out program called "Project Read" has been implemented for those having reading difficulty. Throughout the curriculum, a total physical response, sheltered English approach is used to assist limited English-speaking students achieve success. There are lots of hands-on materials used by teachers and students alike. There is also a home-school library where students may check out material to take home. This material is accompanied by activities developed to help the students use the material that is checked out.

A number of after-school programs have been developed to help students achieve success in both the academic and social curriculum. After-school reading tutorial programs were established for grades four, five, and six. The fifth-grade teachers established a Celebrate Success program for those students who were having some academic difficulty and who wanted help. Students who wanted to be a part of the program had to make an application and be accepted. The program has become very popular. In the sixth grade, a homework club was established where each teacher works with six students who are having difficulty. An approach similar to reading recovery is used to improve their reading skills. Parents must sign a contract guaranteeing that the student will attend. If a student misses two times, he or she is removed from the club.

Two problems had to be resolved in order to conduct such an extensive after-school program. These problems were those of funding the programs and of providing transportation for the students. The first was resolved through the use of Title I funds to pay for the additional costs of the programs. The transportation problem was an important one because many students participating in the program lived a considerable distance from the school. The school district assisted in the solution by scheduling a late bus for those students who are involved in these activities.

Because the principal of the school has tried to avoid the perception that a diverse population requires "redemption," enrichment programs were viewed as being essential. In order to do this a Junior Great Books pull-out program has been developed and an accelerated literacy program implemented.

Some teachers feel that the emphasis has led to an important issue that needs to be addressed. This is the issue of assessment. There seem to be a couple of sub-issues involved. One of those issues deals with the assessment of students who are making the transition from their primary language to English. During this transition period many of them are not yet ready for assessments in English. Assessing these students in English will not give them an indication of the level of success they have achieved. However, accommodating these students in classrooms where English is the main language adds yet another responsibility for the teachers. Many of them attempt to give oral assessments. However, this takes additional time.

Another concern is that assessment is inconsistent across the classrooms in the school. Therefore, a student may develop a set of expectations that creates problems when the student moves to another classroom where the assessment is more rigorous and the student has more difficulty. Some teachers worry that parents may not be getting the message that their youngsters need additional assistance in order to continue achieving success. Teachers, like those in many schools, debate the issues of promotion and retention. Are they promoting students who are not ready to move on? Several teachers indicate assessment is one issue that needs schoolwide attention.

Diversity

The diversity theme is an appropriate one for the school because of a couple of factors. Not only are there students from diverse cultural and ethnic backgrounds in the school, but the school also houses a number of students with special physical challenges. The diversity theme is implemented throughout the school in several different ways.

One of the major events of the year is when the school celebrates cultural diversity. Each year the school holds an international carnival. This carnival brings students and parents together to create displays and booths that focus on their cultural identity and pride. This carnival not only helps individuals to develop a sense of pride in their identity and helps older generations to pass on traditions of their culture, it helps the students, the parents, and the teachers to develop an appreciation for the multicultural nature of the school. Therefore, the idea that diversity is an opportunity rather than a problem takes on a visible form.

In addition to focusing on the cultural diversity, special programs are implemented that help the school population understand and develop a sensitivity to those individuals who have special physical challenges. It is clear that the faculty and staff have looked at students as an opportunity to build a strong curriculum. They have avoided the sense of negativism that is often found in schools that have student populations similar to that of Tynes. Although most of the teachers indicate that working in JTES is demanding and they often feel "burned-out" by the end of the school year, few would choose to teach anywhere else.

THE SOCIAL CURRICULUM: RETHINKING MANAGEMENT

Traditional power-based management approaches would have been an accepted response to management issues at Tynes. There would have been considerable support for this from the local community. The principal indicated that when the population of the school first started to change the parents voiced concerns about security and gangs. It is clear that the community had stereotyped images of students who were moving into the school. It is easy to allow these stereotypes, and other misconceptions, to color our perceptions and influence our actions. This coloring could have occurred at JTES.

That discipline was a major concern of the local community was clear. A nononsense, get tough, authority-based approach to discipline was a choice that many would have viewed by the local community as the logical approach to their stereotypical concerns. The principal believed that a strong discipline program was needed in order to address the concerns of the community and to maintain their support. However, a distinction was made between a strong discipline program and a power-driven or harsh one. She believed that a strong program could still be collaborative, fair, and positive. In other words, a program based on principal and teacher power was not viewed as one being needed at the school. If JTES was to develop the basic themes of *problem solving* and *critical thinking*, emphasize *diversity* and *inclusion*, and create a *positive climate*, then the management dimension of the social curriculum had to be consistent with these basic themes. The management program needed to be formed around concepts of communication and fairness. The emphasis needed to be placed on helping students exercise self-responsibility and learn how to achieve success.

Communication and firmness are implemented early in the school year at JTES. The principal and the vice principal visit every classroom at the beginning of the year and inform the students of the district and school policies regarding zero tolerance of weapons and drugs. They then discuss various forms of harassment and intimidation, including nonverbal signals as well as verbal and physical intimidation. They provide them with concrete examples. They inform the students that harassment and intimidation are not acceptable in the school. This is followed with letters home in both English and Spanish that inform the parents of school policies and places special emphasis on the issues of harassment and intimidation.

Collaboration and inclusion was included at the very beginning by charging the Bilingual Advisory Board with some responsibility to propose management procedures that would be fair to all students in the school. These proposals were used to help construct a management plan that reflected the basic themes of the school. Moreover, the plan provides concrete examples of the metaphors of *management, guidance,* and *mediation* that we have discussed in earlier chapters.

A basic theme of the school—teaching self-responsibility—is consistent with the metaphor of management, as we have described it in this book. Self-responsibility, we argue, should entail the sharing of power and the fostering of cooperation. One example of this idea in practice is the inclusion of the parents and the Bilingual Advisory Board in decisions about school and the management plan. There are other examples of this idea in practice.

Classroom meetings are used by several of the teachers in the school. Recurring problems or concerns that affect the entire class become topics of discussion at classroom meetings where student opinions and recommendations are solicited. The students are then given an opportunity to be involved in problem solving and to share power with the teacher.

The whole climate of the school reflects the management metaphor we have described. The cooperative climate established between administrators and teachers and among teachers models the cooperation for the students and strives to eliminate feelings of alienation.

The guidance metaphor is also visible in the way that behavior management problems are handled in the school. When problems occur, students are provided with the responsibility to work out the problems. They are asked, "What did you do?" "What should you have done instead?" "What do you want the teacher to do?" Students are challenged to consider what they will do differently the next time. However, a clear message is communicated that individuals are not protected from the consequences of their behavior. A clear message given is that rules are for everyone and those who break the rules can be expected to experience the consequences of their actions. Consequences for inappropriate behavior include the use of time-out areas. Such areas, which are monitored by teachers, are located throughout the school. These are used during recess and lunch time when they are needed. In addition, tickets are given to students on the playground for inappropriate behavior. It is considered okay to occasionally get a ticket. However, four tickets during a month triggers an action. One such action might be referral to the *Kindness Club.*

The Kindness Club is an interesting example of the guidance and mediation metaphors in action. The club was originally established as a schoolwide response to persistent or serious discipline problems. It is an after-school program initially intended to be a punitive activity for those students who had serious behavior problems. However, one of the teachers assumed responsibility for it and has turned it into a positive experience. The analogy of the traffic school is one that was used in establishing the Kindness Club.

It is a class that lasts for four weeks. During the club students are taught topics such as anger control and conflict resolution skills. They are involved in participatory activities such as role playing. They openly discuss problems and alternative ways to deal with them. At the end of the month each child develops a plan for how they will avoid future difficulty. A "graduation" ceremony is held, where each student is given recognition and their growth is celebrated.

Prior to any student's "admission" to the Kindness Club, the student's parents and selected teachers meet to discuss targeted problems. The parents sign an agreement ensuring that the student will attend. The result has been that Kindness Club has become a very positive experience. The students enjoy their participation and want to attend, so attendance is not a problem. They are proud of their accomplishments in the club and thus most students leave it feeling positive about their experience and to feel positive about themselves.

Teachers are allowed to develop their individual classroom management plans. A part of the plan can include an office referral. When students are referred to the office the first step is for the students to sit down and write out their point of view in their own words. They then discuss this with the school administrator. In some instances the students may call their parents and tell them what has happened. If the violation is of a serious nature, the parents are asked to come to the school and pick up the student.

Examples of the mediation metaphor are also abundant in the school. These include teaching students how to send "I" messages in order to learn how to communicate their needs and concerns in a respectful and productive manner. Teacher workshops on conflict resolution have been conducted and the students have been taught conflict resolution and building a sense of community.

One example of how the management and mediation metaphors can be applied is one incident that arose when a couple of students moved into the school from another area where gangs and intimidation were the norm. These students were soon involved in a serious confrontation with other students in the school. The various students involved in the confrontation and their parents were called together for a meeting. A child welfare worker and a representative of the local police department were also included. Rather than a confrontational experience, the meeting became one where the parents and teachers were able to share concerns. Suggestions were provided on how to handle situations such as this. The parents were grateful and supportive and there have been no other "gang type" activities at the school.

In summary, the administration and faculty did not succumb to the notion that power and toughness were the appropriate guiding metaphors for management at JTES. They refused to accept the traditional stereotypes and fears of the local community. They believed that all students deserved respect and that themes applied to the academic curriculum should also be applied to the social curriculum. They allowed ideas of fairness, collaboration, diversity, mediation, dignity, and respect to guide the way they interacted with the students. The result is that discipline is not identified as one of the major concerns by the teachers. Teachers and students do not appear to be adversaries and the whole climate of the school is a positive one.

WHAT CAN WE LEARN?

While many important points can be extracted from the case of JTES, there are three particularly salient points that occurred to us as we considered the school's context. The first point that emerges out of the study of JTES is that meeting the challenges of a diverse school population requires teachers to have a positive attitude toward teaching and learning. These need to be teachers who respect students and who understand that academic talent and social responsibility are not limited to given cultural or socioeconomic groups. These same teachers also need to be willing to reflect on accepted practices and to challenge them when they are not appropriate for the students they are teaching. Teachers must have not only the courage but also the felt need to challenge stereotypes and prejudice.

The experiences at Tynes are consistent with those reported by Gillborn, Nixon, and Ruddock (1993). Gillborn et al. (1993) indicate that rethinking the management and discipline dimension requires the rethinking of a range of interrelated aspects of school life. Thus the social curriculum does not exist apart from the academic curriculum but is an integral part of the whole. The same principles that guide the academic curriculum need to be applied to the social curriculum.

Thousand and Villa (1995) further argue the importance of teachers in creating a vision. They define this as an active mental struggle to journey from the known to the unknown (p. 59). Beth Berndt, the principal at JTES, had a vision. Her vision was that of an inclusive school where all children and all parents were respected. It was one where the school was enriched by the diversity of the school population. We challenge you to consider your vision of teaching in a diverse school. Is it an accurate and realistic vision? Is it a limiting vision based on labels, stereotypes, and the teacher as boss? Or, is it an empowering vision based on ideas of equity, fairness, and teacher as leader? Is it a vision of teaching that includes all the children from all of the families or is it a vision that only includes some of the children from some of the families?

A second point that emerges from the JTES case report relates to the challenges posed by increased diversity. Such challenges must be viewed as opportunities rather than as constraints. JTES views diversity as something that creates positive opportunities for teaching and learning. In addition, the attitude was one of using these changes to improve the education of *all* the students. What is needed are teachers who do not view diversity as an educational deficit but, rather, as an opportunity to achieve important educational goals that are not possible in more homogeneous settings. Gillborn, Nixon and Ruddock (1993) reach a similar conclusion about the need for teachers to view diversity as an asset to teaching rather than as a deficit. Like JTES, Gillborn et al. (1993) found importance in demonstrating an understanding and respect for the community.

The third point that emerges from the case of JTES relates to power-based approaches to behavior management. The JTES context contradicts the often heard dictum that power-based approaches are necessary when working with a diverse population. Refining management to include input from students, allowing them some decision-making power, can be an effective strategy for engaging students more readily with the social curriculum. The students at Tynes respond positively to the focus on the development of self-responsibility and problem solving. In fact, the example of the "Kindness Club" indicates that students may actually welcome opportunities for them to learn alternative ways of dealing with their problems. Very often such problems are a matter of a student not knowing how to deal with anger, fear, and threat in a positive manner. When this perspective is understood, discipline is not seen as a set of punishments that are implemented to force compliance to the wishes of the teacher. Rather, it is seen as integral part of the total school experience of building a climate of trust and mutual respect that will help the students learn important skills and attitudes that are of prime importance.

EXERCISE 8.1   Creating a Positive Vision for Teaching in a Diverse Environment

We have attempted to provide a description of how a traditional elementary school in a conservative community has responded to the change from a relatively homogeneous to a diverse student population. We suggest that a critical element in constructing a positive approach to diversity is the vision that teachers have for teaching and management in diverse environments. In chapter 3 we pointed out the importance of your biography in constructing a vision of appropriate educational practice. Your past experiences have an important and notable influence on your vision and your theories of classroom life. We want you to begin to rethink your vision based on the information we have presented regarding Tynes Elementary School. Think about the following questions and write out your responses. Be honest with yourself as you respond to these questions, but also, be willing to challenge assumptions you make about teaching in a diverse classroom.

A. Your Attitude Toward Teaching in a Diverse Classroom

How would you feel about teaching a class of students similar to those found at Tynes?

- What would you expect to be the problems you would encounter?
- Do you think it would be rewarding? In what ways?
- How do you think it would be different from the images you have about the task of teaching?

On what basis have you formed your attitudes about teaching in a diverse classroom?

- To what extent has your personal biography influenced your attitudes?
- To what extent have your attitudes been shaped by what you have heard from others?
- How do you think your attitudes would influence your ability to achieve success in a diverse classroom?
- What actions can you take to develop an attitude that will facilitate your success?

B. Organizing the Academic and Social Curriculum

If you found yourself in a traditional elementary school with the traditional curriculum, what principles would you use in organizing the academic curriculum so that it would be appropriate for your students?

- What parts of the curriculum do you think would be the easiest to change?
- How would you develop the concepts of shared power and mutual respect through the academic curriculum?

How would you apply the basic principles you use in your academic curriculum to the social curriculum?

- What would your management plan include?
- How would you engage the parents in your plan?
- How would you involve the students in your plans?

C. Collaboration, Guidance, and Mediation in Your Classroom

Collaboration and community building throughout the school are characteristics of Tynes. How willing are you to share with other teachers?

- How willing are you to share your failures and concerns with another teacher?
- Are you threatened when someone else gives you advice on how to teach?

How willing are you to collaborate with parents?

- Meeting and conferencing with parents is a major concern of many teachers. What do you fear when working with parents?
- What are some things that you can do to build parental support for your program?

How would you collaborate and build a sense of community and solidarity within your classroom?

What are some specific actions you would take to implement the metaphor of lead manage-ment in your classroom?
How could the metaphor of guidance be applied?
What are your views of the metaphor of mediation?

- How is this idea different from traditional approaches to resolving conflict?
- How comfortable would you be in using mediation?
- What specific skills would you need to learn in order to apply mediation in your classroom?

D. Defining Your Vision

Now put your responses together. Do a little dreaming.

- What vision do you have of the types of classroom and environment that you would have in a diverse environment?
- What expectations would you have for the students?
- What expectations would you have for yourself?
- What would it take to make that vision a reality?

REFERENCES

Gillborn, D., Nixon, J., and Ruddock, J. (1993). *Dimensions of discipline: Rethinking practice in secondary schools.* London: HMSO, Department for Education.

Gonzalez, R. D. (1990). When minority becomes majority: The changing face of English classrooms. *English Journal, 79,* 16–23.

Kohn, A. (1996). *Beyond discipline: From compliance to community.* Alexandria, VA: Association for Supervision and Curriculum Development.

Thousand, J. S., and Villa, R. A. (1995). Managing complex change toward inclusive schooling. In R. A. Villa and J. S. Thousand, *Creating an inclusive school.* Alexandria, VA: Association for Supervision and Curriculum Development.

The Social Curriculum of Brown-Barge Middle School: A Case Report of Guidance and Mediation

by Richard Powell

The far reaching changes embedded in the new middle school movement, although requiring new techniques, cannot be met with traditional, prescriptive "how-to" approaches that attempt to replicate what model schools are like.

(Oakes, Quartz, Gong, Guiton, Lipton, 1993, p. 475)

Classroom management can and should do more than elicit predictable obedience; indeed, it can and should be one vehicle for the enhancement of student self-understanding, self-evaluation, and the internalization of self-control.

(McCaslin & Good, 1992, p. 8)

TOWARD STUDENT SELF-UNDERSTANDING

Think back on your years in school as an early adolescent. These were the years you spent in middle or junior high school. Did your middle school's social curriculum expect predictable obedience from you? Or did you have a social curriculum that didn't necessarily value predictable obedience? Just what kind of social curriculum do you think expects more, and then elicits more, than predictable obedience from students? What changes might traditional schools have to make in order to enhance self-understanding, self-evaluation, and internalization of self-control in students, as McCaslin and Good note above? These are complex questions—there are neither simple nor straightforward answers. The purpose of this chapter is to help you seek these answers.

TOWARD UNPREDICTABILITY IN STUDENT LEARNING

Our nation of schools has long held tightly to a system of classroom management that prizes predictability in student behavior and in external locus of control for fostering such predictability. Because of this tradition, moving toward an alternative system of management where unpredictability of learning is prized and where student learning is based on an internal locus of control—where students personally *want* to learn what is taught—is certainly a pressing challenge, if not a formidable one, for all schools today.

If what Jeanie Oakes and her colleagues claim in the opening quote of this chapter is valid (Oakes et al., 1993), then the kind of far-reaching management changes that schools are expected to make today, most especially changes at the middle level, simply might not be possible if we continue turning to standard, traditional, and prescriptive management models that tend to make all schools alike and most students think and act the same way. If there is anything that we as an educational community have learned over the past few decades from the ongoing debate over student diversity, it is the simple yet profoundly important fact that most students do not think alike, do not learn alike, and certainly do not act alike. So many factors—culture, ethnicity, socioeconomic status, family tradition, nationality, location, religion, ableness, and so on—collectively influence how students act and think. These factors also influence how you, as a classroom teacher, act and think about classroom teaching.

This chapter is about a unique middle school, Brown-Barge Middle School (BBMS), that created a theme-based forward-thinking social curriculum. The BBMS curriculum prizes, at least in part, unpredictability in student learning, fosters student self-understanding and self-evaluation, and affirms the many factors that influence how early adolescents act and think. In responding to the far-reaching changes that are now suggested for middle school curriculum and instruction across the country, BBMS turned away from traditional, prescriptive how-to approaches to school reform and turned toward alternative, integrative, and innovative approaches. Except for the presence of desks, chalk, and noisy hallways filled with early adolescents, BBMS shows little resemblance to most conventional schools that many of us attended at some point in our lives.

BBMS differs notably in its social curriculum from schools that are more conventional. Because of this difference, questions about classroom management quickly surface: How does the idea of management fit into the BBMS context, if at all? How do teachers interact with students in an integrative curriculum environment like BBMS so that student learning is less prescriptive and so that students *want* to be at school? Seeking answers to these questions, which this chapter tries to do, provides you with insight into an alternative and highly engaging social curriculum, and insight into management practices that are part of such a social curriculum. As you read about BBMS, do not think that the school's social curriculum is limited only to that campus. Schools elsewhere have created similar kinds of social curricula for emerging adolescents (Brazee & Capuletti, 1995; Powell, Skoog, & Troutman, 1996).

In the following discussion, I (Powell) first describe BBMS, in particular, its locality, its context, and its curriculum. Second, I provide a brief and very basic description of how we explored the school's context so that we could better understand the social curriculum as it is experienced each day by students and teachers and as it relates to the metaphors of manage, guide, and mediate. Third, I provide a more detailed overview of the school's integrative curriculum, which causes students and teachers at the school to alter their views of conventional schooling practices. The school's curriculum—a curriculum which has important and far-reaching implications for current school reform across the nation—and BBMS teachers' commitment to this curriculum were two significant reasons why we selected BBMS for this book. In this third section of the chapter, we consider the school's written curriculum, and we explore how this curriculum has caused BBMS teachers to use alternative management metaphors when they discuss their teaching. Next, I consider what the idea of management means to teachers at the school, and I see how the school deals with student behavior and discipline. In the final section of the chapter, I describe specific features of the BBMS curriculum that are intended to enhance students' self-understanding, self-evaluation, and the internalization of self-control (McCaslin & Good, 1992).

THE CONTEXT OF BROWN-BARGE MIDDLE SCHOOL

Locality

Brown-Barge Middle School (BBMS) is in Pensacola, Florida, a small city in Escambia County. The city of Pensacola has a city-limit population of 59,000 persons; the whole county, however, has 280,900 persons. Given the overall county population, Escambia County has a total student population of 44,000; approximately 63% of these are white, 32% are African American, and 5% are classified as other. The ethnicity of students in Escambia County is relatively stable, although new immigrants (Hispanic and Asian origin) are continuously moving to the area. Because BBMS is a magnet school for technology it draws students from the entire school district and from all socioeconomic classes.

School Context

I hardly noticed BBMS when I first drove into Pensacola on Interstate 110. The school building is an old somewhat inconspicuous structure just off the interstate. However, when I walked into the school building, the older appearance of the school fell away, and I experienced a reformed schooling context that will probably be unlike any other you've experienced either as a teacher or a student. After exploring the school's social curriculum, I believe that BBMS transcends traditional school contexts entirely; it is a completely engaging learning experience for *every student* who attends there, and for *every teacher* who teaches there.

There are two particularly striking features of BBMS that characterize its learning environment. The first feature is an integrative curriculum (see Beane, 1993). Teams of teachers work together to plan 12-week curriculum units around specific themes. Examples of these themes include environment, global awareness, art exploration, and historical motifs. Each theme is called a *stream,* and a group of students is assigned to one stream for each 12-week unit. More will be said about the formal curriculum of the school below. A second striking feature of BBMS is its multiplicity of technologies. BBMS received a federal grant over a two-year period to develop a magnet school for technology. In order to practice integrative curriculum innovations, BBMS also received a curriculum waiver from the Florida Department of Education. With this funding and with curricular leeway provided by the waiver, principal Camille Barr and a cadre of professional educators at BBMS developed an innovative school curriculum based on educational equity.

Each team of teachers at BBMS sets its own daily schedule for students, creates and selects instructional materials (traditional textbooks aren't part of the BBMS curriculum), and designs numerous field trips, major projects, and group work for the students. Unlike recent curricular reform efforts that have tried to toughen academic standards without addressing cultural conflicts within the classroom, the BBMS curriculum accomplishes this goal. The school changed the content and delivery of instruction while focusing extensively on the social relations between teachers and students. An overarching goal for BBMS was to create a learning environment where students and teachers work collaboratively to attain higher order thinking, then apply these skills to the students' personal lives outside the school.

Other qualities of BBMS that collectively characterize its uniqueness include a noncompetitive environment (e.g., no athletic teams or intramural activities; no traditional letter grades; no traditional yearbook), the removal of standardized test scores for ranking students, the use of alternative assessment strategies, and the use of theme-based issues for teaching content. The BBMS curriculum is also needs based. That is, the stream topics were selected after students and their parents indicated what their greatest needs were for learning.

GETTING TO KNOW BBMS

Over the past four years, I have completed various studies at BBMS. These studies focused on how the school's curriculum was structured (Powell, Zehm, & Garcia, 1996), how the school met the needs of a diverse student population (Powell, 1996), and how the school's culture influences BBMS students' perspectives of learning at the school (Powell & Skoog, 1995). These studies provided me with the background information I needed in order to decide that the BBMS social curriculum could shed important light on alternative management practices, especially practices that seemingly align with current calls for school reform (Quartz, 1996).

To explore the management practices of the school more specifically, I visited BBMS in order to conduct interviews with all teachers at the school.[1] Time constraints and schedule conflicts prevented me from interviewing every BBMS teacher, but I was able to interview 16 out of the 20 teachers at the school. I also interviewed the principal, the guidance counselor, and the director of the resource center. During these interviews, which lasted approximately 60 minutes each, I asked BBMS educators to describe their lives at the school and to talk specifically about their daily relationships with students. I also asked them to tell me about management practices at the school and to pick metaphors (among those we suggested to them) that best fit these practices. Specifically, I asked them to explain which metaphor best reflected their teaching: guide, mediator, or traditional manager. So that I could reflect more upon these interviews, I taped and transcribed what the teachers said.

In addition to these interviews, I reviewed the school's curriculum documents, I observed classroom instruction, and I interacted informally with students. In the brief time I had at the school, I wanted to get a sense of the school's social curriculum; the intense week-long immersion I had at the school helped me accomplish this goal.

---

[1]For a detailed account of this study, see Powell, Skoog, Troutman, and Jones (1996).

THE CURRICULUM

One way to understand the social curriculum of BBMS is to first consider the framework of its written curriculum. The curriculum of BBMS is called *integrative*, following the work of James Beane (1993). It is integrative because content to be learned is selected and integrated on the basis of relevancy to specific themes. The integrative curriculum of BBMS—the curriculum that is taught by teachers and that is negotiated by teachers and students—is the framework for almost every interaction between teachers and students and every interaction among students. The formal curriculum that is taught, therefore, is central to how the social curriculum is structured at the school and, hence, central to the kind of management that is in place at the school. In the discussion below I describe how students become acquainted with the BBMS curriculum when they first arrive at the school, and what they do to get ready to re-enter conventional schools when they have finished the curriculum. I then describe teacher and student roles that are associated with the integrative curriculum that has been implemented at the school. Interestingly, the roles that teachers and students fill at the school are embedded within a form of teaching that is called *stream teaching*. Consequently, I provide a brief overview of stream teaching.

Communities and Transition

The social curriculum at BBMS, including the formalized written curriculum, is so nontraditional in process and product that all students admitted to school must complete an entry-level 12-week course of instruction. This instruction is called the *Communities Stream*. In this stream BBMS students learn to work cooperatively in groups. Students also become accustomed to working productively without the pressures of competition found in traditional school settings, and they learn both computer and audio-visual technology skills that are necessary to successfully complete assignments and projects at the school. When students get ready to move from BBMS to one of the conventional high schools in the district, they complete yet another course of instruction, which is called the *Transition Stream*. In this stream, students become reacquainted with the norms of conventional schooling, such as working more individually, using textbooks, viewing teachers as content authorities rather than as colearners and attending classes that represent courses taught in a traditional curriculum (e.g., science, English, mathematics).

New Teacher Roles

The standard curriculum that most middle schools use[2] and the traditional school day[3] have been restructured entirely at BBMS, thus suggesting the need for new teacher roles. In place of these elements is a theme-based, fully integrated curriculum (Beane, 1993). Unlike more conventional school settings, teachers at BBMS

---

[2]This kind of curriculum is divided into discrete subjects such as science, math, English, and so on.
[3]The traditional high school, for example, is usually divided into specific periods of instruction, such as first period, second period, and so on.

never work alone; rather, they work together collaboratively and collegially in teams to prepare student activities and projects around carefully selected themes. Moreover, teachers at the school view themselves more as generalists than as subject matter specialists. As generalists, BBMS teachers and their students learn content together; they actively negotiate curriculum and instruction during their social interactions in group study. This makes BBMS teachers exemplary role models for learning and causes them to function primarily in nonauthoritarian roles as teachers. Both of these qualities—exemplary role models and nonauthoritarian roles—have a profound influence on the nature of the management that is in place at the school. More will be said about the nature of this management later in the chapter.

New Student Roles

To study and learn specific content that is related to each stream topic, BBMS students are organized into smaller communities of learners. Since each team of teachers has freedom to set and adjust its own daily schedules, students attend teachers' classes at various designated times. That is, there is no one set schedule that the whole school follows except when to arrive at school in the morning, when to go home in the afternoon, and when to have lunch.

Rather than working individually on projects and assignments, students almost continuously work in peer groups. They learn targeted content and skills from each other as well as from their teachers. Content that they are expected to learn is specifically tailored to the stream topic (see discussion below), and all students are expected to engage in original research on stream topics. Consequently, students work together in their peer groups on research projects for a portion of each school day. Students become colearners, facilitators for each other, proactive researchers, and critical thinkers. They are free to challenge teachers about the content that is taught as they engage in research that is personally meaningful.

Stream Teaching

The idea of *stream teaching* is unique to BBMS. It refers to the kind of teaching that is associated with 12-week units of instruction called *streams*. The streams that were taught at BBMS during the 1995–96 school year, including the stream topics, titles, and premises, are shown in Figure 9.1. After studying the stream topics in Figure 9.1, consider which stream (or streams) you are most prepared to manage. Perhaps you feel confident that you could manage at least one stream, perhaps *Bridges*, but what about two streams, or three streams? If you were teaching at BBMS, you would teach at least three different streams during a school year. Each trimester you would be part of a different stream and work with a different team of teachers. You also would teach a different team of students every 12 weeks. You should now be getting a better idea of what BBMS teachers mean when they call themselves *generalists* rather than *subject matter specialists* (e.g., history teacher, science teacher, and so on). You should also begin to better understand when you hear BBMS teachers say that one of the most important personal qualities a teacher must demonstrate at the school is flexibility.

Stream Topic	Stream Title	Premise
		First Trimester
Communities	One for all and all for one	Communities—plant, animal, and human, are connected and interdependent. A sense of community fosters cooperating, pride of place, identity and support.
American Tapestry	There are ties between us	The United States is a culturally diverse society. For people to succeed and prosper in harmonious surroundings, we must work toward understanding the common threads which unite us.
Your Greatest Performance	Your greatest performance	Through creative expression, individuals discover potential and develop confidence which results in respect for self and others.
Futures	We are the future	By observing how the past has influenced the present, students can look toward and impact their future with confidence.
		Second Trimester
How Things Work	How things work	Our everyday world involves many devices which we take for granted and greatly benefit from but which we may not understand.
Conflict Resolution	Conflict and compromise	Examination of the roots of conflict between individuals, groups of people, and nations is essential for students to understand the complexity of relationships, as well as strategies through which conflicts can be resolved.
Robotics	Robotics	Understanding the history, development, and fundamentals of robotic technology is essential to appreciating their role in the future.
Historical Motifs	Your most excellent adventure!	From earliest civilizations, recurring motifs have inspired great art. By making connections with the past we begin to understand the universality of creative expression.
Life Skills	Your life, your business	Being an intelligent consumer with a basic understanding of the business world, we become better prepared to deal with financial responsibilities.
		Third Trimester
Exploring Art	Art Exploration	Knowledge of art and an appreciation of art in its historical perspective are important components of a balanced education.
Flight	Flight	In pursuing his quest for flight, man expands his world and his intellectual abilities.
Global Awareness	We are the world	Due to modern technological advances, our world is becoming a smaller place; everyone will need the knowledge and skills necessary to communicate and cooperate in today's diversified, multi-lingual world.
Transition: Exit to High School	In the end . . . (and the beginning)	As students leave Brown-Barge, their successful transition to high school is dependent on an adequate knowledge of life management skills, academic skills, and an awareness of vocational direction.

FIGURE 9.1

Stream Topics, Titles, and Premises for the 1995–1996 Academic Year at Brown-Barge Middle School

Powell, R., Skoog, G., & Troutman, P. (1996). On streams and odysseys: Reflections on reform and research in middle level integrative learning environments. 19(4), 1–30.

Another interesting feature of stream teaching is that you don't necessarily teach in a conventional linear fashion where some information or content is taught before subsequent content is taught. At BBMS you teach that content which is most germane to the stream topic. Students might or might not have had the content before. Therefore, rather than teaching content out of context, you teach content in the context of the stream. Students then learn holistically; they directly relate content to the stream topic, and this is the manner in which they acquire the expected learnings.

As students learn specific content, they work collegially and collaboratively with peers. They share insights, hunches, and ideas with each other. They solve problems together, and they complete their research projects in small groups. This means that BBMS students construct personal knowledge of the content to be learned socially, which is called the *social construction of knowledge*.

THE SOCIAL CURRICULUM AT BROWN-BARGE MIDDLE SCHOOL (BBMS): RETHINKING MANAGEMENT

Because BBMS so closely resembles recent calls for school reform especially for early adolescents, we believe that the school needs to be more closely considered as a model for 21st century schools across the nation. Moving toward the BBMS model in a wholesale fashion means radical reform for most schools. In a nation that has traditionally demonstrated conservative politics for educational change (Apple, 1996), adopting radical reform in such a widespread manner would most likely cause much concern for many educators, policy makers, parents, and politicians, regardless of the inherent goodness of the reform for students and for society. Such conservative thinking and schooling, however, must in time give way to more innovative and culturally sensitive ways of meeting the needs of learners in today's pluralistic schools. As Apple (1996) argues, we must decide at some point to become "part of a conscious collective attempt to name the world differently, to positively refuse to accept dominant meanings, and to positively assert the possibility that it could be different" (p. 21). The curriculum and instruction at BBMS reflect Apple's argument.

Further reflecting Apple's argument, BBMS has created, implemented, and sustained a curriculum that clearly does more than elicit predictable responses from students (Oakes, et al., 1993; see Powell & Skoog, 1995). After we closely examined the inner workings of the school for this book, and after conducting studies on the BBMS campus over the past few years, we believe that BBMS educators are striving to help students learn the skills and knowledge needed for demonstrating self-understanding, self-evaluation, and internalization of self-control (McCaslin & Good, 1992). To achieve these goals, BBMS educators have had to rethink teaching and learning, rethink teacher roles, rethink student roles, and develop a kind of instruction called *stream teaching,* among other transformations noted above. These factors collectively point to yet another major transformation at the school—namely, *a transformation in management practices.* This is because BBMS educators have had to rethink the whole idea of traditional school management, which is based mostly on the idea that teachers, as subject matter experts and as enforcers of school rules and regulations, have sole authority in their classrooms and power over students.

Now that I have characterized the BBMS school context as one in the midst of real reform and one that has brought about significant changes in the way students learn and interact with each other at school, I shall now consider what teachers at the school think about their social curriculum. As I listened to the teachers and as we read the interview transcripts several weeks after we visited the school, I discovered some very interesting features of the social curriculum at BBMS. In the discussion below, I have organized these features into *themes.*

Before discussing these themes in more detail, I must first mention that I went to the BBMS campus without a preconceived set of ideas about what management was like at the school although I was already familiar with the structure of the curriculum and with students' perspectives of learning at the school (Powell & Skoog, 1995; Powell, Skoog, & Troutman, 1996). Realizing that the written curriculum of the school was radically different from more conventional schools, I assumed that I would discover a form of management that perhaps would vary in important ways from conventional management practices. This form of management was the focus for my visit and the focus of this chapter.

Before going to the school I developed a tentative set of rather loosely structured interview questions that I assumed would help me explore the curriculum structure of the school more closely, particularly as this structure related to issues of management and to the idea of social curriculum (see the appendix to this chapter). In a conversational format, I asked each teacher individually to respond to the interview questions in addition to answering other questions that spontaneously surfaced during the interviews. By interviewing the teachers in this manner, I captured their insights, perceptions, ideas, and beliefs about what school life was (and is) like at BBMS. I also compared and contrasted the idea of management at BBMS with the idea of management at other schools that are more traditional in their approach to management.

TEACHERS' PERSPECTIVES OF THE SOCIAL CURRICULUM AT BBMS

As I talked with BBMS teachers, and later, as I examined the interview transcripts, I discovered four overarching themes relative to the school's social curriculum: organizing content for integrative teaching and learning; organizing and implementing integrative instruction; filling new teacher roles; and filling new student roles. These themes characterize life at the school and depict the kind of tasks that BBMS teachers carry out each day in order to facilitate integrative teaching and learning in an effective and successful manner.

Organizing Content for Integrative Teaching and Learning

As I noted earlier in this chapter, an integrative curriculum like BBMS that is constructed around carefully selected themes (global awareness, art exploration, environment) is structured in a vastly different way than a conventional curriculum that is constructed around discrete subjects (e.g., science, mathematics, history, language arts, and so on). The former is theme-centered and if constructed according to the suggestions of Beane (1993), will be constructed around the expressed needs of students. The latter (i.e., conventional curriculum organized around discrete subjects) is mostly subject-centered, not necessarily student-centered, since instruction is centered mostly around the structure of the content—the needs of students are not explicitly addressed or considered first when planning instruction with such conventional curricula.

Organizing content for learning, which in traditional terms equates to the management of curriculum development, materials development, and instructional planning, differs notably from integrative curriculum contexts like BBMS. In traditional school contexts, organizing content for learning usually involves looking at expected outcomes for learning or at specific behavioral objectives suggested by the local school district, by state educational agencies, or by national standards set by specific organizations such as the National Council for Teachers of Mathematics, the National Science Teachers Association, or the National Council for the Social Studies. Organizing content for instruction in some locations, for example in Texas, also aligns very closely to state-mandated standardized tests; the idea of *teaching to the test* tends to be the prevailing mode of instruction in these locations, thus lending further support to conventional approaches to organizing curriculum for classroom instruction.

The question surfaces: How does organizing content for instruction in school environments where content is highly prescribed, where objectives are preconceived, and where standardized tests prefigure what is taught, differ from organizing content for instruction like BBMS where content is integrative, where objectives are not always preconceived, and where standardized tests do not prefigure classroom instruction? This latter set of factors, where classroom instruction is not prefigured by various factors, comprises many recent calls for school reform (Doll, 1993; Eisenhart, Finkel, & Marion, 1996; Fullan, 1994; McCaslin & Good, 1992; Oakes, et al., 1993; Quartz, 1995). The social curriculum of BBMS provides some answers to this question. We have compiled selected comments made by teachers about organizing content for learning into two themes: *beyond conventional textbooks* and *thinking and planning integratively.*

Beyond Conventional Textbooks

BBMS educators demonstrated a certain pride in not using conventional textbooks in their classroom instruction. This kind of thinking is very different from that of educators in conventional classrooms who use standard textbooks almost exclusively for organizing and implementing instruction (Powell, in press). I talked to Rita, a teacher who had been at BBMS from the time that the school implemented the integrative curriculum, about teachers who might not feel comfortable teaching at BBMS. Below is an excerpt from the conversation I had with her:

Q. *In general, do you think there are teachers that wouldn't work at an integrated school like Brown-Barge Middle School regardless of the circumstances?*

Rita: *Some of the teachers from [a neighboring middle school] came over here. One of them said that she would never come to this school to teach.*

Q.   *Why would the teacher not come here?*

Rita: *She said, "none of the kids are seated in rows." And she said, "The kids don't
have textbooks out and they aren't really doing any school work." After being
here for eight years now, I knew they were doing a lot of work, just different
kind of work. So I said, "Maybe that's what's wrong with students at other
schools. There aren't enough exciting things going on to keep the kids interested. Our kids want to come to school. I don't think that kids at other
schools really want to go to school."*

In Rita's comments above, you can see how deeply entrenched the idea of textbook teaching is for conventional teachers—that if textbooks aren't on the desks and
open, then learning is not occurring. Yet teachers at BBMS clearly are successful at
organizing instruction without conventional textbooks (Powell & Skoog, 1995).

Not having textbooks with which to construct lessons and not having prefigured objectives and goals for planning and implementing instruction, however,
caused BBMS educators to rethink how they actually put together meaningful and
pertinent instruction for early adolescents. They had to rethink not only how to organize instruction, but also how best to organize time when you do this. *Time management* was mentioned by several teachers as a concern when organizing information for classroom instruction. Denise, in particular, was concerned about the
length of time required to prepare integrative lessons. Denise noted:

> You have to spend a lot of time putting lessons together. We don't have lessons that
> are already made by textbook publishers. So we have to spend a lot of mental time
> on thinking. Because we don't have a textbook for what we do, I'm searching all
> the time for content and information. I have likened this to having your own busi-
> ness and when you have your own business, you try to figure out how to use var-
> ious things in the business. That, to me, is mentally exhausting. It can be physically
> exhausting too because I have to go to the library almost every weekend to look for
> more content and information.

In a related comment, Helen Ruth underscored the time constraints that teachers at BBMS have when they work without conventional textbooks and without
prefigured curricula. Helen Ruth said:

> There are periods of time here when I am under so much stress because of time con-
> straints that I've thought I might go back to a conventional school. But really,
> there's no school I would rather be than here. I would rather put up with the pres-
> sure of not having enough time than to be so structured by curriculum that I could
> not do what we do here.

Thinking and Planning Integratively

Despite time management concerns voiced above by BBMS teachers, there was an important reason that teachers at BBMS turned to informational sources other than textbooks. Recall that the BBMS curriculum is theme-centered, not subject-centered (see
Figure 9.1). Conventional textbooks tend to be written for subject-centered curricula
(e.g., biology textbooks, literature textbooks). At BBMS, however, the content to be

taught is selected on the basis of themes (e.g., flight, bridges), not on the basis of subject matter areas. Teachers at the school, therefore, do not necessarily think in terms of traditional subjects; rather, they think in terms of themes. Consequently, they don't think of themselves as subject matter specialists (e.g., biology teacher, English teacher) needing to use subject-centered textbooks, but rather they think of themselves as generalists needing to use multiple and highly varied resource materials. More will be said about teachers' perceptions of themselves later in this chapter.

When the curriculum is theme-centered and integrative rather than subject-centered and linear, and when teachers accept the professional reality of being generalists rather than subject specialists, the whole curriculum planning process changes in at least three specific ways. The first way that the process changes pertains to rethinking the linear arrangement of content; BBMS teachers think in terms of holistic, nonlinear arrangement of content. They also think in terms of students' social, developmental, and academic needs. With a conventional, subject-centered curriculum, educators tend to perpetually prepare students for the next grade level, or for the standardized test, or for the next course (e.g., Algebra II) in a series of courses (e.g., Algebra I, Algebra II, Geometry), and so on. However, working within the integrative, nonlinear curriculum context of BBMS, educators there are striving for meaningful, experience-based learning that has direct relevancy to students' interests and needs at that moment. Brian best summarized this kind of curriculum:

> What we're teaching these children is sometimes far beyond what they would get in a normal middle school course. We are not necessarily preparing them for high school. We are not preteaching what they are getting in high school either.

A second way the whole curriculum planning process changes in a nonlinear school environment is in thinking integratively about what you will teach. At first this might sound rather simple. However, few things about classroom teaching can be more complex than thinking integratively about what you will teach. Bear in mind that BBMS teachers do not use textbooks, which would be organized in a linear, chapter-by-chapter fashion. Rather, they think about how best to bring various kinds of information together so that the most meaningful learning can occur for a specific topic over 12 weeks. The responsibility of this kind of instruction is quite heavy, and the effort expended to create such instruction is equally heavy.

At BBMS, of course, the idea of thinking integratively is cast in terms of an instructional unit called a *stream*. The kind of integrative thinking associated with a stream is mentioned in this conversation we had with Linda:

Q: *What does it take to put a stream together?*

Linda E: *The key is that if a child says to me, "Ms. So-and-so is my math teacher, and Ms. So-and-so is my science teacher, and Ms. So-and-so is my English teacher," then that is not a stream. And that is not how we define integrative instruction.*

Q: *So, what is a stream then?*

Linda E: *A stream like we have at this school is an integrated curriculum. We try to get the kids to say to themselves, "I'm doing this project on the environ-*

> *ment. And in it I have to bring together all kinds of information on the environment like science, math, writing, social factors. All of this is tied together and leads to an important purpose."*

Similarly, Brian noted:

> We're talking about energy right now in one of our streams. Later on in this stream they are going to have to know mechanical advantage, which is mathematics. They are going to have to know the simple machines, which is physics. They are going to need to know how those machines fit together, which is engineering. They are going to have to know what actually drives those machines and what impact the machines have on life, which is history and government.

Rather than thinking only in terms of mathematics or only in terms of physics, Brian, in his comment above, demonstrates the kind of integrative thinking, and consequently the kind of integrative planning, that must be carefully managed by every BBMS teacher to successfully create an integrative learning environment. This view is further supported by the following comment made by Minnie:

> There is so much you have to do here when you think about developing a stream. When the curriculum is integrated, this means you have to be responsible for the kids' math, science, English, social studies, and everything. You are trying to find materials to fit whatever you are talking about and whatever you are doing.

Fitting various pieces of information together so that students can experience integrative thinking and learning is one of the greatest challenges teachers have at the school. A casual observer at the school who just drops in for a day or two and tries to understand what is happening instructionally at the school might miss some of the powerful kinds of cognitive integration that occur in students over time. In the following comment Tee notes what you would have to do in order to better understand the kind of integration that is happening at the school:

> If you stayed at the school long enough you would be able to see how everything fits together. It is kind of hard to see this in only a short period of time. You would have to shadow a student all day for several days to really see how we are fitting everything together. But if you only came to my room and didn't go to my team teachers' rooms, you would think that what we are doing in my class is all we are doing in the whole stream. But you see, the students learn about ratios in my room. They use ratios to do art work in Marilyn's [team teacher] room. And they use ratios to build their structure in Michael's [team teacher] room. It is the fitting together of all of our instruction that is central to our teaching. And you just can't see that if you glance into a classroom here and there.

From the collection of comments above, what becomes clear is that planning and organizing instruction in a nonlinear curriculum environment, which can also be called an *integrative social curriculum*, requires a fully different kind of interaction among teachers and a different kind of thinking about content to be taught than in a conventional subject-centered curriculum environment. Not only must you think integratively, but you must organize and manage your effort in an integrative way. The absence of conventional textbooks which have traditionally organized content in a linear, subject-centered, manner requires BBMS teachers to rethink their classroom instruction and to rethink their interactions with colleagues and with students.

Organizing and Implementing Integrative Classroom Instruction

In schools like BBMS, some of the organization of content for instruction and some of the implementation of actual classroom instruction is actually negotiated with students as the thematic units, or the streams in the case of BBMS, are taught. While you, the classroom teacher, have certain responsibilities to see that instruction is implemented and managed successfully and while students have certain responsibilities to work collaboratively and collegially, how integrative instruction actually unfolds over time contrasts markedly with conventional instruction. The BBMS teachers' comments indicated clear contrasts with conventional instruction in the following areas: *professional autonomy, collaborative and collegial relationships with peers and students, lesson engagement,* and *experience-based learning.* Each of these areas is discussed below.

Professional Autonomy

BBMS teachers have much autonomy when they implement their lessons. Part of this autonomy derives from being able to choose which instructional materials are best suited to the overall theme of the stream, and to choose how they will structure the school day. Another way of understanding the teacher autonomy is through the notion of *voice.* Specifically, we asked teachers about their voice at the school as a means of exploring the level of autonomy they have when implementing classroom instruction. In the following conversation, we asked Brian about his voice at BBMS:

> Q.   *How do you see your voice at Brown-Barge?*
>
> Brian: *I have almost complete autonomy in my classroom. I have never been told how I should teach, and what materials I should use. I've never been told not to do anything. And I really appreciate that. I don't think we could pull off what we do at Brown-Barge if we had strict guidelines from above like other schools have.*
>
> Q.   *So you think it's different here at Brown-Barge than at other schools?*
>
> Brian: *I know it is different. I have friends in the other schools in the district, and they have to follow curriculum guidelines.*

We also asked Linda about the kind of voice she has at BBMS. Linda noted:

> I would certainly say that overall you have much more voice here than at other schools. Of course, that goes back to the freedom that we have within a stream and within the context of our own team. Where else would you be able to set your schedule for each day, to say what it is that you are actually going to teach, and be able to do these kinds of things?

The autonomy that teachers felt and the voice they collectively expressed provided some BBMS teachers with a basis to get more excited about what they were teaching at the school. For example, Tee noted:

I never get bored teaching here because we can do basically whatever we want in our classrooms. Let me give you an example. I have taught the Transition stream three years now, and I don't think I have taught the science aspect of that stream the same way any of those years. When I was teaching high school science, I knew I wanted to do things differently, but you are kind of confined in traditional high schools. But here at Brown-Barge I don't have that kind of confinement.

The comments above about autonomy and voice depict teaching at BBMS to be full of excitement and freedom. While we found teachers to have much freedom and to be very excited about their work, a comment from Marilyn points to a more difficult part of the autonomy issue. When teachers have much autonomy in their teaching, they also feel empowered. Managing their professional lives as empowered teachers, however, brought about new challenges. Marilyn said, "Sometimes we get absolutely overwhelmed with the empowerment we have here at Brown-Barge." When we asked Marilyn to explain this comment more fully, she noted:

Sometimes the kids come in to the class and say, "Can't you just give us notes and let us memorize and take a test?" But at Brown-Barge, our answer to that is "No." It's true that it's much harder to really think about what you are learning than just to memorize facts. It takes more energy to really think critically and deeply about a topic. And we as teachers feel the same way sometimes. And when you don't use textbooks and have to create your own lessons, then you certainly have to think more. But now that we [the teachers at BBMS] have had this freedom and have been empowered, we would probably yell at Camille [the principal] if she would ever begin telling us what to do. And yet the empowerment is so hard. So, it's that double-edged sword of having autonomy versus being told what to do. And the kids go through the same thing.

An interesting part of the autonomy at BBMS is the necessity to let go of more conventional ways of teaching. Autonomy allows BBMS teachers to create instruction that is highly individualized and that varies considerably from one class to another. Martha was one of the teachers who developed the original integrative curriculum at the school. We asked her if there was any part of her former teaching before BBMS that she had forgotten. She reflected:

I have almost forgotten that at most other schools students have to sit in neat little rows and everyone has to do the same worksheet. You know what I mean, that everyone has to be doing the same thing at the same time. You just have to forget that here at Brown-Barge because it really doesn't matter here if we have everybody in the classroom doing something entirely different. But that is really hard for a teacher who is really traditional because that teacher will think she is losing control. That kind of stuff is real hard to let go when you first teach at a school like this one.

Collaboration and Collegiality

Having autonomy and being able to contribute an important voice to the school's momentum do not mean, however, that teachers at BBMS work entirely alone without the assistance of their colleagues, as often happens in schools that are conventional and subject-centered. Collaboration and collegiality were part of the daily lives of teachers at the school. Teachers at the school, therefore, had to be able to manage their professional lives as true collaborators. We asked Helen Ruth to talk about some of the more pressing challenges that teachers have at BBMS. She noted:

> An important challenge here is learning how to get along with each other. We have a saying around here that we have to model behaviors for our students. If we as teachers do not know how to interact with each other, then we can never teach our children how to interact.

Collaborating with each other in a collegial manner at BBMS also meant assuming instructional responsibilities that were at times challenging and that moved beyond teachers' subject matter expertise. Accepting these responsibilities, however, was a necessary part of being a teacher at BBMS. This was reflected in a comment made by Marilyn:

> I've always been on the Arts Exploration stream. Well, usually the science people and the mathematics people work together in a stream that is science-related. In the Arts Exploration stream there were no people who felt comfortable enough to teach the math, so I said, "I'll teach it." I was never particularly good at math, but I know more than middle schoolers. So I took over teaching the math and have now formulated a whole series of my own just working with the kids on an individualized basis.

Lesson Engagement

As teachers worked collaboratively and with much freedom to implement lessons, they created an atmosphere for students that was highly engaging. However, this atmosphere was complex and was filled with much professional commitment from the teachers. A comment from Minnie provided support for high engagement and commitment. Minnie had 32 years of teaching experience before teaching at BBMS. I asked Minnie to compare her former teaching experiences to those at BBMS. She noted:

> In the other schools where I worked, we always had textbooks. If I ever got sick in these other schools, I could always tell my substitute, "Open the book to such and such chapter, have the students read the chapter and answer the questions at the end of the chapter." Here at Brown-Barge you can't do that. Most times, if you are sick, it is just easier to come to work because it is very difficult to write up your substitute plan. This is because we have so many things going on. The kids are doing so many things every minute of the day. They're moving around. They're on the floor doing things. They're moving from one wing of the building to another wing all the time. How can you put all of this in a substitute plan?

The high level of engagement that Minnie mentioned above also created a certain level of stress for some of the teachers. Knowing how to manage this stress became an important issue for teachers at the school. Michael noted this about the stress he felt:

> I feel responsible not just for the kids in my class but for kids in the whole stream or even in the whole school. I have to know where every kid is that I'm responsible for and where they are at every moment. This morning I had some kids working down the hall, some in the library, some videotaping each other, some paint-

ing, some cutting paper, and some going to another room. All of them were on task, but they were on task all over the place. This can be very stressful sometimes, trying to keep up with all the kids.

To an outsider visiting the school, what Michael described might be viewed as utter chaos. However, Donna said:

> People in general think we are not structured. But I see us as very structured. I mean there are people whose structure is not the same as my structure. I have a lesson, I have objectives to my lesson, I know what I want to accomplish, and I know where I want the kids to be from the beginning to the end. It's what happens between the beginning and end that the miracle in learning occurs. At Brown-Barge you usually see students in this in-between-area taking the initiative to learn on their own, and that means they need a lot of freedom to explore. It may look chaotic, but if you look around, that is what I hope you are seeing, that children are engaged in their own learning.

Experience-Based Learning

One reason that there is a high level of engagement at the school, that students may be in various locations for the same class, as Michael explained above, and that the context may appear chaotic, as Donna explained, is because the integrative curriculum at BBMS is experience-based. That is, students are continuously working on projects of various sorts, including original research projects. Teachers at the school must learn how to manage this kind of teaching and learning. As students complete experience-based projects, they acquire necessary knowledge and information to understand the theme that they are studying for the 12-week stream. Experience-based instruction also means extensive individualized instruction, as Tee noted: "We individualize instruction so that we challenge every kid to the highest point we can."

Facilitating the experience-based learning at the school is the multiplicity of technology that is available to students. The technology is particularly helpful in the many research projects that students complete. I asked Rita to compare how she organized her classrooms at BBMS with how she organized her classrooms when she previously taught high school. Rita noted:

> In high school I didn't have all the resources that I have here, especially with all the online resources and the library. Because of these resources, I don't have to give them so much information. They would rather discover it for themselves and use the equipment. The discovery process works better for me here at Brown-Barge. I think it could work in the high schools, but I don't think that they have the resources to allow children to research the way we do here.

As an example of experience-based learning, BBMS students can enroll in a stream called *Bridges*. One part of this stream is actually building a bridge on the BBMS campus. Linda noted:

> When our kids are building bridges, one of the first activities they do is make towers out of newspaper rolled up with glue. And by measuring the angles, they can discover all sorts of geometric concepts. But if I simply lectured to them and told

them, "alternative and interior angles are equal," that wouldn't mean anything to them. But if they discover, "Hey, when I measure the bridge here, this angle equals this other angle," then they really know.

Creating an environment that is experience-based, where students are truly able to discover much for themselves and where a school that appears to be in chaos is clearly structured and meaningful for students, requires considerable energy from teachers. When I asked Debbie what teaching was like at BBMS, she said:

> It is incredibly intense because we are having to produce materials that don't exist in the world today. So we have to go out and make them by putting things together. I just did some materials for the stream I am working on now. Every twelve weeks we create something new.

Filling New Teacher Roles

Another important aspect of the BBMS social curriculum was filling new teacher roles. BBMS teachers filled roles that were mostly unconventional; specifically, they filled roles that aligned with the integrative curriculum that they created and implemented. As they filled these roles, they moved away from traditional management practices where teachers assume sole authority in the classroom and where they are viewed as *the* subject matter experts. While BBMS teachers had to ensure that student behavior was appropriate and while they still had to help students remain on task, they nonetheless viewed themselves as filling different kinds of teacher roles than subject matter experts and classroom police officers.

This section will discuss the roles that teachers viewed themselves as filling at BBMS. We describe certain roles that teachers mentioned in our interviews with them. However, prior to discussing these roles, we first must examine the power relations at the school, particularly the power relations between teachers and students, among teachers, and between teachers and the school's administration. Understanding the power relations at the school also helps you understand the opportunities that teachers had to fill roles other than those they traditionally filled in conventional schools.

Power Relations at School

Think back on the kind of *power* you had as a middle school and high school student. Were you invited to make decisions about what you learned at school? If so, you probably had some power, and consequently some voice, in what content was taught to you. Or were these kind of instructional decisions already made for you, in which case you probably had little or no power in decisions about what was taught to you and consequently little or no voice? If you attended a conventional school where you had little voice in what happened at school and where most of the power was held by those in authority (e.g., school principal for whole school, teacher for classroom, superintendent for whole school district, and so on), then as a student you were likely subordinate to almost everyone else at school.

In such conventional schools, teachers do not always have much power either. For example, in some school locations teachers are mostly told what content to teach and what materials to use when they teach the content. Creative teachers, of course, will supplement the mandated content with additional materials, but the underlying basis for what is taught is nonetheless received by teachers not created by them. In many conventional settings, then, teachers have limited power and limited voice in what (and sometimes how) they teach.

A quick glance inside the doors of BBMS, however, shows a different picture of power relations at school. Indeed, the power relations are so different from those at other schools that students actually have to learn how to interact with each other and with teachers during the first 12 weeks they are at school. They learn these skills in the *Communities Stream*, as I noted earlier in the chapter. And teachers at the school have much decision-making power in what is taught and how it is taught. For example, I asked the school counselor, Carol, to share with me her perceptions of the kind of voice and consequently of the kind of power that teachers have in making decisions about what they teach and in being involved in other decisions about curriculum, instruction, and site-based governance. In response to the question, "What are teachers' voices like at Brown-Barge compared to the traditional school setting where you were before coming here?" Carol said,

> They are more empowered at Brown-Barge than they were at my former school. Teachers here can say more about what they want and need. They discuss things openly all the time with each other, with the students, and with the principal. Sometimes our faculty meetings go on for hours. This is mainly because teachers are able to express themselves and they try to come to a conclusion of how they are going to handle concerns, issues, and other things. The teachers definitely have a voice here, and the voice is always heard.

One aspect of the school that provides teachers with a source of empowerment and with a means to express themselves either explicitly in meetings or implicitly in their instruction is the governance of the school through management committees or through curriculum stream teams which utilize a flexible schedule. Carol explained both:

> The management committees [Curriculum, School Culture, Technology, Teaming, and Marketing/Partnerships] emerged as a result of concerns expressed by the staff. Each person decides which committee [whose members meet bimonthly] is best suited for their work outside their curriculum stream team assignments. The School Improvement Team, which consists of the administration and the chairpersons from each of these committees, acts as the "internal school board" where major school decisions are made at the bimonthly meetings.

Carol also explained about the schedule, which provided BBMS teachers with more decision-making power about how they structured their day and how they structured learning activities for students:

> When the teachers are working on their streams, they pretty much determine what they are going to be doing within their own team area. There is no set curriculum for them to follow. And nobody is hanging over them watching exactly what they

teach. The teachers are the ones who determine how much time they are going to use. The only thing that is set, pretty much, is when they have lunch. The rest of their day is total flexibility to plan as they need.

In Carol's comment above, you can see how BBMS teachers must learn to *manage* their day in ways that teachers at more conventional schools, where there is a pre-set schedule and designated periods, don't have to. Teachers at BBMS felt that this kind of empowerment—the kind that gave them reign over how best to teach selected thematic content—provided them with much instructional freedom.

The empowered roles that teachers have at BBMS were mentioned by Martha, who had been at the school since it started its integrative approach to learning. I asked Martha about her voice at the school. Martha noted:

> Yes, I have a powerful voice here at Brown-Barge. And that was a big change for me. I came here after 20 years of teaching in schools where I was told what to do and where the schedule was always fixed and not flexible. And when I got here to BBMS, I was told that I had to take part in developing the schedule for the school. At first I had no idea what to do, and I said, "No, I'm not going to fix the schedule. That is what the administration does." But I learned very quickly that this school runs a lot on teacher input, not just on administrator input, although Camille (the principal) does have discussions with us and expresses her views and opinions. But she also lets us do the same, and we decide together on what we should do. I've never been worried about giving my opinion here, but I've never worked at a place where I felt my opinion was really taken into consideration and valued like it has been here.

Because BBMS teachers had such flexibility in their scheduling and in what information to teach students during streams, they also had to be willing to give up the kind of power that comes from always being in control of the classroom context and always being in control of what students are learning. I asked Dianna, for example, if there were teachers who wouldn't fit well into the BBMS school context. Dianna noted,

> I would say yes. People who wouldn't fit well here are those who have to be in control, who have to be in charge, people that have a hard time being flexible. By saying people who have to be in control, I mean people who always need everything cut and dried.

An important point to be made from Dianna's comments above is that BBMS teachers, in conventional terms, were not *in control* of students; being in control of students also means having power over them. Rather than having such power over students, BBMS educators tended to share power with their students, as suggested by the following comment made by Tee. I asked Tee to talk about the idea of *control* in her teaching. She said:

> I formerly taught in a high school science situation. It was real hard for me to give up control, you know, like I was in charge of the classroom all the time, and I had to set up labs and all of that. When I came to Brown-Barge I had to give up the idea of control that I had in high school. Because of the way we have the curriculum set up here at Brown-Barge the students look up most of the things on their own. I'm not the same kind of teacher here. You see, at this school it's not so much like, "Here

is the teacher in charge of the class, and here is the class." Instead, it is all just one big group and if we contribute what we know and what we can do to make it better for everybody, then all of us will benefit.

The idea of sharing power with students was also noted by Rita in the following comment. Rita compared classroom management at BBMS with her former high school teaching. She said:

> In the high school where I taught before, most of the teachers, including me, sort of talked down to students so that there wasn't a lot of meaningful conversation going on. It was also a one-way communication, from teachers to students, but not really from students to teachers. We really never asked for student input on much of anything. But here at Brown-Barge, we never do that kind of teaching. We get student input on almost everything. When I talk to students here, I talk to them many times as if they are adults. It's kind of hard for me to describe the kind of teaching I do here at Brown-Barge because I never really taught this way until I came here a few years ago. The tone that the teachers at Brown-Barge use in the classroom is also different than where I taught before. It's not the tone that says, "I have power and you don't." It's a tone that says, "Let's share all this power and learn together."

The comments above clearly suggest that the power relationships and, consequently, the interpersonal relationships between teachers and students at BBMS and among teachers at the school, were notably different than such relationships between teachers and students in conventional schools and classrooms. That the power relationships at BBMS were unique and provided teachers and students alike with a feeling of empowerment is clear. Because power was shared more by teachers and students at the school, teachers no longer managed students in the same way as they did in their former teaching in conventional schools.

Shifting of power relations at BBMS prompted a corresponding shift in how educators at the school viewed themselves as teachers, thus suggesting the need to rethink traditional approaches to classroom management. In the interviews and conversations we had with BBMS teachers, most of the comments we heard were about their roles at the school. Below is a discussion of these roles.

Teacher as Proactive Learner

The metaphor of teacher-as-learner is certainly not new. One expectation that all teachers have is to continuously update and enrich their own knowledge about teaching and about the content being taught. The idea of teacher-as-learner, however, takes on a new dimension at BBMS because teachers don't always have a broad and deep background in the stream they are teaching. This means that teachers, along with their students, are put into a position of being authentic learners and, most importantly, of being role models for learning content that is being taught. The idea of being teacher-as-learner in the BBMS tradition was typified by the following comment made by Wendy:

> When you teach a stream, the topic might take you places you have never studied or explored before as a teacher. The stream might not be your area of expertise as far as your academic preparation or even as far as your avocation are concerned.

Whatever your experience is, you might be learning something right along with your students. If that happens, the only thing you've got that your students don't have is a little more experience. And you might know where to find stuff out that they don't. Many times I have found myself being side by side with my students while we were finding it out together. If you need to know all the answers as a teacher, if indeed that is your comfort zone, then you don't need to be at this school.

A similar comment was made by Linda:

When the kids ask you a really hard question, you have to have enough security in yourself to be able to say, "Well, I don't know the answer to that, but why don't we find out together." It's OK that the teacher not know everything; this is a learning process where the kids and you can learn together and you can share that. If you feel like you as a teacher can't do that, if you are uncomfortable with knowing that you don't know most of the things the students will ask, then that's a problem here at Brown-Barge.

Teacher as Content Generalist

Not only was the idea of being a learner at BBMS an ongoing reality for teachers, so was the idea of being a generalist. Moving from being a content specialist (e.g., mathematics, social studies, English) to being a content generalist was a major transformation in the role of teacher at the school. This transformation was necessary because of the nature of the written curriculum, which is comprised of thematic streams. This does not mean, however, that BBMS teachers had to give up entirely their favorite areas of study; rather, they had to be willing to teach not only their area of study, but other areas as well. BBMS teachers therefore teach in areas they may be less familiar with, thus causing them to learn about specific information along with students, and requiring them to be flexible enough to teach in areas outside of a preferred area of study.

The flexibility needed to teach in other areas, and the consequences of this teaching, were mentioned by Michael. When I asked Michael to describe teachers who might be unwilling to teach at BBMS, he said,

Teachers who would have great difficulty teaching here are those that have to feel that they are an expert in their field. Sometimes at Brown-Barge you just have to be willing to say, "I don't know what's going on," and ask for help. You have to be willing to say, "Hey, I'm willing to try, and although I don't know where to begin teaching this stuff, I'm looking for resources anyway." That's really harder for some people to do than to say, "I know the subject and I know what to do. So just leave me alone in my own classroom and I'm comfortable."

Moving out of the comfort zone of knowing deeply and broadly about the subject in order to become a generalist was mentioned explicitly by Brian, who said,

The teacher that doesn't fit at this school is the subject-oriented teacher. If they are so proud of themselves and so stuck on their subject orientation, then they would not help this school at all. You must be a generalist here. You cannot be a specialist. If you think and act like a specialist at this school, then you have lost half of your effectiveness.

In a conversation I had with Helen Ruth, I learned that being a generalist at BBMS was why several teachers returned to conventional schools to teach. Helen Ruth noted,

> We have had a few teachers who left Brown-Barge because they were really dedicated to their subject area where they received their training. They wanted to teach in a setting where they could teach, for example, only science or where they could teach only math. I would say that teachers who are very committed to only one subject area should not teach in an environment like this because they would find it hard to move beyond their subject area. They probably would not be able to give and take: They might have a hard time sharing information. And they probably would not want to be a proactive lifelong learner in an area that is different from the area in which they had chosen to pursue their studies.

Teacher as Collaborator

Being content generalists and proactive learners also caused BBMS teachers to be collaborators with each other. The need to collaborate with colleagues was particularly important when teachers taught in streams where they were less certain about the content, and where they had to create instructional materials and daily lessons that were fully integrated. When I asked Marilyn to describe her relationship with other teachers at the school, especially those she taught with in streams, she said,

> I am constantly working with other teachers here. And I constantly learn from them too. Every day I turn to my stream teachers and seek advice, ask about what to teach, get more information in certain areas. We always brainstorm together about what we are teaching.

About working with other teachers at the school, Michael noted, "As far as the curriculum is concerned, I feel very collaborative with the teachers. We work together and share everything." And Martha related how teaching at Brown-Barge requires all teachers to interact with each other in supportive ways.

> When I first came to Brown-Barge, I had to change from being the only teacher in the classroom to being one of three or four teachers in the classroom. This is because at Brown-Barge we are always in each other's classrooms. This was a little bit hard at first, but now I don't think I could teach any other way. You get so much support from the other teachers. And the ideas you get working with others are wonderful. I wouldn't take anything for that.

Teacher as Facilitator, Guide, and Negotiator

In each conversation I had with the teachers, I asked them in what ways, if any, did they fill the roles of facilitator, guide, or negotiator with students. The selected responses below typified the responses given by many of the teachers. I asked Brian to tell me what it was like teaching at Brown-Barge. Brian viewed teachers at the school as being *facilitators*. He noted,

> It's very challenging teaching here because you're no longer the teacher; you are the facilitator. I believe that very strongly. I try to get the best out of the students by helping them and by suggesting ways to do projects. Of course I still have to impart

some knowledge to them because of the acquisition skills that we teach. But there is no question that I am a facilitator. I'm certainly not a traditional teacher and traditional classroom manager.

Wendy, however, viewed teachers more as *guides* to student learning. I asked Wendy the question, "If I watch you for a while in your classroom, would I see you as a manager of students, or would I see you as a negotiator or as a guide?" Wendy responded,

Wendy: *You would probably see all of those things.*

Q.   *What would be the most predominant, if any of them?*

Wendy: *Of those three, probably guide.*

Q.   *What would we see if you are a guide for your students?*

Wendy: *If we have a particular problem to solve in class, I usually present the problem initially. Then the problem I presented creates other problems. You determine which problem you are going to pursue. After you choose the problem, I will try to guide you in the direction of learning that would be most relevant to the problem. Sometimes the students and I have to find the direction together since I don't always know which way to go.*

In addition to being guides and facilitators, teachers also believed they were *negotiators* with their students. As I discussed earlier in this chapter, in conventional school contexts students have little negotiating power about what content they learn and about how they learn it. Rita provided me with insight into how students and teachers at BBMS, on the other hand, negotiate various aspects of classroom life. I asked Rita if the idea of negotiation had any meaning at BBMS. Rita noted,

Rita: *Negotiating for what?*

Q.   *Negotiating for what to learn, how to learn, why to learn?*

Rita: *Probably how to learn. We negotiate that a lot. Because no one teaching approach works with all kids, I will sit down with my students, and I say, "This is what we need to learn. How can I best get you there? What works? What are you really interested in? What are your goals?"*

I asked Linda if some things at school were open to negotiation with students. Linda said,

They can negotiate a lot of things and they know that. For example, if I'm giving an evaluation on a project and if they think it is an unfair evaluation, then they can come to me and they can say, "I don't think this is fair." I sit there and listen to them. If their argument is well-stated, then I will change the evaluation. I have done that several times.

Filling New Student Roles

The teacher roles described above, which were central to the social curriculum of BBMS, suggested the need for new student roles. Moreover, shifts in the distribution of power at the school, especially power about how content is taught and how students are evaluated, suggested the need for students to be highly proactive and thoroughly engaged in learning-expected content. This meant that BBMS students, just like teachers at the school, had to be proactive learners.

Students as Proactive Learners

Central to being a proactive learner, where students take charge of much of their learning at school, was the relationship between students and teachers. This was mentioned by Carol, the school counselor, who noted,

> I think the relationship between the students and teachers at Brown-Barge is very different than at a lot of other schools. Here the students are able to discuss, to verbalize their thoughts and their ideas and their opinions to a very great extent without any kind of backlash from the teachers. Because of this, the students feel more comfortable expressing themselves so they are more open to coming out with some ideas that they might not come out with in a traditional school for fear of being put down by the teacher or by students.

One factor that enabled students to express themselves openly at the school, as Carol noted above, was shared power, which was discussed earlier in the chapter. Linda talked about this power when she discussed how students worked together at the school. Linda noted,

> Kids come to Brown-Barge from other schools and from other environments where they haven't really been responsible for their own learning. When the kids begin school here they have to figure that out—they have to figure out how to be responsible for their own learning. They need help getting used to this at first, but then after they have been at Brown-Barge a while, they need less and less help in carrying out their own projects and assignments. The kids really cooperate in groups and work together, but you have to have power to do that. And a lot of kids at first don't know what to do with the power that we give them. So we guide them at first, then pretty much turn them loose to direct their own research and other projects.

Students as Collaborators

Linda's comment above—that students "really cooperate in groups and work together"—reflects yet another role that students were expected to assume at the school, namely *collaborator of learning*. I asked Linda to tell me what I would observe about the school's beliefs about how students learn if I was at the school for an extended period of time. Linda noted,

> You would see the students getting very involved with other students in collaborative groups. You would see them get involved with me some but not as much as with each other because they are involved with each other and with the technology.

The practice that students continuously demonstrated of working collaboratively in groups was perhaps one of the most salient features of the school context. I observed this collaboration and corresponding shared power among teachers and students in each classroom I visited. Once students acquired suitable collaboration skills in the Communities Stream during their first 12 weeks at the school and once they practiced these skills in all other streams, they became highly capable of directing their own learning (Powell & Skoog, 1995), which suggests that many students at the school acquired the kind of internalization of self-control for learning that McCaslin and Good (1992) called for at the beginning of the chapter.

Students as Social Constructionists

When students work together collaboratively over time, when they learn to share knowledge and information about targeted content, and when they willingly do this because it is a naturally flowing part of the school environment and not out of coercion or contrived cooperative grouping, they become what Gergen (1985) calls *social constructionists.* That is, they build their personal knowledge of targeted content, themes, and projects from sharing insights with each other in their ongoing collaborative groups. In these collaborative groups are educative and communal interchanges between and among students. This is mostly opposite of what is expected in many conventional school settings, where sharing insights openly and in a trusting manner is hindered by intense individualism that predominates such school settings.

By becoming social constructionists, BBMS students received certain benefits, as reported by Powell and Skoog (1995). Students' confidence increased for learning and for expressing themselves openly. They also developed strategies for learning from other students, including respectful listening and appropriate sharing of personal perspectives. Students also reported that their understanding of concepts and ideas was enhanced when multiple viewpoints from peers and from teachers were expressed and considered.

Dealing With Student Behavior and Discipline

Although BBMS differs from most conventional schools in its curriculum and instruction, the school is like other schools in that it must also deal with student behavior and discipline problems of emerging adolescents. As a middle school, BBMS is filled with learners who are overflowing with energy and enthusiasm and also who have a very great need to discover themselves and their independence in the world around them.

BBMS does not have a dean of students, who in most schools takes care of student discipline and misbehavior. This means that BBMS teachers must be prepared to deal with most behavior problems as they occur in the classroom or as they see them occurring elsewhere. Helen Ruth talked about the responsibility she had in dealing with student behavior. Helen Ruth noted,

> We don't have a dean of discipline at the school. So as far as discipline is concerned, we're responsible for that. I think that if a teacher is mostly responsible for discipline, then she needs to really get to know the child in order to find out why they're acting the way they are. I mean you have to get to know the whole child, where they're coming from, what they come to school with. Then you can individualize how you address that child. You don't necessarily change the rules for every student, but by knowing the students personally might change how you enforce the rule.

After observing students and teachers interacting at BBMS, we surmised that students at the school have much freedom, certainly more freedom than at conventional schools that are not social constructionist in orientation. Linda talked about how this freedom was related to maintaining proper student behavior. Linda noted,

> The kids have a lot more freedom here most of the time, so if they have to go to the bathroom, then they get up and go to the bathroom. If they want water, then they get up and go get water most of the time. If they abuse that privilege, then the privilege is taken away, and they know that.

Linda also mentioned another challenging instructional task that comes with student freedom.

> We really don't have any major problems at the school with student misbehavior. I think that probably if I had to choose one thing, however, that can become a problem, I would say that is trying to keep all of the kids on task and motivated and excited about what we are doing. We have a lot of freedom, and because of that we expect kids to stay on task much of the time by themselves. But invariably, we all have to face students who have a hard time staying on task, and not every student can stay on task 100% of the time. But that doesn't really lead to major discipline problems. Usually I just have to remind students to get on task, and they do.

Like emerging adolescents at any school, BBMS students at times press the limits and challenge teachers' patience. Tee told me what she often did in these situations:

> Students know that if they get too far out of hand I'll call their parents at home. And there have been times because of bad behavior I have had to walk a student out to a car after school where a parent was waiting. But these are usually last-minute measures since I always talk to students before I turn to these kind of things to correct their behavior. I will always give them first chance to fix it; then if that doesn't work, I'll go to the more extreme measures to correct the behavior.

Helping BBMS Students Understand Conflict and Compromise

An important dimension of the BBMS social curriculum, a dimension that is directly germane to this book, is helping students understand the notions of conflict and compromise. In chapter 6 we discussed the ideas of conflict and compromise as they cut across various school cultures. At Brown-Barge Middle School, students can (and many do) study these things more formally. One of the streams at the school is called *Conflict and Compromise,* and it deals directly with conflict resolution strategies. The premise for the Conflict and Compromise stream, which is stated in one of the school's curriculum documents, is to enable students to conduct an:

> examination of the roots of conflict between individuals, groups of people, and nations [which] is essential for students to understand the complexity of relationships, as well as strategies through which conflicts can be resolved.

Students who complete this stream of study practice conflict resolution strategies at the school, and they demonstrate a broader understanding of conflict and compromise in the world around them. What is often an implicit part of some school curricula, namely rules and regulations that students must follow in order to avoid conflict and in order to build compromises with students and teachers, is an explicit part of the BBMS curriculum.

Another stream that in some ways is closely related to *Conflict and Compromise* is entitled *American Tapestry.* The overall topic for this stream is *There Are Ties Between Us.* The premise for this stream relates to living in a culturally diverse society which is often filled with cultural conflict and which often requires many compromises from members of society. The stream premise states:

> The United States is a culturally diverse society. For people to succeed and prosper in harmonious surroundings, we must work toward understanding the common threads which unite us.

As students complete the American Tapestry stream, they learn about racism, stereotyping, and related topics. They learn how culture is an inherent part of every person, and they acquire strategies for affirming and respecting various cultures.

The descriptions above of *Conflict and Compromise* and *American Tapestry* are unfortunately very brief. The important point from providing you with a brief glimpse of these two streams is to demonstrate how one school—BBMS—is helping its students understand how they can contribute to harmony in the world both locally and globally by managing their own behavior and by monitoring how they interact with persons whose backgrounds differ from their own. It is these two streams that also provide students with many opportunities to enhance self-understanding and to learn about the place of self in the society. Few schools have made such student self-understanding an overt and well-developed part of their curriculum. Yet students in all schools today are faced with so many kinds of conflict and must know how to reach compromises for this conflict every day of their lives.

EXERCISE 9.1   Building an Integrative Social Curriculum

I have tried to depict a rather comprehensive view of the social curriculum of BBMS in this chapter. I have also highlighted a social curriculum that strives to align its curriculum and instruction with recent calls for school reform, particularly the reform of school management. These calls include, for example,

- moving beyond traditional "how to" approaches that merely replicate what model schools, in conventional terms, should be,
- creating instruction that enhances student self-understanding,
- moving away from a focus on drill and practice and toward a focus on critical problem-solving and decision-making,
- fostering internalization of student self-control
- helping students and teachers become proactive learners
- helping students monitor their own learning over time through self-evaluation.

To achieve these goals, educators at BBMS envisioned, created, and implemented whole school reform. There was no attempt, as there often is in conventional schools, to infuse piecemeal changes to a school's existing curriculum, which would lead at best to minor modifications in classroom instruction (Quartz, 1996). However, the kind of wholesale changes made at BBMS would be considered radical by educators who prefer more conservative educational practices. We can't expect, therefore, that every school could or even would make the kind of transition to integrative curricula that BBMS made. On the other hand, we cannot continue supporting schools which uphold conventional curriculum and instruction. Such schools maintain the status quo of traditional education and traditional management practices. Traditional management practices and conventional curriculum and instruction, however, do not necessarily engage students from all cultural and ethnic groups equally well. Changes in classroom curriculum and instruction and changes in traditional classroom management must be made if *all* students are to feel they belong in our schools.

Because BBMS offered one alternative to conventional teaching (and management) practices, we would like you to consider for yourself how many of the changes made at BBMS might be suited to a classroom you might now be familiar with, or a classroom that might be your own in the future. Below are questions that reflect the discussion we offered of BBMS. The questions collectively represent the social curriculum of BBMS, and thus how teachers at the school organized and maintained classroom life as it unfolded each day. As you think about the questions and as you write your responses, look back over corresponding parts of the chapter. After completing all questions, compare and contrast your responses with those developed by your peers.

A. Organizing Content for Learning

Beyond conventional textbooks

- In what ways, if any, will you be able to move beyond textbook-centered instruction in your classroom?
- What resources might you gather and use, other than traditional textbooks, to present your lessons?
- What obstacles might you need to overcome if you choose not to use traditional textbooks in a school (or school district) that requires their use?

Thinking and planning integratively

- What major factors will influence how you organize content for instruction? District-mandated curriculum? State-mandated standardized testing? Professional colleagues in same school? Textbooks?
- How might you change from subject-centered instruction to theme-centered instruction like that in place at BBMS, if such theme-centered instruction is indeed a valued enterprise?
- How might you organize the content that you are required to teach around broad themes? (NOTE: See Figure 9.1 for examples of themes used at BBMS to organize instruction.)
- What specific colleagues might you invite to plan and implement integrative lessons?

B. Organizing and Implementing Integrative Classroom Instruction

Professional autonomy

- How much autonomy will you have in choosing the instructional materials you will use to present your lessons? Stated another way, how much *voice* will you have in choosing materials?
- What factors might limit your professional autonomy for organizing and implementing classroom instruction?

Collaboration and collegiality

- How willing are you to work closely, and in an ongoing manner, with professional colleagues?
- What is the difference between collaboration and collegiality at BBMS and at schools that are more conventional?
- Educators at BBMS continuously worked with each other to strengthen their instruction. In what ways could you turn to your colleagues each day to strengthen your own classroom instruction?
- Are you willing to open your classroom doors to other teachers at any time of the day?
- How can you work with other teachers when you plan and implement your lessons?

Lesson engagement

- Earlier in this chapter was a comment by Minnie. She mentioned that coming to work at BBMS when she was ill was actually easier than writing plans for a substitute teacher. This is because the daily lessons at BBMS are so highly engaging for both teachers and students that providing a detailed lesson plan for a substitute is very complicated. How might you make your lessons this engaging?

Experience-based learning

- BBMS used extensive experience-based learning activities, whereas conventional schools tend to use more book-based learning activities. How does BBMS define experience-based learning? What are advantages to experience-based learning? What are disadvantages?
- How might you incorporate experience-based learning, as used at BBMS, in your classroom?

C. Filling new teacher roles

Power relations at school

- Compare power relations at BBMS to power relations in schools that you have attended. When you make this comparison, consider such areas as instructional decision-making, curriculum decision-making, professional autonomy, and teacher voice.
- At BBMS, both teachers and students share power in certain areas. This sharing means that teachers and students at the school have greater

responsibility in deciding what and how to teach. Would you like to have this kind of responsibility? Why or why not?

- How does the distribution of power in conventional schools influence what and how content is taught?
- What kind of power are you willing to share with your students? How might this sharing of power influence your classroom management? What kind of voice will you give them in classroom decision-making?

Teacher as proactive learner

- How are BBMS teachers proactive learners?
- In what ways, if any, will you demonstrate being a proactive learner for your students?
- Are you willing to explore various content areas with your students that you don't know a lot about? How might you do this?

Teacher as content generalist

- Many teachers in middle school and in high school prefer to think of themselves as content specialists (e.g., mathematics teacher, English teacher, and so on). At BBMS, teachers prefer to think of themselves as content generalists, thus teaching in various thematic areas rather than in only one or two areas. Are you willing to become a content generalist and teach more broadly to your students about the content?
- If all teachers were required to be content generalists instead of specialists, how do you think this would change the entire educational system?

Teacher as facilitator, guide, and negotiator

- Teachers at BBMS view themselves as facilitators and guides of student learning. They also believe that they often negotiate various aspects of their classroom life with students. How is the social curriculum of BBMS conducive to teachers' perspectives of themselves as facilitators and guides?
- Teachers in most schools would rather think they are more like facilitators and guides than traditional classroom managers. Yet there are many aspects of the school classroom that must be managed if learning is to occur for all students. In what ways, then, will you be a traditional manager of your classroom? In what ways will you be a facilitator? In what ways will you be a guide?
- Are there aspects of your classroom life, including curriculum and instruction, that you will negotiate with your students?

D. Filling new student roles

Student as proactive learner

- At BBMS, students as well as teachers are viewed as proactive learners. Students and teachers alike have moved beyond textbooks at the school, and they complete many experience-based projects. What does proactive learning mean to you? How will you help your students become proactive learners and critical thinkers like BBMS has done? How will you manage a classroom that is organized to foster proactive learning in students?

Student as collaborator

- At BBMS, students are helped to learn how to work with peers productively. This is because BBMS students work continuously in collaborative groups, where they solve problems together, complete experience-based projects, and do group brainstorming. In what ways will you help your students become collaborators with each other?

Student as social constructionist

- BBMS students worked continuously together in groups to construct personal meaning of content. Earlier in this chapter we called this the *social construction of meaning.* How does managing a social constructionist classroom differ from managing a traditional classroom?
- In what ways, if any, will you create a social constructionist classroom?

E. Conflict, Compromise, and Multicultural Education

An interesting part of the BBMS curriculum were two instructional streams: Conflict and Compromise, and There Are Ties Between Us. The first stream helps students understand conflict and compromise locally and globally. The second stream, which focuses on cultural differences, helps students understand the many interesting dimensions of a multicultural society. How might you include these things in your classroom curriculum, if at all?

CONCLUSION

The social curriculum of BBMS has provided the educational community with a successful alternative framework for organizing classroom life. Consequently, the BBMS social curriculum has given us an alternative to traditional classroom management practices, although teachers at this school clearly stated that those who lack flexibility, who are less willing to work collaboratively with peers on a daily basis, and who are less willing to go the extra mile to find pertinent instructional materials for a nontextbook-centered learning environment, might feel uncomfortable teaching in such a setting.

Using comments made mostly by BBMS teachers, and using observations of the school

context, you were provided with a rather simplified overview of life at the school. Comprising this overview were various features such as lesson engagement, experienced-based learning, teacher as collaborator, and so on. Clearly, BBMS is not totally unique in some of these features. Many teachers in conventional schools, for example, have organized classroom life so that students are highly engaged in what they are learning. And many successful teachers in these same conventional schools have moved beyond traditional use of textbooks. The real uniqueness and the real forward-thinking of BBMS is the collective effectiveness of all of these features which happen continuously and simultaneously in the midst of an integrative, theme-based curriculum. Because of this uniqueness, whole new relationships at BBMS have emerged between teachers and administrators, between teachers and students, and among teachers. Consequently, a new system of management is now at the school.

REFERENCES

Apple, M. (1996). *Cultural politics and education.* New York: Teachers College Press.

Beane, J. (1993). *A middle school curriculum: From rhetoric to reality.* Columbus, OH: National Middle School Association.

Brazee, E., & Capuletti, J. (Eds.). (1995). *Dissolving boundaries: Toward an integrative curriculum.* Columbus, OH: National Middle School Association.

Doll, W. (1993). *A post-modern perspective on curriculum.* New York: Teachers College Press.

Eisenhart, M., Finkel, E., & Marion, S. (1996). Creating the conditions for scientific literacy: A re-examination. *American Educational Research Journal, 33*(2), 261–296.

Fullan, M. (1994). Coordinating top-down and bottom-up strategies for education reform. In R. Elmore, & S. Fuhrman (Eds.), *The governance of curriculum* (pp. 186–202). Alexandria, VA: ASCD.

Gergen, K. (1991). *The saturated self: Dilemmas of identity in contemporary life.* New York: Basic Books.

McCaslin, M., & Good, T. (1992). Compliant cognition: The misalliance of management and instructional goals in current school reform. *Educational Researcher, 21*(3), 4–17.

Oakes, J., Quartz, K., Gong, J., Guiton, G., & Lipton, M. (1993). Creating middle schools: Technical, normative, and political considerations. *The Elementary School Journal, 93*(5), 461–480.

Powell, R. (1997). Teaching alike: A cross-case analysis of first-career and second-career beginning teachers' instructional convergence. *Teaching and Teacher Education 13*(3), 341–356.

Powell, R. (1996). The music is why I teach: Intuitive strategies of effective teachers in culturally diverse classrooms. *Teaching and Teacher Education, 12*(1), 49–61.

Powell, R., Skoog, G., & Troutman, P. (1996). On streams and odysseys: Reflections on reform and research in middle level integrative learning environments. *Research in Middle Level Education Quarterly, 19*(4), 1–30.

Powell, R., Zehm, S., & Garcia, J. (1996). *Field experience: Strategies for exploring diversity in schools.* Columbus, OH: Merrill.

Powell, R., Skoog, G., Troutman, P., & Jones, C. (1996, April). *Standing on the edge of middle level curriculum reform: Factors influencing the sustainability of a non-linear integrative learning environment.* Paper presented at the annual meeting of the American Educational Research Association, New York City.

Powell, R., & Skoog, G. (1995). Students' perspectives of integrative curricula: The case of Brown-Barge Middle School. *Research in Middle Level Education, 19*(1), 85–115.

Quartz, K. (1996, April). *Becoming better: The struggle to create a new culture of school reform.* Paper presented at the annual meeting of the American Educational Research Association, New York City.

Quartz, K. (1995). Sustaining new educational communities: Toward a new culture of school reform. In J. Oakes, & K. Quartz (Eds.), *Creating new educational communities: Ninety-fourth yearbook of the National Society for the Study of Education* (pp. 240–252). Chicago: University of Chicago Press.

10

Diversity and Management:
The Case of Estacado High School
by Richard Powell

Students will not work hard for a teacher who is not firmly embedded in their quality worlds.

(Glasser, 1992, p. 66)

Schools, like other social institutions, are shaped by cultural values and practices.

(Hollins, 1996, p. 2)

TEACHING, LEARNING, AND CULTURAL FILTERS

The purpose of this chapter is to help you better understand the relationship between student diversity and classroom management. This is not necessarily an easy relationship to clarify, nor is there an easy set of strategies to simply put into place that addresses this relationship. This is why we have chosen to demonstrate this relationship between diversity and management with a case report of a culturally diverse high school. By reading about a case like this you should be better able to consider how your own classroom management might be affected by culturally diverse students. The school we have selected for this case report is Estacado High School, a medium-sized high school in the West Texas town of Lubbock. An important element of this chapter, besides its attempt to demonstrate how diversity influences classroom management, is that the chapter—along with the previous two chapters—demonstrates how classroom management is intimately connected to all aspects of school life, including student diversity (chapter 10), the structure of the curriculum (chapter 9), and the socioeconomic status of the community, parents, and their children (chapter 8).

Various reports on teaching and learning over the past few decades have helped us better realize that the practice of teaching and learning is far more complicated than pouring information into students' minds. The educational community is beginning to more widely accept that if you actually tried to *pour information into students' minds* the information would pass through a number of highly personalized filters before it could be learned. These filters, which we alluded to in chapters 8 and 9, include socioeconomic class, gender, ethnicity, race, religion, family life, biography, developmental readiness for specific school-taught information, religion, and the list goes on. On an individual basis, these filters create personal perspectives through which learners learn and through which teachers teach. On a school level, the filters collectively create school cultures that vary from one school to another even within the same school district. The purpose of this chapter is to help you better understand the relationship between cultural filters and the social curriculum of your classroom.

Working With Cultural Filters

Skillful teachers in today's classrooms know about and are willing to work with the many filters listed in the preceding paragraph on a moment-by-moment basis. When you first begin teaching you might not know how the filters listed above, as well as others you might think about that we haven't listed, influence your interactions with students. To successfully reach students, however, you must continuously learn about and negotiate these filters with students over time to help them be successful in school. This negotiation process is not always easy especially when the many life experiences and consequently the many cultural filters you have acquired differ notably from those your students are now acquiring (and have previously acquired) when you teach them.

At Estacado High School (EHS) approximately 40 teachers and approximately 800 students continuously negotiate some very powerful cultural filters through which teaching and learning occur.[1] EHS is in Lubbock, a mid-sized western town of approximately 200,000 citizens on the Texas high plains. With agriculture and oil as its economic infrastructure, Lubbock is nearly 300 miles from the nearest metropolitan area and is geographically located on the southern plains.

The cultural filters that are especially salient at EHS are *socioeconomic class* (henceforth called social class), *ethnicity, race, family background,* and *geographical boundaries* within the local school district. These filters are further complicated by the cultural mismatch that has occurred at EHS. This mismatch reflects the lack of alignment between racial and social class dimensions of teachers and their students, a mismatch that holds potential to separate teachers from students in counterproductive ways.

A quick glance at EHS students and teachers illustrates the mismatch mentioned above. We must emphasize here that the mismatch is not exclusive to the EHS school environment, but typifies many school environments across the nation. Students at EHS are predominantly African American, Hispanic, and come from lower-class living conditions; teachers at the school are mostly white and middle class—none of the teachers live within the geographic boundaries set by the school district. These district-set boundaries delimit which students in the town must attend EHS. Moreover, the state-mandated tests have been criticized as being culturally insensitive to minority students, and further criticized as being constructed in such a way that privileges the successful performance of mainstream students on the test. Yet EHS, like other schools in the state, is required to administer the test to students every year.

Despite cultural differences—especially social class differences—between teachers and students, and despite cultural concerns over state-mandated tests, most EHS teachers earnestly strive to understand the barriers that some cultural filters create for separating them from EHS students. We do not want to give you the impression that every EHS teacher and every EHS student succeeds in negotiating the filters. Yet many EHS teachers try to better understand constraints to

---

[1] A more complete discussion of the context of EHS is in a later section of this chapter.

effective communication with students. They also try to understand the personal challenges at home and in the community that students face and must transcend in order to be successful in school. Before describing the context of EHS, we first consider two of the more pressing issues—what we called *filters* above—that so strongly influence how teachers think about management at EHS: social class and ethnicity.

Social Class as a Cultural Filter

Think about the questions in this section which are about lifestyle and social class, especially as these questions pertain to schools like EHS. As you think about the questions consider how your answers might influence your personal style for creating a social curriculum in your classroom and for setting up a system of management that corresponds to this social curriculum.

Most students who attend EHS live in neighborhoods that are called low-income. Have you ever lived over a long period of time in conditions that could be considered low-income? Can you credibly describe a low-income or lower-class lifestyle? Would you describe yourself as now being lower class, middle class, or upper class? Regarding your biography, were you raised in an environment that could be described as lower class, middle class, or upper class? Did the person or persons who raised you have an annual income of approximately $5,000–$10,000, approximately $40,000–$50,000, or approximately $150,000 or more? What do you believe the values, lifestyles, and future aspirations are for school-aged persons who live in the three aforementioned income brackets? What are your stereotypes for students who live in the three brackets? Regarding the income brackets above, which bracket(s) of students would you prefer to teach? Why?

Although we—as authors of this book—are first to agree with the age-old saying that "money isn't everything," we are also first to agree with the truism that money unquestionably creates certain lifestyles and consequently creates certain opportunities (or the lack of opportunities) in our society. This is especially true as Kozol (1991) for example, has demonstrated for educational opportunities. As an example, think for a moment about students who might live in one or more homes where the combined average income of guardians is barely $5,000. How might this student's life differ from another student, perhaps at a different school, who lives in a home or in several homes where the average income is 10 or 20 times that amount? Students who live such different lives based on their social class will have certain values and needs, including educational ones, that determine how they will be able to interact with you at school, and that determine whether they will even be willing to interact with you and the content you teach.

Race and Ethnicity as Cultural Filters

Like social class, the racial status and ethnicity of students and teachers can also be viewed as formidable cultural filters that must be continuously negotiated in school. *Minority* and *ethnicity* are concepts that refer to particular groups in our society. Banks (1993) suggests that persons who belong to the same *ethnic group* share a common sense of values, culture traits, and peoplehood (e.g., Irish, Jewish, Italian American). Persons who belong to the same *minority group* may or may not share common values and cultural traits. However, minority group members share physical/racial traits that distinguish them from persons without these traits, and that differentiate them from persons who are members of the dominant social group.

The dominant social group in the United States is comprised of middle class European-Americans—a group that is more commonly called the majority population, the mainstream, or white middle class. Although demographically the majority, there are numerous areas of the nation where white middle class is actually a minority, and where other societal groups traditionally known as the minority actually comprise the majority of the population. When a school has this kind of student population, the school is often termed a *majority minority school*, thus suggesting that its students are comprised mostly of one or more traditional minority groups (Powell, Zehm, & Garcia, 1996).

The on-campus dynamics that are created by a majority minority situation point to important questions about the idea of management. If, for example, the overwhelming majority of students are Hispanic, the social curriculum will—or arguably should—fundamentally differ from a school where the majority of students are African American, Asian, or white. In some schools, however, two or more nationalities may comprise the student population. In the case of EHS, for example, African American and Hispanic students are equally predominant. In this case, the social curriculum will reflect a meeting and mingling of two predominant cultures. As another example, Mark Keppel High School in Al Hambra, California, is comprised primarily of Asian and Hispanic students, thus creating a need for the school to acknowledge, affirm, and incorporate personal and educational needs from both Asian and Hispanic students, as well as other students at the school.

The argument that can be made about nationality, ethnicity, and race can be made for social class. That is, if the majority of students in a school are from lower-class neighborhoods, the social curriculum of the school will reflect these students and their personal and academic needs. Social values, personal values, family customs, oral communication patterns, and so on, that are more consistent with the prevailing student culture in a school will therefore be predominant in the social curriculum. Teachers who have more empathy for the prevailing student culture will presumably be more responsive to the kind of interpersonal dynamics they establish with students (Ladson-Billings, 1994; Powell, 1997). Related to the idea of management is the idea that the prevailing student culture creates a certain social curriculum; the social curriculum in turn suggests the need for certain kinds of management practices that might not be consistent with another school where the student population and social curriculum varies culturally. In the remainder of this chapter we apply the theoretical ideas above to the context of EHS.

THE CONTEXT OF EHS

Students and Their Parents

As noted above, EHS is a low-income majority minority school with approximately 800 students. Although actual percentages of student backgrounds vary slightly from year to year, 47% of students are African American, 44% are Hispanic, 9% are white, and 3% of the students are members of other societal groups.[2] At least 75% of EHS students are considered to be at risk economically. Economic at-riskness of EHS students is further complicated by other issues, including, for example, racial segregation in the town and limited upward mobility of minorities as demonstrated by a historical precedent of job hiring practices and by an exceedingly low population of middle class minorities in the town and in surrounding rural communities.

Only one percent of EHS students who are white live in the school's neighborhoods. The remaining white students are from middle and upper-middle class neighborhoods in other parts of the city; these remaining white students from other neighborhoods choose to attend EHS in order to be part of its magnet programs. EHS magnet programs are discussed more fully below.

Another important dimension of the EHS student population is the number of students who have their own children. Although exact figures for the number of students who have children are unavailable, teenage motherhood and fatherhood is a very real and ongoing part of the school environment. The school holds parenting classes for students who are interested in attending such classes. These classes help teenage parents learn parenting skills and provide them with needed encouragement to continue in school as full-time students. The tendency for teenage parents in lower-class communities to drop out of high school is high. The deeply caring attitude of the EHS administration and faculty helps teenage parents at the school feel like they are an important part of the school environment.

Another dimension of EHS, certainly a challenging dimension, is getting students' parents involved in school-related activities. During the time that this chapter was written, the school opened a parent liaison office. Mrs. Davis, the parent liaison whom I (Powell) visited with, said that her primary responsibility was to get parents academically involved in their children's education. Mrs. Davis, however, was realistic in her appraisal of what she could actually accomplish for EHS. She noted, "Basically this year we are just trying to get parents into the building. For whatever reasons exist out there, parents just don't come to this school. And we want to change that." The challenge facing Mrs. Davis was clear when she said, "Earlier this year we were having an important event at school and we wanted parents to attend. To invite parents to the event I sent out 800 letters to parents. At least one letter was sent to every home where a student lives. But only one parent showed up for the whole event."

---

[2]Based on student records during the 1996–97 academic year.

In trying to search for ways to connect parents to the school and thus to connect students to the school more directly, Mrs. Davis was in the process of sending questionnaires to all students' homes. These questionnaires, she hopes, will provide her with valuable information for understanding how to better connect parents to school, and to make parents feel comfortable when they visit the school. Mrs. Davis believes that much of the lack of parental involvement is rooted in parents' own feelings of inadequacy in school.

EHS Educators

The backgrounds of EHS professional staff (i.e., teachers, administrators, counselors, and other professionals) vary notably from backgrounds of students. On the average, the ethnic composition of professional staff is approximately 76% white, 10% Hispanic, and 13% African American. The turnover rate of teachers at the school is remarkably low, although the school hires some teachers who are new to EHS each year. As I had conversations with teachers at the school, I discovered that some of them had been teaching at the school for many years. For most EHS teachers there is a deeper level commitment to working with EHS students; to helping them in every way possible to succeed in school. Novice teachers, however, especially those who are privileged middle class persons and who have never lived or worked in low-income neighborhoods, are initially challenged to learn the social curriculum of a low-income majority minority school.

The Standard Curriculum

The EHS curriculum—what teachers are expected to teach and what students are expected to learn—is mostly standard for a subject-centered high school. The local school district as well as the Texas Education Agency (TEA) gives EHS educators little opportunity to be innovative in the content they teach despite the almost desperate need for such innovation in schools such as EHS. State-level officials in the TEA seemingly hold tightly to the myth that *what is good for one student is good for all students.* Despite the growing body of evidence that this myth actually pushes some groups of students away from school, the myth predominates Texas schooling and consequently the EHS curriculum.

Grade-level and subject-specific learning objectives are determined mostly by state-level officials; teachers are accountable for teaching not only these objectives, but also for preparing students for the high-stakes mandated test known as the *Texas Assessment of Academic Skills* (TAAS). Some courses also have end-of-course exams that further prefigure the content that teachers must include in their lessons. Despite state guidelines on curriculum content, teachers at EHS can be and are highly creative for their students.

Among the greatest challenges for EHS teachers is to develop strategies that connect students to state-mandated content without disconnecting them from school because of the irrelevancy that students feel for what they are expected to learn. Given this challenge, teaching in schools such as EHS is clearly some of the most challenging and, unquestionably, some of the most important teaching that exists in the whole profession. After observing teaching at EHS for over three years and after observing other similar schools in urban areas, I remain convinced that only the very best, the most creative, and the most deeply compassionate teachers can succeed in helping transcend the students' perception of content irrelevancy. Common sense suggests that overcoming this perception helps to connect students with school in needful ways. These teacher traits—*very best, most creative, deeply compassionate* (however these traits might be defined)—were clearly evident for some of the teachers I observed at EHS.

Magnet Programs

Because of the medical and law magnet programs at EHS, the school attracts a limited number of students from around the entire district, not only students within the neighborhood school boundaries set by the district. Over half of the students who attend the magnet programs are middle class, white, and economically advantaged compared to most disadvantaged students who live within the local neighborhood. These aforementioned students do not live in the EHS neighborhood. One reason that the magnet programs at EHS, and at other schools in the district, were put into place was to provide an alternative to forced integration of schools (i.e., bussing of students) in the district. On a legalistic level this was somewhat successful: Of the 9% white students at EHS, 8% of these are from other neighborhoods and attend EHS for the magnet programs.

Although EHS magnet programs have diversified the racial make-up of the school, the programs are unquestionably tailored to the academically talented students. To be admitted to the magnet programs EHS students must have a 3.5 grade point average (GPA) on a 4.0 scale. This kind of GPA qualifies students for the school's academic honors program. Despite the opportunities that the magnet programs create for honors students, the programs can also be viewed more critically as creating yet another form of segregation at the school—the segregation of honors students from those in other academic tracks. As an example, I asked one of the EHS teachers who had been at the school only one year but who also had years of experience elsewhere what her professional life was like teaching students at the school. I asked her to tell me the essence of her Estacado teaching experience. I was, of course, especially interested in her instructional management practices. She said,

> If you are wanting to know what it is like for me to teach kids from this specific neighborhood I don't think I can answer that. Because I teach only honors students who are mostly in the magnet programs I really don't know what it's like to teach real EHS kids—you know, the kids from this neighborhood. Most of the kids I teach come from other parts of town, not from around here.

I interpreted this teacher's comment above to mean that she and the honors students that she teaches are separated academically and bureaucratically from the mainstream culture of EHS. This school's mainstream culture, which is a minority, disadvantaged, and lower social class culture, is an inherent part of the local neighborhood.

It is this culture that is essentially the real pulse of the school, but a pulse that because of academic tracking not every teacher can feel, and thus respond to in culturally responsive ways.

Despite the inherent segregation in the school's magnet program and the school's tracking practices, educators at the school are rightfully proud of their magnet programs. Students who are admitted to the magnet programs are involved both in extensive field trips to selected sites outside of the local area and with medical-oriented and law-oriented facilities in the local community. Consequently, the magnet programs connect EHS to the community in very important ways.

TELLING ABOUT EHS

In this chapter I tell a descriptive account of EHS's attempt to create a social curriculum that reaches high school students who live mostly in low-income neighborhoods. As the school searched for successful ways, EHS gradually began implementing some of the central ideas that framed the model of the Quality School management described by Glasser (1992). This implementation, according to vice principal Jerry Lee, reportedly brought about a more congenial school atmosphere within only a few years and significantly reduced the number of classroom behavior problems that were being referred by teachers to the principal's office.

In telling the story of EHS in this chapter, I am reminded of the work of respected ethnographer Alan Peshkin (1986), who writes:

> Given the range of objectives that characterize a school, the number of questions that can be raised about these realities, and the diverse perspectives created by the personal biographies of different researchers, it is clear that no story told about any school can be everyone's story. (p. ix)

Following Peshkin's quote above, the story I tell about Estacado High School (EHS) is indeed my story—as understood through my perspectives and beliefs—and thus cannot be "everyone's story." I am fully aware, just as you are, that every teacher and every administrator at EHS, because of their personal biographies, would very well offer a story that varies from mine, and would justifiably disagree with some of the claims I make about school, especially claims about management and the social curriculum.

The reason that I talk about personal dimensions of story-telling here is to let you know about the personal and professional limitations I have in writing this chapter. As a child growing up in a small and isolated western Kansas town, I was raised in a lower social class neighborhood that was racially and ethnically diverse. In some ways my childhood and school experiences were similar to students at EHS. However, my teaching career took place in schools where students were predominantly white and middle class; students at EHS represented predominantly racial minority and lower SES societal groups. While I believe that I had at least some understanding of how EHS students' lower SES home and community conditions influenced their school lives, my white perspective clearly limits the understanding I am capable of gaining from students' experiences as racial minorities in EHS and in the local community.

GETTING TO KNOW EHS

If I have both personal and professional limitations for writing about EHS, then how did I get to know the school well enough to credibly report on its management practices and to apply the notion of social curriculum to its school context? This is a very important question that I will briefly address here. Over a period of three years I became better acquainted with EHS. This period of time enabled me to more broadly explore management in the school and to consider EHS as one model for working with low-income students. My interest in the school continued to build as I held my field-based university teacher education classes there. These classes focused upon classroom management, cultural diversity, and classroom teaching strategies.

As discussions over the nature of this book on social curriculum and management unfolded with my colleagues (McLaughlin, Savage, Zehm), I realized how EHS would more specifically be able to contribute to our understanding of school-based management in contemporary society. EHS is, at least in some ways, similar to other schools I have visited and have taught in across the nation. However, in very important ways EHS is also atypical of other schools, thus suggesting the need to rethink traditional models of management and student discipline in such atypical school sites. This idea of rethinking management for site-specific, community-specific, and culture-specific school environments—a notion that questions generalizability of management models and a notion consistent with the idea of site-based social curricula—was particularly suited to our goals in this book.

CULTURE, THE SOCIAL CURRICULUM, AND MANAGEMENT

Reconsider for a moment a few of the dimensions of EHS that were highlighted above:

- low-income school located in a low-income neighborhood,
- school district is in a small remote city that has traditionally been segregated by race and remains racially and economically segregated today,
- majority minority school comprised of mostly lower-class African American and Hispanic students with corresponding values, needs, and cultured predispositions,
- academic tracking based on multiple criteria, most particularly based on intelligence tests and other forms of standardized testing,
- minimal parental involvement in school-related activities,
- multiple first languages spoken by students, and
- mainstream teaching staff, representing mostly white middle-class values, needs, and cultures.

From the list above, think about all the different values that are present in EHS at any one moment of a school day and that comprise the social curriculum of the school. Think also about how you, as a classroom teacher, would *manage* the mixing and mingling of these values so that your students might interact more genuinely with you as a person and thus interact more genuinely with the content you are expected to teach. These were the things that educators at EHS had to very seriously think about and take action on if they were going to create a social curriculum that would enable students to feel valued, needed, and successful. Teachers also had to take action if they were going to transcend the latent racial and economic segregation that yet prevails in Lubbock. The traditional ideas of *controlling* student behavior and *enforcing* student learning with practices such as assertive discipline, corporal punishment, and stern rules and regulations weren't working at EHS.[3] The dropout rate at EHS was increasing, standardized test scores continued to drop, student behavior problems had escalated, and educators at the school got more and more frustrated as their middle class values for education, and the values of the school district, clashed with the educational values and personal needs of their students.

There follows an account of how EHS began turning away from a management system based on the ideas of *controlling* and *enforcing* a traditional school environment, and toward a social curriculum where student respect, dignity, and responsibility were viable options. As a way of introducing you to this account of EHS, I first consider the recent movie and corresponding book called *Dangerous Minds*.

PRECONCEPTIONS, STEREOTYPES, AND MANAGEMENT

On *Dangerous Minds*

In her book, *Dangerous Minds*[4], LouAnne Johnson (1992) offers a gutsy 'snapshot' of how she, as a mostly inexperienced classroom teacher, met and mingled with disadvantaged high school students who were bussed to a school that was not in their own neighborhood. How Johnson's book depicts selected students, and how the movie version of the book in particular depicts these students, creates somewhat negative stereotypes for students in general and for disadvantaged students in particular. The book also creates a rather scary description of one person's approach to *managing* students whose need for traditional school-based information, and whose school-based behaviors, vary markedly from students whose need for traditional school-based information is more consistent with college-bound high school students in middle class and upper-middle class communities.

The kind of stereotypes that a reader (and prospective teacher) can potentially acquire for students depicted in *Dangerous Minds* (both book and movie versions) is most accurately reflected in the following quote taken from the back of the book's cover[5]:

> They were called the class from Hell—thirty-four inner city sophomores she inherited from a teacher who'd been "pushed over the edge." She was told "those kids have tasted blood. They're dangerous."

This quote, while obviously marketing hype to get people immediately interested in the book, is an unfortunate circumstance of furthering the kind of stereotyping

---

[3]This claim was made by Mr. Jerry Lee, the vice principal of EHS.
[4]The book *Dangerous Minds* was originally published with the title *My Posse Don't Do Homework*.
[5]Based on: Johnson, L. (1992). *Dangerous Minds*. St. Martin's Press, New York. On the front cover of the book is a picture of Michelle Pfeiffer, who played the part of Johnson in the movie version of the book, and who is depicted as seemingly tough-skinned and unconventional in her attire. Also in the picture of the book cover are students who are situated behind Pfeiffer.

that has been associated with students who live in low-income neighborhoods, and who traditionally and socially have not been able to link upward social class mobility with successful educational experiences.

Despite the negative stereotyping of students that is associated with *Dangerous Minds* and its marketing hype, Johnson's story of the students she taught has an important positive point as well: Her students are young adults who have educational, social, and personal needs that are equally important to all other students. A related point—perhaps an unnecessarily complicated point in the way Johnson tries to make it in her book—is that by using teaching strategies that are consistent with students' cultures, however gutsy and nontraditional these strategies might need to be, a teacher might better create a classroom social curriculum that more readily engages students in successful school experiences. However, the majority of teachers who enter the teaching profession are not predisposed to be gutsy and nontraditional (Powell, 1997) in the way Johnson depicts herself in *Dangerous Minds,* and there are many schools that would not endorse the classroom strategies used by Johnson to reach her students.

Teachers in general enter teaching because they like kids and believe that they can make a difference in some kids' lives (e.g., Veenam, 1984). Few prospective teachers would immediately like kids, and would choose to become a teacher, if they really believed that these kids had indeed "tasted blood" and were universally "dangerous." Moreover, Johnson (1992) implicitly suggests that teachers who are successful with the students that she teaches in her story must be tougher than the kids being taught. Being tougher than students and showing students this toughness, however, is not a universally agreed-upon classroom strategy regardless of how much this approach might have been lauded in the earlier part of this century and regardless of the success that LouAnne Johnson had with this approach. This also is not an approach we endorse in this book.

Dangerous Minds and EHS

Although the classroom strategies that are depicted in *Dangerous Minds* are not those we can freely endorse in this book, I still have need to mention Johnson's book since I (Powell), as a teacher educator of both undergraduate and postbaccalaureate teacher education students, must deal with these student stereotypes continuously. The following scenario, which happened very recently in one of my postbaccalaureate teacher education classes that was taught at a university in Lubbock, exemplifies this kind of *Dangerous Minds* student stereotyping.

As noted earlier in this chapter, EHS has been a location for my field-based teacher education classes to meet each semester. With the assistance of principal Ken Wallace and vice principal Jerry Lee, we meet in a designated classroom at the school. Throughout the semester we make many classroom observations at EHS, talk with teachers and administrators, do action research projects about cultural diversity issues, and consider how to best engage students at the school using suitable instructional strategies. We also examine the school's behavior management system, and we discuss various writings that are related to this system.

At the beginning of every semester when prospective teachers in my classes learn that we will be doing field-based work at EHS, I am asked the same questions by them: Why are we going to EHS when there are other high schools in the district that seem to be doing so many better things? Why do we have to go to a school with so many minority students? Clearly, these kinds of questions point to the image problem—especially the stereotyping—that surrounds EHS. Part of this image problem, however, does not have its roots in what actually happens inside the school; rather, the image problem has its roots in the latent segregationist tendencies of the town and of the whole geographical area, of prospective teachers' lack of experiences with and naive understanding of other societal groups, and with the media's negative depiction of minority youth in general (see, for example, Giroux, 1997).

Despite the many "roots" of the EHS image problem, the roots are realities that I, as a teacher educator, must deal with and that I must help prospective teachers address. This was most evident when I asked one of my classes during the second class session of the semester to write a few paragraphs about EHS. I asked students to note what they knew about the school, what they have heard others say about EHS, and what they expected to see when they first enter the school building (assuming, of course, they haven't been in the building before this time). After a few minutes of writing I asked for volunteers from the class to explain what they wrote. Jim (not his real name)—a student who was deeply committed to becoming a teacher—said:

> I haven't ever been in the school, and I attended a much smaller rural school than the size of EHS. But I've heard about EHS, and the only thing I know to expect when I go into Estacado is what I saw in the movie *Dangerous Minds*. I'm really kind of afraid to go into EHS right now and I wish we could go to another school that, well, is like the one I attended so I can be around people mostly like me [white, middle class]. I know that students will have guns at EHS, that they will want to fight all the time.

Importantly, no mention was made of *Dangerous Minds* in my class up to the point that Jim made his comment. Yet this is what came to Jim's mind when I asked him to write about EHS. However, Jim was unaware that after EHS began implementing a new system for student behavior, the school had fewer student fights than any other school in the district. Jim also had a misconception about the use of guns at the school. Jerry Lee, the vice principal, noted that the only gun they were aware of at the school was left by a student one time in a tree outside the school. Jim also had no knowledge of the population of EHS students who had their own children, and thus was unaware of the special needs of student-parents.

In many ways Jim's stereotypes of EHS and his image of the students in the school are a social construction. Jim had never been in the school, yet he had strongly negative images of EHS, images that were created by the local society in which he lives and by the larger society in which he receives a multiplicity of media-driven images and messages. Had Jim not been asked to do field-based work in EHS, he would have retained his negative stereotype of the school and kept his "gangster" image of EHS students. Toward the end of the semester Jim admittedly was humbled by the school's hospitality, by the friendliness of students, and by the school's attempts to help students be successful in school despite the local town's segregationist practices. I was pleasantly surprised when Jim requested to do his student teaching at EHS, which he completed successfully.

Jim is obviously a success story—a story I purposefully selected for this chapter—for how some students can overcome the negative stereotypes they unintentionally acquire for majority minority schools like EHS. Not every student, however, is as successful as Jim was in overcoming his or her misconceptions and negative stereotypes for some student groups. Important questions related to the social curriculum, and to the idea of management, surround the case of Jim. Consider the questions below.

- Had Jim not had an opportunity to have a field-based course at EHS and thus to face his fears and misconceptions for teaching at EHS, what kind of classroom social curriculum might he have initially established when he began teaching?
- How might have Jim's fear for teaching students at EHS, and for interacting with some students whom he believed would be carrying guns to school, influenced his interactions with students at the school?
- What kind of management system would Jim have most likely set up in his classroom had he not developed a better understanding for his students? As part of this management system, what might have been his classroom norm for instructional strategies? What might have been his classroom norm for overseeing student behavior?

Without knowing Jim and his personal qualities better (i.e., his personality, his degree of flexibility, his level of empathy for other social groups, and so on) these questions become somewhat academic. Yet for virtually hundreds of first-year teachers who enter classrooms as professionals for the first time, the questions above are not academic at all—they are totally real and must be faced on a moment-by-moment basis as novice teachers and their student stereotypes are brought to the classroom.

UNDERSTANDING EHS STUDENTS' QUALITY WORLDS

One way that Jim (in the discussion immediately above) began to move beyond his *Dangerous Minds* stereotypes for EHS students was to explore what the school was doing, on the whole, to help its own novice and experienced teachers better understand the needs of EHS students. Several years prior to Jim's early field experiences at EHS—the same experiences that were part of the field-based course he was taking from me at the time—EHS principal Ken Wallace and vice principal Jerry Lee began exploring the *Quality School* concept described by William Glasser (Glasser, 1992). They believed that this concept and its related assumptions might be one means for teachers to understand the personal, social, financial, parental, and academic needs of EHS students, thus fostering more successful management practices. A central idea of a Quality School, as described by Glasser, is to "manage students without coercion," thus creating a school where students take more responsibility for their own learning, for their own behavior, and for their own decision-making. A related idea of the Quality School model is that students will have more choice in how they engage in school-related activities.

Although Mr. Wallace and Mr. Lee believed that the Quality School idea was well suited to EHS, they also were aware that experienced teachers often are reluctant to try out new approaches to teaching and learning. This reluctance comes from years of being asked to—and in some schools required to—try out yet another quick-fix innovation for perceived problems in school. Mr. Wallace and Mr. Lee, however, believed that the Quality School idea was more than just another quick-fix innovation. The two administrators wanted EHS teachers at the very least to be introduced to the key concepts of the Quality School model.

Because of budgetary constraints for EHS, the school could not really afford highly expensive consultants for putting on workshops about how to implement and sustain Quality School practices. To begin implementing Quality School into the EHS social curriculum, Mr. Lee attended training institutes for Quality School and for reality therapy. This kind of therapy is the fundamental basis for the Quality School model of management. Mr. Lee is now a certified trainer of Glasser's work. Mr. Lee, then, along with the assistance of a professor in a nearby university, delivered in-service workshops to EHS teachers on Quality School management.

What Mr. Lee has tried to help EHS teachers understand is that every student has a very personal world outside of school where certain cultural, social class, and family traits comprise a quality situation for him or her. According to Mr. Lee, if you really want to reach EHS students, then "you have to get to know the students' quality worlds." Knowing about and understanding students' quality worlds also means knowing what is personally important for EHS students, and most importantly knowing how you can connect students to positive learning experiences by being sensitive to students.

Glasser believes that the idea of Quality World is the most important concept associated with this model of schooling. Glasser (1997) writes:

> This small, very specific, personal world is the core of our lives because in it are the people, things, and beliefs that we have discovered are most satisfying to our needs. (p. 599)

Associated with the Quality World idea is what Glasser earlier called *control theory* and now calls *choice theory* (Glasser, 1997). Choice theory is further framed by four psychological needs:

- the need to belong
- the need for power
- the need for freedom
- the need for fun

At EHS, Mr. Lee has taught teachers enough choice theory and enough about the Quality School idea so that most EHS teachers know at least theoretically how students need to be treated if they are to put teachers and the school in their quality worlds. Most importantly, the four needs are generally culture-specific, but they are also universal. Following the work of Glasser (1992), this means that you can expect all students to have these needs. However, you can also expect these needs to vary from person to person, from school to school, from ethnic group to ethnic group, from one social class to another, and so on. The key to opening the door to students' quality worlds—the same key that EHS teachers use daily—is to understand the four needs as they exist for EHS students, and understand how to make these needs part of classroom instruction. This requires you to understand what students' quality worlds are like outside of school and to understand the dimensions of these worlds that they bring to school.

Let us return for a moment to our discussion of Jim above. As Jim began to understand the concepts of Quality World and choice theory, he then began to realize that EHS students had psychological needs that were similar to his own. Jim also realized that in order to understand better how students' needs play themselves out in school, he would need to gain a much better understanding of students' quality worlds outside of school. To accomplish this, Jim visited neighborhoods surrounding the school, and he tried to broaden his awareness of students' cultural backgrounds by getting to know students more personally, by reading about diversity issues, and by reading about poverty in schools. Jim also completed an action research project where he explored EHS students' perspectives of teaching and learning. When Jim finally completed his various projects at EHS and when he considered the school in terms of Glasser's Quality World concepts, his preconceptions of EHS students as "dangerous," as being "pushed over the edge," and as having "tasted blood" changed dramatically. That some students at the school might be dangerous in certain ways and that in some aspect of their personal life they have been pushed over the edge could very well be true. But as Jim discovered, this kind of student stereotype does not reflect the majority of EHS kids, and certainly does not set them up to be universally feared.

STUDENT BEHAVIOR AT EHS

One of Jim's greatest initial fears over being at EHS was his fear of student misbehavior. Not only did his initial student stereotype frighten him of the students, but his general fear of not being able to "control" a classroom in general bothered him. However, as Jim learned, when EHS began implementing aspects of the Quality School model, they also implemented a student behavior program that greatly minimized student misbehavior and that gave students much responsibility for their own behavior. This began moving the behavior program away from one of coercion and to one of cooperation.

The student behavior and discipline policy for students at EHS is straightforward. The policy essentially has consequences for three classes of misbehavior. Class A and B misbehaviors are serious offenses; they usually are related to illegal activities such as carrying drugs in school, carrying weapons, and so on. Removal from school and being turned over to law enforcement officers can result from these misbehaviors. Class C misbehaviors are the less serious, off-task kind of behaviors that disrupt the normal flow of classroom teaching. Class C misbehaviors are further defined as those that keep the teacher from effectively teaching and other students from learning. The class C misbehaviors also include being tardy to class or skipping class altogether.

When a teacher feels that a class C misbehavior has occurred, she or he sends the student to *time out* for that class period. Before the student who was sent to time out can return to that specific class where the misbehavior occurred, the student is required to make *restitution* with the teacher. One approach for making restitution, which is a central part of the school's attempt to help students become more responsible for their own behavior, is for students to write a five-paragraph essay while they are in time out. In the essay the student explains why he or she was sent out of the classroom and specifies a plan to avoid this in the future.

Restitution is made when the student, either before or after school, visits the teacher to discuss the essay. If a student is sent out of a teacher's classroom a third time, the student cannot return to the class for the remainder of the semester. The student goes to permanent time out unless another class is available. The first time that a student goes to time out, documentation is made. The second time a student goes to time out he or she talks to the vice principal, Mr. Lee, who also calls the student's guardian.

Although some educators might disagree with the EHS approach to dealing with classroom behavior issues, Jim was relieved that the school had a well-established means for dealing with such issues. This further alleviated some of his fears and initial concerns about organizing his classroom social curriculum so he would have greater potential for success as a teacher and so his students would have greater potential for success as learners.

THE REALITY OF MANAGEMENT IN EHS: EXPERIENCED TEACHERS' PERSPECTIVES

The above story of Jim, a preservice teacher who was initially very afraid of EHS and its students and who held negative stereotypes for EHS students, provides one means to consider how his fear would have become part of the social curriculum of his classroom. This same fear, if left unchallenged when he began his first year of teaching, would likely have framed how he negotiated, guided, and facilitated student learning.

Jim's perspective of EHS was that of a preservice teacher yet professionally uninformed about how daily life in classrooms unfolds and how the social curricula of individual classrooms and whole schools take shape. In this section of the chapter we explore what experienced EHS teachers' perspectives are for teaching at the school. The contrast between Jim's somewhat naive perspective of EHS students and the teachers' experienced perspectives of EHS students is striking and consequently warrants consideration here.

Selecting Experienced EHS Teachers

As I began focusing on EHS for the purpose of writing this chapter, I realized that experienced teachers' perspectives were needed in order to understand more fully what daily life was like at EHS. I also needed to talk with EHS teachers in order to understand how, if at all, they were trying out the ideas that reflect the Quality School model of management. I talked to Jerry Lee about which EHS teachers might be best suited to the needs of this chapter. He made several suggestions of teachers whose classrooms, in his best judgment, embodied Quality School ideals.

Of the teachers Mr. Lee suggested, Delores Martinez and Dave Dickerson agreed to talk with me in depth about their classroom social curriculum, about their ideas related to management, and about the Quality School model as it applied to their interactions with students. When I reported to Mr. Lee who would be participating in my study for this chapter, he noted that Dave is one of the few teachers who performs most of the Quality School ideals without necessarily knowing Quality School theory. He further noted that Delores continuously explores various aspects of the Quality School theory, but that she also has raised important questions about the limitations of the Quality School model.

Both teachers allowed me to observe their classroom teaching over time so that I could get a better understanding of the relationship between their perspectives of teaching at EHS and how these perspectives became transformed into actual classroom life. Consequently, I observed their classroom teaching on various occasions, and I observed their interactions with students between classes. I also had several lengthy conversations with them about the social curriculum of their classrooms. To ensure that I represented what Delores and Dave said in these conversations more credibly, I taped and transcribed our comments during each conversation.

Delores Martinez and Dave Dickerson

Of the two teachers, Delores had taught at EHS the longest length of time, nine years, whereas Dave had taught there two years. Delores is Hispanic and was raised in Lubbock. Dave, on the other hand, recently moved to Lubbock from the Eastern coast of the United States. Delores, who teaches art at EHS, and Dave, who teaches government, both have classrooms that would strike a casual observer as being somewhat comfortable and easy-going but not off-task and uneventful. Despite the rather relaxed climate of their classrooms, both teachers also demonstrated a high degree of *withitness*, a term that is often used to describe teachers who are intuitively aware of most everything that is going on in the classroom at any particular moment.

As I observed their teaching and their classroom social curricula, and as I began comparing their teaching approaches, I detected some common themes of their teaching. I briefly discuss four themes here that reflect the perspectives and related practices of the classroom social curricula of Delores and Dave:

- knowing and reaching students,
- reflecting on self as teacher,

- understanding the idea of Quality School, and
- dealing with student and school stereotypes.

Knowing and Reaching Students

Central to the Quality School model is the notion of *really* knowing students. In a school that has adopted the Quality School model, this means more than knowing only their names and how they interact with you for part of each school day. Indeed, knowing students in a Quality School way means knowing how they live out their lives at home and in their neighborhoods—that is, knowing what comprises their quality worlds in local neighborhoods and knowing what compromises they have to make just to get through a day in their own neighborhoods.

A comment made by Delores reflects the theme of *knowing and reaching students* in order to teach them in the classroom. Delores noted:

> You have got to be able to reach the kids. But you've got to be able to know how to reach them and that's where a lot of teachers here get so frustrated. Because some teachers just don't know how to reach them because they don't know who they are. When these teachers feel they are unable to reach the kids, they say to themselves, "What do I do? I just don't know." So what they do is they get upset at the kid and the kid gets upset with them. Then there is no learning going on and the discipline problems start. A lot of fear that some teachers have when they come to Estacado comes from the fact that they don't know the culture of the kids. They don't know the Mexican and African American cultures. They only know what they have been raised in. And many of these teachers were raised in and now live in white and middle class cultures.

Another comment by Delores further suggests her deeper-level awareness of EHS students and her understanding of their lives outside of school:

> Our students at EHS are challenging and one reason they are challenging is because parents in this neighborhood don't have a lot of the money and they don't have a lot of the out-of-school experiences that kids at some other schools have. It's not that kids at Estacado are any less intelligent or less smart. It's just that the kids lack in experience. This means that the traditional content we teach them can be real hard for them to relate to. I don't mean that every kid has to relate to everything taught in school. That is ridiculous to think that. But some kids we have here really can't relate to anything in school at all.

Like Delores, Dave has striven to get to know students outside of school. In one of our conversations he told me:

> In order to connect with them in school I have to get interested in their lives out of school. I am interested in them out of school and I know about many of their lives. I have talked to many of their parents. I know maybe 75-80 percent of their parents. And I make a real effort to be here for them if they have a problem.

Dave also mentioned the special needs that some of his students have because these students have their own children. In order to be more understanding of these students' situations at home, Dave has talked to many of them to find out about their home lives. Dave noted:

At first I was really surprised when I came to Estacado how many students have their own children. But now I take all this in stride. But knowing who these people are, and knowing that they have some very demanding needs at home helps me connect with them more and helps me teach them better.

The comments above by Dave and Delores are first glimpses at their felt need to really know students well before they could begin reaching them in the classroom. By putting the practice of knowing students well as a priority in their classroom life, they also viewed themselves as more than only content specialists (i.e., government specialist, art specialist) as the next theme below suggests.

Reflecting on Self as Teacher

To help Delores and Dave reflect on themselves as teachers, I asked each of them individually to choose three words that would best describe them as teachers at EHS. Delores chose the words "compassionate, understanding, and flexible." Dave chose the words "friend, parent, and confidant." The words that they chose clearly reflect their desire to know students before they can reach them. Perhaps most importantly is that the words they chose are all on a humanistic level rather than subject matter or academic level. This does not mean, however, that Delores and Dave put learning content as a secondary goal in their classrooms. Rather, this means that both teachers believed firmly—just as EHS administrators believed—that in order for students to learn content successfully, they must first connect with students on a personal, compassionate level. Establishing trust-filled and respectful relationships with EHS students is foremost in establishing a positive classroom social curriculum and foremost in the Quality School model of classroom management.

Another point can be made here that is related to creating trust-filled relationships. Recall the story of Jim earlier in this chapter. Jim's initial fear of EHS students would have clearly interrupted the process of creating the kind of relationships that Dave and Delores suggest are necessary before content can be successfully taught at EHS, and before lessons can be managed in such a way as to ensure positive learning experiences for all students. However, not all preservice teachers like Jim have field-based teacher education experiences in minority schools which can help them confront their fears, stereotypes, and biases for teaching students from other societal groups. Preservice teachers who have such experiences, however, reportedly enhance their sensitivity for teaching societal groups (i.e., race, class, ethnic) other than their own (Cochran-Smith, 1995; Powell, 1997).

Creating trust-filled relationships with students—the kind of relationships that Delores and Dave have created—clearly is not a new idea for high school teachers. Most any educator would agree with the need for this dimension of classroom teaching. And certainly such relationships are central to Glasser's Quality School model. However, not every high school teacher is willing to demonstrate other qualities that Delores and Dave believed they demonstrated with their students, such as being compassionate, understanding, flexible, a friend, parent, and confidant. Yet these qualities, Delores and Dave believed, must come first at EHS, and at other schools like EHS, before successful teaching and learning of content can be realized on any level.

Understanding the Idea of Quality School

At EHS, presumably like at other schools, the overall premise of helping teachers understand the Quality School idea and helping them implement some of its practices is to enable EHS teachers to look more deeply into the cultural and family backgrounds of students. A related idea is that when teachers really begin to understand students' backgrounds—when they really begin to understand what the concept of *quality* means for the students they are teaching—then they begin relating to students' backgrounds in their lessons and in their daily interactions with students. A hoped-for outcome of this is for teachers to move away from *controlling* student behavior with *coercive* classroom practices, and move toward *negotiating* and *mediating* student behavior with *noncoercive* classroom practices (Glasser, 1992). By using negotiated and noncoercive approaches to management, at least on a theoretical level, students have more of a choice about their involvement in classroom and school activities. As a function of their personalities and as a function of their deep-felt commitment to helping young learners be successful in school, some teachers use negotiation and noncoercive strategies without knowing theoretically about the Quality School model (for example, see Powell, 1997). Dave and Delores are such teachers, although Delores is more familiar than Dave with the theory and practice of the Quality School model.

There is, of course, a theoretical model to follow for becoming a Quality School as suggested by Glasser (1992), and for becoming a Quality School teacher. If you walked into EHS at any given moment during the school year, you might or might not see evidence of the Quality School model. Not every EHS teacher, of course, is as deeply committed to the Quality School model as Mr. Lee and Mr. Wallace. However, if you visited with each teacher you would find that the EHS faculty in general is aware of how the idea of quality in students' lives can be applied to their teaching. And you can clearly see evidence of how teachers apply this to their teaching as students have taken more responsibility in making choices about their behavior and their learning.

Delores, in particular, had some important comments to say about the school's attempt to become a Quality School. Delores told me, "The Quality School thing is so easy to say and to talk about, but it's so very hard to do." Delores further explained:

> If you are going to reach a child in his or her quality world then you have got to know where that child is coming from. You've got to know where that child lives. Instead of sitting in one of these classrooms for eight hours of in-service listening to some consultant trying to find out why Johnny can't read, teachers should go where Johnny lives. Go walk the neighborhood. You know, have teachers walk the neighborhood and find out where Johnny lives, or where Trashonda lives. Find out exactly where these children come from and then go back to school and lay it out on the table and say, "Okay, this is where all my kids live and now I know why Trashonda often

doesn't respond in my class." Knowing about Trashonda and knowing about Johnny like this takes a really sharp awareness of kids, and you just can't get that awareness sitting in a workshop listening to consultants who *think* they know our neighborhood. This awareness comes from getting into the neighborhood.

Delores, however, is not naive in the kind of classroom challenges—and certainly the kind of serious questions—that underlie the Quality School model. Delores further noted:

> When Mr. Lee introduced the Quality School idea I went along with it because I thought, "Okay, I need to work with students' Quality Worlds and I need to see where they're at." So when this child has drugs or when that child has a non-structured Quality World at home, I thought, "Now, how do I get into that world in order to reach them?" I guess what I am asking here is, Do I need to know all about drugs and do I have to know just where he is with drugs in order to reach him in my classroom? But if their world of drugs and nonstructure is really and truly all they know, then I need to be able to identify with that in order to pull them out of that. But students see that you are trying to identify with where they are coming from and then they try to pull you into their Quality World because that is absolutely all they know. If drugs is making them feel good, then that is what their Quality World is about.

Delores also had a very comprehensive understanding of the neighborhood in which EHS was located. An important part of Delores's description of the EHS's neighborhood is that the Quality World of the neighborhood doesn't necessarily include success in education as a foremost ideal. In the next comment Delores refers to East Lubbock's lower socioeconomic class living conditions. Delores noted:

> A lot of kids who live near this school don't even travel very far from where they are raised. So one thing about east Lubbock is that students feel like this is everything to them. This is where they have their friends. This is where they have their social times, every aspect, because a lot of them don't feel good about going into west Lubbock or south Lubbock where the wealthier kids live. They feel like east Lubbock is it for them. As far as a social life, there really is no social life for east Lubbock kids other than watching movies. And while I hate to admit it, getting pregnant is also part of that social life since there are no other distractions. So for many kids in east Lubbock there are just no things for that academic development that might be more available in other parts of the city.

In another comment Delores also relates the lack of academic support at home for many students who live in the EHS neighborhood:

> One-hundred percent of the problem for many of our kids at EHS is that nobody at home supports them in their academic endeavors at school. To teach in this school you have to understand that. What you do is you encourage them, you try to somehow help these students see how school and how being successful in school can be part of their quality worlds out of school. So you really have to focus on supporting the kids to the point that you get what you want out of them. But if you don't know who they are and where they are coming from you will get nothing from them in the way of success at school. Knowing and relating honestly to the kids comes first. And this relating has to be honest; it can't be fake or they'll see right through you.

Delores' insight that enabled her to reach students in a Quality School manner was derived partly from her biographical experiences as a Hispanic growing up in east Lubbock, partly from her professional experiences teaching in the community, and partly from her theoretical and practical experiences with the Quality School model.

Dave's natural predisposition to reach students, according to Mr. Lee, aligned with the Quality School model of teaching. However, Dave's insight that enabled him to reach students in a Quality School manner was derived presumably from an inherent ability to connect personally with students rather than from compliance with the theoretical aspects of the Quality School model.

Perhaps the most pressing question that must be asked here, however, relates to Jim, the preservice teacher who was discussed earlier in this chapter. For example, what experiences might Jim have that would best prepare him to emulate the teacher and student relations that Delores and Dave established with their students? And where is the most appropriate place for Jim to get these experiences? Clearly, the experiences that Jim acquires must help him overcome the stereotypes he had for EHS, its students, and its neighborhood.

Dealing with Stereotypes

Stereotyping students like those at EHS is almost pervasive in our society. And few social problems are more important to overcome in the immediate future than this kind of stereotyping. Almost every teacher in practically every location faces the challenge of student and school stereotyping; Dave, Delores, and Jim stand before this same challenge. Jim (white, middle class), for example, had never been in EHS before his teacher education program and he believed the students were dangerous and should be feared. When Dave (white, middle class, second-career teacher) took the job at EHS, he was firmly committed to being an outstanding teacher, but he admitted that teaching in a majority minority school at first intimidated him.

In the section above on the Quality School model Delores depicted life for students who live in the EHS neighborhood. A significant part of this depiction was the minimal opportunities and experiences these students have outside school for enriching their educational endeavors in school. One reason for this minimalist existence in east Lubbock is the low-income status of many persons who live there—essentially, eastern Lubbock is a lower-class neighborhood, a fact that has been noted throughout this chapter. As time passed, east Lubbock also became a predominantly minority community and remains this way today. Hence, east Lubbock is a lower class, predominantly minority community. Moving out of east Lubbock to other parts of the town has historically been limited, thus curtailing opportunities for upward mobility, and creating a situation where minorities from the east side of town have filled many of the lower paying, working-class jobs in the community.

Education is not viewed by Lubbock's eastsiders as a means to improve upon their living condition since a very low percentage of those from the neighborhood who manage to graduate from high school go to higher education. Concomitant with this historical situation has been a decline in student motivation and lack of student interest in EHS. Moreover, as evidenced by recent trends at EHS, teachers in the town's school district are mostly white and middle class, and few if any live within EHS neighborhood boundaries. Not surprising, then, is the stereotype among district educators that EHS students don't want to learn, rarely come to school, don't care about improving their condition, and so on. Although the trend is now changing in the district, educators of the past traveled into EHS from other parts of the town, spent the usual amount of time with students as students passed from class to class, then returned to their home neighborhoods far removed from the poverty that surrounded their students.

Clearly, the class and race stereotyping in the case of EHS, and we presume other schools in similar situations, have, in general, profound influence on how the school is managed, how instruction is delivered, and how teachers either do or do not develop an interest in fostering student success in school. Contemporary school practices in theory are not intended to allow such stereotyping to get in the way of equitable educational opportunities. The teachers and administrators I interacted with at EHS are committed to helping EHS students move beyond these stereotypes. But they are doing this in the midst of latent racism that clearly has divided and continues to divide Lubbock by race and class, in the midst of leftover stereotypes about minorities (especially African American and Hispanic persons), and in the midst of some ever-present beliefs about the dangerous nature of students who attended EHS (recall the case of Jim above).

One of Delores' comments related another way that Lubbock maintains its stereotype for EHS. When I asked Delores about stereotyping and the school, she replied:

> When it comes right down to it, it's the media. I'll give you an example. Recently a lady got raped on this side of town and the media mentioned Estacado High School. It wasn't an Estacado student and wasn't even on the Estacado campus. But the papers and the television reporters said "near Estacado High School." So when you read that or hear that your mind automatically connects crime to Estacado.

Dave's comments highlighted what happens when such stereotyping goes unchallenged. When I asked Dave to suggest a few words that best describe the EHS students, he quickly replied with three words: "unchallenged, deserving, and unmotivated." I asked him to explain these words. He noted:

> They are unmotivated because they are not challenged. Because nobody expects them to be motivated. I think people expect less of these kids because of who they are and where they come from. When I say "people," I mean faculty, the community, the town.

Dave then noted that the EHS kids come from a different world. He noted:

> They come from the east side of Lubbock. And there is this whole east side persona thing which is poor, minority, high crime, violence, you know, everybody is having sex with everybody else, all the teenagers are pregnant or getting someone pregnant, no morals, all that kind of stuff. Of course all of this is just silly stereotypical thinking, but this persona is a very real phenomenon in Lubbock. I don't think I've ever lived anywhere in my life that had so many stereotypes dumped on one school as dumped on EHS by the greater Lubbock community. If there is a

crime in our society, then that crime is all the stereotypes that are dumped on EHS. This kind of crime that nobody takes the blame for, but that is always there, is the real crime. And it is this real crime of stereotyping that somehow keeps the tangible and explicit street crime alive and well. I know that might sound like a pretty big accusation, but all you have to do is teach EHS kids for a short while to see what I'm talking about.

The kind of stereotyping mentioned by Dave and initially believed by Jim leads to certain kinds of classroom management, including instructional and behavioral management. Such management of students who are perceived to be low achievers, unmotivated, lower-class trouble makers, minority, and so on, includes drill and practice, highly structured classes, tight control of learning through behavioral objectives, tight control of behavior through severe penalties for infraction of rules, watering down of content, and so on. Key words for this kind of management are *control, dominate,* and *oversee.* On the other hand, some EHS educators have sought to overcome the stereotyping that had surrounded EHS for decades, and in some instances still surrounds the school, by implementing a model of noncoercive management called Quality School. Key words for this kind of management are *negotiate, mediate, choice,* and *engage.*

The Quality School model of management—a model that creates a certain social curriculum in the school—is clearly not the only model that strives for negotiation with students and for giving students choice so they can be more highly engaged in school activities. But for now the Quality School model is a feasible alternative for traditional management at EHS. Teachers at the school realize that the world of quality they return home to after a long but promising day of teaching is clearly unlike the world of quality their students' return home to. This realization might not solve all instructional and managerial issues at the school, but it clearly connects teachers to students in important cultural and educational ways.

TOWARD A CULTURALLY RESPONSIVE KIND OF MANAGEMENT

Little doubt remains that in today's classrooms there is a pressing and unprecedented need for a kind of management that could be described as culturally responsive. What the shape of this management might be, however, is illusive and clearly difficult to define. If a definition can be created for one school, trying to impose that definition on another school, say, for example, from an upper-middle class, predominantly white school to a school like EHS, would arguably be ethnocentric and racist unless this definition allows for variations in cultural, class, ethnic, and racial dimensions of student life. Glasser's definition for Quality School allows for this.

If a culturally responsive kind of management, as we argue here, is illusive, is difficult to define, and is more relative (i.e., changes from school to school) than generalizable (i.e., what is mostly good for one school is mostly good for all schools), then what has this chapter, and what has my research on EHS, taught us about being culturally responsive teachers? Perhaps the first lesson learned from this work at EHS is that before we can begin thinking in terms of *managing* students, we must first begin thinking in terms of *negotiating* with students. This, of course, supports the claims we have made throughout this book, and thus seems to be a self-serving claim here. Yet EHS educators could simply not manage in the traditional sense (e.g., control, dominate, etc.) before they negotiated their cultural and academic space with students. In negotiating this space, teachers theoretically were also negotiating students' worlds of quality. Hence, negotiate-then-manage becomes a prerequisite to manage-then-negotiate.

A second lesson we can glean from reflecting on the EHS experience, a lesson that reflects the need for cultural responsiveness in management practices, is that classroom instruction is, as Hollins (1996) so aptly writes, "shaped by cultural values and practices" (p. 2). Such instruction, however, cannot be primarily shaped by just one set of cultural values and practices, but rather by a meeting and mingling of values and practices as students and teachers create a social curriculum in the presence of expected content to be learned. EHS administrators and faculty used the concept of Quality World as both a conceptual and practical means to create a social curriculum at school where teachers better understood the place of students' personal lives in school and in classroom teaching. Delores knew very well the place of cultural values and practices in her teaching; her students were an extension of her own persona.

A third lesson that can be derived from the EHS experience relates clearly and explicitly to the notion of *caring*. As we noted in chapter 2, there exists many models, approaches, algorithms, styles, and orientations to what is called *management* in our schools. Some of these relate more to *content*, others relate more to *process*, yet others relate more to *learning outcomes*. What was needed at EHS, however, according to Mr. Lee, was a caring approach to instructional and behavioral management that began with students' own lives, not with content nor process nor outcomes. Although the local school district, in conjunction with state mandates, placed content and outcomes as foremost instructional considerations, a social curriculum was needed in EHS where students felt like they *belonged* and that someone genuinely *cared* about them. Although many models of management exist (as noted above), the Quality School approach appeared to be a model that held potential for connecting EHS teachers to students' own worlds, perhaps enabling teachers to create an ethic of caring in EHS (e.g., Colsant, 1995) that would be felt by many students and that would help students feel like they really belonged there.

The three lessons learned above, among others, are powerful and important for creating social curricula in today's schools and for creating an atmosphere of management that is culturally responsive and positive. That the process most EHS educators use to reach kids is called a *Quality School process* matters very little. What matters most is that this process, whatever name it bears, has brought EHS educators closer to students' personal lives, and this consequently has brought students closer to successful school experiences.

I have elected to end this chapter with a positive tone because after being on the EHS campus for over three years as an observer, college instructor, and a former public school teacher in the same state, I am confident in saying that many EHS educators are honestly trying to make a difference in the lives of students who are and continue to be marginalized by the town of Lubbock, which is essentially castelike in its social class orientation.

All too often we read negative and doomsday accounts of schools with seemingly no hope remaining for students, teachers, or parents. EHS, in my judgment, provides hope. I do not mean to suggest, however, that everything is perfect at EHS. Contrariwise, students are still sent to the office for misbehavior, teachers still have to comply with state regulations for teaching specific content, thus feeling disempowered and controlled, the school still has to combat stereotyping of both school and students from the local community, a few teachers remain to be convinced that the Quality School model is worthy of adopting, the school continues to struggle with lower than average standardized test scores (a measure that has extremely high stakes in the local district and throughout the state), and so on. Yet underneath these daily struggles has emerged a feeling of connectedness between teachers and students, and among teachers—that somewhere there really does exist a utopian world of shared quality that could become a practical reality. That EHS has more work to do before its students can realize the same benefits as students in other parts of Lubbock is clear. That they have begun working diligently on this is also clear.

EXERCISE 10.1   Reflecting on the Idea of Students' Quality Worlds

This chapter, which focused on Estacado High School, was intended to help you consider various cultural dimensions of the social curriculum and consequently various dimensions of classroom management and student negotiation. The whole idea of *quality* might have taken on new meaning for you as you read the chapter and as you concurrently considered your interaction with students within a quality world framework.

For this activity, identify a school or schools in a neighborhood nearby that perhaps, like Jim in this chapter, you have heard about but have not visited. If you attended mostly middle class schools, this other school you have heard about might be in a lower class or upper class neighborhood. Or if you attended mostly lower class schools, this other school you might have heard about should be in a middle or upper class neighborhood school. Seek to gain the necessary approval to visit this school.

Before you visit the school take an inventory of your beliefs, perspectives, stereotypes, and impressions of students, teachers, the neighborhood, the school, and so on. Write your beliefs and clarify any stereotypes you have for the school and its students. Also determine what fears, if any, you have for being a teacher at the school. Try to determine the source of these fears, and explore whether these fears are valid or are merely misconceptions.

Regarding the idea of quality world, before you visit the school write a paragraph or two that you believe best describes *your* world of quality. To do that, consider these questions: Who are the most important people in your life? Who are your most important positive role models? Who are your negative role models? What do you like doing with your friends? What opportunities do you have to socialize with your friends in your neighborhood? Where do you socialize with friends? What hours of the morning, afternoon, evening, or night do you socialize with friends? Why this particular time? Are you able to eat at a variety of restaurants and go to a variety of movies? Are these things part of your quality world? How much is *education* part of, or has been part of, your quality world? After answering these questions for yourself, try to answer them for the students who attend the other school you identified above.

After answering the questions above and after making a personal inventory, explore the social curriculum of the school you have selected to visit. Who are the students? Where do they live? What is their neighborhood like? What might comprise a quality world in this neighborhood? Could you live comfortably in this neighborhood? Why or why not? Arrange to talk with a teacher and some students at the school. Determine how the school, if at all, reflects students' cultural orientations.

After gathering information about the school, speculate on how your preconceptions about the school and its students would have hindered or fostered the development of a system of management where all students feel like they belong and are cared for in your classroom. What preliminary fears, if any, might have interfered with the development of a social curriculum in your classroom where students feel like they belong and feel like you genuinely care for them?

REFERENCES

Banke, J. (1993). The canon debate, knowledge construction, and multicultural education. *Educational Researcher, 22*(5) 4–14.

Cochran-Smith, M. (1995). Color blindness and basket making are not the answers: Confronting the dilemmas of race, culture, and language diversity in teacher education. *American Educational Research Journal, 32*(3), 493–522.

Colsant, L. (1995). Hey man, why do we gotta take this? Learning to listen to students. In N. Nicholls and T. Thorkildsen (Eds.), *Reasons for learning*. New York: Teachers College Press.

Giroux, H. A. (1997). *Channel surfing: Race talk and the destruction of today's youth*. New York: St. Martin's Press.

Glasser, W. (1997). A new look at school failure and school success. *Phi Delta Kappan, 78*(8), 597–602.

Glasser, W. (1992). *The Quality School: Managing students without coercion*. New York: Harper Collins.

Hollins, E. R. (1996). *Culture in school learning: Revealing the deep meaning*. Mahwah, NJ: Lawrence Erlbaum.

Johnson, L. (1992). *Dangerous minds*. New York: St. Martin's Paperbacks.

Kozol, J. (1991). *Savage inequalities: Children in America's schools*. New York: Crown Publishers.

Ladson-Billings, G. (1994). *The dreamkeepers: Successful teachers of African American children*. San Francisco: Jossey-Bass Publishers.

Peshkin, A. (1986). *God's choice: The total world of a Fundamentalist Christian school*. Chicago: University of Chicago Press.

Powell, R. (1997). Then the beauty emerges: A longitudinal case study of culturally relevant teaching. *Teaching and Teacher Education, 13*(5), 467–484.

Powell, R., Zehm, S., and Garcia, J. (1996). *Field experience: Strategies for exploring cultural diversity in schools*. Columbus, OH: Merrill.

Veenam, S. (1984). Perceived problems of beginning teachers. *Review of Educational Research, 54*(2), 143–178.

P A R T

IV

EXPLORING CLASSROOM MANAGEMENT FROM A PERSONAL PERSPECTIVE

CHAPTER

11

Inquiring Into Classroom and School Life: An Action Research Approach

Antonio Faundez: I would want to stress that the source of knowledge lies in inquiry, in questions, or in the very act of asking questions. I would venture to state that the earliest form of language was the question, that the first word was at one and the same time question and answer in a simultaneous act.

Paulo Freire: . . . [W]e must make it clear once again that our interest in asking questions, about asking questions, cannot remain simply at the level of asking questions for their own sake. What is supremely important is whenever possible to link question and answer to actions which can be performed or repeated in future. . . . I think it important to note that there is an undeniable relationship between being surprised and asking questions, taking risks and existence.

(Freire & Faundez, 1989, pp. 37, 38, 40)

We certainly agree with the aforementioned comments by Freire and Faundez (1989). Questioning is central to our knowledge of management in culturally diverse classrooms, and questioning ought to influence our actions in some way. Being surprised and taking risks—those are earmarks of many outstanding teachers who are not always content with longstanding traditional approaches to teaching and who are willing to ask important questions about classroom teaching.

Questioning is one aspect of *inquiry,* a term we use to capture the wide range of professional thinking that you can do in your classroom. Teachers are constantly inquiring about what is happening. In this chapter we view inquiries as being made up of the questions you ask yourself, based upon what you experience, and the questions you ask students and others. To teach well is to consider and reconsider your own questions about your own teaching. Consider, for example, the following questions about a single lesson: How have I just taught this lesson? Was it the best way to teach it? I wonder what the students thought about that final question I asked during the lesson; there didn't seem to be much discussion. What was Tony doing during the lesson, anyway? He passed that note and then, when I confronted him, he tried to pretend he couldn't hear me. What's the right way to handle that one?

When, as a teacher, you ask these kinds of questions, you may have a number of different goals in mind. You might simply want to find a short-term solution that will enable you to get through the following day without a confrontation or a worsening problem, or you may be searching for a more consistent approach to solving a common problem.

Stevenson (1986), a scholar dedicated to enhancing educational opportunities for early adolescents, writes the following about teacher inquiry:

> Teacher inquiry is an integral part of every lesson or unit taught. Each time we solicit student reactions to an idea, activity or speculative question, we are inquiring-attempting to assess perceptions, understandings and beliefs. Sensitive teachers know that no matter how teaching is carried out, learning is always idiosyncratic and personal. The processes of inquiry are simply processes of assessment, i.e., strategies designed for finding out what the state of affairs may be as our students or others perceive them. (p. 3)

The purpose of this chapter is to help you explore how you might inquire about the social curriculum in a conscious way, so that you can increase the chances for the long-term growth of everyone involved. In the following pages we provide examples of actual questions asked, and inquiries carried out, by preservice and in-service teachers, and we highlight how teachers can conduct *participant action research*, a form of inquiry whose express purpose is to take action in response to what you have learned from asking specific questions about your teaching. In this chapter we provide you with a framework by which you can not only ask specific questions about your social curriculum, but act on the answers you might find from asking these questions.

THE GOALS OF INQUIRY

Among the many possible goals of inquiring into school life, we want to highlight four:

(1) The first goal, which is consistent with the chapters in Part III of this book, is to *understand who your students are.* You can do this by examining students' actions and their interpretations of classroom life. This may involve doing case studies of students and their perceptions of school. This can also involve classroom ethnographies that describe interactions over time. Both of these inquiries might require you to conduct interviews and to make classroom observations over a designated period of time.

(2) The second goal is to *examine your practices and what you value*—and the match between the two (Elliott, 1991). This entails being self-aware and being willing to openly examine and criticize your own personal theories for teaching and learning (Bullough & Gitlin, 1995, p. 180). If this were your goal, you might write an autobiography, keep a teacher journal, or videotape yourself teaching.

(3) The third goal is to *improve your social curriculum*—and the teaching skills necessary to accomplish that goal. To do this, you would examine how different classroom activities influence students' interactions. For example, you might audiotape class meetings or small group work, conduct a survey to uncover students' judgments about class rules and procedures, or keep careful notes during student-led conferences and see whether the students' sense of responsibility in the classroom increases.

The first three goals all involve improving teaching and enhancing students' social learning and development in classrooms. There is another goal that takes you beyond the classroom walls, into the school halls and offices and amid the community life around the school.

(4) The fourth goal is to *examine how school policies and programs affect school life.* Your goal in this case is to "participate in the development of the school" (Bullough & Gitlin, 1995, p. 226). Central to this goal is trying to understand what other teachers and school staff, parents, administrators, and community members think about school policies and programs. For example, you could analyze observational, interview, or survey information derived from conflict resolution sessions, from student support team meetings, from what occurs during in-school suspension, and from various methods of communicating with parents.

THE PROCESSES OF INQUIRY

Participating in Inquiry

The roles that you play and the forms that your inquiries take reflect the explicit or implicit goals you have in mind. Anderson, Herr, and Nihlen (1994) have ably described the range of roles that teachers can play when conducting inquiries. We think of them, figuratively, as positions taken along a continuum, beginning with being only an *observer* and ending with being a full *participant* in classroom activities.

Let's first examine the forms of inquiry that can help you, as an observer, learn about classroom life. Observing as an "outsider," perhaps during a practicum prior to student teaching or as part of a peer coaching project, means that you are not teaching in that classroom at the time. Your observations consist of *watching, listening,* and *thinking* about what is occurring. There is value in being an outside observer, but only if you are clear about what questions you want to ask, and if you have an idea of how to document and analyze what you see and hear. Your observations can also influence your thinking and perhaps your colleagues' thinking too.

We shall now consider the various forms that your inquiry might take. As a preservice teacher, you could interview the classroom teacher, complete a sociogram that depicts classroom relationships, do an ethnographic study of classroom life, conduct a case study of one or a few students, shadow students as they interact inside or outside of school, write a school history, or create a community profile. As a practicing teacher, you might videotape a colleague's classroom as you both teach together and then analyze what happened. Later in the chapter, we will give a more complete list of these data sources. For now, let's go into a bit more detail about the inquiry process.

The best way to begin an inquiry into your social curriculum is by establishing the context and documenting what seems to be happening, which leads to generating questions about *why* certain things are happening. If you then wish to study some aspect of classroom or school life related to your initial questions, you will determine a research focus by specifying what questions you want to ask. You gather some sort of information (what we will call *data*) which is related to your focus, and analyze the information to make sense of what it

FIGURE 11.1
The Inquiry
Process

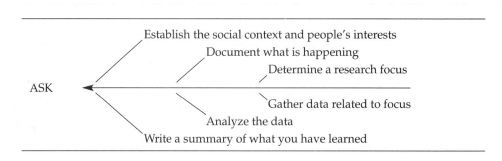

Establish the social context and people's interests

Document what is happening

Determine a research focus

ASK

Gather data related to focus

Analyze the data

Write a summary of what you have learned

means to you. Even this part of the process involves asking questions, only now they are questions about the best sources of data and the best ways to analyze the data. Finally, if you want to report (or are required to report) what you have learned from the inquiry process, you write a summary of your findings. We really shouldn't say "finally", however, for several reasons. There is not necessarily a final point in the inquiry process, because many teachers who do the kind of research we are describing in this chapter use their results from one first study to inquire more deeply into the same issue in a following study. Also, as we will describe shortly, practicing teachers may conduct *practitioner action research*, in which the final step of the process we just described is to take action in response to what they have learned. To help you envision the inquiry process, examine the diagram in Figure 11.1.

The diagram, read clockwise from the top, portrays a set of activities that are carried out when you inquire. Though we believe that the activities in the order presented form a workable sequence, this is not a linear process. Documenting what is happening may require analysis, for example, and you might gather data about people's interests in the early stage of an inquiry. No matter how the activities are sequenced, throughout the process of inquiry you will be asking questions. That is why *ask* is placed on the far left, and all of the activities are related to it. The activities shown in Figure 11.1 are described below.

ACTIVITY 11.1   Establish the Social Context and People's Interests

Every classroom and school has a *context*, a historical and social background that influences interactions in the environment. Developing understandings about the school and community, about what has happened before you came into the class, and about the students are essential elements of your inquiry. On a school level, Bullough and Gitlin (1995, pp. 75–101) offer helpful descriptions of how to do a school history, which can contribute to the aforementioned understandings. In exercise 11.1 you explore the history of a school by examining the school context and by developing a profile of the school's community.

EXERCISE 11.1   Learning the School Context

Developing a Community Profile

A community profile is a rather comprehensive depiction of a specific school's community. Examples of community profiles were given for John Tynes Elementary School, Brown-Barge Middle School, and Estacado High School in chapters 8, 9, and 10, respectively. Working with a group of your peers, seek permission to study a selected school that your group will visit during a two-day period of time. You will also take your own self-guided tour of the neighborhoods that circle the school, and then talk with some local parents and community leaders at, for example, a Boys and Girls Club or a YMCA/YWCA. The purpose of this exercise is for your group to construct a community perspective about the school, including the students, the teachers, the curriculum, and the environment. You and your peers should try to collect data about the following:

1. A description of the structural impressions—the drive to the school, the neighborhood, community, school, and classrooms.
2. A description of the culture(s)—demographic data from several sources, examples of diverse people, and your impressions of the school, community, and classrooms. (How do different people talk about the school?)
3. A description of the resources you found in the school, community, and classrooms that could be helpful in teaching and learning.
4. A description of what this exercise helped you learn about teaching and learning, and the importance of learning about the community.

Now that you have thought more about developing a community profile of a specific school site, respond to the following questions: What else might *you* include in a community profile? What do you think are some benefits of doing this profile? How would you present what you have learned to peers, to school administrators, or to parents in the community?

Developing an Understanding of the Students

Another way of thinking about the matter of context is to consider who your students are, both inside and outside of school. In a university course on middle school curriculum, one of us (James McLaughlin) asks preservice teachers to observe the life of young adolescents outside of school. A version of the assignment that guides these observations is below:

> For this assignment you will observe and talk with an individual or a group of students. The purpose of the interaction is to enable you to think about how people who are this age act and talk, and to consider how physical, intellectual, social, and emotional development are interrelated. Your interaction will include a minimum of one hour of observations in a site of your choosing, for example a mall, a playground, a park, downtown, a store, or someone's house. Please do not observe in a school. I want you to learn more about what students do outside of schools, to give you a better understanding of who they are.

You will take notes about what you have seen and heard, either during or after observing the adolescents. At some point in the proceedings, you must talk with one or more of the people you are observing, and ask them questions designed to learn about their ways of thinking and acting.

The following format can serve as a framework for reporting the results of your observations:

(1) *Introduction*—briefly describe who you are observing, the setting, their activities, and other background information necessary to understand the people's actions.

(2) *Observations*—describe the interactions observed. Make some judgments about the kind of thinking reflected in the interactions. Include the manner of speaking, pertinent quotes (if applicable), body language, movement, and the nature of relationships between the people if they are in a group.

(3) *Reflections*—think carefully and thoughtfully about what you observed. What characteristics of the persons did you see (physical, intellectual, social, and emotional)? Did their actions seem to be typical or atypical? Why? What did you learn that might be important to consider as a teacher?

You will, of course, always have only a partial picture of the context, or, more accurately, a collection of descriptions that do not necessarily relate a unified story. That is alright; this is an introduction to thinking about context, and you will gain more insights the more often you do this sort of investigation.

ACTIVITY 11.2   Document What Is Happening in the Classroom

For preservice teachers, one way to begin thinking about and documenting what is happening in the classroom is to conduct a case study about a particular event or about a certain group of students. While doing a case study can help you understand the classroom context and find out students' interests, such a study can also help you formulate questions about some aspect of classroom life. There are innumerable questions you might ask. Many of them are quite specific, like the kind of daily self-questioning with which we began this chapter. But there are some general questions that can help you document what is happening in your classroom. Below is a case study format you can use to formulate questions about classroom life.

Case study of a selected classroom. Plan to visit a selected classroom over an extended period of time. You should try to make regular and consistent observations of teaching and learning in this classroom. Each day that you visit the classroom take careful notes about what is happening there. Consider the *formal, interpreted, enacted,* and *hidden* social curriculum in your field notes. For the case study, choose an event that will, for example, elicit discussion about how to teach, about issues related to schooling and being a teacher, and about students' learning. Describe the setting of the event, the participants in the setting (for ethical reasons, use pseudonyms when you describe participants), and the events as they unfold. Then, develop a set of questions that can guide a discussion about the classroom event. Finally, determine several choices of action for the teacher in this situation, and offer your judgment about the best choice that could have been made, given the context.

This case study format might seem rather simple to you, but as you become more involved in making observations and recording careful notes, you will soon realize that the case study is exceedingly complex. You will also realize that determining alternative choices of action is equally complex given the cultural and biographical backgrounds of students. Additional factors that further complicate the case study are the beliefs, perspectives, and biases for teaching that are demonstrated by the teacher. We now ask you to consider the questions below, which will help you look more deeply into the classroom you observe for your case study.

What is happening here? The first question you might ask during a case study is "What is happening here?" On the surface this question always *appears* to be so easy to answer. But underneath the surface this question becomes detailed and complex. This complexity is further increased when you realize that what is really happening in the classroom, as we noted above, involves the continuous interaction of so many factors, including cultural and biographical factors of everyone in the classroom. The value of this seemingly simple question, therefore, depends on your ability and willingness to observe not only what is obviously happening—that is, what everyone is clearly and plainly doing—but also to observe how factors such as culture, biography, and personal biases profoundly influence the social curriculum. In the course of skillfully addressing this question, you will begin to raise many other questions that may become central to your case study.

Below is one example of a preservice teacher's effort to inquire about classroom life during the first part of a preservice practicum. Note the details in the portrait that Aronica draws in her case study (this version is edited and shortened from the original).

Aronica's Case Study

The class in which I have been involved during my practicum is a seventh-grade social studies class. There are 17 students in the class and the socioeconomic backgrounds of the students range from upper middle class to lower class. Most of the students are in the gifted track, with three students who are behind in reading ability, but are able to work at the pace of the rest of the class. One student in this group caught my attention and is the subject of my case study. A 12-year-old from an upper middle class home, James [not his real name] is unpopular with the rest of his classmates and suffers socially in spite of his academic success.

James suffers from an attitude of "always having to be right" in any given situation, challenging students and teachers alike. During a Teams-Games-Tournament session [a technique of cooperative learning], in which the class was divided between boys and girls, a great deal of team animosity was directed toward him by his fellow teammates. He tried to answer all of the questions directed at his team, with no conferencing with his teammates. Furthermore, when James answered incorrectly, he was met with names from his classmates and tried desperately to prove his answer was indeed correct, while engaging in defensive name-calling to his peers. In a strange way, I saw that he wanted his classmates to accept the fact that he, too, could make mistakes.

At other times, James puts an immense amount of pressure on himself to succeed academically. However, he is impatient and unwilling to search for answers for a long period of time. When given a map exercise in which he could not immediately find all of the places, he commenced to argue with the instructor, asserting that the answers could not possibly be found. It is disturbing to see a student who pressures himself so strongly to excel at such a young age.

In contrast to the grim picture presented in the previous paragraphs, James is a responsible young man. He always wants to be cognizant of missed assignments and strives to take care of his personal responsibilities. He participates actively in most class discussions. However, the challenging aspects of his personality overshadow the positive aspects in such a way that he is looked at as an annoyance to students and teachers.

Now that you have completed reading Aronica's case report, what questions do *you* want to raise about the situation Aronica described? Do you have any suggestions about how she might proceed, both with the individual student and with the rest of the class?

What do others think is happening? After exploring the question, What is happening here? you can then compare your perceptions to those of your peers by asking, What do others think is happening? In responding to this question you should try to represent the perceptions of teachers, students, and other school participants. *Shadow studies,* in which you would walk in the *shadow* of a student or a group of students during most or all of a school day, provides an opportunity to re-experience school life as a young student experiences it and to talk informally with students about how they perceive school (Bullough & Gitlin, 1995, pp. 105–126). There are many other ways to talk with students, including interviews, which we will discuss later in the chapter.

An intriguing inquiry was done by Candace Jordan, an elementary special education teacher, with two of her students named Angela and Latoya. Ms. Jordan was interested in what her students thought about small group work, so she simply turned on a tape recorder when Angela and Latoya were discussing their work. These two students were having difficulty collaborating as they worked together; they discussed this problem as the tape recorder was running. Angela thought that Latoya had not been doing her share of work. Angela challenged Latoya, and Latoya explained her actions. Here is an excerpt from the taped conversation:

"[When collaborating] the person has to see that it's OK to work with that person," says Angela. "I usually pick the right people. . . . I picked a new partner [Latoya] now, and she's *not* working very nicely, but I'm getting her good. Before she was not working very good, but I've gotten her on the horsey and now we're taking a ride!"

Latoya responds to this apparent criticism cheerfully, "If you are stuck on something, and you're working with somebody, the person that knows it may help you with it. Like my friend [Angela], she helps me with a lot of stuff, and I think it's really nice for her to do that."

"Thank you, Latoya," says Angela with an audible sigh of relief. "I think I have been helping her a lot, too. But I think the most thing she has been helping me about is being my friend." In accepting Latoya's explanation, Angela seems to have come to value friendship in itself. (Nicholls & Thorkildsen, 1995, p. 154)

For these two students, there was a dynamic between the personal relationship and the collaborative tasks required in the group work. How the tasks and personal relationship turn out is unclear, but by being privy to their conversations, the teacher learned how to monitor and arrange group work for the two girls and for other students.

Why are things as they appear to be? A third question you can ask about the case study you conduct is, Why are things as they appear to be? An important dimension of observing in schools is to do speculative thinking about *why* things are as you see them. The next case study by Pam is an example of speculative thinking.

Pam's Case Study

Lydia is a member of the self-contained, fifth-grade class that was the subject of my observation. I noticed her on the first day of my observation and thought that she was physically more developed than many of her peers. I later learned that she had been retained. One day she came in and said she would not be in school for five days because her mother's car was broken and the ride her mother had to work could not bring her to school. I later found out that she had been suspended from the bus for a week because she had been fighting. On another day, her friends came in from lunch discussing Lydia's weekend routine of spending Friday, Saturday, and Sunday at the skating rink. I was struck by the innocence of the discussion because there is a reason behind a child being farmed out to the skating rink for three days in a row.

After a discussion with my cooperating teacher, I found out that she is the daughter of an unwed teenage mother. She has a brother who is supposedly a hellion in the fourth grade, taking Ritalin due to his behavior disorders. According to my supervising teacher, the atmosphere in Lydia's home does not quiet down until around 10 P.M. because of the behavior problems with her brother. Therefore, her home life is not conducive to completing homework assignments, and in general is not academically supportive.

After reading Pam's case report, what do *you* think may be the problem(s) in this case? What questions would you raise? If Pam is correct, and the home atmosphere is not conducive to academic success, what role can you play in influencing the situation? What might be the limitations on your actions? How might the social curriculum in your classroom help to improve Lydia's situation?

ACTIVITY 11.3   Determine a Research Focus

The next activity in the inquiry process shown in Figure 11.1 is to determine a research focus. To begin determining this focus, ask yourself, What is an issue that
really interests me? Formal inquiries usually begin with a relevant question about
which you can gather information. For example, you *can* gather data to address the
question: What do students think are the benefits and drawbacks of working in cooperative groups in this class? However, a question such as, Are cooperative
groups the best way for students to learn in this class? is quite difficult to answer.
What are some questions that you might pose?

ACTIVITY 11.4   Gather Data

After determining a research focus, your next step is to collect data related to this
focus. The ultimate purpose of this data is to provide some kind of *evidence* that answers the questions you asked about your research focus. Evidence, of course, is
comprised of the data you gather, and the first issue in gathering data concerns
whom you will gather it from—that is, who will participate in this activity. People
participate in two ways: by helping you gather data, and by providing data to you.
Participants can include students, teachers, other school staff, administrators, parents, and community members. In some cases, even in an informal inquiry as part
of a preservice practicum, you may need to get formal approval from those who
participate, while other informal hallway conversations or whole-class observations need no explicit approval.

Another aspect of gathering data relates to the sites in which you will gather
data. Depending of course on the questions you ask, you can glean valuable information about students' social lives and interests by observing and talking with
them in malls, school halls, athletic fields, or the school media center, just as we described earlier in the observation assignment.

When you gather data you must also be concerned about the *quality* and the
usefulness of the data you collect. To begin thinking about the issues of quality and
usefulness, you can ask these two questions: What data sources would be the best
to use? Why would these sources help me to understand what is happening in the
classroom? The data sources you choose usually depend on the nature of your research questions. Table 11.1 lists some common types of data sources.

EXERCISE 11.2   Explore Data Sources

In Table 11.1 we offer you some sample analytical comments about general types
of data. However, you will also notice that in Table 11.1 we have not provided
comments for every data source. Working with a group of peers, generate at least

one strength, one limitation, one question, and one suggestion for the data sources we have not discussed. The purpose of doing this is to help you develop an over-all set of guidelines for the data you may collect as you carry out a research project. Keep in mind that the data which are listed in the table are intended to help you learn more about students, about classroom and school interactions, and ultimately about your teaching—with the general goal of creating the best social curriculum possible.

OBSERVATIONS

Types (observations)	Strengths	Limitations	Questions/Suggestions
Field notes of class interactions, student conferences, etc.	You can shift the focus whenever needed; more open-ended and subject to observer's judgment about what to see and hear; may require minimal rewriting compared with audiotapes	Observer must be skillful and clear about what the observational focus is; usefulness depends on whether observer is honest about entering perspectives and biases	Leave 1/3 of the field note page blank, to write later in response to your notes; think and write in response as soon as possible, or you may lose your sense of what occurred
Videotaping	Captures more movement and sound than any notes can; may provide a chance for students to be involved	Can't always shift focus to where you want; time-consuming to transcribe and analyze	When might videotaping be most useful? Who should do the taping, and should the camera be stationary or movable?
Mapping the room			
Checklists and/or logs of student and teacher actions			

TABLE 11.1
Sources of data
Sources: See especially Good and Brophy (1994) on ways to look in classrooms (including checklists, logs, and other instruments that have already been tried), Hubbard and Power (1993) on observational techniques, and Anderson et al. (1994) on guidelines for interviewing.

INTERVIEWS			
Types (interviews)	**Strengths**	**Limitations**	**Questions/Suggestions**
One-to-one	Can go into more depth and can develop strong relationships with a few people over time	Limits greatly the number of participants who can be interviewed because more time is needed for each interview	How will you choose whom to interview, if they are to represent a group you want to learn about? How will you explain the purpose and establish trust during the first interview?
Whole class	Can get a wider range of responses that may be more representative of the group's commonality and differences	Difficult to take notes or audiotape, with so many participants responding; may need help to keep up with notes	Will you do a "focus group" interview, in which all participants respond to each question (this could be difficult, though it is quite useful for small groups), or will you let the discussion take its course? How will you keep track of what is being said?
Small group			
Student-to-student			
Parent			

TABLE 11.1 cont'd.
Sources of data

WRITTEN/RECORDED RESPONSES OF PARTICIPANTS

Types (written response)	Strengths	Limitations	Questions/Suggestions
Survey (yes/no or agree/disagree statements)	Easy to develop and measure; makes respondents take a clear stand	Can't determine *why* respondents answered "yes" or "no," and doesn't allow for qualitative judgments about the topic	Keep initial surveys short; field test the survey with a small group to see how they respond before giving it to a larger group. Did you get responses that will help you learn what you want?
Survey (rating or ranking scale; for example, 1 represents lowest rating and 5 represents highest rating of an item)			
Survey or questionnaire (statement completion)			
Survey or questionnaire (open-ended questions)			
Student journals			
Class suggestion box, or letters to teacher			
Webbing and sorting activities related to students' ideas and knowledge			
Sociograms that portray students' interrelationships			

TABLE 11.1   cont'd.
Sources of data

STUDENT OUTCOMES/PRODUCTS

Types (student outcome)	Strengths	Limitations	Questions/Suggestions
Tests (standardized)			
Tests (teacher-made)			
Student-made products			
Attendance records			
Referral records			
Grades			

TABLE 11.1 cont'd.
Sources of data

Triangulation. Another important feature of gathering data is called *triangulation*. This feature pertains to getting more than one kind of data, perhaps at various times and using various strategies. Most researchers who attain triangulation get at least three different sources of information. For example, to adequately respond to your research questions, you might need to gather observation, interview, and student outcome data. While good, credible studies are those which demonstrate triangulation, you must also keep the amount of data you gather manageable. You can easily get lost in a virtual mountain of data that you may not have the time (or the inclination) to analyze.

Two practicing teachers, Sandra and Anne, collaborated on a research project in Sandra's elementary school classroom. Their proposal—their plan for inquiry—which includes the participants, the sites, the data sources, the research question, and the research schedule they designed, is described below.

Sandra and Anne's Plan

What and Why What are the different ways children solve word problems when working in groups? We're interested in this question because we want to know whether group work is more effective than individual work when dealing with word problems.

How We will focus our study on four students in Sandra's sixth-grade mathematics classes in Riverbend School (not real name of school). We will select two boys and two girls. There will be two students from one class and two from the other.

We will observe the students as they work in groups during mathematics class. The children will be working in the same groups every day during our study, and each group will consist of students of varying ability levels. While the focus of our data collection will be group work, we also plan to collect data through an individual interview with each of the four children. During such an interview, we will present a few word problems to the child and ask him or her to explain the procedures he or she would go through to solve the problems.

Approximately 15 minutes will be spent at the beginning of class for Sandra's instruction on the topics of area and perimeter (and perhaps volume). Then, 30 minutes will be spent on group work. The students will work on word problems related to the topics which Sandra has covered during her instruction time. Our in-class observations will be documented through notes and through audiotape recordings.

When Sandra's classes meet from 11:45 A.M. to 12:35 P.M. and 12:38 P.M. to 1.25 P.M. We will conduct our observations during these class periods over a one-week period, from Wednesday, May 4, to Tuesday, May 10. We will evaluate data from Monday, May 9, to Friday, May 13. The first draft of our report will be written by Tuesday, May 17. The second draft will be written by Tuesday, May 31.

ACTIVITY 11.5   Analyze the Data

After you gather data, and in some studies as you gather data, you are faced with two questions: How will I learn from the data I have gathered? What is a good approach to analyze the data I have gathered? There are many good sources of information about data analysis, which you can find in the chapter reference section. In this section, we want to offer you some ideas about ways to analyze two types of data, namely *quantitative data* and *qualitative data*. Quantitative data more often reflects numbers and statistics; qualitative data more often reflects narrative or case reports.

When you are generating data that is quantitative, there are various sorts of analysis. If you have developed a survey, (for example, there may be statements asking for agreement or disagreement), then you might use a quantitative analysis to discover the percentages of agreement or disagreement. Perhaps you have used a four- or five-point scale to obtain a more complex picture of students' views about a class incentive system. In this case you might find the mean (average) score for each statement and compare the means of different statements. If you have asked respondents to rank or rate a list of items in relation to one another (e.g., *number these from 1 to 10 in order of your preference, with 1 being the most preferable*), then you might also determine an average, or mean, ranking. The examples above might be included on a presurvey and a postsurvey, in which case you could find the change in the percentages or means from the presurvey to the postsurvey. There are accompanying statistical procedures that you can use to compare the means over time within a particular group (say, one class of students), or across groups (comparing one class with another).

Qualitative data are generated from sources such as interviews, open-ended questions on surveys, and observational field notes. These kinds of information aren't easily reduced to numerical scores without sacrificing much of their possible meaning. However, you can do a simple procedure called *frequency counts* as part of analyzing responses from student journals concerning how students view themselves as learners, for example. Even if we had comparative data to show whether the frequencies of such responses changed from September to December, we could not necessarily answer a number of quite important questions simply in terms of frequencies. Why did the students *not* talk about learning in groups or about their social learning? Why did they include certain ways of learning, but not others? How did their beliefs about themselves as learners change over time? In order to answer these questions we must seek out qualitative data, which might be the most *discernible patterns* of qualitative responses. One way you can discover these patterns, which are often called *themes*, is to look for the most powerful responses given by individual students.

We offer three ideas to help you think more about qualitative data analysis. The first idea relates to coding the data. Codes can be abbreviated symbols that represent your thoughts about important ideas within the data. The categories represented by your codes may be derived from your research questions *before* analyzing the data (what may be called *a priori* codes) or developed *after* you have begun reading through the data. For example, you may be coding your notes from classroom observations you have made of students' interactions during a small group science lab activity. Some questions you might first ask for these observations are: What do students talk about during science labs? How do the students' personal relationships seem to influence the conversation and the nature of the work they accomplish?

You could have already determined several possible categories for *topics of conversation* and several possible ways that personal relationships might influence lab work. Or, you may have decided to read through the first transcript in its entirety. As you read the first transcript, you record personal insights you develop about your research questions, and you begin developing categories related to topics of discussion and personal relationship patterns during science labs. Using the categories you generated from the first set of transcripts, you would then code the remainder of your observational notes.

A second idea related to analysis of data relates to *writing* in response to certain sets of qualitative data. Baumann, Schockley, and Allen (in press) describe the process that Allen and Schockley developed when they collaborated to learn about students in an elementary classroom:

1. Each researcher reads a transcript of the observations and informal interviews with a certain student and also examines the student's cumulative portfolio of work.
2. Each researcher writes a one–two page narrative response to the data.
3. The researchers read aloud the narratives they have written.
4. As they read aloud and discuss what they have written, one researcher keeps an ongoing chart of their different interpretations of the data.
5. They summarize the main points from their "interpretive dialogue" and decide what they might read about the practices of other researchers and teachers.

A third idea for data analysis is to *read aloud* an interview transcript or field notes with a group of people, in order to collectively analyze and "check" the data (the following ideas are from the Prospect Inquiry Process, as described in Branscombe, Goswami, & Schwartz, 1992, p. 84). Here is the process:

1. One researcher reads aloud an entire transcript (whatever the group has agreed to analyze).
2. Each person gives his or her impression or interpretation of what is meaningful from the transcript.
3. One person takes notes and summarizes the discussion.
4. Someone chooses a "small chunk" of data to describe and discuss, again in turn.
5. The notetaker again summarizes the discussion.

The processes just presented incorporate both individual and collective methods of analysis and both written and oral forms. There are also other ways to analyze qualitative data (for example, developing rubrics to analyze students' writing). If you generate qualitative data—and every teacher in the course of teaching *does*—try to adapt some of these methods for your interests and needs.

ACTIVITY 11.6   Write a Summary

The overall purpose of gathering and analyzing certain kinds of data is to write a summary about what you have learned. This summary can then be shared with colleagues. To think about writing a summary, consider these questions: How might I write up and report what I have learned? Whose interests will be served by the summary report I write? Who will benefit most from the report? Who will be disadvantaged by the report?

The first question above concerns method and audience, while the second one concerns the matter of goals. For whom are you writing the summary? Will your findings help you to understand better how to teach? Will they help students understand better how to get along? Will they help another teacher understand better how to hold class meetings with students? The format for your written summary depends on your answers. We have already shown you several examples of assignments for case studies and community profiles, and in the next section on participant action research we will provide a format for writing a summary of your inquiry.

PARTICIPANT OBSERVATION ACTION RESEARCH

The Inquiry Process—Revisited

Much of the discussion above describes what you, as an observer, do to gather and analyze information about the social curriculum. Now we want to explore the process of being both a participant and an observer, what is commonly called a *participant observation,* when you conduct research into your classroom or school.

The idea of teachers and other professionals conducting research on their own work arose early in this century, but there was not much serious talk about it until the 1950s. In fact, only in the last 15 years or so has site-based teacher research been given serious consideration. There are many more people talking about it, or attending conferences where it is discussed, than there are teachers conducting formal inquiries over a period of time. Still, we find an increasing number of teachers inquiring about life in their schools, and an increasing commitment by school leaders to consider action research as a vehicle for better understanding school life as it unfolds each day.

How is participant observation action research, as carried out by teachers in their classrooms, different from what teachers already do? This form of action research involves a more systematic approach to data collection and analysis, research questions that are directly related to practice and everyday actions, and a somewhat different role as teacher and researcher. One of the most important features is that the focus throughout the inquiry process is on *acting* as well as *asking.* At any point in the process, an inquiring teacher may wish to take action, perhaps to change a method of calling on students or a structure for holding class meetings. Figure 11.2 shows the recursive nature of asking and acting in this process of learning.

In the following pages we want to describe some action research inquiries made by preservice and practicing teachers. You will see that there are a variety of questions raised, topics considered, methods utilized, and data gathered. We have

FIGURE 11.2
The Inquiry
Process—
Revisited

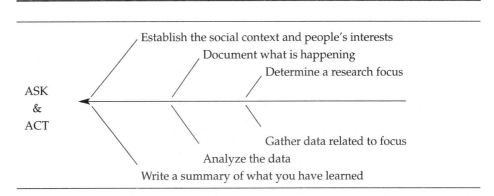

ASK & ACT

Establish the social context and people's interests
Document what is happening
Determine a research focus
Gather data related to focus
Analyze the data
Write a summary of what you have learned

organized this discussion into four themes: focusing on oneself as a teacher; focusing on individual students; focusing on group or whole-class interactions; and focusing on team or school issues.

Focusing on Oneself as a Teacher

Lee Colsant (1995), an experienced high school French teacher, became disturbed by the lack of student engagement in his classes.

> This year my hopes are dashed. During the next few weeks my well-honed syllabus fails to achieve its effects. . . . A tug of war ensues. The few, who are willing to handle the rigors of systematic grammar drills and memorization of vocabulary, take a back seat to a growing, vocal minority. . . . I come face to face with the illusion that I am contributing to the well-being of my students. (pp. 64, 68)

Colsant is discouraged, but he decides to take action by really talking with the students, and to document what he does by keeping a journal of his efforts.

> The new effort of collaboration is paying off. Though I'm tense, this lessens. They are accepting me more, but now it is on more mutual terms. I observe the class closely. They are working relatively well. I feel less need to be the source of control. . . . A feeling of warmth toward the class grows. (pp. 70–71)

As the year goes on, Colsant experiments by negotiating with students for their grade (they assign part of it), and by trying to use the social networks already in place among the students, rather than assigning them to seats and establishing arbitrary small working groups.

> I try to understand the personality of each emerging group and the individual that contributes to each. That endeavor alone needs vigilance and patience. . . . Each reform is a story. But it resides in the toil of quiet listening. To be present to the students' inconsequential chatter, their silence, their voice. It is to live the conversation, to walk not into the classroom but into the world of the students. (p. 87)

In this piece of eloquent writing, Colsant seriously questions his assumptions not only about conventional methods of teaching French, but about who his students are. And his careful documentation of how students talk—or don't talk—is essential to his understanding of what to do to reform his own classroom.

There are two other noteworthy examples we will include. First, Pergande (Pergande & Thorkildsen, 1995, pp. 21–35) described her efforts to monitor students' conversations with her and with each other. As she thought about students' talk she saw the need, as had Colsant, to listen more closely to students. She came to believe that teaching is a form of moral inquiry. As a second example, Sonja, a student teacher whose journals and interviews are chronicled in Bullough and Gitlin (1995, pp. 191–196), was concerned with how to *become an authority* in the classroom. Her journals offer testimony of that struggle, which is both personal and professional.

Focusing on Individual Students

Grindler, Stratton, McKenna, and Smith (1995) have written the account of how they tried *bookmatching* in Smith's kindergarten classroom. This is a teaching strategy in which the teacher chooses a book for class reading and discussion that addresses issues faced by one or more students in the class. It is intended to be informational for everyone and therapeutic for some. Smith and her colleagues tried to help a student named Tommy who was troubled because of an abusive family situation. To help Tommy, teachers developed a teaching unit that dealt with the problem of family abuse. They interviewed students before and after the unit to determine what the students thought they knew and what they believed about such situations.

> On the day the unit ended, a dramatic event occurred. Tommy sought out Paige and spent half an hour explaining what had happened and asking her for help. Her communication with the psychologist—greatly facilitated by the action research project—contributed substantially to the nature and effectiveness of the counseling Tommy received. (p. 54)

For another example, Moscoe (1994) pursued an inquiry related to conferences. She kept a written record and tape-recorded student conferences over a two-month period. Moscoe learned about students' purposes in seeking conferences, about the value of publishing the students' writings, and about a conference technique of playing tape recordings of the child reading a story, to discuss their reading further.

Focusing on Group or Whole-Class Interactions

Vicki, another student teacher, conducted an interesting inquiry into power relations in the classroom (in Bullough & Gitlin, 1995, 185–191). She describes her approach:

> [I recruited] a fellow cohort member [to do] observations to help identify a problem. These observations did reveal some management concerns, and upon reflection I identified some students who seemed to be very alienated, others who were "testing the limits," and still others who seemed to be engaged very minimally if at all. I wanted to develop a plan which preferably would address all of these concerns. (p. 185)

In order to build her *referent power* in the classroom, which is the kind of power that comes from knowing about and caring for one another, Vicki decided to hold individual conferences with each student to enhance her classroom's social curriculum. Her hope was that this would "enhance my rapport with the students, decrease power struggles and management problems, and create a classroom climate more conducive to learning" (p. 187). Another cohort member, the cooperating teacher, and one of the university supervisors observed the individual conferences in the fourth period. Their continuing observations of classroom interactions, a final student evaluation of Vicki's teaching, and her teacher journal with field notes about class events, led Vicki to believe that "I have in fact achieved some success in establishing referent power in these classes" (p. 189). The summary of her project concludes with her comments:

> I am very glad I conducted this project. It helped me to reflect on my teaching in a way I know I would not have done otherwise. . . . In my first year of teaching, I would like to set some specific goals and objectives for establishing and maintaining both order and a comfortable ambience in my classroom. . . . (p. 191)

Although Vicki's project dealt with her effort to have an impact on the whole class, other examples that more directly relate to group dynamics have been noted by Stevenson (1986), who briefly summarized how a number of middle school teachers in Vermont conducted inquiry projects. Gene Szatkowski, for example, gave students a survey about teasing that convinced him that students did take it seriously. Amy Demarest made observations and distributed questionnaires focusing on how students learned responsibility, and she learned that "the clarity of teachers' statements of expectation was the single-most important ingredient in students acting responsibly" (p. 37). Dean Witham used questionnaires and small group interviews to determine what students thought about a self-management system. "He concluded that the system needed increased visibility and that students who had not held a card [a token representing self-controlled behavior] needed more direct assistance in earning one" (p. 37). As a final example of group dynamics reported by Stevenson (1986), Sharon Baack explored students' perceptions of the school detention system through interviews and a survey that utilized the skills of a "student research team." She found that most students judged the suspension and detention procedures to be unfair, and that clearer definition and outline of procedures was necessary.

Did the teachers above make *lasting* changes at the classroom and school levels? We hope so, and we think that they represent some of the potentially valuable classroom-based inquiries that can be accomplished. Other possible readings for you include Allen (1992), who used numerous data sources to learn what happens when high school language arts students lead class discussions; and Richards (1989), who also used varied sources to consider what might motivate a difficult group of middle school students.

Focusing on Team or School Issues

There has been far less writing related to this focus than to the focus on teachers or students in individual classrooms. Emily Calhoun (1994), in her writing about the League of Professional Schools and its emphasis on schoolwide action research, described what some school-level groups were doing and offered guidelines for others wanting to do something similar. McLaughlin, Earle, Hall, Miller, and Wheeler (1995) did an action research project that had both classroom and team ramifications. They used longitudinal interviews to develop profiles of middle school students' beliefs about what they were learning and how they learned best. The students then read the profiles and added their ideas about themselves, so that the teachers could know more about how to engage the students during classroom interactions and how to adapt some of the team policies and procedures.

Several of the resources we list at the end of the chapter further deal with the school level. We hope that more published studies by collaborative groups of teachers working at the team and school levels will surface soon, particularly studies in which administrators are involved. That is *really* a missing piece of this picture.

Writing Your Summary

Now that you have read about some action research projects, we want to focus on writing your summary. The sample format for the action research summary, which is shown below, consists of a series of questions and a possible organizational scheme. Note two facets of this format that differ from summarizing a purely observational inquiry described earlier in the chapter. First, embedded in the format are questions that ask about the *changes* you might have made in your questions, data sources, and means of analysis. The traditional view of research is that these parts of the process are determined before entering the site, and that they remain unaltered throughout the study. We know from our experiences, however, and the experiences of teacher researchers, that more provocative and important questions may be raised, richer sources of data may be located, and more illuminating means of analysis may be created in the process of doing an action research project. You certainly have to have a solid rationale for changing any of these aspects, but there are sometimes compelling reasons to do so.

The other difference relates to the centrality of action. Sharing the information and trying to *act* on what you have learned, as a teacher in a classroom and as a member of a school community, lie at the heart of practitioner action research. Questions in the last section of the format ask you to consider how you might act on what you have learned.

FORMAT FOR AN ACTION RESEARCH SUMMARY

Introduction

What is the topic of your inquiry?

Why did you want to know more about this topic when you began the project?

What have you read that influenced your thinking about the project? (Set the question in the context of what you've been reading and thinking)

What is the structure of this summary paper?

Methods

What question(s) were you asking? Were there any changes in your questions?

Why did they change?

Why was your original question important to you?

Who were the participants? How many were there? Why and how were they chosen?

What was the setting?

How did you collect the data? Why did you choose those sources? Were there any changes in your way of analyzing the data? Why did you make changes?

What was the schedule?

How did you analyze the data? Why did you choose this approach? Were there any changes in your way of analyzing the data? Why did you make changes?

Results/What You Have Learned

What did you learn from analyzing the data? (Use evidence to support your analysis, interview quotes)

Discussion and Follow-up Action

What were the limitations of your study (methods and analysis)?

What are the implications for your practice and thinking, and for your institution?

What do you want to share with others? How should you share it? What suggestions would you offer for further research?

How has this project influenced your practice and thinking?

What might you do next year in response to what you have learned?

Problems You Might Face

In terms of potential problems you might face with your inquiry project, try to think of an inquiry project as existing in three parts: *entry, implementation,* and *exit.* We will offer some thoughts about possible problems in each phase. For example, entry involves gaining access to a site while also establishing initial trust with those with whom you will interact. To what extent will you be a *participant* as well as an *observer*? Are there school, district, or university guidelines for what universities call *human subjects review*? Are they pertinent to this situation? From whom do you have to ask permission to do what you want? What sort of proposal may be required?

Let's say that there are certain requirements for doing action research. You developed the proposal and then you convinced school personnel that what you intend to do is to their advantage. Getting the permission of key school personnel gives you formal entry into your study. During implementation you may run into problems related to data gathering. There may be difficulty in gaining access to the data you believe you need, or in gaining permission to do things such as audiotaping interviews or videotaping class sessions. If you decide to try a different data source because the data you are getting is not what you need, you may have to renegotiate access to data sources.

Exiting the project brings its own hurdles to overcome. How will you deal with the issues of anonymity and confidentiality? There may be political concerns over who will have control of the data and who might be affected by your findings or by any written summary. You may want some of those who participated in your inquiry to have the chance to see what you have written, or perhaps you made promises of access to your data analysis when you began the project. Be careful to allow others to *influence* your study and your summary report, but not *veto* your analysis.

Finally, how will you report and share the results? If this inquiry is a university practicum requirement, then the instructor will have a plan for reporting what you have learned. But if you are doing a formal inquiry during student teaching or if you are a practicing teacher, with whom should this summary be shared? Particularly with participant observation action research, there may be a commitment that the results of the data analysis will have some impact on what happens in the school, so you must determine the best way to share your summary.

CONCLUSION

In concluding this chapter, we want to return to the point from which we started. The opening conversation between Faundez and Freire challenged you to place *asking* and *acting* at the center of your social curriculum. Initially, you must have the courage to *ask* questions about what you are doing and what you believe about students, parents, ways of teaching and learning, school issues, and the needs of the community in which the school operates. You must also ask questions of others—your students, other teachers, school leaders. Asking questions means taking a risk and it means being open to surprises.

If the questions that are the basis of your inquiries are to give you important and relevant answers, then you must also *act* as an inquirer. That entails gathering data about what goes on in your classrooms and possibly other places in the school, analyzing carefully what the data may mean for your teaching, and altering what you and your colleagues do in response to what we have learned from the whole process of inquiring. This is not a neat, linear process. It is messy ("so, what actions *should* we take?"), and it is discontinuous and recursive ("since we haven't really learned much from what we've done, what other questions could we ask, or what other data could we generate that might help?"). Even so, inquiry offers us a way to learn and a way to become better teachers and thinkers.

YOUR TURN TO PLAN AN INQUIRY

Now, it is your turn. How would you conduct an inquiry into the social curriculum within a classroom and a school?

Inquiry for Preservice Teachers:

1. Read in full several of the pieces cited in this chapter, or examples from other resources, that tell the story of preservice teachers conducting inquiries. Discuss in a group your judgments about the inquiry: What did you think about the process they described? (Refer, if you wish, to the process described in this chapter.)
2. In response to the following questions, write first individually and then share your writings and ideas with other classmates:
   What would you do to establish the social context and people's interests?
   How would you document what is happening?

What questions would you inquire about?
Why are those questions important?
Who would participate in the inquiry?
What sort of data would you gather to provide evidence for what you have learned?
How might you analyze the data?
What are some of the problems and difficulties you might have to face? How would you deal with them?
How would you write it up or share the results?

Inquiry for Practicing Teachers:

1. Do the same two activities as the preservice teachers.
2. Following that, think about how the inquiry might benefit you as a teacher, other people at your school, and even teachers in other schools.

REFERENCES

Allen, S. (1992). Student-sustained discussion: When students talk and the teacher listens. In N. A. Branscombe, D. Goswami, & J. Schwartz (Eds.), *Students teaching, teachers learning* (pp. 81–92). Portsmouth, NH: Heinemann.

Anderson, G. L., Herr, K., & Nihlen, A. S. (1994). *Studying your own school: An educator's guide to qualitative practitioner research.* Thousand Oaks, CA: Corwin Press.

Branscombe, N. A., Goswami, D., & Schwartz, J. (Eds.). (1992). *Students teaching, teachers learning.* Portsmouth, NH: Heinemann.

Bullough, R. V., Jr., & Gitlin, A. (1995). *Becoming a student of teaching.* New York: Garland Publishing.

Calhoun, E. F. (1994). *How to use action research in the self-renewing school.* Alexandria, VA: Association for Supervision and Curriculum Development.

Colsant, L. C., Jr. (1995). "Hey, man, why do we gotta take this? . . ." In J. G. Nicholls, & T. A. Thorkildsen (Eds.), *Reasons for learning: Expanding the conversation on student-teacher collaboration* (pp. 62–89). New York: Teachers College Press.

Elliott, J. (1991). *Action research for educational change.* Milton Keynes, UK: Open University Press.

Freire, P., & Faundez, A. (1989). *Learning to question.* New York: Continuum.

Good, T. L., & Brophy, J. E. (1994). *Looking classrooms* (6th ed.). New York: HarperCollins College Publishers.

Grindler, M., Stratton, B., McKenna, M., & Smith, P. (1995). Bookmatching in the classroom: How action research reached the lives of children through books. *Action in Teacher Education, 16* (4), 50–58.

Hubbard, R. S., & Power, B. M. (1993). *The art of classroom inquiry: A handbook for teacher researchers.* Portsmouth, NH: Heinemann.

McLaughlin, H. J., Earle, K., Hall, M., Miller, V., & Wheeler, M. (1995). Hearing from our students: Team action research in a middle school. *Middle School Journal, 26*(3), 7–12.

Moscoe, T. (1994). Conferences: Planned transactions. In G. Wells (Ed.), *Changing schools from within: Creating communities of inquiry* (pp. 61–80). Toronto, Ontario: OISE Press.

Nicholls, J. G., & Thorkildsen, T. (Eds.). (1995). *Reasons for learning: Expanding the conversation on student-teacher collaboration.* New York: Teachers College Press.

Pergande, K., & Thorkildsen, T. A. (1995). From teachers as experimental researchers to teaching as moral inquiry. In J. G. Nicholl & T. A. Thorkildsen (Eds.), *Reasons for learning: Expanding the conversation on student-teacher collaboration* (pp. 21–35). New York: Teachers College Press.

Stevenson, C. (1986). *Teachers as inquirers: Strategies for learning with and about early adolescents.* Columbus, OH: National Middle School Association.

Professional Resources

Note: In addition to the references above, we hope that the following resources will be useful for university-level, K–12, and preservice teachers. We have reviewed them and have chosen them because they are well-written and potentially valuable.

1. **Journals devoted to action research, or to publishing teachers' research articles; there are many articles in these publications that we have not listed in the resources**

Educational Action Research

Triangle Journals Ltd.
P.O. Box 65
Wallingford, Oxfordshire OX10 OYG
United Kingdom

Teacher Research Journal

Ruth Hubbard
Campus Box 14
Lewis and Clark College
Portland, OR 97219

Teaching and Change

Sage Publications
2455 Teller Road
Thousand Oaks, CA 91320
(805) 499-0721

Research and Reflection (an e-mail journal)

Contact: EDITOR@Gonzaga.edu

2. **Edited books that contain chapters describing action research projects; chapters are coauthored or authored by K–12 teachers**

Branscombe, N. A., Goswami, D., & Schwartz, J. (Eds.). (1992). *Students teaching, teachers learning.* Portsmouth, NH: Heinemann.

Burnaford, G., Fischer, J., & Hobson, D. (Eds.). (1996). *Teachers doing research.* New Jersey: Lawrence Erlbaum.

Goswami, D., & Stillman, P. R. (Eds.). (1987). *Reclaiming the classroom.* Portsmouth, NH: Boynton/Cook.

Nicholls, J. G., & Thorkildsen, T. A. (Eds.). (1995). *Reasons for learning: Expanding the conversation on student-teacher collaboration.* New York: Teachers College Press.

Noffke, S., & Stevenson, R. (Eds.). (1994). *Practically critical: Explorations in educational action research.* New York: Teachers College Press.

Wells, G. (Ed.). (1994). *Changing schools from within: Creating communities of inquiry.* Toronto, Ontario: OISE Press.

3. **Action research collaborations between university professors and teachers in K–12 schools; coauthored or authored by K–12 teachers**

Books

Allen, J. B., Michalove, B., & Shockley, B. (1993). *Engaging children: Community and chaos in the lives of young literacy learners.* Portsmouth, NH: Heinemann.

Gitlin, A., Bringhurst, K., Burns, M., Cooley, V., Myers, B., Price, K., Russell, R., & Tiess, P. (1992). *Teachers' voice for school change: An introduction to educative research.* New York: Teachers College Press.

Articles

Allen, J., Michalove, B., Schockley, B., & West, M. (1991). "I'm really worried about Joseph": Reducing the risks of literacy learning. *The Reading Teacher, 44*(7), 458–472.

Hunsaker, L., & Johnston, M. (1992). Teacher under construction: A collaborative case study of teacher change. *American Educational Research Journal, 29*(2), 350–372.

Stanulis, R. N., with Jeffers, L. (1995). Action research as a way of learning about teaching in a mentor/student teacher relationship. *Action in Teacher Education, 16*(4), 14–24.

4. Research articles authored by K–12 teachers only

Awbrey, M. (1989). A teacher's action research study of writing in the kindergarten: Accepting the natural expression of children. *Peabody Journal of Education, 64*(2), 33–64.

Ballenger, C. (1992). Because you like us: The language of control. *Harvard Educational Review, 62*(2), 199–207.

5. Writing about student teachers and university practicum students conducting action research

Book Chapters

Cochran-Smith, M., Garfield, E., & Greenberger, R. (1992). Student teachers and their teacher: Talking our way into new understandings. In N. A. Branscombe, D. Goswami, & J. Schwartz (Eds.), *Students teaching, teachers learning* (pp. 274–292). Portsmouth, NH: Heinemann.

Noffke, S. E., & Brennan, M. (1991). Action research and reflective student teaching at the University of Wisconsin-Madison: Issues and examples. In B. R. Tabachnik & K. Zeichner (Eds.), *Issues and practices in inquiry-oriented teacher education* (pp. 186–201). London: Falmer Press.

Articles

Clift, R., Veal, M. L., Johnson, M., & Holland, P. (1990). Restructuring teacher education through collaborative action research. *Journal of Teacher Education, 41*(2), 52–62.

Gore, J., & Zeichner, K. (1991). Action research and reflective teaching in preservice teacher education: A case study from the United States. *Teaching and Teacher Education, 7*(2), 119–136.

Lovat, T. J. (1995). Bio-teaching ethics and the researcher teacher: Considerations for teacher education. *Action in Teacher Education, 16*(4), 71–78.

Nath, J. M., & Tellez, K. (1995). A room of one's own: Teaching and learning to teach through inquiry. *Action in Teacher Education, 16*(4), 1–13.

Ross, D. D. (1989). Action research for pre-service teachers: A description of why and how. *Peabody Journal of Education, 64*(3), 131–150.

6. Books about how to do action research, not written by K–12 teachers

Cochran-Smith, M., & Lytle, S. L. (1993). *Inside/outside: Teacher research and knowledge.* New York: Teachers College Press.

Holly, P., & Southworth, G. (1990). *The developing school.* London: Falmer Press.

Kemmis, S., & McTaggart, R. (1982). *The action research planner.* Geelong, Victoria, Australia: Deakin University Press.

Miller, J. (1990). *Creating spaces and finding voices: Teachers collaborating for empowerment.* Albany: State University of New York Press.

Newkirk, T. (Ed.). (1992). *Workshop by and for teachers (4): The teacher as researcher.* Portsmouth, NH: Heinemann.

Oja, S. N., & Smulyan, L. (1989). *Collaborative action research: A developmental approach.* London: Falmer Press.

C H A P T E R

12

Synthesizing Your Personal Theories for Management in Contemporary Classrooms

Some educators now realize that [students] cannot simply be viewed as representatives of groups and categories and, at the same time, as living beings with subjectivities and distinct vantage points.

(Greene, 1994, p. 2)

Teach these boys and girls nothing but facts. Facts alone are wanted in life. Plant nothing else, and root out everything else. You can only form the minds of reasonable animals upon Facts.

(Dickens, 1989, p. 1)

CREATING YOUR CLASSROOM SOCIAL CURRICULUM

One of the key functions of most college textbooks related to teaching—certainly a key function of this textbook—is to help you become familiar with current trends in specific areas of teaching and learning. These trends, when related to specific domains of knowing (e.g., management, curriculum development, instructional design) can take the shape of processes, products, new ways of thinking about classroom life, and so on. In other words, one of the key functions of most texts is to pull together and synthesize a collection of some of the main ideas in a certain field and, wherever appropriate, restructure these ideas. This kind of restructuring is intended to help you more successfully interact with students as you live out your life as a professional educator.

This is the goal that we have tried to attain in this book—to help you think about your classroom in such a way as to help you be more successful in creating a positive and productive social curriculum. An important point related to this goal that we have also tried to make salient throughout the book is that you can no longer wait until later in your professional career to rethink how you:

- interact with students in culturally diverse classrooms,
- work with students to create certain culturally responsive social curricula,
- *manage* your professional lives each day, and
- negotiate your classroom social curriculum with your students.

Viewing students in stereotypical ways—that is, as members of larger groups and categories—is a practice that has been, and continues to be, challenged today by many social groups. This is why we have opened this chapter with the writing of Maxine Greene, who suggests that every student has distinct subjectivities and vantage points from which they understand their place in school. We believe that you have no alternative as a culturally responsive teacher in today's society than to:

- restructure traditional ideas about management so that these ideas align more suitably with less traditional classrooms of today,
- consider the place that culture, ethnicity, and nationality have in your classroom setting,
- develop new ways of understanding how you interact and "manage" students, and
- create anew your classroom social curriculum.

These items above are those that we have advocated throughout this book.

Thinking About Classroom Life From Contemporary Perspectives

On Creating Classroom Life Anew

We—as authors of this book—are keenly aware of just how difficult this *creating anew* can be in daily classroom practice, especially in the midst of long-standing traditional, subject-centered, top-down, and nonnegotiable ways of working with students. Not only is creating some *new ways of interacting* with students a challenge even for the best of teachers, creating some *new ways of thinking about interacting* with students is even more challenging. This latter process—developing new ways of thinking about interacting with students—was the very challenge we struggled with when we began thinking about writing this book, when we actually wrote it, and when we revised various drafts of the book after it was written.

On Developing a Shared Vision for Classroom Management

As a team of authors, we initially began writing this book with a shared vision of how we might accomplish the goals we had for the book. As the writing process continued we began to really struggle with what to do with traditional ideas like those espoused by such scholars as Gagne and Briggs (1974) and Hunter (1994). These traditional ideas were not aligning well with the contemporary perspectives we wanted to incorporate in the text. Such perspectives, we felt, would help you better understand classroom life today.

Some of us wanted to keep more of the traditional ideas and ease them into new ways of thinking, while others of us wanted to discount traditional ideas and stay only with new ways of thinking about classroom life. Out of this meeting and mingling of the *traditional ideas* with the more *contemporary ideas* a somewhat healthy yet troublesome tension arose. The tension was healthy in that we had to think more deeply about the purpose of the book and how it might best be designed. The tension was troublesome in that we did not always agree on how ideas should be expressed, and on the place that *management* now has, and should now have, as a way of thinking and as a way of carrying out classroom teaching. This is the same kind of tension that happens in classrooms when the more traditional ways of understanding classroom life meet the more contemporary multicultural ways of understanding classroom life.

On Addressing Issues of Diversity

One idea that we agreed upon when we began writing this book was that given the rise of cultural diversity in classrooms across the nation, traditional ideas pertaining to management are less sensitive to cultural diversity.[1] Traditional ways of thinking about students tend to put them into more comprehensive groups and categories, thus giving less attention—at least theoretically—to the subjectivities and vantage points that were mentioned by Greene (1994). To say simply, even glibly, that "times have changed and so, too, must we as educators," is trite. Nor is this the kind of simple slogan that rallies educators to try out new ideas about classroom management, or that warrants the publishing of books like this one. To say, however, that the whole infrastructure of society has become more complex, more diverse, more multicultural, and more personally demanding relative to tolerance and acceptance is more at the center of this book.

These complexities of society in general and of schools in particular that were noted in the aforementioned sentence are more at the center of the felt need we had when we first decided to write this book, and when we decided thereafter to bring it to its completion. Also at the center of this felt need is the widely held truism that teachers in schools everywhere must accommodate many varying definitions of diversity. These same teachers must also determine how to transform these definitions into culturally relevant practice for their students (Ladson-Billings, 1994; Powell, 1997).

Focusing on the idea of diversity turns our attention once again to Greene's quote at the beginning of the chapter: Sensitive teachers today know about students' subjectivities and vantage points, and about students' personal needs that emerge from these subjectivities and vantage points. These same teachers will also very likely admit that some traditional ideas about management—those that are explicitly behavior-centered—just do not fit most classrooms anymore. The interpersonal demands on all educators regarding diversity issues have created a pressing need for culture-centered ideas about management. Such ideas do not have to replace all behavior-centered ideas entirely, but culture-based ideas clearly cause all of us to rethink how we interact with students, and what subject matter content is best suited to teaching students in a multicultural society. This content, to follow the work of Banks (1991), for example, should represent a multiplicity of perspectives.

Creating a Collage of Perspectives

The metaphor of *collage* best describes the multiple perspectives that we—as authors of this book—used to write about social curriculum in today's schools. The metaphor of collage, we believe, is highly appropriate for any book on teaching

---

[1]This argument has been made by various authors, including Bullough (1994), McLaughlin (1994), Hollins (1996), Nieto (1992), Bennett (1990), Banks (1991), Powell, Zehm, & Garcia (1996), among others.

today, and particularly appropriate for a book such as this one that deals with classroom life and traditional concepts related to management. However, we would be remiss if we did not mention the theoretical struggles we encountered as we developed this collage.

As a team of four authors, our ideas met and mingled in unique, sometimes complementary, and sometimes antithetical ways as we combined our perspectives to write the text. Tom Savage has written extensively using ideas that are, in some ways, more traditional in their orientation (for example see Armstrong & Savage, 1998). Throughout the writing of this book Tom upheld the traditional value of *management* as a classroom phenomenon, although he agreed that a pressing need exists to move beyond the traditional conception of management in contemporary classrooms. While the psychological and behavioral dimensions predominated Tom's ideas in the book, he also acknowledged the cultural dimensions of schooling, most especially the dimension related to social class. That Tom acknowledged social class as a cultural dimension is clear in chapter 8.

Jim McLaughlin (1994), on the other hand, represented the belief that the traditional notion of management is far less useful today than it was in the past (see also chapter 2 of this textbook). Jim also held firmly to the belief that newer and fresher approaches to classroom instruction are needed. As the writing process unfolded, Jim consistently preferred to use terms such as *mediate, guide,* and *facilitate* rather than *manage.* Jim also preferred using the concepts of *social curriculum* and *classroom life* rather than *social control* and *classroom order.* The bottom line of Jim's arguments rested in issues of equity, diversity, and empowerment of students and teachers. Richard Powell, on yet another hand, found value in traditional uses of the *management* metaphor *and* in phrases suggested by coauthor McLaughlin. Foremost for Richard were issues of diversity and equity (see Powell, Zehm, & Garcia, 1996; Powell, 1997). Finally, Stan Zehm brought a humanistic orientation to the book as demonstrated in chapter 7 (see also Powell, Zehm, & Kottler, 1996; Zehm & Kottler, 1993). This orientation did not necessarily negate traditional notions of management, but was nonetheless better tailored to ways of understanding classroom life that were related to student-centeredness and teacher empowerment.

While writing this book, we were in a continuous state of theoretical negotiation; no one person and no one set of ideas or values predominated other ideas or values. We also guided each other's learning and thus each other's understanding about alternative ways of viewing classroom management. Ultimately the ideas of mediate, guide, and facilitate became as important as the more traditional idea of management. However, we continuously strove to move the traditional idea of management into contemporary classroom discourse, and into the spirit of multicultural life, thus moving the idea of *management* into cultural as well as behavioral dimensions.

In creating the collage for this book yet another phenomenon occurred: namely, a blurring of management genres.[2] A function of such blurring, and a func-

---

[2]The idea of "blurring of genres" was taken from the work of Denzin and Lincoln (1994) and Denzin (1997). This represents a time in the history of ideas where no one idea predominates, and no one idea can be said to be more valid than other ideas, even those ideas that have been long-held as predominate ways of knowing.

tion of the collage we developed with ideas represented in this book, is that no one idea for classroom management seems to be suited to all students. While this claim clearly is not surprising, we believe it is worth reiterating here. Subjectivities and vantage points, social class standing and privilege, academic tracking and ability grouping, standardized testing and generalizing ability, are all very real parts of our students and our classrooms, and consequently are all calling for a blurring of genres for management. As an author team, we represented a blurring of genres thus providing a strength for the book that in more traditional times would have been viewed as a weakness. Although we had a shared vision for the book—for how the collage might look when we were finished—we clearly differed as demonstrated in the discussion above, in how we might best attain our vision for you as a teacher. This, too, is your challenge as a prospective teacher: to understand students' subjectivities and vantage points, and to realize that because of these student features, single approaches to organizing your classroom social curriculum might be ill suited to creating a classroom context where all students—to the extent possible—feel engaged in learning targeted content.

The purpose of the foregoing discussion, which was about our journey in writing this book, is to suggest to you that in order to create new ways of interacting with students, you must at some point ask serious questions about how more traditional ideas are suited to your classroom. This means you have to reflect on traditional ideas that you hold, examine how these ideas foster your personal theories for management, and rethink those theories that may be less suited to the students you teach. This is what we had to do about the whole idea of management, and it is what educators had to do at each of the schools we described in chapters 8 through 10 of this book (i.e., Tynes Elementary School, Brown-Barge Middle School, and Estacado High School).

Making changes in how you teach comes only after asking probing questions about the status quo. After completing this book, and after participating in an action research project in chapter 11, we believe and hope that you are in a better position to:

- think more thoughtfully about your interaction with students,
- consider the place that your preconceptions about management and classroom life have in today's classrooms, and
- think about the value of knowing students' subjectivities and vantage points.

IDENTIFYING YOUR PERSONAL THEORIES ABOUT CLASSROOM MANAGEMENT

From Collage to Personal Theories

In the preceding section we discussed how a collage of ideas about management was assembled in such a way as to develop this book about classroom management. As a team of authors we allowed our ideas to meet and mingle in order to develop a book that we believe aligns with the needs of teachers who are preparing to teach in classrooms that are culturally diverse, and who must grapple with many managerial issues. Some of these issues, for example, multiple first languages other than English spoken in individual classrooms, were less challenging only a few decades ago. But today linguistic diversity is just one of many challenges you face.

In this chapter we ask you to focus more specifically on your collage of ideas—what we will now refer to as your *personal theories*—about how you manage your classroom, including the management of teaching, learning, and student behavior. Various research reports suggest very clearly that the personal theories you have about classroom teaching are embedded deeply within your biographical experiences, including both in-school and out-of-school activities. For this reason we asked you in chapter 3 to reflect on some of these experiences; specifically, we asked you to reflect on the labels you carried throughout your school years as a student.

Before moving into the discussion below, we need to explain about the idea of personal theories. Taken from the work of Hunt (1987), the idea of personal theories refers to a collection of personal perspectives, beliefs, attitudes, and predispositions that you have for teaching. These things collectively influence how you interact with students, how you teach targeted content, how you feel about yourself as a teacher, and so on. In short, almost everything about you can be somehow tied to your personal theories.

Closely related to the idea of *personal theory* is the idea of *personal practical philosophy*. Connelly and Clandinin (1990) describe personal practical philosophies as "what [you] respond with when someone asks [you] what [you] believe about children, about teaching and learning, or about curriculum . . .[it is your] beliefs and values contextualized in [your] experience" (p. 70). Clearly there is overlap between the work of Hunt (personal theory) and the work of Connelly and Clandinin (personal practical philosophy). Although both terms are valuable and useful heuristics for helping you examine your beliefs about management, we will finish the book using Hunt's ideas about personal theories below.

GETTING IN TOUCH WITH YOUR PERSONAL THEORIES FOR MANAGEMENT

At one time or another you have talked about your personal theories for managing students. In fact, if you are like so many other prospective teachers, one of the things you have talked about most is dealing with the behavior of your students. Many prospective teachers are fearful that they won't be able to *control* student behavior—that students will "run all over them." But as we have suggested throughout this book and as we have described in chapters 8 through 10, when you build your teaching around other concepts such as *facilitate, guide,* and *mediate,* you will be more likely to gain the respect of your students than if you approach them thinking that you have to *control* every move they make. This is what many teachers at Estacado High School have done, namely to build their teaching around the concept of *quality world* (see chapter 10).

To understand the idea of personal theory, think about the activities you completed in this book. Some of the activities were done alone, some were done with your peers in school classrooms, and others were done as you visited various community settings. As you completed these activities you explored how your personal beliefs about teaching influenced your classroom interactions with diverse learners, and you constructed a personal knowledge for how diversity influences your social curriculum. The personal knowledge you constructed about teaching, which is embedded in the school classroom context, has a prevailing practical dimension. Because you constructed this knowledge in ways that were meaningful to you, you personally own it, and now you have the moral responsibility that comes with this ownership. Your personal knowledge base, which is developed from being a student for so many years in school classrooms, and which is coupled with your prior beliefs about teaching as well as your ability to transform these beliefs into practice, comprises your personal theories for classroom management.

We also need to mention that your set of personal theories for management is clearly much more than a single verbal expression. It reflects what you do in the classroom as a function of your personal history, your former teacher role models, and your current beliefs. This is why you must also consider your biographical experiences when you synthesize your personal theories for teaching diverse learners. One way— certainly a very important way—to get in touch with your personal theories for managing school classrooms is to think reflectively about who you are as a prospective teacher, and who you might become as a beginning and also as an experienced teacher. To help you think reflectively about who you are as a prospective classroom manager, we refocus your attention below on selected parts of this book.

THINKING REFLECTIVELY ON SCHOOL MANAGEMENT

As you completed the activities throughout this book, you participated in teacher-research projects, and you formulated questions about teaching diverse learners. To answer these questions you gathered, explored, and interpreted selected information. If you completed chapter 11 then you carried out an action research project. Doing this helped you continue the process of reflective thinking. The activities below which focus on each part of this book are intended to extend and deepen this thinking.

Developing a Classroom Perspective of the Social Curriculum

A central part of your personal theories about classroom management are the perspectives you hold about teaching and learning, particularly about how you best interact with students, and about how students best learn content. In the first chapter of this book we asked you to begin rethinking your role as classroom manager—to begin thinking of yourself as a worker who continuously interacts with a highly diverse group of young people. To help you begin this rethinking process we offered other ways of thinking about interacting with highly diverse learners; namely, we suggested that you begin imagining yourself as guide, mediator, and facilitator within the context of your *social curriculum.* Importantly, we also asked you to reflect critically on the labels you wore as a precollege student and then as a college student.

A rather broad set of questions surfaces from the preceding paragraph. These questions, when addressed thoughtfully, can help you articulate more clearly the personal theories you have for classroom management. Working with a group of peers, explore the following questions:

- In what ways, if any, have you begun to rethink your role as a classroom manager after completing this book?
- What insights into classroom teaching have you derived from the metaphors of *guide, facilitator,* and *mediator?*
- What place, if any, do traditional student labels have in contemporary classrooms? How might the labels you carried throughout your school days influence how you interact with students?

Dealing With Daily Life in Culturally Diverse Classrooms

The three aforementioned questions are intended to help you think more broadly and deeply about issues pertaining to management. The second part of the book, however, dealt with daily life in culturally diverse classrooms. The broader ideas related to management—the very ideas represented in the questions above—help to frame your daily practice. Sometimes, however, teachers get so busy in the daily events of teaching that they forget about the relationship between broader ideas and daily practice. The relationship, however, is very real.

In chapter 4 you were introduced to selected ideas about organizing classroom life with your students. We further suggested that however classroom life might be organized, cultural diversity and culture-based issues must become part of your decision-making about how you will organize your teaching days. The questions that readily surface from issues of diversity are:

- How will you begin organizing your classroom social curriculum?
- What part will the concepts *guide, mediation,* and *facilitation* play in this or-ganization? What part will the concept *management* play in this organization?

In chapters 5 and 6 you explored the reality of conflict and compromise. We of-fered you some specific suggestions for how you might best address conflict and compromise as issues related to teaching, learning, student behavior, and student needs surface. Questions for you to consider include:

- Have you thought about strategies for compromise when conflict surfaces?
- What are some types of cultural conflict that could surface, and how might you best compromise this conflict with students?
- What are some types of behavioral conflict that could surface, and how might you best compromise this conflict with students?

Also in Part II of the book, we asked you to examine special issues related to management. In particular, we discussed issues related to infusion, gifted education, and special education.

- In what ways are you prepared to deal with these kinds of issues in your classroom?

Developing Local Understandings of Social Curricula

Part II of the book was intended to help you think more about daily life as it unfolds at school. Part III was intended to help you better understand how daily life in your classroom, and similarly in other teachers' classrooms in the same school, creates a distinct social curriculum for students who attend the school. We purposively selected three schools to help you better understand what we mean when we say *a local understanding* of a school. This is because schools, while very similar in some ways, can be very different in other ways, thus requiring you to have a local understanding of a school in order to teach there. This was very clear for all three schools we described in Part III.

- Which of the three schools described in Part III felt more familiar to you, if any?
- Aside from grade level, which of the schools would be easiest for you to negotiate your classroom social curriculum with students? Why?

EXPLORING YOUR PERSONAL THEORIES IN ACTION

Answering the questions above by yourself, then comparing notes with a colleague, help you think more deeply, certainly more theoretically, about the underlying beliefs that frame your personal practical theories for classroom management. This kind of thinking also helps you become aware of the historical and professional experiences from which you have constructed, and continue to construct, your theories for management. An important point to remember is that each teacher's personal theories allow for both strengths and weaknesses in classroom teaching. This is why you must continuously think about, and whenever necessary reconsider, the status of your set of ever-developing personal theories.

Although the processes of critical thinking and open discussion help you understand the teaching beliefs that underlie your personal theories, these processes reveal only part of the mental scaffolding that frames your personal philosophy. To more fully understand your own theories you must explore how they are enacted in actual classroom teaching. Hunt (1987) notes that your personal theories are brought to life when your underlying beliefs, whether expressed or unexpressed, are transformed into classroom practice. How you transform your beliefs into practice, either consciously or unconsciously, in the face of political, administrative, and curricular constraints of your local school context is a crucial factor in determining the degree of alignment between your beliefs as expressed explicitly and your beliefs as enacted in real classroom life.

An important point must be made here regarding personal practical theories. You do not construct these by yourself; you socially construct them. That is, you construct such theories for teaching through personal and professional interactions in and out of school. Your theories are always embedded, therefore, in a specific social context, and are given life by this context. To adequately explore your personal practical theories for teaching you must examine your actions within the social context of school classrooms as you actually teach students.

CONCLUSION

This chapter and those that preceded it have been an attempt to help you understand your beliefs, predispositions, and personal theories for managing classrooms in a pluralistic society. This book has also been an attempt to help you learn about distances: the cultural distances you might be keeping from some of your students, either through your personal interactions with them, your classroom curriculum, or your classroom learning environment.

Underlying this book is our conviction that you, as a classroom teacher, must make a sincere, passionate attempt to help every one of your students be successful in school. While this is complicated even for the best of teachers, your attempt to do this will be more successful when you better understand personal factors (e.g., beliefs, values, classroom behaviors) that widen any existing gaps between you and your students.

Understanding any potential distances between you and your students through self-searching and critical reflection over many months makes you continuously wonder about your teaching. Boomer (1992) explains the value of this kind of wondering:

> To know "what is going on," or even to wonder what might be going on, means having an all-encompassing fish-eye-lens taking in the backgrounds, capabilities and aspirations of the learners and their parents, knowing the structures, habits and values of the school, reading the wider pol-

itics of the system and society (particularly its economics), and understanding the ebb and flow of interactions and struggles in the arenas of gender, race, ethnicity and class. (p. 281)

Teachers who are deeply committed to their work continuously wonder about their classrooms. They think critically about their practice, always looking for ways to begin anew. They do this because they understand, as Boomer does above, that any distance between them and their students, regardless of the cause, interferes with learning.

Throughout this book you should have come to realize that becoming a culturally sensitive teacher may require you to make a transition from one kind of thinking about teaching (e.g., traditional, authoritarian, content-centered) to another kind (e.g., contemporary, negotiable, student-centered). Do not think, however, you must make this transition over night, or even in a few weeks. Moving from one kind of professional thinking to another can be threatening to your sense of security as a teacher, thus causing you to quickly retreat to what feels secure and what protects your self-confidence as a teacher. Making the transition to being a more culturally sensitive teacher should be approached carefully and thoughtfully, with determination and wholeheartedness. About the idea of transition Silko (1977) writes, "It is a matter of transition, you see: The changing, the becoming must be cared for closely" (p. 130). As you move toward becoming more culturally sensitive in your curriculum and instruction, continuously reflect on your personal practical philosophy for teaching diverse students. This will help you nurture and care for changes in your teaching practice without running back to ways of teaching that might be less effective for your students.

A final note needs to be mentioned about what you have learned from this book and from doing the activities and research projects we suggested in various chapters. We have clearly taken a culture-oriented approach to management. We avoided lock-step procedures for management, and we encouraged you to think about alternative ways of interacting with your students. One goal we had—a goal we hope we reached—is that you now know both strengths and limitations of your own personal theories for addressing the management dimensions of your classroom that you must carry out almost every minute of your professional life at school. What you have learned about managing culturally diverse classrooms will be evident in the daily decisions you make about how best to engage all learners in your classroom social curriculum. An important dimension in making these decisions is *discernment*. Another way of thinking about discernment is knowing what to do and what to say at the right classroom moment. You will acquire this kind of discernment with time in the classroom, with various experiences, and with an openness and willingness to learn about yourself.

In past years theory-based courses in classroom management that were taught for prospective teachers were taught exclusively at the university, and tended to use behavior-oriented approaches to managing and controlling students and related learning. Seeing connections between what was taught about management at the university and what was happening in real-world classrooms was remote, and for many prospective teachers, not possible. Teacher education programs today are more centered on practical experiences in professional development schools which means you can more quickly explore the relevancy of management models. What works and what does not work are now more obvious, and the limitations of management models—the same models often depicted in textbooks as good theory—sometimes are not necessarily good practice. This is why we have tried to mix and mingle various perspectives in the theoretical collage of this book. This is also why we have included three schools in part III of this book—to let you see the value of knowing about the local understandings you must have about individual schools despite their superficial similarity to other schools.

A fitting way to end this book on culture-centered management is to turn to the classical work of Charles Dickens who, through one of his characters, depicts the antithesis of culture-centered teaching and learning. At the beginning of his novel, *Hard Times*, Dickens introduces a certain Mr. Gradgrind, a teacher whose sentiments and classroom strategies are presumably reflective of that day and time. Opening *Hard Times* with a quote from Mr. Gradgrind, Dickens (1989) writes:

> Now, what I want is, Facts. Teach these boys and girls nothing but facts. Facts alone are wanted in life. Plant nothing else, and root out everything else. You can only form the minds of reasonable animals upon Facts: nothing else will ever be of any service to them. This is the principle on which I bring up my own children, and this is the principle on which I bring up these children. Stick to the facts, Sir! (p. 1)

While the aforementioned quote was published in 1854, we are sure that one of your K–12 teachers still resembled the attitude of Mr. Gradgrind. Teaching to the facts is as present today as it was in 1854, and with this kind of teaching come methods and strategies that are clearly behavior-centered: drill and practice, mastery learning, and so on.

Schools are clearly some of the most conservative institutions we have in our society, and there is merit, we admit, in holding on to some long-standing traditions in schools. Yet the sentiment of Mr. Gradgrind and the lock-step drill-and-practice teaching that goes with it, although stated in an extreme way by Dickens, appears to be reaching fewer and fewer students today. Mr. Gradgrind, we assume, had fewer challenges than you have today; for example, challenges with linguistic diversity, with infusion of students with special needs, with tracking, and the list goes on and on.

At no other time in the history of our country have we been faced with so many *voices* wanting to be heard (Powell, 1997); at no other time have we been saturated with such a multiplicity of technology; and at no other time have we been "globalized" like we have been at the present. Managing classrooms using Gradgrind's tactics simply will not work anymore. As you enter the doorsteps of your very own classroom as a professional teacher the first time, your challenge will be to move beyond the Gradgrind syndrome—to step over some traditional methods that privilege some students but marginalize others. The system of management you implement must move toward a culture-sensitive social curriculum. When that happens, more students will be engaged in learning targeted content, and more teachers will prove to be successful at what they do.

REFERENCES

Armstrong, D., & Savage, T. (1998). *Teaching in the secondary school* (4th ed.). Upper Saddle River, NJ: Prentice Hall.

Banks, J. (1991). Teaching multicultural literacy to teachers. *Teaching Education, 4*(1), 135–144.

Bennett, C. (1990). *Comprehensive multicultural education: Theory and practice* (2nd ed). Boston, MA: Allyn and Bacon.

Boomer, G. (1992). Negotiating the curriculum reformulated. In G. Boomer, N. Lester, C. Onore, & J. Cook (Eds.), *Negotiating the curriculum: Educating for the 21st century* (pp. 276–289). Washington, DC: The Falmer Press.

Bullough, R. V. (1994). Digging at the roots: Discipline, management, and metaphor. *Action in Teacher Education, 16*(1), 1–10.

Denzin, N. (1997). *Interpretive ethnography: Ethnographic practices for the 21st century.* Thousand Oaks, CA: Sage Publications.

Denzin, N., & Lincoln, Y. (1994). Introduction: Entering the Field of Qualitative Research. In N. Denzin & Y. Lincoln, (Eds). *Handbook of qualitative research.* (pp. 1–18). Thousand Oaks, CA: Sage Publications.

Dickens, C. (1989). *Hard Times.* New York: Oxford University Press. (First published in 1854)

Gagne, R. M., & Briggs, L. J. (1974). *Principles of instructional design.* New York: Holt, Rinehart and Winston.

Greene, M. (1994). *Beginnings, identities, and possibilities: The uses of social imagination.* Paper presented at the annual meeting of the American Educational Research Association, New Orleans.

Hollins, E. (1996). *Culture in school learning: Revealing the deep meaning.* Mahwah, NJ: Lawrence Erlbaum.

Hunt, D. (1987). *Beginning with ourselves.* Cambridge, MA: Brookline Books.

Hunter, M. (1994). *Enhancing teaching.* New York: Macmillan.

Ladson-Billings, G. (1994). *The dreamkeepers: Successful teachers of African American children.* San Francisco, CA: Jossey-Bass.

McLaughlin, H. J. (1994). From negation to negotiation: Moving away from the management metaphor. *Action in Teacher Education, 16*(4), 75–84.

Nieto, S. (1992). *Affirming diversity: The sociopolitical context of multicultural education.* New York: Longman.

Powell, R. (1997). Then the beauty emerges: A longitudinal case study of culturally relevant teaching. *Teaching and Teacher Education, 13*(5), 467–484.

Powell, R., Zehm, S., and Garcia, J. (1996). *Field experience: Strategies for exploring cultural diversity in schools.* Columbus, OH: Merrill.

Powell, R., Zehm, S., & Kottler, J. A. (1995). *Classrooms under the influence: Addicted families, addicted students.* Thousand Oaks, CA: Corwin Press.

Silko, M. (1977). *Ceremony.* New York: Penquin Books.

Zehm, S., and Kottler, J. A., Jr. (1993). *On being a teacher: The human dimension.* Newbury Park, CA: Corwin Press.

AUTHOR INDEX

SUBJECT INDEX